# The Mission
## of the Triune God

# The Mission of the Triune God

Trinitarian Missiology in the Tradition
of Lesslie Newbigin

ADAM DODDS

Foreword by Murray Rae

☙PICKWICK *Publications* • Eugene, Oregon

THE MISSION OF THE TRIUNE GOD
Trinitarian Missiology in the Tradition of Lesslie Newbigin

Copyright © 2017 Adam Dodds. All rights reserved. Except for brief quotations in critical publications or reviews, no part of this book may be reproduced in any manner without prior written permission from the publisher. Write: Permissions, Wipf and Stock Publishers, 199 W. 8th Ave., Suite 3, Eugene, OR 97401.

Pickwick Publications
An Imprint of Wipf and Stock Publishers
199 W. 8th Ave., Suite 3
Eugene, OR 97401

www.wipfandstock.com

PAPERBACK ISBN: 978-1-4982-8346-5
HARDCOVER ISBN: 978-1-4982-8348-9
EBOOK ISBN: 978-1-4982-8347-2

*Cataloguing-in-Publication data:*

Names: Dodds, Adam, author. | Rae, Murray, foreword.
Title: The mission of the triune God : trinitarian missiology in the tradition of Lesslie Newbigin / by Adam Dodds ; foreword by Murray Rae.
Description: Eugene, OR : Pickwick Publications, 2017 | Includes bibliographical references and index(es).
Identifiers: ISBN 978-1-4982-8346-5 (paperback) | ISBN 978-1-4982-8348-9 (hardcover) | ISBN 978-1-4982-8347-2 (ebook)
Subjects: LCSH: Newbigin, Lesslie. | Missions—Theory. | Trinity.
Classification: BV2063 .D63 2017 (paperback) | BV2063 .D63 (ebook)

Manufactured in the U.S.A.                                              07/26/17

# Contents

*Permissions* | vi
*Foreword by Murray Rae* | vii
*Acknowledgments* | ix
*Abbreviations* | xi
*Introduction* | xiii

**Part One: The Trinitarian Missiology of Lesslie Newbigin**

CHAPTER 1
The Contours of Newbigin's Missiology | 3

CHAPTER 2
Newbigin's Theology of the Trinity | 58

**Part Two: Constructing a Trinitarian Missiology in the Tradition of Lesslie Newbigin**

CHAPTER 3
Trinitarian Missiology: The Triune Being of the Missionary God | 121

CHAPTER 4
The Mission of the Son and Spirit | 183

CHAPTER 5
*Missio Ecclesiae* | 252

CHAPTER 6
Conclusion | 288

*Bibliography* | 305
*Index of Persons* | 325
*Index of Subjects* | 329

# Permissions

Unless otherwise stated, biblical quotations are taken from the New Revised Standard Version Bible: Anglicized Edition, copyright 1989, 1995, Division of Christian Education of the National Council of the Churches of Christ in the United States of America. Used by permission. All rights reserved.

Scripture quotations marked NIV are taken from The Holy Bible, New International Version®, NIV®. Copyright © 1973, 1978, 1984, 2011 by Biblica, Inc.tm Used by permission. All rights reserved worldwide.

Scripture quotations marked NASB are from The New American Standard Bible®. Copyright © The Lockman Foundation 1960, 1962, 1963, 1968, 1971, 1972, 1973, 1975, 1977, 1995. Used by permission.

Scripture quotations marked ESV are from the ESV® Bible (*The Holy Bible, English Standard Version®*), copyright © 2001 by Crossway. Used by permission. All rights reserved worldwide.

All references to archival Newbigin material are from the *The Papers of Lesslie Newbigin (DA29)*. Cadbury Research Library: Special Collections, University of Birmingham, Edgbaston, Birmingham B15 2TT, UK. Catalogued at http://www.special-coll.bham.ac.uk/index.html. Used by permission.

Quotations from *Mission's Flame* by Matt Redman (Song ID 36333) and *Jesus Is Alive* by Ron Kenoly (Song ID 60495) are both by permission of Capitol CMG Publishing. License: Lyric Reprint in Book, License No. 588681

# Foreword

LESSLIE NEWBIGIN DESERVES TO be recognized as one of the great churchmen of the twentieth century. Missionary, evangelist, pastor, ecumenist, and prophet among his own people, Newbigin held fast to the truth of the gospel and articulated that truth with deep insight, humility and compassion. Newbigin repeatedly denied being a theologian, but that denial holds true only if being a theologian is conceived in the narrow sense of someone whose call to bear witness to the gospel is exercised primarily in the realm of the academy. That, however, is not a satisfactory definition of what it is to be a theologian. Newbigin was a theologian in the much more important sense that he sought always to think, and speak, and act in obedience to the biblical story. His life's work was to bear witness, in thought and in deed, to the God whose loving purposes for the world are made known and enacted among us through his Son and Holy Spirit.

Although the renewal of Trinitarian theology was taking place around him, notably in Newbigin's own Reformed tradition through the prompting and example of Karl Barth, Newbigin did not manage to read Barth until relatively late in his career. When, on 'retiring' to Britain in 1974, he finally found time to read Barth's *Church Dogmatics*, Newbigin discovered in Barth's resolutely Trinitarian theology refreshing confirmation of what he himself had known throughout his career: the doctrine of the Trinity was not an arcane summation of matters that could be treated just as well in advance of, or even without, any consideration of God's triunity. The Trinity belongs rather to the very heart of the gospel. Newbigin knew, and said so early in his career, that all Christian thinking, especially our thinking about mission, had to be done in the light of the triune God's presence with us through his Son and Spirit. Mission is not something that we do in response to the directives of a remote God, but is rather to be understood as the action of God himself exercised through the Son in the power of the Holy Spirit. Any talk of the Church's mission is but a confession that the people

Christ calls to be his Church are graciously enabled by the Spirit to participate in the work that God is already about.

Guided by this conviction, Newbigin called for the development of an explicitly Trinitarian missiology. Only with a proper recognition of the work of the Triune God is it possible for the Christian Church to be faithful in mission. Newbigin himself never articulated in systematic or comprehensive form the Trinitarian missiology which he considered to be essential for the Church. That task would be left to others. We do find in Newbigin's writings, however, the repeated application of elements essential to a Trinitarian construal of the missionary endeavor.

Much attention has been paid in recent years to Newbigin's career and to the literary legacy that he has left for us. Among such work, particular attention has been given to his prophetic and profoundly perceptive engagement with Western culture. Many have sought to follow Newbigin's lead in addressing the widespread cultural resistance to the gospel in the Western world, and a good number of studies have emerged that attend to various aspects of Newbigin's theological writing. But the task of developing an explicitly Trinitarian missiology such as Newbigin called for is still in progress and can benefit yet from drawing Newbigin into conversation with the ecumenical tradition of Trinitarian theology. That is the task undertaken by Adam Dodds in this volume. Beginning with a thorough study of Newbigin's own writings, and of the contexts from which these writings emerged, Adam then proceeds to explore the doctrine of the Trinity itself and to show how Newbigin's insights might be developed into a more thoroughgoing Trinitarian missiology. He offers a careful exploration of how it is that the missionary work of the Son and Spirit sent among us by the Father becomes the basis and context for a proper understanding of the mission of the Church.

While ready to acknowledge some of the criticisms that have been levelled at Newbigin's writing, Adam presents a compelling case for the enduring fecundity and truthfulness of Newbigin's conviction that Christian mission has always to be understood as a participation in the work of the triune God. The fruitfulness of that conviction, furthermore, is amply demonstrated in the book you have in your hands. Adam's work will not be the last word on the matter, simply because the agenda of thinking through and indeed of taking up the call of God to share in his work in the world is always before us and remains unfinished yet. The present work is, however, a very worthy contribution to the task that Newbigin himself encouraged of developing a missiology that is determined in every aspect by the mission that the Father, the Son and the Spirit first undertakes among us.

Murray Rae

# Acknowledgments

THIS BOOK STARTED LIFE as a doctoral thesis. During the extended period of time in which this doctoral project was carried out I am grateful for the companions God provided along the journey who were also completing their own doctorates. These include Dr. Euan Rodger, Dr. Matt Easter, Dr. Keron Niles, Rev. Dr. Andrew Nicol, Dr. Chris Caradus, Dr. Andrew Torrance, Dr. Katharina Völker, Dr. Deborah Bower, Dr. Jacky Zvulun, Dr. Robert Wayumba, Dr. Kirsten Cheyne, Dr. Lesley Gill, Dr. Andre Muller, Rev. Dr. Selwyn Yeoman, Dr. Mark Gingerich and Dr. Chris Roome.

As Ravi Zacharias has said, a book is, amongst other things, a documentation of the thought life of the author on a particular subject. Recalling all the influences upon my thought life is an impossible task. Thus there are many more people to whom I owe a debt of gratitude than I can specifically mention, and so I will name only a few.

To those who have discipled me in the grace of God, Phil Kingham and Olu Robbin-Coker—thank you for investing in me and imparting to me your love for the Lord Jesus and your desire to learn more of God and His ways. To my theological mentors in the grace of God, Alan Torrance (in person) and Greg Boyd (through his books and sermons online)—thank you. Of course this book would not have been possible were it not for the steady faithfulness, ceaseless productivity, and prayerful, prophetic and pioneering life of Lesslie Newbigin whom I never had the privilege of meeting.

To Ps. Mike Griffiths, who kept encouraging me to finish this project. And to the elders of Dunedin Elim Church past and present (Andrew Smith, Peter Sara, Then Hon Chew, Dan Gibbons, Euan Rodger and Tony Pantel), who arranged cover for a busy pastor and graciously gave me study leave in order to finish the corrections, even though it took longer than anyone expected—thank you.

To my doctoral supervisor, Professor Murray Rae, whose unswerving support and guidance, and patience (longsuffering) in reading and re-reading and re-reading portions of this book has helped make it what it is—thank you.

To my parents, John and Judy Dodds, who birthed in my brother and I a love for books and the desire to learn, and who supported me through the entire higher education journey—thank you. To Dr. Joseph Dodds—we will make it back to Applecross with our children one day. And to Rev. Canon Arthur Dodds, big grandpa, who with Letty Dodds encouraged me in my faith and in studying theology—may I also be pastor-theologian in my eighties.

To my sons Elias John Dodds, Micah Whitfield Dodds, and Peter Isaac Dodds—I love you and I am so proud of you. Become all God has called you to be, and I know that you will, because you've got what it takes.

To my wife Kylie, who did not mind having Lesslie Newbigin become a part of our marriage for eight years. Your companionship and continual supply of encouragement, home baking, and coffee kept me going until the finish line. I love you.

And lastly, to King Jesus, Holy Spirit my Life-giver, and gracious Father God; may this work bear a not inaccurate witness to your eternal loving personal reality, and may it inspire others to participate in Your Triune mission of love.

# Abbreviations

| | |
|---|---|
| BCC | British Council of Churches |
| CD | Church Dogmatics |
| CSI | Church of South India |
| CWME/DWME | Commission/Division for World Mission and Evangelism |
| GOCN | Gospel and Our Culture Network (UK and US) |
| IBMR | International Bulletin of Missionary Research Journal |
| IMC | International Missionary Council |
| IRM | International Review of Mission(s) Journal |
| SCM | Student Christian Mission |
| URC | United Reformed Church of Great Britain |
| WCC | World Council of Churches |

# Introduction

### INTRODUCING LESSLIE NEWBIGIN

BISHOP LESSLIE NEWBIGIN IS commonly regarded as one of the twentieth century's most outstanding Christian missionary statesmen, ecumenical leaders, and missiologists. However, it is also true to say that Newbigin is a theologian, for "Everything he saw in his long career, he was gifted to see as it truly was: in the uncreated light and eternal reign of the Pantocrator, the Lord Jesus Christ."[1] Whichever single adjective one selects to describe Newbigin will prove to be insufficient, due to the range of roles that he ably fulfilled in his long and fruitful career. Drawing on Geoffrey Wainwright's chapter headings in his theological biography of Newbigin, Timothy Yates describes Newbigin as "confident believer, direct evangelist, ecumenical advocate, pastoral bishop, missionary strategist, religious interlocutor, and Christian apologist: all these he was."[2] Therefore, it is quite natural that over a decade since his death, there is a growing field of Newbigin studies, with several monographs devoted to engaging with his thought. In addition, Paul Weston has produced a 'Newbigin Reader' as an aid to Newbigin studies in general.[3] However, some scholars suggest that this dialogue with Newbigin's thought is still peripheral to the missiological mainstream. N. T. Wright suggests that Newbigin's missiological contributions are being ignored,[4] whilst David Kettle regrets that Newbigin's thought "does not widely receive attention," and "is not often subject to careful reflection . . . In Britain, at least, he seems to have been relegated to the margins."[5] Whether or not this

1. Work, "Witness," 352.
2. Yates, "Lesslie," 45.
3. Weston, *Lesslie Newbigin*.
4. Wright, "Review," 3.
5. Kettle, "Unfinished Dialogue?," 19–20.

assessment is fair, it is certainly true that Newbigin's thought remains highly pertinent to the theology of mission and deserves an important place in the ongoing missiological conversation.

## NEWBIGIN'S CALL FOR A TRINITARIAN MISSIOLOGY

In the early 1960s Newbigin recognized the need for theologically grounding the ongoing missionary enterprise and so called for the development of a robust trinitarian missiology.[6] The timing of this call coincided with both a crisis in the missionary movement and the theological rediscovery of the importance of the doctrine of the Trinity (particularly through the work of Karl Barth and Karl Rahner) by the Western church. This call for a trinitarian missiology is vitally important because, among other reasons, it concerns the justifying authority of the missionary movement. In an age where past justifications of the Christian missionary enterprise were being exposed as inadequate and problematic, Newbigin understood the necessity of developing a carefully thought-through trinitarian theology of mission to undergird the ongoing mission of the church. In this regard it is interesting to observe Hunsberger's comment: "I never was around Bishop Newbigin when he was not working hard to cultivate for the church a sense of its authority to preach the gospel, and its authority to believe that it is true."[7] It is not surprising that Newbigin wrote his major work on trinitarian missiology in the 1960s, which arguably represents the decade of the last century when the church's mission came under the most intense and damaging assault.

Much has changed since the 1960s but the issue of the authority of the church to carry the gospel to the ends of the earth has not. For much of Newbigin's life, and still today, there exists a form of religious pluralism that rejects the morality and necessity of missions because it teaches that "the various world religions [need to] accept one another as fellow-climbers of the cloud covered mountain on whose summit in the mists God dwells unseen."[8] Modernity, with its plausibility structures stemming from the En-

---

6. Tennent says "Newbigin's prophetic realisation about the need for a Trinitarian missiology remains one of his important legacies" (Tennent, *Invitation to World Missions*, 68).

7. Hunsberger, "Apostle," 2.

8. Watt, *Islam and Christianity Today*, 146. More recently, Pratt suggested that the message of Christianity and the message of Islam have their source in the same universal revelation. "Jesus and Mohammad are different historic personalities, who lived in different times and different situations, and who were—and are still—differently understood; yet they are equally bearers of revelation, equally messengers of God" (Pratt,

lightenment, rejects outright the claims of the gospel, thereby undercutting the legitimacy of the missionary movement. Many associated with what is commonly called late- or post-modernity further emasculate the missionary movement by positing that ultimate truth cannot in fact be known. They maintain that there is no overarching metanarrative which is true for all, and argue that any attempt to promote one's views to others is simply the 'will to power'. Newbigin's missiological work can be understood as a response to each of these challenges regarding the validity of Christian belief and missionary praxis, and restoring a 'proper confidence' in the church to believe and proclaim the gospel.

Behind this most practical of concerns lies the biblical and theological imperative to exposit robustly the theology of mission. From his reading of the gospels and the rest of Scripture, Newbigin knew that the commissioning of the church for mission was accompanied by Christ's giving of the Holy Spirit and that both Christ and the Spirit were themselves given and sent by the Father. The import of this for Newbigin can be grasped when one is aware that he displays "the impulses of the systematic theologian in his press for a cogent and coherent theological perspective . . . yet remains distinctly biblical in his approach."[9] Newbigin contends that to think through missiological questions in a theological manner requires an understanding of the *missio ecclesiae* in terms of the doctrine of God as Father, Son and Spirit.[10] To locate and ground the church's mission apart from the mission of the Triune God is to misunderstand it. Furthermore, Newbigin also knew that everything in theology is determined by one's doctrine of God, and so he would agree with his contemporary Colin Gunton who spoke of "doing theology from the Trinity" because "everything looks—and indeed is—different in the light of the Trinity."[11]

In summary, Newbigin called for the development of a trinitarian missiology out of faithfulness to the gospel, the drive to think through the theology of mission with clarity and precision, and to provide a permanent theological justification for the church's mission.

## NEWBIGIN'S OWN CONTRIBUTION

Newbigin's own contribution to the project of developing a trinitarian missiology came chiefly in his 1963 book, *Trinitarian Doctrine For Today's*

---

"Islam," 8).
    9. Hunsberger, *Bearing the Witness of the Spirit*, 43.
   10. Newbigin, *Trinitarian Doctrine*, 82.
   11. Gunton, *The Promise*, xxix, 4–5.

*Mission*, which will be examined in chapter 2. He attempts to develop this trinitarian missiology in his later missiological work *The Open Secret*, but "Newbigin's project was never fully worked out." He "never attempted anything more than the broad outlines of a Trinitarian theology of mission."[12] His own insights are not insignificant or without profundity, of course, but his main contribution towards developing a trinitarian missiology lay not so much in the content of his own work but in his call for others to take up this task. This work is a response to that call.

As a missionary and missiologist Newbigin's writing was always occasional and completed 'on the run'.[13] Fully aware of this, Newbigin insisted that he was not a systematic theologian.[14] Therefore, his own contributions to the development of a trinitarian missiology are indicative rather than comprehensive. Nevertheless, his work is valuable in numerous ways. He acted as a theological and missiological scout, who went ahead of the missionary church, reporting back with advanced knowledge and pointing it in the right direction. In other words, to change the metaphor, Newbigin was something of a prophet,[15] despite rejecting that designation,[16] because "He had the ability to see what lies ahead and articulate it. More than that, Newbigin clarified the issues and laid out an agenda."[17] In accordance with these observations, Wilbert Shenk has characterized Newbigin as a 'strategic thinker'[18] whilst Michael Goheen says his theology is chiefly '*ad hoc* and contextual', since Newbigin engages with the burning issues of the day within the crucible of missionary engagement.[19] It is in this way that Newbigin fulfilled his prophetic office of calling God's people forward. My own

---

12. Tennent, *Invitation to World Missions*, 68.

13. Shenk, "Lesslie Newbigin's Contribution," 3.

14. Stults comments "while he never developed a systematic theology, it is evident upon reading his work that he is a systematic thinker with certain core theological convictions that dominate his thinking" (Stults, *Grasping Truth and Reality*, ix). Nevertheless, it is also true that "Virtually everything Newbigin wrote was 'on assignment', that is, in response to a request to speak or write for a particular occasion. He found no time for leisurely and detached reflection. He spoke and wrote 'on the run'" (Shenk, "Lesslie Newbigin's Contribution," 3).

15. So called by Rt. Revd. Sandy Millar. "Foreword," Newbigin, *Discovering Truth*, vi. See also the title of the proceedings of the 1998 "After Newbigin" international conference, *A Scandalous Prophet*.

16. "I am no prophet" (Newbigin, "Mission in the 1980's," 154).

17. Shenk, "A Tribute," 4.

18. "Rather than a systematic scholar attempting to provide a comprehensive account, he is best characterized as a strategic thinker" (Shenk, "Lesslie Newbigin's Contribution," 4).

19. Goheen, "As the Father Has Sent Me," 6, 271.

task in this work is to take up his challenge to develop a robustly theological trinitarian missiology.

## SECONDARY WORK ON NEWBIGIN

This enquiry into Newbigin's thought not only differs from, but also complements the existing corpus of Newbigin literature. Most of the major works that engage heavily with Newbigin focus on a specific aspect of Newbigin's thought, except for three multi-authored volumes,[20] and Geoffrey Wainwright's excellent theological biography of Newbigin. The first major monograph on Newbigin, by George Hunsberger, is entitled *Bearing the Witness of the Spirit: Lesslie Newbigin's Theology of Cultural Plurality*. It focuses on Newbigin's theology of culture, which "attempts to respond theologically to the phenomenon of culture, cultures, and the plurality of cultures found in the world."[21] Two monographs, Paul Weston's *Mission and Cultural Change: A Critical Engagement with the Writings of Lesslie Newbigin* and Donald LeRoy Stults' *Grasping Truth and Reality: Lesslie Newbigin's Theology of Mission to the Western World*, specifically take up Newbigin's summons for a Christian missionary engagement with Western culture. Sijo Jacob's *Religious Pluralism and the Finality of Christ: Christological Reflections from Lesslie Newbigin* and Samuel George's *The Gospel as Public Truth: An Indian Multi-Religious Perspective on Lesslie Newbigin* focus on the theology of religions, whilst Jürgen Schuster's *Christian Mission in Eschatological Perspective: Lesslie Newbigin's Contribution* examines the eschatological dimension of Newbigin's missiology. Michael Goheen studies Newbigin's missiology from the perspective of his ecclesiology,[22] as does Jukka Keskitalo, but unfortunately the latter's work is only available in Finnish. There is also a growing set of literature studying Newbigin in dialogue with other significant thinkers, including Kenneth Cragg,[23] John Howard Yoder,[24] John Hick,[25] and C. S. Lewis.[26]

---

20. Foust et al., *A Scandalous Prophet*; Laing and Weston, *Theology in Missionary Perspective*; Sunquist and Yong, *The Gospel and Pluralism Today*.

21. Hunsberger, *Bearing the Witness of the Spirit*, 9.

22. Goheen, "As the Father Has Sent Me."

23. Wood, *Faiths and Faithfulness*.

24. Nikolajsen, *The Distinctive Identity of the Church*.

25. Adams, *Christ and the Other*.

26. Feddes, *Missional Apologetics*. In addition to published works, Kenneth Gordon is conducting his doctoral research at Spurgeon's College, UK, on evangelical and ecumenical perspectives in the life and work of Lesslie Newbigin and Willem Visser 't Hooft.

The variety of studies on Newbigin's thought reflects some of the depth and range of his work. The number and variety of these publications on Newbigin substantiates Kettle's claim that Newbigin's thought is neither out of date nor belonging to a past age; rather, its relevance invites further dialogue.[27] This further dialogue is especially important since some crucial areas of Newbigin's thought still require further development, including his trinitarian missiology. Among the existing corpus of Newbigin literature there is no work that attempts to develop a trinitarian missiology in the way I attempt to in this present work. Thus Yong is incorrect in stating "to my knowledge, to date, Newbigin scholarship has focussed on his trinitarian theology."[28] Rather Newbigin scholarship has focused largely in three areas: missionary engagement with Western culture (the interface between the gospel and culture), the theology of religions, and missionary ecclesiology. The lack of significant engagement with Newbigin's trinitarian missiology is the *raison d'etre* of this present work, which I hope will contribute to the ongoing dialogue with Newbigin's thought, and fill a gap in existing literature in both Newbigin studies and trinitarian missiology.

## THE CONTRIBUTION OF THIS STUDY

For several decades now, there has been a widespread renaissance in trinitarian theology, catalyzed by the contributions of Karl Barth, Karl Rahner, and Vladimir Lossky. This trend shows no signs of abating because theologians continue to recognize the central importance of the doctrine of God for all areas of theology. In addition to a plethora of studies concerned directly with the doctrine of the Trinity itself, there have been numerous studies that have explored the implications of the doctrine for other areas of Christian theology, including: Christology,[29] Pneumatology,[30] the doctrine of creation,[31] theological anthropology,[32] soteriology,[33] ecclesiology,[34]

---

27. Kettle, "Unfinished Dialogue?," 25–28.
28. Yong, "Pluralism," 147.
29. Sanders and Issler, *Jesus in Trinitarian Perspective*; Cook, *Trinitarian Christology*; Habets, *The Anointed Son*.
30. Del Colle, *Christ and the Spirit*.
31. Gunton, *The Triune Creator*.
32. Bellinger, *The Trinitarian Self*; Grenz, *The Social God*.
33. Sherman, *King, Priest, and Prophet*.
34. Volf, *After Our Likeness*; Treier and Lauber, *Trinitarian Theology for the Church*.

doxology,[35] ministry,[36] proclamation,[37] the theology of religions,[38] and the interaction of theology and science.[39] Given this extent of trinitarian theological publishing, the dearth of work on the trinitarian theology of mission is surprising; indeed the first two books on the doctrine of the Trinity and mission only appeared in 2010.[40] I surmise the reason for this is the broader neglect of missiology within the discipline of theology.

David Bosch notes that in the early church mission was the "mother of theology" (Kähler), but as Europe became Christianized theology lost its missionary dimension. This is because as the early church movement became increasingly institutionalized, "The impetuous missionary torrent of earlier years was tamed into a still-flowing rivulet and eventually into a stationary pond."[41] For much of church history missiology has been largely absent from the mainstream theological enterprise, and even when it was included it became the theological institution's "department of foreign affairs," exotic but peripheral. Edinburgh missionary historian Andrew Walls concurs, suggesting that at the theological banqueting table ". . .mission studies are roughly the equivalent of after-dinner mints."[42] Reflecting on his own theological education at Cambridge, Christopher Wright recalls "there seemed to be little connection at all between theology and mission in the mind of the lecturers, or of myself, or, for all I knew, in the mind of God either."[43] Theology and mission seemed to be concerned with two very separate endeavors. Writing for the The Catholic Theological Society of America, Stephen Bevans notes that the marginalizing of missiology is analogous to neglect of the doctrine of the Trinity.

> Like the doctrine of the Trinity until very recently— and, I believe, in a not-unrelated way—mission has long been marginalized and isolated in Christian theological reflection; and while it might no longer be true of the Trinity, it is still true that, should

---

35. Torrance, *Worship, Community*.
36. Seamands, *Ministry in the Image of God*.
37. Pasquarello, *Christian Preaching*.
38. Heim, *The Depth of the Riches*; Lai, *Towards a Trinitarian Theology of Religions*.
39. Polkinghorne, *Science and the Trinity*.
40. Flett, *The Witness of God* and Tennent, *Invitation to World Missions*. These are both complementary and welcome contributions to the area of trinitarian missiology. Substantial and important differences remain, however, with this present work, in methodology, in scope, and in detail.
41. Bosch, *Transforming Mission*, 53.
42. Walls, *The Cross-Cultural Process*, 273.
43. Wright, *The Mission of God*, 21.

mission have to be dropped as false, the major part of religious literature could well remain virtually unchanged.[44]

This is disastrous for the integrity of theology, for theology is the study of the self-revelation of God in the missions of the Son and the Spirit. Furthermore, theology, says Jenson, is "the church's continuing communal effort to think through her mission of speaking the gospel."[45] Missiology is not just one subdiscipline within the theological enterprise but is part of the fabric of every branch of theology, permeating the whole and all its parts. Theology is missionary by definition, therefore, "theology ceases to be theology if it loses its missionary character."[46] Thus the resurgence in trinitarian theology needs to be accompanied with the restoration of missiology as integral to systematic theology. Newbigin himself made a considerable contribution to restoring mission back at the heart of the theological enterprise.[47] It is my hope that this study, which develops a constructive trinitarian missiology that builds on Newbigin's work, will further contribute to this endeavor.

This study, which started life as a PhD thesis, is a constructive work of trinitarian missiology[48] in which I seek to make two particular contributions to current missiological discussion. First, I hope to deepen and extend our understanding of Newbigin's trinitarian missiology. Second, I hope to provide a systematic account of the central features of the mission of the Triune God in the tradition of Lesslie Newbigin. This will particularly include a consideration of the being of God *ad intra* in which mission is grounded, and the being of God *ad extra* through which mission is enacted. I will further consider the person and work of the Son, the person and work of the Holy Spirit, and the incorporation of the church into the mission of God. I hope, thereby, to heed the recent call for deliberation on Christian mission to be retrieved from the theological margins and placed where it belongs as centrally important to systematic theology.

This study falls neatly into two parts. Part One first examines the main contours of Newbigin's missiology (chapter 1). This lays the foundation for an examination of Newbigin's own trinitarian missiology (chapter 2). In

---

44. Bevans, "Wisdom From the Margins," 22.

45. Jenson, *Systematic Theology*, 1:22. Bosch concurs: "theology, rightly understood, has no reason to exist other than critically to accompany the *missio Dei*" (*Transforming Mission*, 494).

46. Bosch, *Transforming Mission*, 494. See also Kirk, *The Mission of Theology*, 49–51.

47. Notable also is Karl Barth, with whom I frequently engage throughout this work.

48. Schmidt-Leukel argues that "there is no such thing as the trinitarian model for understanding mission" ("Mission," 57). I hope that my own work will show that there is a proper foundation for mission, indeed the only proper foundation, in the doctrine of the Trinity.

Part Two I develop a constructive and systematic trinitarian missiology that builds on Newbigin's trinitarian missiology presented in Part One. I first focus on the doctrine of the Trinity proper and its relevance for the theology of mission by discussing the Triune being of the missionary God (chapter 3). In chapter 4 I propose an explicitly trinitarian account of the mission of the Son and the mission of the Holy Spirit, and in chapter 5 I develop a trinitarian account of the mission of the church as participation in the *missio trinitatis Dei*. In my concluding chapter (chapter 6) I will offer my own appraisal of Newbigin's missiology. I will also suggest how further work in trinitarian missiology might proceed. In pursuing this project, I have drawn especially upon my own evangelical Protestant tradition.

PART ONE

# The Trinitarian Missiology of Lesslie Newbigin

CHAPTER 1

# The Contours of Newbigin's Missiology

## INTRODUCTION

JAMES EDWARD LESSLIE NEWBIGIN was born in England in 1909 and was educated at Cambridge University, where he became a Christian. In 1936, after postgraduate theological study at Cambridge, the Church of Scotland sent Newbigin as a missionary to South India. He participated in the 1947 formation of the Church of South India (thereafter CSI), a church reunion of Presbyterian, Anglican, Methodist and Congregational churches. In that same year he became a Bishop in the CSI, where he remained (with the exception of approximately 6 years[1]) until 1974. Throughout his mission to India, Newbigin saw his task as primarily that of teacher, pastor and evangelist. He carried out his teaching role through the publication of many books concerning ecclesiology,[2] soteriology,[3] missiology,[4] secularism,[5] the theology of religions,[6] and books on the Christian faith that were addressed specifically to his Indian context.[7] In 1974 Newbigin retired from his role as the

---

1. From 1959–1965 Newbigin was seconded by the CSI to the IMC in London (1959–1961), and upon its merger with the WCC, to the DWME of the WCC in Geneva (1962–1965).

2. *The Reunion of the Church*; *The Household of God*.

3. *Sin and Salvation*.

4. *A South India Diary*; *One Body, One Gospel, One World*; *Trinitarian Doctrine*.

5. *Honest Religion For Secular Man*.

6. In 1958 Newbigin gave the Noble Lectures at Harvard University, later published as *A Faith For This One World?*; *The Finality of Christ*.

7. *Christ Our Eternal Contemporary*; *Journey Into Joy*. Both are transcripts of addresses given as part of teaching missions at the Christian Medical College, Vellore.

CSI Bishop of Madras and returned to England. There he embarked upon a new and arguably more difficult mission, his mission to Modernity; it is for this missiological contribution that he is most well-known. In this mission his role as teacher, pastor and evangelist continued unabated. His writings focused on critical engagement with modernity's plausibility structures that undermine the veracity of the gospel, and restoring to the Western church a proper confidence in the gospel and in its missionary identity and calling.

The purpose of this chapter is to sketch the contours of Newbigin's theological framework, identifying and explicating its main themes and key doctrines. This will then serve as a context in which to study the place of the doctrine of the Trinity in Newbigin's thought (chapter 2).

## ELECTION IN NEWBIGIN'S MISSIOLOGY

### Missional Election

For Newbigin, "The Bible is primarily the story of election,"[8] of "God's choosing (election) of a people to be His own people, by whom He purposes to save the world."[9] As with all Newbigin's theology, he expounded the doctrine of election as found in the biblical narrative.[10] We join that narrative in Jesus' calling of the twelve disciples.

> It has often been pointed out that it was significant that Jesus chose twelve men—the number of the tribes of Israel. This is a representative number. He did not simply invite anyone who cared to join. He chose twelve. The twelve in some sense represent Israel; but in what sense? They are the *pars pro toto*, the part which represents the whole. But in what sense do they represent the whole? . . . [I]s the Church the *pars pro toto* in the sense that it is sent in order that the rest of the world may be converted? That certainly seems to be the sense implied in the story of the calling of the first apostles, who are promised that they will become fishers of men.[11]

*Firstly, election for Newbigin signifies God's strategy[12] of choosing some on behalf of all, choosing some for the sake of all.* Thus, the biblical doctrine

---

8. Newbigin, *A Faith For This One World?*, 77.
9. Newbigin, "Why Study," 75.
10. Hunsberger comments that in Newbigin's theological method he is "distinctly biblical in his approach" (*Bearing the Witness of the Spirit*, 43).
11. Newbigin, *Finality of Christ*, 97, emphases original.
12. This language comes from Forster and Marston, *God's Strategy in Human History*.

of election is for Newbigin inextricable from conversion and mission. Accordingly, "Conversion will always be wrongly understood unless it is remembered that the Church is the *pars pro toto*. God converts a man not only that he may be saved, but also that he may be the sign, earnest and instrument of God's total plan of salvation."[13]

In the chapter on election in his dogmatics, Emil Brunner begins his discussion with a warning: "The history of the doctrine of Predestination itself teaches us that with the question of the Divine Decrees we have entered the danger-zone, in which faith may suffer severe injury, and theological thinking may easily stray into disastrous error."[14] Brunner had in mind Augustine as interpreted and developed by Calvin and the Calvinist tradition, which taught that God predestined some persons for salvation (the elect) and passed over others (the reprobate). Although identifying with the Reformed tradition, Newbigin does not approach this doctrine within these parameters. Rather, his reading of the doctrine of the election is decisively missional.

Newbigin was aware of the errors in the history of this doctrine and so warned, like Brunner, that election "is so basic to the biblical doctrine of the church and yet capable of such terribly unbiblical distortion."[15] In line with his Reformed heritage Newbigin accepted that God chooses some and not others, whilst he emphatically rejected other elements of the tradition such as double predestination.[16] In Newbigin's view, mission was the heart of the doctrine of election, but historically this had been transplanted by spiritual elitism and privilege. He says,

> And we can see that wherever the missionary character of the doctrine of election is forgotten; wherever it is forgotten that we are chosen in order to be sent; wherever the minds of believers are concerned more to probe backwards from their election into the reasons for it in the secret counsel of God than to press forwards from their election to the purpose of it, which is that they should be Christ's ambassadors and witnesses to the ends of the earth; wherever men think that the purpose of election is their own salvation rather than the salvation of the world: then God's people have betrayed their trust.[17]

13. Newbigin, *Finality of Christ*, 113.
14. Brunner, *Dogmatics*, 1:303.
15. Newbigin, *The Household of God*, 100.
16. Interestingly, one is hard pressed to find any references to predestination in Newbigin's writings. This is surprising given that election is so central to Newbigin's theology and is traditionally discussed in conjunction with predestination.
17. Newbigin, *The Household of God*, 101.

Given Newbigin's theological context, it was necessary for him to articulate his doctrine of election as responsibility against a background of election as spiritual privilege. Indeed, it might have been the repugnancy of the distortion that awakened him to the doctrine's missionary dimension; one cannot be sure. Having said this, Newbigin's doctrine of election was not primarily responsive to and corrective of other deficient doctrinal articulations, but constructive. Newbigin admits it is an unknowable mystery why God chooses (elects) some, but one can know the purpose, and it is here that his accent falls. "When . . . she [the church] thinks of her election in terms of spiritual privilege rather than missionary responsibility, then she comes under His merciful judgement as Israel did."[18] *Secondly therefore, Newbigin's doctrine of election is about missionary calling and responsibility.*

The context of divine election is Jesus Christ. "God's purpose proceeds by way of election, of choosing; and the Chosen and Beloved is none other than Jesus Christ."[19] Although reminiscent of Karl Barth, I believe this aspect of Newbigin's thought originated primarily from his study of Scripture.[20] As early as 1953 Newbigin wrote,

> It is He [Jesus] who is the elect of God, His beloved, His chosen One. Our election is only by our incorporation in Him. We are not elect as isolated individuals, but as members in His Body. The instrument of His choosing is precisely the apostolic mission of the Church. 'I chose you,' says the incarnate Lord to His apostles, 'and appointed you, that ye should go and bear fruit' (John 15:16).[21]

*Thirdly, it is evident that Newbigin's doctrine of election is both christocentric and ecclesial in nature,* and furthermore, it leads directly to a relational theological anthropology.

## *Relational Theological Anthropology*

To rightly explicate a theological anthropology, Newbigin insists that one must begin with the doctrine of the Triune God because God enjoys ontological and epistemological priority. Describing the divine life, Newbigin

---

18. Ibid., 132.

19. Newbigin, *Trinitarian Doctrine*, 51.

20. Newbigin did not extensively read Barth until immediately after the India period in 1974. Although he had heard elements of Barth's theology prior to this he had found him "totally unimpressive" (*Unfinished Agenda*, 241).

21. Newbigin, *The Household of God*, 102.

states that "Interpersonal relatedness belongs to the very being of God."[22] Then, as if out of the gratuitous overflow of the trinitarian perichoretic love that is the divine interpersonal relatedness, God created humanity. Therefore human life corresponds, to some extent, to the divine life.

> It is that human beings are created in love and for love, created for fellowship with one another in a mutual love which is the free gift of God whose inner life is the perfect mutuality of love—Father Son and Spirit; that happiness consists in participation in this love which is the being of God.[23]

Drawing on Dutch philosopher Van Peurson and Greek orthodox theologian John Zizioulas, Newbigin understands God's being to be a Being-in-relatedness.[24] The doctrine of the Trinity grounds the origin, nature and purpose of human life. Newbigin sees this especially in his understanding of the *imago Dei*. It is "being-in-relatedness for which God made us and the world and which is the image of that being-in-relatedness which is the being of God himself."[25] Drawing on Genesis, Newbigin affirms that

> the nature of man is that he was made in love, by love, and for love. Love is the source and end of his being. Therefore man cannot live alone. For this reason, in the very same verse in which the Scripture tells us that God created man in His own image, it goes on to say 'male and female created he them.' When God created man He did not create an individual; He created man-and-woman. For God is not an individual; God is personal but He is not a person. He is a Trinity, Father, Son and Holy Spirit, one God; one personal being in whom love is perfect and complete because love is both given and received. The Father loves the Son and the Son loves the Father, in the unity of the Holy Spirit. When we say 'God is Love', we mean that the fullness of love exists in God. But fullness of love only exists where love is both given and received. Fullness of love cannot exist in an individual. Therefore also when God created man in His own image, He created him male and female. The image of God is not seen in an individual man, but in man-and-woman bound

---

22. Newbigin, *The Open Secret*, 70.

23. Newbigin, *The Welfare State*, 11.

24. I develop this in "Being Is in Communion: God Is Love" in chapter 3. Newbigin, "Human Flourishing," 405.

25. Although Newbigin does not use this language he is content to see vestiges of the divine activity in creation, in particular in those creatures made in the divine image. Newbigin, *The Open Secret*, 70.

together in love. Thus God has placed in the very constitution of man the need for and the possibility of love.[26]

Newbigin realized that 'no man is an island' (John Donne), and instead, the essential nature of what it means to be truly human is found in relationships of love. Thus, "The image of God is present in this relatedness-in-love (Gen 1:27)."[27] This human being-in-relatedness is directed to God, to fellow human beings, and more broadly to creation itself.[28] *Fourthly, human life is inherently interdependent and social by divine design.*

Placing theological anthropology within this context of creation's materiality is important for Newbigin, who develops his theology of being human in relation to a competing anthropology prevalent in both Indian and Western cultures. Making sweeping generalizations, Newbigin argues that Indian and Greco-Roman anthropology is idealistic wherein the human is essentially spiritual in nature; the physical is incidental at best and evil at worst. The human being is conceived of as a spiritual monad and consequently the soul is of greater significance than the body. Newbigin observed this same view of humans is being strengthened in the West through its contact with Indian religion and culture, and prominently features in both Enlightenment thought (Descartes)[29] and modern thought (John Hick).[30]

In the Bible, this mind-body, spirit-flesh dichotomy is simply absent and all of life is viewed as a unified whole that includes physical, mental and spiritual dimensions. For Newbigin, we *become* human beings through shared relationships with other humans as part of the world of created order.[31] We have no knowledge of souls that have not become known to us as embodied persons.[32]

> In contrast to those forms of spirituality that seek the 'real' self by looking within, the Bible invites us to see the real human life as a life of shared relationships in a world of living creatures and created things, a life of mutual personal responsibility for the

26. Newbigin, *Sin and Salvation*, 17–18.
27. Newbigin, *The Open Secret*, 69.
28. Newbigin, *Living Hope*, 16–17.

29. Descartes' *cogito* is thoroughly individualistic because he can define himself without reference to any other person. Relations with others are not, for Descartes, constitutive of what it means to be human. Furthermore, Descartes' anthropology is dualistic because he views a human being as a mind disconnected from its body and the rest of the material world; "a disembodied objective eye," to use Newbigin's description. Newbigin, *Discovering Truth*, 7–8.

30. Newbigin, *The Open Secret*, 102. See also John Hick, *Death and Eternal Life*.
31. Newbigin, "Salvation," 1.
32. Newbigin, *The Open Secret*, 102.

created world, its animal and vegetable life and is resources of soil and water and air. This, and no other, is the real human life, which is the object of God's primal blessing and of his saving purpose.[33]

In the Old Testament there is a pagan myth of the primeval conflict, in which the dragon is murdered and the world made from its corpse. "It is a primal myth where violence is seen as the origin or basis of human life. In our own time, through various supposed implications of Darwin's theory of evolution, there is the idea that human life is to be understood as a power struggle," survival of the fittest. By contrast,

> The doctrine of God as Trinity gives us a completely different picture of what the ultimate meaning of human life is. It means that the primordial reality from which all things come, and to which all things are directed, is that shared communion of love and bliss which is the being of the Trinity. This makes an enormous difference to the way we understand the human situation.[34]

Hence, out of all the Old Testament divine imperatives, Jesus highlights, in Mark 12:30–31, loving God with all your heart, mind, soul and strength, and loving your neighbor as yourself.

> Human beings find fulfilment not in the attempt to develop themselves, not in the effort to better their own condition, not in the untrammeled exercise of unlimited covetousness, but in the experience of mutual relatedness and responsibility in serving a shared goal.[35]

This shared goal is the *missio ecclesiae*, which is a participation in the *missio Dei*. To summarize, Newbigin's theological vision of humanity is that the human only exists in relationship with other persons and only as part of the world created by the Triune God.

---

33. Ibid., 69.
34. Newbigin, *Living Hope*, 15.
35. Newbigin continues, "shared commitment to a common purpose. That is what brings human beings to their very best, and most of us know it. Part of the terrible irony of war is that it enlists the best in human nature for purposes of mutual destruction" (*Foolishness To The Greeks*, 122).

## Relational Theology of Election

Newbigin most often contrasts a Christian theological anthropology and soteriology with what he calls Indian thought, which conceives of salvation as ultimately a matter between each individual soul and God. In this theological framework election appears to be arbitrary favoritism. However, based on his relational conception of what it means to be human, election is quite the opposite. Newbigin writes,

> once it is understood that salvation is corporate and cosmic, and that therefore the means which God employs for our salvation must be congruous with that end, it becomes clear that God must deal with us according to the principle of election. One race is chosen in order that through it God's salvation may be mediated to others, and it may thus become the nucleus of a new redeemed humanity.[36]

In divine election God chooses some that they be the channel of divine grace for others. God chose this method rather than communicating with each soul directly through general or special revelation—a separate communication to each individual.

> But a salvation whose very essence is that it is corporate and cosmic, the restoration of the broken harmony between all men and between man and God and man and nature, must be communicated in a different way. It must be communicated in and by the actual development of a community which embodies—if only in foretaste—the restored harmony of which it speaks. A gospel of reconciliation can only be communicated by a reconciled fellowship.[37]

God's purpose is that human beings should have a concern for their fellow human beings. Therefore, God chooses one to be sent to another, and so on, so that all may be knit together in one redeemed fellowship. Thus the church becomes "His reconciled and reconciling people."[38] For Newbigin, salvation depicted a making whole, a unifying of all creation whose source and pattern is the love within the life of the Triune God, "the summing up of all things in Christ."[39] Therefore, there can be no private salvation; we cannot experience salvation in its fullness until all for whom it is intended

---

36. Newbigin, *The Household of God*, 100.
37. Ibid., 141.
38. Ibid., 101.
39. Eph 1:10, NASB.

have it together.⁴⁰ Correctly describing Newbigin's understanding of election, Hunsberger says "God's method of choosing particular witnesses is congruent with the social nature of the gospel which envisions the healing of the nations."⁴¹ Election is God's mission strategy, and that is why Newbigin cannot conceive of election without mission; the two are entirely interconnected.⁴²

Newbigin's missiology is inextricably bound up with divine election, for that is the divinely chosen method of mission. Jesus is the one who is elect and the church is elect in him. The church has been chosen and reconciled to God in order to be instrumental in reconciling all humanity, and thus is by nature missionary. Summarizing missional election, Newbigin says,

> The source of election is in the depths of God's gracious will 'before the foundation of the world'; its context is 'in Christ'; its instrument is the apostolic mission to the ends of the earth; its end is to sum up all things in Christ; and its means, seal and token is the presence of God's Holy Spirit—opening men's hearts to believe the Gospel, knitting them in love into the fellowship of the body of Christ, giving them in foretaste the powers of the age to come, and sealing them as Christ's until His coming again.⁴³

The doctrine of election is foundational to all of Newbigin's missiology.⁴⁴ Hunsberger notes "in the 'missionary significance of the biblical doctrine of election' we find a thread that runs . . . throughout the range of his writings."⁴⁵

## REVELATION AND THE KNOWLEDGE OF GOD

God savingly reveals himself by acting in history, in the exodus from Egypt, and supremely in the incarnation of his Son. Knowledge of these salvific events is communicated by the work of the Holy Spirit, through the community of Jesus Christ and through Scripture. When God does reveal himself in

40. Newbigin, *The Household of God*, 140.
41. Hunsberger, "Renewing Faith," 12.
42. Newbigin, *The Household of God*, 141.
43. Ibid., 103.
44. Hunsberger contends that election is Newbigin's primary missiological theme, and there is much evidence to support this claim. Hunsberger, *Bearing the Witness of the Spirit*, 67. See also ibid., 45–112.
45. Hunsberger, "Renewing Faith," 12.

history,[46] God is still Lord of his self-disclosure. Newbigin holds to a strong doctrine of divine sovereignty, and emphasizes that God does not choose to reveal himself to all people simultaneously, but to some for the sake of all. Thus, Newbigin remarks "that it must be both a veiling and an unveiling if it is to be true."[47] This is why he entitles one of his major missiological works *The Open Secret*. The truth of God is open to the eyes of faith but is veiled, secret, to those outside of this company. Although knowledge of God belongs only to the church, when this is combined with Newbigin's missionary doctrine of election, it is understood that through the church's mission all are to be invited to become participants in this knowledge.

However, humans are not readily receptive to this invitation, to God's self-introduction, because they are enslaved by sin. "The world is not free as it thinks it is." Newbigin continues, "We are not honest inquirers seeking the truth. We are alienated from truth and are enemies of it. We are by nature idolaters, constructing images of truth shaped by our own desires."[48] Since the unregenerate mind is at enmity with God (Rom 8:7), Newbigin argues that the truth of God cannot be incorporated into any pre-existent human structure of meaning, for all human knowing, when encountered by divine revelation, will be exposed as faulty and inadequate.[49] For this reason he writes, "the mark of a true revelation of God is that it will be rejected by the world . . . revelation must create a crisis for the world because it destroys the world's estimate of itself. Revelation must involve contradiction."[50] For the recipients of revelation, knowledge of God involves deconstruction before it involves construction. This is where human responsiveness to God's self-revelation is of paramount importance.

In God's self-revelation he is seeking to draw humans into personal engagement with himself, and this engagement then becomes the source and foundation of all knowledge. Newbigin frequently reminds his readers that in God's self-disclosure he is seeking a personal response; in other words, human knowledge of God involves a trusting obedience. As the starting point for this knowledge he writes, "The act of turning in trust to Jesus—however far short it may fall of full understanding—is the indispensable starting point for understanding."[51] Regardless of whether someone is

---

46. Whilst affirming this claim, Barth rightly and carefully qualifies it in Barth, *CD* I/1, 325–6.
47. Newbigin, *The Light Has Come*, 97.
48. Newbigin, *Proper Confidence*, 69.
49. Newbigin, *The Light Has Come*, 69.
50. Ibid., 93.
51. Ibid., 51.

turning to Jesus for the first time, or has been a Christian for decades, "It is only as we obey the light that we see in them that we shall be granted further light."[52] Newbigin's teaching is based on his understanding of Scripture and no doubt upon his pastoral and personal experience, but he also cites Liberation Theology to support his contention. In agreement with Gutierrez, he asserts "that there can be no dualism between a timeless 'spiritual' truth and the time-conditioned concrete historical situation. Therefore, true theology does not begin in the realm of ideas. It begins with praxis."[53] Newbigin is concerned to hold together both theory and praxis, truth and action, particularly against the ancient and modern philosophical traditions, including Plato and Lessing, which posit an 'ugly ditch' between historical happenings and eternal truths. Against this history of Western dualism, Newbigin maintains that "Salvation is God's action in history, and therefore truth can be known only through participation in this action."[54] Knowledge of God belongs to the realm of ideas and of history, because they are aspects of the same created reality. The response of obedience to God in his self-revelation will consist of a spiritual response that is expressed in action, similar to the disciples' response to the invitation of Jesus: 'Follow me' (Mark 1:17 and parallels).

In Newbigin's theology, knowing God by faith and obedience is trinitarian in shape: "knowing God means following Jesus the Son on his path of love and obedience to the Father in the power of the Spirit who is the Spirit of the Son, and who is ever showing us new things as we faithfully follow."[55] One might add that following Jesus involves following him in his mission to the world,[56] thus it is unsurprising that Newbigin specifies that *missionary* obedience in particular brings about further knowledge of God. Jesus' promise (in John 16:12–15) that the Holy Spirit will guide the disciples into all truth "was at the very heart of the mission of the church." He continues, "As they went out in the power of the Spirit to take the gospel to all the nations, the Spirit would show them the fullness of what it meant that Jesus was, and is, Lord."[57] Elsewhere he writes, "The promise that the Holy Spirit will lead the church into the fullness of the truth is set in the

---

52. Newbigin, *The Good Shepherd*, 142.

53. Newbigin, *The Open Secret*, 95. See also *Trinitarian Doctrine*, 26.

54. Newbigin, *The Open Secret*, 96. In making this affirmation Newbigin necessarily rejects the claim of Cartesian dualism that the human senses are unreliable, and he affirms the happenings of history can be reliably known. Newbigin, *New Birth Into A Living Hope*.

55. Newbigin, "The Bible and Our Contemporary Mission," 16.

56. For an exploration of this subject, see Dodds "The Centrality."

57. Newbigin, *Living Hope*, 44.

context of the missionary commission. So the insights given in the exercise of cross-cultural mission are essential to the fulfilment of that promise."[58] Missionary praxis leads uniquely to greater illumination concerning what it means to know God.

For Newbigin, the Bible functions as an irreplaceable 'means of grace' in knowing God, though he does not use this precise language. For Newbigin, always consciously biblical in his theology, knowledge of God comes through dwelling and participating in God's story as revealed in the Scriptures.[59] Newbigin teaches that as Christians continuously live, read, study, digest, and reflect upon the Bible, they find that they participate in its story and grow in their knowledge of God.

> We need to learn to know God as he is. There is no way by which we come to know a person except by dwelling in his or her story and, in the measure that may be possible, becoming part of it. The person who allows the biblical story to be the all-surrounding ambience of daily life and who continually seeks to place all experiences in this context finds that daily life is a continuous conversation with the one whose character is revealed in the biblical story taken as a whole.[60]

Central to God's story is his formation of the church. The Bible is not a series of infallible statements to be read apart from the community which is uniquely shaped by it, the church. Thus, knowledge of God is an ecclesial knowledge. Ecclesiocentric in much of his theology, Newbigin observes that Jesus made the Father known not by uttering a series of inerrant statements but by forming a community of friends, sharing his life with them, and leaving them to be his witnesses. "To wish that it were otherwise is to depart from the manner in which God has chosen to make himself known. The doctrine of verbal inerrancy is a direct denial of the way in which God has chosen to make himself known to us as the Father of our Lord Jesus Christ."[61] Newbigin sees the doctrine of biblical inerrancy as severing the strong ties between church and Scripture. No doubt he would approve of Trevor Hart's suggestion that Scripture and church are mutually definitive,

---

58. Newbigin, "The Enduring Validity," 53.

59. Describing Newbigin, Wainwright says "He prayed with the Bible, he preached with the Bible, he thought with the Bible, he wrote with the Bible" (*Lesslie Newbigin*, 390). At the Service of Thanksgiving for the Life of Lesslie Newbigin in Southwark Cathedral on 28 March 1998, Rev Murdoch MacKenzie said of Newbigin "He lived and moved, and had his being soaked in the words of Scripture" (quoted in Gordon, "Newbigin," 88).

60. Newbigin, *Proper Confidence*, 88–89.

61. Ibid., 89.

for "'Scripture' is that text which functions authoritatively within the church, and 'church' is that community which treats Scripture as authoritative for its life and faith, and allows it to shape its own distinctive identity."[62] This is not only a reflection of the nature of the Bible but also a reminder that God is known through the community that has been called out by him and lives in fellowship with him.

For Newbigin, knowledge of God is in marked contrast to the philosophical knowledge of eternal truths, which involves rational reflection and 'Socratic recollection.' It also differs from a modern scientific account of truth derived from 'objective' study following the empirical method. Knowledge of God does not merely consist in cerebral information but is an interpersonal relating. Due to the relationship between knowledge of God and obedience, "there can be no revelation apart from reconciliation."[63] The *telos* toward which all true knowledge of God moves is reconciliation. Revelation in the Christian tradition "is more than the communication of information; it is the giving of an invitation."[64] Newbigin then goes further still, "When we speak of God's self-revelation . . . we are speaking of reconciliation, of atonement, of salvation."[65] Expounding this further, John Webster explains that revelation is God's self-presentation to us, his speaking out. The history of that speaking out is the history whereby God establishes *saving fellowship* with his creatures.

> It is a history of *fellowship* because at the center of the history is 'God with us'; it is a history of *saving* fellowship because it is a history which triumphs over the opposition to fellowship with God which is sin. Revelation is therefore reconciliation; indeed, reconciliation is the more comprehensive communicative concept for what we mean by revelation.[66]

That the Giver cannot be dissociated from the gift enabled P. T. Forsyth to say that divine "revelation is His Self-donation."[67]

In summary, knowing God involves a trusting obedience, and this knowing takes a trinitarian shape of following Jesus in his loving obedience to the Father as enabled, and led by the Spirit. In particular, *missionary* obedience leads to further knowledge of God, because one cannot know and obey God without participation in the ongoing trinitarian missions of

---

62. Hart, "Tradition, Authority," 193.
63. Newbigin, *The Light Has Come*, 17.
64. Newbigin, *Proper Confidence*, 65.
65. Ibid., 67–68.
66. Webster, *Word and Church*, 27, emphasis original.
67. Forsyth, *The Soul of Prayer*, 18.

God to the world. Concretely, God is known by dwelling in his story, in the ongoing life of the church, and by reflecting on Scripture. Lastly, revelation and reconciliation include and require the other, and the *telos* toward which all true knowledge of God moves is reconciliation.[68]

## *The Bondage and Freedom of the Will*

God has given humans freedom, which Newbigin defines as "the power to choose between real possibilities."[69] This is in order that they may love others and join together in their shared goal of participating in God's mission to the world, and so freedom is freedom *for* loving service of God and others. However, Newbigin is also faithful to both the Scriptures and his Reformed tradition in affirming the bondage of the human will, that the person who sins is a slave to sin (John 8:34).[70] Briefly put, Newbigin teaches both that only Jesus can set people free from sin by way of a death and new birth,[71] and that God the Father "preserves . . . sufficient human freedom to enable men to accept Jesus as their Lord, or reject him."[72]

Human freedom is an important part of Newbigin's missiological enterprise because it is a key battle ground between the aforementioned competing anthropologies. Newbigin believes that in the Western context "The ideology which we have to recognize, unmask and reject is an ideology of freedom, a false and idolatrous conception of freedom which equates it with the freedom of each individual to do as he or she wishes."[73] Newbigin believes that the only proper Christian response to this false, individualistic ideology is to set

> against it the Trinitarian faith which sees all reality in terms of relatedness. In explicit rejection of an individualism which puts the autonomous self at the center and sees others selves as limitations on our freedom, we have to set the basic dogma entrusted to us, namely that freedom is to be found by being taken into that community of love given and received which is the eternal reality from which and for which all things exist. The rejection of relatedness as the true road to freedom is seen

---

68. See "Conversion and Regeneration" below.
69. Newbigin, "Socialism," 1.
70. Newbigin, *The Light Has Come*, 112.
71. Newbigin, *Proper Confidence*, 68; *The Light Has Come*, 112.
72. Newbigin, *Trinitarian Doctrine*, 52.
73. Newbigin, *Truth To Tell*, 75–76.

in the easy dissolution of the marriage bond, in the breakup of families, and in the massive development of consumerism.[74]

Newbigin's method for theological assessment, here as elsewhere, is to evaluate the topic in question; in this case human being and freedom, as contextually present in the divine economy. This is the basis of his own theological approach and the foundation from which he criticizes and exposes false doctrine. More than once Newbigin quoted fondly from the opening paragraph of Augustine's Confessions: "You have made us for yourself and our hearts are restless until they find their rest in you." Newbigin comments, "It is the simple truth that human beings cannot live forever without God ... people cannot live forever ... without meaning, without direction, without something worth dying for ... a secular society ... cannot satisfy the human spirit."[75] In marked contrast to, and with intentional rebellion from this, Newbigin writes,

> our [modern Western] society is—in its central thrust—governed by a false creed, namely, that human beings are made for self-fulfillment apart from God, for 'happiness' on terms that they are free to decide for themselves and apart from any consideration of what may be the ends for which God created us ... Human beings exist for God and for responsible relations with each other under God. The church is required to affirm this as public truth, which must govern public life even if it is contradicted by the majority. If the church fails to make this witness, it is guilty of complicity in the destruction of the nation.[76]

Articulating a theologically sound anthropology is thus an essential part of Newbigin's mission to Western culture, and one in which his doctrine of the Trinity is foundational and instrumental.

## Regeneration and Conversion

In Newbigin's mission to Modernity he sought to correct Modernity's false epistemology and anthropology. However, at the center of his mission was the summons to the 'enlightened' inhabitants of Modernity to Christian conversion. Unlike election, ecclesiology, and epistemology, Newbigin does not devote any one section or subsection of any of his major works to the

---

74. Ibid., 75–76. See also Kirk, *The Meaning of Freedom*.
75. Newbigin, *The Christian Message*.
76. Newbigin, "Response to David M. Stowe," 152.

doctrine of conversion/regeneration.[77] This has led one scholar of Newbigin, Donald Le Roy Stults, to criticize him for under-emphasizing this central missiological subject.[78] Stults' criticism, however, is mistaken because it misunderstands the nature of Newbigin's work and because it does not adequately reflect the importance that Newbigin attaches to evangelistic work, the intended outcome of which is personal conversion.[79]

Taking the latter first, Newbigin frequently spoke about the importance of personal conversion to faith in Christ. Reflecting on the integration of the IMC and WCC two decades after the event, Newbigin was concerned that missions as classically understood were being replaced by development work and inter-church aid. He reflects, "I had to . . . sustain the conviction that 'it matters supremely whether or not a person comes to know Jesus Christ', whatever their involvement in development, and that no proposed earthly utopia is a substitute for that."[80] This is not an isolated statement but is representative of Newbigin's sustained effort over decades to ensure that evangelistic work remained central to the work of the WCC. This concern surfaces frequently in Newbigin's life, such as in his debate with Konrad Raiser whom he criticizes for "total amnesia in respect of the missionary and evangelistic work of the churches" that comprises the WCC. Newbigin objects that although "Raiser speaks much of the basic significance of the confession of faith and baptism . . . there is no sign of any concern about the fact that the great majority of the world's people have not made this confession and have not been baptized."[81] To suggest, as Stults has done, that Newbigin says little about personal conversion is mistaken.

Stults is right, however, that an emphasis on personal conversion is not prominent within Newbigin's writings. This is because Newbigin's theological role was more strategic than systematic. In a private conversation on another subject with Newbigin's friend and the former leader of Holy Trinity Brompton the Rt. Rev. Sandy Millar, of Newbigin's writings he said, "Some things in life are adequately covered." Newbigin perceived that what was not 'covered' and what was the pressing need for the Western church were issues of the gospel and public truth, and Newbigin saw his job as "filling in the gaps."[82] Western missiological texts, such as those produced by the

77. For my purposes I use these two words interchangeably.
78. Stults, *Grasping Truth and Reality*, 276.
79. Newbigin, "Crosscurrents," 149.
80. Newbigin, "Integration," 248.
81. Newbigin, "Ecumenical Amnesia," 5.

82. Conversation with Bishop Sandy Millar at 1 Moray Road, Tollington Parish, Finsbury Park, London N4 on Monday 4th January, 2010. Millar's comments were in response to my question about why in Newbigin's writings he so rarely speaks about

'Church Growth' movement, already emphasized personal conversion and so this was not an area requiring Newbigin's attention. Instead, due to his aversion to Western individualism, Newbigin repeatedly emphasized that the converted "person must be immediately incorporated in a community of faith that indwells the story."[83] Rather than concentrating on personal salvation Newbigin thought it more pertinent to emphasize "there is no true giving of the self to Christ which is not at the same time a giving of the self to those for whom Christ died."[84] Absence of emphasis, however, does not mean absence altogether.

Newbigin published a journal article on conversion, and the subject of conversion pervades his writings and is particularly evident in *The Light Has Come*. Newbigin speaks movingly about the moment of his own conversion as "the acceptance of the grip of Christ's pierced hand upon the hand that pierced Him."[85] Offering a more technical description of conversion's personal nature, "Conversion . . . involves the replacement of alienation by a loving personal relationship, constantly renewed, between the self and the source of its being."[86] Consequently, criticizing Newbigin for under-emphasizing personal conversion is inappropriate. Of course conversion involves personal salvation and joining the church, but, for Newbigin, "it is these things only secondarily."[87] In writing about conversion his primary interest lay elsewhere.

I have already touched on conversion/regeneration in speaking of revelation as reconciliation, and the need for God to bridge the divine-human epistemic gulf by overcoming the human bondage of the will. When examining knowing God by dwelling in his ongoing story, the ecclesial character of conversion was discussed.[88] Further reflection on the doctrine of regeneration/conversion in the Newbigin corpus reveals several notable features.

First, commenting on John 1:18 Newbigin says "only God can make God known."[89] The fact that anyone knows God must be due to God's desire

---

signs and wonders, miracles, deliverance, healings, and prophecy. Millar's reply highlighted the strategic nature of Newbigin's ministry, which also applies to the present matter.

83. Stults, *Grasping Truth and Reality*, 276.
84. Newbigin, *The Reunion of the Church*, 97.
85. Ibid., 91.
86. Newbigin, *Finality of Christ*, 112.
87. Newbigin, "From the Editor," 149.
88. Conversion "involves an inward relationship of faith, it involves a way of behavior, *and it involves a visible companionship*" (Newbigin, "Conversion," quoted in Goheen, "As the Father Has Sent Me," 277, emphasis added).
89. Newbigin, *The Light Has Come*, 11.

and decision to make himself known, for it is a preposterous idea that the omnipotent God might be known against his will. Elsewhere Newbigin harshly treats any notion of natural theology[90] and strongly asserts the necessity of divine self-revelation as the primary prerequisite and condition for human regeneration. Elaborating on this Newbigin writes, "Only the action of the Spirit can reveal who Jesus is."[91] Salvific human faith in Jesus originates in the will and work of the Triune God. Only God *can*, and indeed *wills* to make himself known. Commenting on John 15:16—"You did not choose me but I chose you" (NASB), Newbigin says, "He [God] Himself is the one who converts."[92] Human regeneration is firstly and necessarily a work of the Triune God. God is both the author and the subject of this revelation. Echoing Karl Barth, Newbigin writes, "But if it is God himself who is revealed, the revealer and the revealed are one, not two."[93]

Second, Newbigin understands conversion in a missional way, leading inexorably to a missional ecclesiology and a missional Christian identity. In the New Testament the context of conversion is the announcement of the coming kingdom. "Conversion, in this context, is a turning round in order to participate by faith in a new reality which is the true future of the whole creation. For Newbigin, this "turning of a man to Christ [is] so that he may become a partner in Christ's work and a witness to God's Kingdom. It is the enlisting of men in God's service for the fulfilment of His purpose for the world."[94] Newbigin's concept of missional election pervades his understanding of conversion, placing it in the context of the *missio Dei*. He uses this to critique popular ecclesio-centric or anthropo-centric views of conversion as adding to the church or the individual 'being saved.' For Newbigin, the missional dimension of conversion is a necessary constituent of what

---

90. "For, if one thing is obvious, it is that the 'god' whose existence natural theology claims to demonstrate is not the God whose character is rendered in the pages of the Bible, not the God and Father of our Lord Jesus Christ, not the blessed Trinity. It is hard to deny this 'god' is a construct of the human mind and that therefore has the essential character of an idol. One has to ask whether idolatry is a step on the way to the worship of the true God, or a threat to it. If our starting point is the kind of reasoning provided by 'the Philosopher' or his many successors, it becomes difficult to accept the possibility of a true incarnation and almost impossible to regard the blessed Trinity as anything other than a piece of mystification. If this is so, must we not say that the knowledge of God given through 'natural theology' is not merely a partial knowledge but is a distorted and misleading knowledge?" (Newbigin, *Truth And Authority In Modernity*, 18–19).

91. Newbigin, *The Light Has Come*, 16.

92. Newbigin, "Conversion," 313.

93. Newbigin, *The Light Has Come*, 17.

94. Newbigin, "From the Editor," 421. Accordingly, he says, "'I will make you fishers of men', must mean 'I have converted you in order that you may go and convert others'" ("Conversion," 313).

'conversion' is, so that "If we are not willing to join Him [Christ] in inviting all men to share it; if we are content to have His love for ourselves and do not wish to share it with all, then at the end—like the elder brother—we shall be left outside."[95]

Third, Newbigin reflects on the epistemological problem of divine revelation. How can one authenticate the ministry of Jesus? How can one *know* that Jesus has truly been sent by the Father? For Newbigin, "The epistemological question has to have a theological answer;"[96] it is the activity of the Spirit who is, in the memorable words of John V. Taylor, *The Go-Between God*. It is "the Spirit of the Father and the Son by whose sovereign and gracious action my reason and conscience are enabled to acknowledge the Son and through him to join in glorifying the Father."[97] This enabling of the human conscience and reason is cruciform in character. "There has to be crisis, judgement, a breaking down and a building up, a dying and a new birth. In the end it is only through a new birth that the revelation can be received. And before there can be a new birth there must be death. The Son of man must be lifted up."[98] This death to self is related to repentance, hence conversion "includes both the inner reorientation of the heart and mind and the outward reorientation of conduct in all areas of life."[99] From the standpoint of the human recipient, knowledge of God follows the way of the cross.

Newbigin is aware that any doctrine of regeneration/conversion must account for both divine and human activity. Fourth, therefore, he stresses creaturely responsibility in conversion. "It would certainly be wrong to suggest that this new relation is established apart from any decision to accept it."[100] Here though, Newbigin is clear to emphasize the divine priority. "God's initiative precedes and evokes our search. 'You did not choose me, but I chose you' (15:16). But this does not mean ours is a passive role. On the contrary, we are questioned, challenged, called upon to take responsibility for the direction of our seeking."[101] Jesus often asks questions such as 'What do you think?' What do you want me to do for you?' In John 1:38 Jesus said "'What are you looking for?' It is a question put to everyone. At some point one has to answer it."[102] The nature of a person's participation in

---

95. Newbigin, *Sin and Salvation*, 125.
96. Newbigin, "Christianity and Culture."
97. Newbigin, *The Light Has Come*, 69.
98. Ibid., 164.
99. Newbigin, *The Open Secret*, 135.
100. Newbigin, "Christ and the World of Religions," 27.
101. Newbigin, *The Light Has Come*, 19.
102. Ibid., 19.

their conversion is not blind faith, not "an irrational leap into the unknown, but . . . the responsible acceptance of a personal invitation: 'Follow me.'"[103] The call to conversion "is a call to concrete obedience . . . to behave differently here and now in all sorts of private and public responsibilities."[104] Or, drawing on a different biblical picture, Newbigin writes, "in company with the believing community and in the communion of the Holy Spirit, we allow ourselves to be drawn, not coerced."[105]

Fifth, stressing the importance of human co-operation in conversion opens the door to what has been called the human 'power to the contrary',[106] that is, the human ability to resist the divine work of regeneration. Accordingly, Newbigin rejects an understanding of irresistible divine grace in favor of a traditionally Arminian theology of divine grace in regeneration.[107] Commenting on John 3:16–21 Newbigin is clear that trinitarian "love does not coerce. It is addressed to men and women who must receive it by a willing belief, and who can also withhold that belief and therefore choose death rather than life."[108] The Son came not to judge the world but to save it, nevertheless, those who do not believe have been judged already. "The coming of Jesus, who is the 'only Son' of the Father, thus confronts those to whom he comes with the possibility of refusing the gift and choosing death. The purpose of his coming is to bring life, not death. Yet the gift of life must be accepted and can be refused."[109]

Sixth, in affirming human participation, Newbigin espouses a form of synergism and thus logically rejects divine monergism.[110] Admittedly, the relationship between divine and human activity is notoriously difficult to describe and Newbigin is not one to indulge in speculative metaphysics. Aware of the inscrutability of the subject Newbigin says, "Evangelism is the telling of good news, but what changes people's minds and converts their wills is always a mysterious work of the sovereign Holy Spirit and we are not

---

103. Newbigin, *Truth And Authority In Modernity*, 21.

104. Newbigin, "Conversion," 310.

105. Newbigin, *Truth And Authority In Modernity*, 79.

106. So described in the New Haven Theology of Taylor, *Lectures on the Moral Government of God*.

107. See Arminius, *The Works of James Arminius*, 724.

108. Newbigin, *The Light Has Come*, 43.

109. Ibid., 43.

110. For monergism the divine will is the sole determining factor in regeneration/conversion, whereas for synergism, in addition to God's work, active human willing is necessary for regeneration/conversion to take place, and this can be withheld. For more on this, see Dodds, "Regeneration and Resistible Grace."

permitted to know more than a little of his secret working."[111] Newbigin's first point about divine priority underscores that he does not adhere to a simplistic synergism where God and the human person are equal partners in and contributors to the work. God's initiative always precedes and stimulates the human response. Discussions of synergism often raise the problem of how human participation does not equate to contributing, and thus to some extent, meriting one's own salvation. Newbigin does not discuss this in detail, but in a related thought he states, "To believe is to have been brought to the place where one knows that one has to rely completely on Jesus, and on Jesus alone."[112] Newbigin was sufficiently theologically astute and biblically faithful to avoid such heterodox pitfalls.

Finally, conversion for Newbigin is irreducibly eschatological. He views conversion within the grand sweep of God's purposes in history that will culminate in Christ's return. Thus he rejects individual salvation as the *primary* meaning of conversion because, "The accent falls on the privileges of membership in the saved community."[113] Not only does this relapse to the false understanding of election primarily as spiritual privilege, but also the "eschatological dimension of the biblical idea of salvation slips out of sight; one forgets that 'being saved' means being made a participant in the mighty saving work of God which is not complete until all things have been summed up in Christ."[114] Newbigin's doctrine of conversion is theo-centric rather than anthropo-centric, for "the content of conversion must be understood in the light of *God's* purpose for the world."[115] The call to conversion looks forward to the consummation of God's righteous purposes in the future.[116]

Newbigin's doctrine of regeneration/conversion retains the divine priority; God is the author and subject of revelation. This revelation imparts missional momentum as a person is swept up into God's salvific purposes for the world. God's self-revelation has the mark of contradiction and cannot be authenticated by unaided human reason and conscience; it remains a secret except to those who have the eyes to see and ears to hear. God the Holy Spirit enables the human mind and conscience to acknowledge the Son, and through him glorify the Father. Humans actively participate in

---

111. Newbigin, "The Pastor's Opportunities," 356.

112. Newbigin, *The Light Has Come*, 90. For a more detailed discussion of this topic see Evans, "Salvation."

113. Newbigin, *Finality of Christ*, 112

114. Ibid., 112

115. Newbigin, "From the Editor," 149, emphasis added.

116. Newbigin, "Conversion," 311–12.

their own conversion by responding to the divine invitation issued through the church. Since God does not coerce, but rather his grace is resistible, humans have 'power to the contrary', and tragically can refuse the gift of life. In accepting the divine gift of grace a person is active in his or her own conversion, but in this activity the person knows he or she must rely on Jesus alone. Nevertheless, a person's regeneration/conversion is ultimately a mystery in which God alone is glorified, as the person looks forward to God completing his purposes in the future. Newbigin's understanding of conversion directly relates to his understanding of the nature of the church. On conversion persons become incorporated into God's gracious purposes for humanity and are caught up in the *missio Dei*, central to which is the church.

## ECCLESIOLOGY I—CHURCH IDENTITY AND MISSION

### *The* Missio Dei *and the Church*

The theological and biblical context of Newbigin's missiological thinking is the divine purpose that centers on "the summing up of all things in Christ" (Eph 1:10, NASB), which relates to Christ's abiding promise, "And I, when I am lifted up from the earth, will draw all people to myself" (John 12:32).[117] Newbigin understands Christ's drawing action as carried out through the church, his Body, and therefore Newbigin's missiology is ecclesially located. John's Gospel pronounces that Jesus came to save the world (John 3:17). Newbigin says, "if we ask, what was the explicit provision which Jesus made for the extension of His saving power to the whole world, we must answer that it was the fellowship which He called, trained, endowed, and sent forth."[118] Jesus left behind no infallible written code containing within it the true way of salvation and correct observance of the Sacraments. "What He left behind was a fellowship, and He entrusted to it the task of being His representative to the world."[119] This ecclesiocentrism accords well with Newbigin's understanding of the divine strategy of election.

Newbigin's ecclesiocentrism does not solely depend upon his understanding of election. He affirms both the typically Protestant emphasis on the church as witness to the Gospel and the typically Roman Catholic emphasis on the church as bearer of the Gospel. The church "is not merely the reporter of the divine acts of redemption; it is also itself the bearer of God's

---

117. Newbigin, *The Household of God*, 17.
118. Ibid., 52.
119. Ibid., 51.

redeeming grace, itself a part of the story of redemption which is the burden of its message."[120] Newbigin warns that either truth, taken in isolation, leads to distortion, and so counsels that both truths need to be affirmed in balance. Concurring with this typically Roman Catholic emphasis underscores his already high view of the church. The church is the witness to and is the bearer of the gospel, because the Gospel always reaches people through the church, whether represented in parent, teacher, preacher or friend. Newbigin approvingly quotes Calvin who followed Cyprian in saying, "Those who have God as Father must have the Church as Mother."[121] Furthermore, Newbigin says, "There is no reconciliation to God apart from reconciliation with the fellowship of His reconciled people."[122] Newbigin's ecclesiology is thoroughly missional and his missiology is thoroughly ecclesial.

## Church Is a Mission

The church has been given a mission that is "none other than the carrying on of the mission of Christ Himself. 'As the Father has sent me even so send I you.'"[123] For Newbigin mission is not merely an activity of the church but, taking his cue from the Apostles' Creed, Newbigin asserts that it is "the *esse* of the Church that it should be holy, and that it should be apostolic, which I take to mean both holding the apostolic faith and prosecuting the apostolic mission to the world."[124] Thus, "the Church's very being is the continuation of Christ's redeeming mission in the world."[125] This view, now standard in twenty-first-century missiology, was a radical departure from nineteenth-century-missiology. Then, missions were primarily carried out by missionary societies that were peripheral to the life of the churches.[126]

In asserting that "the Church *is* a mission"[127] Newbigin is aware that it is possible to take this statement too far. By defining the church solely in instrumental terms vis-à-vis its missionary task J.C. Hoekendijk implies

---

120. Ibid., 85.

121. Newbigin, *The Reunion of the Church*, 29. See Cyprian, *On the Unity of the Church*, 6, cited in Calvin, *Institutes*, IV.I.1, 1012.

122. Newbigin, *The Reunion of the Church*, 28.

123. Newbigin, *One Body*, 17; see John 20:21. Clearly this claim needs to be qualified by disavowing the doctrine that the Church is the *Christus prolongatus*, and by explaining both the continuity and discontinuity between the missions of the son and the Church (which I discuss in chapter 4).

124. Newbigin, *The Household of God*, 85.

125. Ibid., 85.

126. Richmond, *Daring To Believe*, 20.

127. Newbigin, *One Body*, 17, emphasis original.

that the church is merely a means to an end. By contrast, Newbigin observes that the church is both a means and an end. "This life in Christ is not merely the instrument of the apostolic mission, it is also its end and purpose."[128] The life of faith, church life, is life in the Spirit which Newbigin summarizes as "a sharing in the life of the Blessed Trinity itself."[129]

Newbigin developed his missionary understanding of the church within the context of the Protestant missionary movement, in which para-church missionary societies played a leading role. These societies, such as the London Missionary Society and the Basel Mission, did not claim to be 'churches', though they drew their membership from churches, and churches were formed as a result of their work. Newbigin argues that these societies came into existence because, in general, the church did not accept its missionary responsibility or acknowledge its own missionary identity.[130] Newbigin is not critical of these mission agencies *per se*, but he is critical of the situation they bequeathed. The churches formed as a result of the mission agencies often had unbalanced ecclesiologies which overemphasized the instrumental nature of the church for mission. Conversely, the 'sending', 'older' churches of the West had still not recovered their missionary character. Seeking to correct the erroneous tendencies on both sides, he says,

> It is helpful to recall the distinction made earlier between mission as *a dimension* of the Church's whole life, and mission as the primary *intention* of certain activities. Because the Church *is* the mission there is a missionary dimension of everything that the Church does. But not everything the Church does has a missionary intention. And unless there is in the life of the Church a point of concentration for the missionary intention, the missionary dimension which is proper to the whole life of the Church will be lost.[131]

Newbigin was greatly concerned and tirelessly called for a recovery of the true nature of the church, a central facet of which is its missionary nature.[132] "What is needed is the widespread and deep recovery throughout the churches, old and young alike, of the truth that to be a Christian is to be part of a universal fellowship in which all are committed to participation

---

128. Newbigin, *The Household of God*, 147–48. Newbigin mentions Hoekendijk but does not specify which article or book of his that he is responding to.

129. Newbigin, *The Reunion of the Church*, 47–48.

130. The reason for this situation will be discussed below.

131. Newbigin, *One Body*, 43.

132. "The Church is only properly understood as a missionary body" (Newbigin, "Missions").

in Christ's reconciling work for the whole world."[133] This fulfilled a corrective and prophetic function of issuing the call to return to an orthodox ecclesiology.

Since the church is a mission then it "is essentially something dynamic and not static."[134] For Newbigin the church is *"in via*, in that she must always be pushing out beyond her frontiers to draw in new members into fellowship with Christ."[135] The church is *in via* to the end of the world—eschatologically—and to ends of the earth—geographically—for "in its life and mission it deliberately and systematically transgresses the boundaries of nation and culture."[136] This is the context of the church's missionary obedience. Moreover, the task is urgent. "There is only one general directive: the Gospel must be preached to the farthest corner of the earth at once and without waiting."[137]

## ECCLESIOLOGY II—THE CHURCH & THE HOLY SPIRIT'S WITNESS

### *The* Missio Dei *and the Holy Spirit*

Newbigin ardently maintained that the church's mission is first and foremost *God's* mission, specifically, the mission of the Triune God. "All our missionary acts . . . are subordinate to and logically posterior to this reality of God's mission."[138] That Newbigin's emphasis is arguably more pneumatological than trinitarian is because he sees this as a biblical emphasis. To be sure, foundational to all of Newbigin's missiology is the Father's work of summing up all things in Christ. After the life, death, resurrection and ascension of Christ, he continues his mission to draw all people to himself through the Holy Spirit. The Spirit's missionary work is "the continuing work of Christ Himself through the Holy Spirit."[139] However, for Newbigin, a central teaching of the New Testament is "that properly speaking the

---

133. Newbigin, *A Word In Season*, 12.

134. Newbigin, *One Body*, 42. Hence, he repudiates the concept and term 'mission station.' "'Mission' means sending, and 'Station' means standing still; the phrase 'mission station' would seem to epitomize neatly the man in our Lord's parable who said 'Sir, I go', and went not" (ibid., 45).

135. Newbigin, *The Reunion of the Church*, xxxi.

136. Newbigin, *One Body*, 31.

137. Ibid., 19.

138. Ibid., 21.

139. Ibid., 18.

mission is the mission of the Holy Spirit."[140] Newbigin observes this in the ministries of both Jesus and the church. He says, "the gift of the Spirit is always for mission, is always the equipping of God's people for their witness to the world, exactly as the gift of the Spirit to Jesus at his baptism was his anointing, for his mission as the Messiah."[141]

Newbigin's missiology has a strongly trinitarian framework but its content largely consists in a high Pneumatology.[142] He does write on the mission of the Son (*Sin and Salvation*, and later *The Light Has Come*) but the accent in his writings certainly falls on the mission of the Holy Spirit. This is probably because the church's mission, one of his main concerns, is most closely linked with the person and mission of the Spirit. It is also because Roland Allen's missiology, with its strong emphasis on the Holy Spirit, is a major influence on Newbigin. It is also likely due to the influence of the growing Pentecostal movement which Newbigin acknowledges in his threefold typology of the church in *The Household of God*.[143] By placing greater emphasis on the mission of the Son as well as the Spirit, and by theologically relating the two, Newbigin's missiology would have been better-rounded and theologically balanced.

In John 20:21–22 Jesus says "'Peace be with you. As the Father has sent me, so I send you.' When he had said this, he breathed on them and said to them, 'Receive the Holy Spirit.'" This passage, so central to Newbigin's missiology,[144] describes Jesus commissioning the apostles. The heart of the Lord's apostolic commissioning of the (proto-) church to continue his mission was the bestowal of the Holy Spirit.[145] Accordingly, therefore, "The Church participates in the mission only by virtue of its participation in

---

140. Newbigin, *A Word In Season*, 21.

141. Newbigin, *Journey Into Joy*, 46.

142. This is contra Amos Yong who asserts, regarding Newbigin's pneumatology, "it would still be more accurate to identify his more as a christological rather than pneumatological trinitarianism." Explaining this assertion, Yong is correct that in the development of trinitarian theological discourse, "the bulk of the work accomplished in the twentieth century lay across the christological rather than pneumatological register." However, this criticism is not specific to Newbigin, and I maintain is not true of him. Yong goes on to fill out helpfully omissions in Newbigin's pneumatology, but he never does justify his initial claim. Yong, "Pluralism," 150, 151.

143. His threefold typology is the Church as Catholic, Protestant, and Pentecostal; he specifically focuses on the latter in chapter 4—"The Community of the Holy Spirit." Thus Amos Yong correctly identifies the influence of Pentecostalism on Newbigin as a cause for Newbigin's strong pneumatology. Yong, "Pluralism," 150.

144. Goheen, recognizing the centrality of John 20:21–22 to Newbigin's thought, entitled his PhD thesis on Newbigin's missionary ecclesiology "As the Father Has Sent Me, I Am Sending You."

145. Newbigin, *The Household of God*, 95.

the Holy Spirit."[146] Given that the Holy Spirit is the missionary Spirit, "The characteristic function of the Spirit is witness."[147] What, then, is the relation between the witness of the Holy Spirit and the witness of the church? Newbigin contends that "witness is essentially a witness borne to Jesus by the Holy Spirit, and that the part that the Church plays is a secondary instrumental part."[148] Newbigin's point is that the Holy Spirit is the principal witness to Christ, therefore the burden of the church's missionary task does not fall primarily on the church. The church is the proper locus of Christ's mission to the world that is carried out by the Holy Spirit, and the church can therefore be confident that God will complete his mission.[149] The Holy Spirit goes ahead of the church "preparing men's hearts in ways that no man could have planned, so that the Church has all that it can do to follow after to make open and visible what the Spirit has already begun in secret before any churchmen knew of it."[150] This, for Newbigin, is the 'open secret'.

## ECCLESIOLOGY III—CHURCH UNITY AND MISSION

### Mission Comity and Newbigin's Contextual Background

Newbigin was an active participant in the ecumenical movement, the beginning of which is conventionally identified with the World Missionary Conference at Edinburgh in 1910. "The missionary passion, the longing that the world might know Jesus as its Savior, led directly to the longing for unity."[151] Newbigin's commitment to church unity originated during his formative years as an undergraduate student at Cambridge[152] and continued throughout his life. However, Newbigin's theology of mission and church unity was principally shaped by the conditions created by mission comity in his context of the church in Southern India.

The exigency of world evangelization and the huge numbers living in unevangelized lands in relation to the relatively small number of ambassadors for Christ committed to reaching them, created the conditions in which mission comity was born. The principle of mission comity, simply

146. Newbigin, *One Body*, 18–19.
147. Newbigin, "The Work of the Holy Spirit," 25.
148. Newbigin, *A Word In Season*, 22.
149. Newbigin, *One Body*, 28.
150. Newbigin, *Unfaith and Other Faiths*.
151. Newbigin, "Unity and Mission," 5.
152. In his third undergraduate year he was part of the Madingley Group which prayed regularly for Christian unity. Newbigin, *Unfinished Agenda*, 14.

stated, is that mission agencies and churches would avoid overlapping with each other in the mission field because, as Newbigin says,

> The fields to be occupied were so vast, and the forces available so infinitesimally small, that it seemed natural that each Church or Society should choose a distinct area in which to begin its missionary work, and that competition which would be wasteful of effort and harmful to the work should be avoided.[153]

In the eighteenth and nineteenth centuries mission comity arose out of a desire for world evangelization and during this time this principle was generally accepted and practiced. It is out of this that the CSI emerged.

Mission comity "laid the foundation for the movement towards unity, because it produced a situation in which the normal form of the Christian church in any locality was not a series of rival congregations, but one congregation facing one area."[154] In these towns or villages, to be a Christian meant simply to belong to the local Christian congregation. Although adequate for a relatively stationary population, as the number of migratory workers significantly increased this situation became problematic. Inevitably, Newbigin explains,

> because the Churches belong to different denominations the cause of Christ is represented in one place by Episcopalian, in another by Presbyterian, in another by Baptists, and so on, each denomination having its own rules regarding church membership and church government. Because in each place there is, normally, no rivalry of different groups, each local Church tends to regard its neighbors in the adjoining area as its partners and fellow workers, and when Christians go from one area to the others they are commended to the fellowship of the Church to which they go. But as such contacts multiply, the illogicality of the situation becomes more and more apparent. A Methodist who comes into an Anglican area is not, by the rules of the latter Church, entitled to receive communion. A Presbyterian baptized in infancy will not count as a full member of the Church if he goes to live in a Baptist area. In practice what frequently happens is that the rules of the different Churches are simply not applied. But it is a sure way to corrupt sound church life to have rules on paper which are not kept, and the Church cannot be content to leave things as they are. What, then, is to be done? Two ways only are open. One is to work for the establishment

---

153. Newbigin, *The Reunion of the Church*, 11.
154. Ibid., 14.

in every center of the full range of denominational Churches, so that any Christian, as he moves about the country, may find wherever he goes a congregation which abides by the ecclesiastical rules and practices in which he has been brought up. The other is to seek for reunion.

That is the issue which the Church in South India has faced. It has chosen the second alternative and the result is the Scheme of Union.[155]

Mission comity created the conditions that in any one place, town or village, there was one Christian congregation which bore the responsibility for the evangelization of its immediate vicinity. "If they behave unworthily, their neighbors will have no other epistle in which they may read the truth of Christ."[156] Where a plurality of denominations exist each congregation is likely to become more concerned with the maintenance of its own distinctive life thus undermining the evangelistic imperative, and so, "the desire of the South Indian Churches for union cannot be understood except on the basis of their concern for the task of evangelism."[157] In his *A South India Diary* Newbigin states that, for the CSI, "the purpose of our union [is]—'that the world may believe.'"[158] The concern for evangelism that both gave rise to mission comity and resulted directly from it led to a concern for church unity that became expressed in the CSI church reunion.

Both worldwide and in South India the strands of the missionary and ecumenical movements are historically interwoven. Newbigin incorporates this entwining into his own personal life and into his missiology. Through Newbigin, the CSI church reunion impacted the world church, as Goheen explains, "His formulation of the church in terms of organic unity that remains inscribed in the proceedings of New Delhi is one of his most significant contributions to the 20th century church."[159] Throughout his lifetime Newbigin was absolutely committed to both the missionary and ecumenical movements which, for him, are part of the one mission of Christ.

## Mission and Unity in Newbigin's Missiology

In a verse that is central to Newbigin's theology, John 12:32, Jesus said— "And I, when I am lifted up from the earth, will draw all people to myself."

155. Ibid., 20–21.
156. Ibid., 15.
157. Ibid., 14.
158. See John 17:21. Newbigin, *A South India Diary*, 26.
159. Goheen, "As the Father Has Sent Me," 225.

Jesus is drawing all humanity to himself, including those who are outside of, and those that are within, the church. To those outside of the church, this leads to the prosecution of mission, and within the church it leads to movements toward church reunion. Newbigin approvingly quotes from the WCC Central Committee which met at Rolle, Switzerland in 1952,

> The obligation to take the Gospel to the whole world, and the obligation to draw all Christ's people together, both rest upon Christ's whole work and are indissolubly connected. Every attempt to separate these tasks violates the wholeness of Christ's ministry to the world.[160]

Commenting on John 12:32, Newbigin says, "Mission and unity are two sides of the same reality, or rather two ways of describing the same action of the living Lord who wills that all should be drawn to Himself."[161] In Newbigin's ecclesiology, mission and unity are both part of the church's nature. Put abruptly, "When the Church ceases to be one, or ceases to be missionary, it contradicts its own nature."[162] Therefore, "mission and unity cannot rightly be separated from each other" because both "belong to the intrinsic nature of the Church until the End."[163]

In Newbigin's theology, mission and unity mutually inhere in a perichoretic fashion. He describes mission as part of the quest for unity and unity as a constituent of world mission. However, there is no equality in this binity but rather hierarchy, with the accent falling on mission. Newbigin almost always conceived of the mutual relation between unity and mission thus: "unity is in order that the world may believe."[164] Offering a salutary warning to the ecumenical movement should it forgo and forget the church's missionary nature,

> "The quest for unity is misunderstood if it is thought of in isolation from the fulfilment of God's whole purpose 'to unite all things in Christ, things in heaven and things on earth' (Eph 1:10) . . . The unity of the Church is wrongly sought unless it is sought from a missionary point of view."[165]

---

160. Newbigin, "The Missionary Dimension," 208.

161. Ibid., 208–9. Newbigin says, "The connection between the movement for Christian reunion and the movement for world evangelization is of the deepest possible character. The two things are the two outward signs of a return to the heart of the Gospel itself" (*The Reunion of the Church*, 18–19).

162. Newbigin, *The Household of God*, 26.

163. Newbigin, *The Reunion of the Church*, xxi.

164. Newbigin, *The Household of God*, 149.

165. Newbigin, "The Nature of the Unity," 187.

Newbigin recognized the indissoluble connection between the gospel, which claims to be the final truth of human existence, and this particular society, the church. Since ecclesiology is so central to Newbigin's theology, including his theology of mission, the reputation of the Gospel is at stake when the reputation of the church is at stake.[166] Although Newbigin greatly cares about the church's reputation in its own right, it is fundamentally Newbigin's concern for the propagation of the gospel—for world mission—that drives his ecclesiocentricity and his ecumenical concerns.

## *Unity and the High-Priestly Prayer of Jesus*

Arguably the center of Newbigin's concern for church unity is the high-priestly prayer in John 17:22–23, "that they may be one, as we are one, I in them and you in me, that they may become completely one, so that the world may know that you have sent me." Thus for Newbigin his theology of church unity first derives from the doctrine of the Trinity, and second is for the purpose of mission.

The unity of Christians rests upon the fact that the name of God has been given to them in Jesus Christ. Newbigin says, "God's act of holy love in Jesus Christ, by which his own inner nature is revealed, constitutes the ground of Christian unity. As God is one, so those who bear his name and the impress of his character must necessarily be one."[167] Church unity is a spiritual unity that derives from a participation in the being of the triune God—"that they may be one, as we are one, I in them and you in me, that they may become completely one." This unity "is a total mutual reconciliation which is the result of being born anew by the Spirit. It is a unity of mutual love given by God."[168] The unity is not organizational or by agreement in doctrine but simply arises out of Christ's indwelling in his people and their being in him. Newbigin says, "[The church] derives its character not from its membership but from its Head, not from those who join it but from Him who calls it into being. It is God's gathering."[169] In other words, church unity is not an achievement 'from below' but a gift of God 'from above' through Jesus Christ. Church unity is already a spiritual reality deriving from participation in the Triune God, and it is also something to be

---

166. Newbigin, *The Reunion of the Church*, 28.

167. Newbigin, "The Nature of the Unity We Seek," 182.

168. Ibid., 185. For an unrelated but complementary account of church unity grounded in the doctrine of the Trinity and for the sake of mission in the theology of Jonathan Edwards, see Pryor, "The Trinitarian Missiology of Jonathan Edwards."

169. Newbigin, *The Household of God*, 27–28.

sought. The "unity we seek," Newbigin explains, "is a visible unity—visible to the world, a sign by which the world may be brought to faith in Christ."[170] Church unity must be visible for the purpose of mission—"that the world may know"—for the world cannot recognize divine action in a merely *spiritual* or *invisible* church unity.

For Newbigin, "'that the world may know', is the true center of the concern for unity."[171] Church unity, therefore, is part of the task of world mission, the urgency of which Newbigin gleaned from Greek Orthodox missiology. The Greek Orthodox Church cannot but painfully nod to the truth that every kingdom divided against itself is brought to desolation. Therefore, "The Orthodox Church . . . believes that only a unified Church and 'sanctified through the truth' can effectively proclaim Christ and bring the nations to Him . . . The Orthodox Church will therefore continue to believe that unity belongs to the mission."[172] Sharing this conviction Newbigin says, the "disunity of the Church is . . . a public abdication of its right to preach the gospel to all nations."[173]

For Newbigin this was true for the church, local and universal. The credibility of the church's witness is dependent upon its unity. Newbigin narrates,

> In a South Indian village a visit from the bishop is quite a public occasion. He is met at a convenient spot two or three hundred yards from the edge of the village by an official deputation of the elders of the church. There are garlands of flowers, trays of fruit, and other tokens of greeting. There will be a band and a choir, or possibly two choirs singing different lyrics at the same time. Just in case there should be any moments of silence, there will also be fireworks.
>
> The entire body will then form into a procession, singing as they go, and letting off a rocket every few yards. Soon they will be pushing their way through the narrow streets, and by the time the procession has reached the church, most of the inhabitants of the village will have turned out to see what is happening. At this point it is quite probable that the bishop will be asked to say something to the nonChristians before going into the church for the Christian service.

---

170. Newbigin, "The Nature of the Unity We Seek," 186.

171. Newbigin, "Unity and Mission," 4.

172. Metropolitan James of Melita quoted in Newbigin, "From the Editor," 276. Newbigin says, "A universal Gospel demands as its sign and instrument a universal fellowship" ("The Summons," 186).

173. Newbigin, *A Faith For This One World?*, 81.

And so it has often happened that I have found myself standing on the steps of a village church, opening the Scriptures to preach the Gospel to a great circle of Hindus and Moslems standing round, while the Christian congregation sits in the middle. When I do that, I always know one thing: the words which I speak will only carry weight if those who hear them can see that they are being proved true in the life of the congregation which sits in the middle. When I hold up Christ as the Savior of all men, and repeat his promise, 'I, when I am lifted up from the earth, will draw all men unto myself,' I know that my hearers are only likely to believe this promise if they can see in fact that the Savior of the world is drawing men of all sorts into one family.

If they can see in the congregation in the center not a new clique, or a new caste, or a new party, but a family in which men and women of all cliques and castes and parties are being drawn in mutual forgiveness and reconciliation to live a life which is rooted in peace with God, then there is a possibility that they may believe. If, on the other hand, they see only a series of rival groups competing with one another for influence and membership, they are not likely to be impressed by the message of our Savior.[174]

The unity of the church, for Newbigin, directly impacts upon the church's missionary outreach. It was with this in mind that he says, "Everything about such a missionary situation conspires to make Christian disunity an intolerable anomaly."[175] In a missionary situation the church proclaims the Gospel, the heart of which is the reconciling atonement of Christ. "[Y]ou cannot engage in world mission without being compelled to face questions of unity" because "How can we, unreconciled to one another, proclaim one reconciliation for the world?"[176] Newbigin calls this an "intolerable scandal."[177] In so far as the church proves itself "unwilling and unable to agree together in one fellowship, we publicly proclaim our disbelief in the sufficiency of that atonement. No one who has shared in the task of seeking to commend Christ to those of other faiths can escape the shame of that denial."[178] Those engaged in mission "must eventually face the question 'Mission for what?' Into what are we inviting the men of all nations—into a new complex of divisions in place of their own, or into the one family

---

174. Newbigin, "Unity and Mission," 3–4.
175. Newbigin, *The Household of God*, 17.
176. Newbigin, *One Body*, 54.
177. Newbigin, *The Household of God*, 18.
178. Ibid., 150.

where at last they may know themselves one in the Father's house?"[179] As an evangelistic sermon from a visiting bishop only has credibility when the congregation's life mirrors the message, therefore, the church's witness is crippled and compromised by its disunity. Newbigin questions whether Christians have the right to preach a Gospel of reconciliation when they cannot be reconciled to one another.

Conversely, toleration of Christian disunity coexists with a non-missional ecclesiology. Newbigin reasons,

> It is not possible to account for the contentment with the divisions of the Church except upon the basis of a loss of the conviction that the Church exists to bring all men to Christ. There is the closest possible connection between the acceptance of the missionary obligation and the acceptance of the obligation of unity. That which makes the Church one is what makes it a mission to the world.[180]

This is the situation of the European church since at least the Reformation.

The force with which Newbigin conveys his theology of church unity reflects his sense of urgency in this regard.

> The Church faces the world not as one fellowship but as a fantastic medley of splintered fragments divided on grounds of race, of tradition, of doctrine. Instead of seeing the face of its one Savior, the world sees a monstrous gallery of caricatures . . . [T]hese divisions . . . are a plain denial of the Gospel. By them we publicly proclaim to the world that we do not believe in the sufficiency of Christ to reconcile all men in one body to the Father. The divisions of the Church are a standing and public contradiction before the world of the very heart of the Gospel which we preach.[181]

In summary, Newbigin says, "I believe that missionary obedience in our day requires of us that we should treat the issue of such visible churchly unity as an issue not for tomorrow but for today."[182] For him "the unity of the Church is a burning issue at the very heart of its world mission," it is "literally the most crucial issue facing us in relation to the world mission of the Church."[183] This is because, "the world will [not] believe that Gospel until

---

179. Newbigin, *One Body*, 54.
180. Newbigin, *The Reunion of the Church*, 11.
181. Newbigin, *The Mission and Unity of the Church*, 17–18.
182. Newbigin, *One Body*, 55–56.
183. Newbigin, "The Nature of the Unity We Seek," 188.

it sees more evidence of its power to make us one."[184] Eloquently conveying the urgency of Christian unity, Newbigin says,

> We still deal with these matters as though we had all eternity before us. We do not. God has work in hand, and He does not allow us to fiddle about for ever while we decide whether or not to do His will. We are blind both to the realities of the Gospel and to the facts of the present world, if we imagine that the question of Christian unity is one that can be left over till tomorrow. And we are indeed fools if, like Augustine before his conversion, we pray: 'God give us unity, but not yet.' The question of Christian unity for the sake of the Church's mission to the world is a question not for tomorrow but for today.[185]

## *Divine Providence and the Church's Mission*

Newbigin consistently taught that the Bible is concerned with the beginning and end of all things and so there must be real meaning to all that happens. Therefore, there cannot be an absolute separation between church history and the history of humanity. Indeed, he asserts, "The Bible does not make such a separation."[186] Newbigin believes the mission of God is worked out through a providential ordering of world history, whose determinative center is Christ.[187] God the Father plans to sum up all things in Christ. Therefore,

> The coming into the midst of history of Him who is the end of history precipitates a polarization of human affairs. We see this happening in the pages of the Gospels themselves. Men and women who come within the range of His influence are brought gently but inexorably to the point where they have to make a decision about Him . . . Once He has come, the question of man's salvation becomes the inescapable question. *All history narrows down to the single issue—salvation in Jesus, or the false offer of salvation in some other name,* some other system, some other program. *The final issue is: Christ or Antichrist. All nations are inexorably brought to this choice.*[188]

184. Newbigin, *The Household of God*, 152.

185. Newbigin, *Mission and Unity of the Church*, 17–18. For a recent articulation of the importance of church unity within Newbigin's missionary ecclesiology, see Weston, "Ecclesiology."

186. Newbigin, *Trinitarian Doctrine*, 26.

187. Newbigin, *Mission of the Church to All the Nations*, pages not numbered.

188. Newbigin, *The Mission and Unity of the Church*, 15, emphasis added.

When God the Father sent the Son on his redeeming mission, God initiated a sequence of events that will culminate in the final judgement and mercy of God. Newbigin talks about the mission of Jesus, and particularly its climax on the cross, as the crisis of human history. "The terrible fact is . . . that in Christ you are presented with a claim to absolute kingship."[189] In Jesus, God presents all of humanity with the possibility of receiving or rejecting the end for which he created all things. The crisis, "the ultimate issue [is] of absolute surrender or final rejection."[190] Since Christ has come, the whole of human history is the pressing of this choice to the final issue.[191] "There can in the end be no neutrality. Every soul must be finally given to Christ or wholly surrendered to the devil."[192] The pressing of this choice is the continuing work of Christ through his instrument the church. "Hence, the promise of conflict, of suffering, and of division. 'These things must come to pass.'"[193]

Newbigin bases much of his theology of mission, in relation to world history, on sustained reflection of Mark 13. From verses 5 to 6 and 21 to 23 he concludes, "The coming of the true Messiah leads to the appearing of the false ones."[194] If one does not accept Christ then one must find another absolute authority, for "An absolute claim can only be met by an absolute counterclaim."[195] The choice is between "Christ or Antichrist, the true Savior of the world, or the bogus saviors who purport to offer mankind final security and wellbeing in terms which belong to this world, that is to say, which belong this side of death."[196] Newbigin sees other religious claims and political movements such as Marxism as examples of these 'bogus saviors' which claim to offer total welfare for humanity. It is a notable feature of these 'bogus saviors' that their emergence is tied to knowledge of the

189. Newbigin, "The Gathering Up," 87.

190. Ibid., 87.

191. Newbigin, *Trinitarian Doctrine*, 27.

192. Newbigin, *Unfaith and Other Faiths*. Despite the duality of this statement concerning the eschatological destiny of humanity, elsewhere Newbigin is more ambiguous on this subject. He says, "But love in the end claims all," whilst also saying, on the same page, "Every soul must in the end be wholly given to Christ or wholly given to the devil" (*A Faith For This One World?*, 104). In his writings from the India period universalistic tendencies are in the minority but reveal a potential tension in Newbigin's own theology.

193. Newbigin, *Mission of the Church to All the Nations*, n.p.

194. Newbigin, *The Mission of the Triune God*, pages not numbered. Although Newbigin makes the point that it is the coming of Christ that has precipitated these movements, he maintains that these "are movements which would be inconceivable as products of the ancient religions of Asia or Africa" (*Trinitarian Doctrine*, 44).

195. Newbigin, "The Summons to Christian Mission Today," 185.

196. Ibid., 185.

coming of Christ, in other words, that they are post-Christian phenomena or post-Christian developments of the ancient religions.[197] It is unsurprising that Newbigin later identifies two post-Christian movements, secular modernity and Islam,[198] as the most gospel-resistant and thus the most difficult challenges for the missionary church.

The church carries out its mission in the geographical and eschatological context of taking the gospel to the ends of the earth and the end of the world. "Rightly understood, the end of the mission is the end of history," says Newbigin. This is because Jesus said, "This gospel of the kingdom shall be preached in the whole world as a testimony to all the nations, and then the end will come" (Matt 24:14, NASB). Newbigin continues, "According to the New Testament, the completion of God's purpose for the world waits upon the completion of the mission. The Christian mission is not rightly prosecuted except with the ends of the earth and the end of the world in view."[199] Consequently, "the Church's mission to the nations is the clue to the real meaning of world history"[200] because it points back to the cross of Christ as the crisis of history, and points forward to Christ's triumphant return. When the disciples asked Jesus concerning the end, the answer he gave "is not a theoretical one but a practical one. Ye shall be my witnesses. Go ye unto all the world."[201] Thus, this eschatological tension between the first and second coming of Christ "cannot be understood apart from the tension of the missionary obligation."[202]

God providentially rules over all of history. In *Trinitarian Doctrine for Today's Mission* Newbigin describes three false ways in which the Christian mission and world history are related. First, history is not a conflict of fate and virtue because God's providential reign rules out fate. Second, history is not steadily progressing toward the kingdom of God so that the historical process is somehow deified, and the work of missions goes 'with the stream.' Third, "However God may direct and use the forces of secular history, these forces do not contain any alternative or supplementary way of salvation."[203] The Bible knows of only one name by which people may be saved, the name of Jesus. Newbigin contends that the relation of God's work through the

197. Newbigin, *Trinitarian Doctrine*, 49.

198. See Newbigin et al., *Faith and Power*; Taylor, "Lesslie Newbigin's Understanding of Islam"; Wainwright, *Lesslie Newbigin*, 231–36.

199. Newbigin, *One Body*, 23–24.

200. Newbigin, *Mission of the Church to All the Nations*, n.p.

201. Newbigin, *The Household of God*, 139. See Acts 1:6–8.

202. Newbigin, *The Household of God*, 141. "The implication of a true eschatological perspective will be missionary obedience, and the eschatology which does not issue in such obedience is a false eschatology" (ibid., 135).

203. Newbigin, *Trinitarian Doctrine*, 51.

church and secular history can only be rightly answered in the framework of the Christian doctrine of the Trinity.[204]

The Father is he that rules over all, rules over history, and orders its events. Therefore "Neither imperialism nor anti-imperialism is a mere work of the devil. God rules and uses them all."[205] The Son submits to the Father's ordering of events as the form of which his mission, and that of his followers, is to be fulfilled. The Father has so ordained it that the coming of the Son precipitates the crisis of human history bringing all things to the point of decision—rejection or acceptance, judgement or salvation. The Spirit anoints the Son at his baptism and inspires Jesus' ministry. Likewise, the Spirit is the witness through the church's witness. He is the Spirit of adoption and the earnest of the church's inheritance. The Holy Spirit "is he who is, properly speaking, the missionary."[206]

## MISSIONAL CHURCH STRUCTURE AND MISSIONARY METHODS

### Christendom, Church Structure and the Missional Nature of the Church

Newbigin calls for the recovery of the missionary nature of the church because he perceives that for most of its history the church has forgotten this aspect of her being. He was disturbed by the lack of prominence of the church's missionary identity and responsibility in Europe and North America. Newbigin's historical analysis of this fact comprises the historical context for his missiology. He says, "I do not think that we reflect sufficiently upon the fact that, even after 200 years of foreign missions, the foreign missionary task remains strictly peripheral in the consciousness of western Christendom."[207] Newbigin detected the cause of the problem to be Christendom, the Christian sacral society that has its *roots* in the fourth century and developed much of its *character* in medieval Europe.

"This deep and disastrous distortion of the Church's life has its roots," Newbigin explains, "far back in history,"[208] specifically, during the reigns of Roman Emperors Constantine and Theodosius. Newbigin draws largely on Charles Cochrane's *Christianity and Classical Culture*, which describes how,

---

204. Ibid., 33.
205. Ibid., 40.
206. Ibid.
207. Newbigin, *Mission and Unity of the Church*, 7.
208. Newbigin, *One Body*, 16–17, emphasis original.

before Emperor Constantine, the church was a minority confession that carried out its mission of evangelism and service without political power. After the church-state alliance instigated by Constantine and consolidated by Theodosius, Cochrane describes how the majority of the Empire became, in name, Christian. Christian identity became co-extensive with the Roman Empire's geo-political boundaries. This rendered traditional forms of mission obsolete because, identifying empire and church, all were considered Christians. Emperors Constantine and Theodosius had effected a change that profoundly altered the character of the European church.

Describing the character of the European church, Newbigin says,

> We have to face the fact that the fundamental structure of our churchmanship was created during that 1,000 year period when Christendom was not expanding but contracting, when—sealed off from contact with the greater part of the world's people by the power of Islam—the Church lived in almost total isolation from the non-Christian cultures. In this situation, the illusion that the age of missions is over became almost an integral part of Christianity.[209]

Newbigin maintains that this illusion has been perpetuated in the parish structure, in church life, in the conception of ministry, in theological curricula,[210] and vitally, in the ordinary consciousness of most church members. Christendom gave birth to non-missional church structures, which survived into Newbigin's lifetime thus perpetuating the lack of missionary consciousness. Newbigin believed that these structures differed significantly from those of the New Testament.

> [I]n the New Testament the Church is depicted as a body of people chosen by God and trained and empowered for a missionary task. It is a task force which exists not simply for the sake of its members, which would be absurd, but for the sake of the doing of God's will in the world. The visible structures of church life which we have inherited from the *corpus Christianum* of mediaeval Europe do not correspond very obviously to that description.[211]

---

209. Newbigin, *Mission and Unity of the Church*, 7.

210. "Even our theological curricula bear eloquent testimony to this illusion. Our church history is normally taught not as the story of the triumphs of the Gospel; but as the story of the internal quarrels of the Church; our systems of dogmatics are not directed towards the nonChristian systems of thought, but against rival statements of the Christian faith. The training of the ministry is not for a mission to the world, but almost exclusively for the pastoral care of established Christian congregations" (ibid., 7).

211. Newbigin, *Honest Religion For Secular Man*, 105.

The process of secularization beginning with the Enlightenment has broken the sacral unity of the Christendom society in which everyone was Christian by default, to one where each must make a decision for his/herself. This reversal of the effects of the church-state alliance "has been the precondition for the recovery of a biblical, that is to say, a preConstantinian, understanding of the Church as a missionary community."[212] Newbigin believes that, "As the established churches of Europe face the deeper implications of the ending of the 'Constantinian era', and recognize the missionary situation in which they are really placed, the inherited pattern of the ministry comes under sharp criticism."[213] Hence, Newbigin calls for "a profound transformation in the accepted patterns of congregational life, of ministry, of Christian action in the world"[214] so that "true pastoral care, true training in the Christian life, and true use of the means of grace will precisely be in and for the discharge of this missionary task."[215] Newbigin's historical accounting of the absence of ecclesiastical missionary awareness is an important feature of his missiology. Indispensable to his missiology is a biblical ecclesiology which is oriented towards the church's mission. This includes a reformation of church structures, ministry, training, and congregational life in accordance with a missional ecclesiology.

The rediscovery of the centrality of missions as evidenced by the modern missionary movement is both a partial rediscovery of biblical mission and a catalyst towards its further rediscovery. As a foreign missionary, Newbigin was aware that the aforementioned deficient church structures of Christendom had been reproduced and multiplied in the missionary movement. Combined with the more negative aspects of colonialism this further amplified the already unbiblical distortions. Thus, correcting missionary methods forms an important part of Newbigin's missiology. In this task Newbigin heavily relied upon one who had already contributed much to this goal, Anglican missiologist Roland Allen.[216]

## *Missionary Methods and Roland Allen*

In Newbigin's articles and books written around 1960 he made frequent reference to Roland Allen's books, especially *Missionary Methods: St. Paul's*

212. Ibid., 104.
213. Newbigin, *The Pattern of Ministry*, n.p.
214. Newbigin, *One Body*, 16.
215. Newbigin, *The Household of God*, 146.
216. Newbigin acknowledged, "Readers of the writings of Roland Allen will have recognized many of his ideas in what I have tried to say so far" ("The Work of the Holy Spirit," 32).

*or Ours?* and *The Spontaneous Expansion of the Church*, for which he wrote Forewords. Newbigin says, "The modern missionary movement has not been successful in following the example of St. Paul who could leave behind a living church at the end of a few months or years of work, and move on to new regions."[217] This same achievement usually takes modern missionaries many decades or sometimes even centuries. Missions have failed to produce, in the measure that the Gospel leads one to expect, spontaneous multiplying Christian communities among the peoples of Asia and Africa. Newbigin asks, "Why are the resources of the missionary movement today so largely exhausted in the support of dependent churches and why is so little energy available for fresh advance?"[218] He continues, "The profound theological reasons for this failure have been brilliantly analyzed by Roland Allen in his wellknown books."[219]

Allen, Newbigin explains, believed only that which is essential to the gospel and must be passed on: "the Scriptures, the Sacraments of baptism of the Lord's Supper and the Ministry."[220] Accordingly, everything else passed on by missionaries he deemed to be unnecessary and damaging 'cultural extras.'

> Roland Allen therefore waged war against everything that missions had tried to bring apart from these—the whole apparatus of a professional ministry, institutions, church buildings, church organizations, diocesan offices and all the rest of it, everything from harmoniums to archdeacons.[221]

Concurring with Allen, Newbigin agrees that there must be continuity and discontinuity between the missionaries and the new community of faith. For Newbigin, the essential elements of continuity are "the things mentioned in Acts 2:42, however we may interpret them." That they are fundamental means "that they belong to the *tradendum*, that they are part of that which is involved, in the transmission of the Gospel. In other words, if they are not transmitted the Gospel has not been transmitted."[222] These are the apostles teaching, fellowship, the breaking of bread, and prayer. Regarding discontinuity, Newbigin offers a more moderate view: "I would not say with Roland Allen that everything else is excluded. I will simply

217. Newbigin, *One Body*, 45.
218. Newbigin, *Trinitarian Doctrine*, 68.
219. Newbigin, *One Body*, 45.
220. Newbigin, "Conversion," 321.
221. Ibid., 321.
222. Ibid., 322.

say that everything else is subject to debate, and guidance according to the circumstances."[223]

Drawing on Allen, Newbigin suggests at least two reasons why the methods of the modern missionary movement have, in general, not led to the spontaneous expansion of the church. First, *"missions relied from a very early stage upon a professional agency controlled and paid by the mission"*[224] leading to unhealthy dependence upon both the mission and ministry professionals. As is well documented, Western foreign missions often went hand in hand with European colonial expansion. European colonial attitudes of condescension and paternalism towards those colonized often transferred over to Western missionaries. The younger churches, which were the fruit of missionary work, usually displayed an unhealthy dependence upon the mission boards or parent churches back in Europe. Western missionaries controlled these churches so that indigenous Christians were often not consulted over matters decided by their Western leaders. Newbigin often mentions the classic example of the handing over of the work of the Tranquebar Mission in South India to the Society for the Propagation of the Gospel early in the nineteenth century, as the result of which (to quote Bishop Sandegrer), "all the Christians in South India went to bed one night as Lutherans, and woke up next morning having become, without knowing it, Anglicans."[225] Newbigin explains,

> If you constantly treat a body of people as a sort of outstation, as the branch of an organization whose headquarters are elsewhere, they will behave accordingly; and the result will be that distressing attitude of dependence, that deep spiritual insecurity, and that lack of real selfhood which we so often deplore in our churches.[226]

This lack of selfhood includes financial dependence. Since a new congregation is a liability and not an asset, a major evangelistic opening would be a major financial disaster. "For practical purposes the Great Commission has to be rewritten: 'Go ye into all the world and make disciples of all nations subject to budgetary requirements.'"[227]

Second, there is *"a failure sufficiently to believe that the preaching and hearing and believing of the Gospel releases in those who believe the very power of the Spirit of God himself to create his own forms of obedience and holiness,*

---

223. Ibid.
224. Newbigin, "The Work of the Holy Spirit," 26, emphasis original.
225. Quoted in Newbigin, *The Pattern of Ministry*.
226. Newbigin, "The Work of the Holy Spirit," 26.
227. Ibid., 26.

*and to bear his own witness to Christ?*"²²⁸ Newbigin speaks of a phrase in Acts 14:23 which he finds deeply moving. The context is the apostle Paul returning to Antioch at the end of his first missionary journey. "And when they had appointed elders for them in every church, with prayer and fasting they committed them to the Lord in whom they believed" (ESV). Newbigin comments, "Is it not the real taproot of the difficulty with which we wrestle in the missionary movement, that we have not been willing from the very beginning to do just that, to commit them to the Lord in whom they believed?"²²⁹

The reason the modern missionary movement is far less successful than that of the apostle Paul is because it differs from him not only in method but fundamentally because of a lack of faith in the Holy Spirit. In New Testament the newly planted living congregations became, in turn, centers of missionary advance. Churches planted by the apostle Paul were not dependent upon the 'Antioch mission' for leadership and finances. Fresh missionary advance did not depend on resources from outside. Rather, the newly established congregations "have in themselves—or rather in the Holy Spirit who is with them—the essential resources for witness and growth."²³⁰ Newbigin believes Paul's whole 'method' rests upon a single point—"that the Holy Spirit of God is himself the missionary; that his presence and blessing are given to those who receive the Gospel . . . and that where the Spirit is, there is all the power and all the wisdom and all the grace that man needs or can expect for the life in Christ."²³¹

Newbigin is aware of movements that overemphasize the role of the Holy Spirit and reminds his readers that mission is the mission of the Triune God. He cautions that "The recovery within the missionary movement of faith in, and experience of, the centrality of the Spirit in missions will be distorted if it is not within the context of the full Trinitarian faith."²³² Nevertheless, Newbigin insists that a recovery of the centrality of the Holy Spirit is vital for the missionary movement, the Spirit whose work it "is to enable us to participate in Christ's Sonship, to be one with him in his obedience to the Father."²³³ This recovery will stimulate and require a corresponding rediscovery of Pauline missionary methods.

228. Ibid., 29, emphasis original.
229. Newbigin, "The Pattern of Partnership," 39.
230. Newbigin, *Trinitarian Doctrine*, 70.
231. Ibid., 71.
232. Ibid., 79.
233. Ibid., 81.

Reflecting on his own experience, Newbigin contrasts the immobilizing effect of modern missionary methods with how effective the Pauline apostolic method is. He concluded that a high practical doctrine of the Holy Spirit leads to the spontaneous expansion of the church.[234]

> I have seen this [modern missions] system come to a practical standstill: funds were not available to increase the number of salaried workers. New areas could not, therefore, be occupied. Teachers could not be offered to new villages. Enquirers who came to ask for a teacher to be sent to their village had regretfully to be turned away. Only if some fresh resources came from 'home' could the mission become a mission again. As it was, it was plain that any talk of 'winning India for Christ' was not serious. I was compelled to ask myself whether it is really true that the Church's obedience to the Great Commission is intended to be contingent upon the accident of a budgetary surplus.[235]

Newbigin identified five steps in his own missionary methodology, which he developed from his study of the New Testament as stimulated and guided by Roland Allen, and from his own ministry experience. The context in which Newbigin followed this new methodology was rural southern India, where the gospel was spreading through the witness of new converts. As a result, groups would often come from villages where no agent of the church was present and request instruction and baptism.

The first step, Newbigin said, "is to find out what the Holy Spirit had already done among them and build on that."[236] Typically behind such a request was an experience of the gospel through the witness of a Christian, a dream or a vision, a providential deliverance, or the reading of a portion of Scripture. Second, it is crucial to acknowledge that the person who the Holy Spirit has touched is, at least for the present, the chosen minister of the Gospel to that community. Third, once the group has made a decision to follow Jesus, baptism should not be delayed. Fourth, baptism should be followed by the fullest possible instruction. Fifth, because learning and witnessing go together, during the months the new congregation is learning the essentials of the faith it is at the same time bearing witness to its neighbors.[237] The result

> was that the churches began to multiply themselves by a kind of spontaneous growth which was not dependent upon increasing

---

234. Newbigin, "The Pattern of Partnership," 39.
235. Newbigin, *Trinitarian Doctrine*, 75.
236. Ibid., 76–77.
237. Ibid., 76.

outside resources. In an area almost entirely pagan, the number of Christian congregations rose from 13 to 55 in 12 years. The secret of growth was the spontaneous witness of the new Christians themselves . . . In the midst of a movement of this kind, one could speak seriously about winning India for Christ.[238]

Newbigin's missiology incorporates a high and practical pneumatology, set within a trinitarian framework, with a commitment to the practice of the priesthood of all believers.

I have described how, through his books, Roland Allen mentored Lesslie Newbigin in missiology. Through Allen's influence and his own experience as missionary and bishop Newbigin was convinced that "The very core of our need . . . is that we recover a more biblical understanding of what mission is."[239] Newbigin traces the unbiblical distortion of ecclesiology and missiology, and the adoption of missionary methods different from those of the primitive church, to European Christendom. This conviction, and the indelible stamp of Roland Allen, remained a part of Newbigin's missiology throughout his India period. Having examined different facets of Newbigin's missionary ecclesiology, we now turn first to the content of mission work—what he calls evangelism and service, and second, to the missionary church's understanding of other faiths.

## MISSION, EVANGELISM AND SERVICE

Newbigin most clearly discusses mission as evangelism and service in his 1958 book *One Body, One Gospel, One World: The Christian Mission Today*. For him mission is first and foremost the mission of the Triune God.[240] Thus, Newbigin conceives of the church's mission theocentrically, as "a participation in the work of the Triune God."[241] As the *missio Dei* is broader than evangelism, so also is the church's mission. Although at times Newbigin seems to use the terms *mission* and *evangelism* synonymously,[242] in general he makes the distinction "that 'missionary' is not synonymous with 'evangelistic.' The mission is wider than evangelism if the word is used in its proper sense, though evangelism is an indispensable part of it."[243] Service is

---

238. Ibid., 77.
239. Newbigin, "The Pattern of Partnership," 43.
240. Newbigin, *One Body*, 21.
241. Newbigin, *Trinitarian Doctrine*, 54.
242. Newbigin, *The Reunion of the Church*, 10–11.
243. Newbigin, *One Body*, 22–23.

the other indispensable part of the church's mission, for it gives a "witness which includes word and deed."[244] Newbigin realized the importance of the evangelistic *and* the social dimensions of mission early in his life.

As a postgraduate student of theology at Cambridge, Newbigin participated in a combined work camp and evangelistic campaign, which brought together those concerned about direct evangelism and social justice. In July 1935, in a village near Swanwick, a large group of Cambridge students including Newbigin labored with pick and shovel to provide a playground for children in the village. Newbigin recalls,

> It was very hard work. We started each day at 5.30, did eight hours of hard labor, and preached, argued and answered hecklers for a couple of hours each night . . . At the end our hands were blistered and our throats were hoarse. But . . . we ourselves had learned a lot both about the world and about the Gospel. Probably all of us were changed by that experience.[245]

Newbigin observed that sceptics and critics had become friends, and he experienced first-hand the value of both evangelism and service as part of the *missio Dei*.

## Evangelism and Service

Newbigin says, "Evangelism is an activity of the mouth or pen by which the good news of God's redeeming acts is communicated." He continues, "It confuses important issues to extend this word beyond its proper meaning."[246] He retains a narrow definition because, in his experience, "a loose use of the word 'evangelism' has been used to cover a real betrayal."[247] Newbigin believes evangelism is an extremely high priority for the church. "There is not and there cannot be any substitute for telling the story of Jesus."[248] Speaking from his missionary experience, he says,

> In the old days we used to do a lot of street preaching. I have done a lot of it myself, and I believe in it. I cannot accept the view that would seek to downgrade evangelism. Anyone who has a faith that he really believes—whether he is a Marxist or a Muslim or a disciple of the Maharashi—wants to persuade

244. Ibid., *Body*, 40.
245. Newbigin, *Unfinished Agenda*, 35.
246. Newbigin, *One Body*, 22–23.
247. Ibid.
248. Ibid.

others to believe it too. If you do not want to share it with others, it is not your real faith.[249]

Immediately after saying this Newbigin adds that evangelism *must* be coupled with practically caring for your neighbors.[250] Following her Lord's example the church is a servant church; this belongs to her nature.[251] Service for Newbigin simply means practically caring for your neighbors. In Newbigin's missionary context schools and hospitals exemplified the church's service. These education and healing services, along with other activities such as emergency relief, food distribution, and improving sanitation, simply flow out of God's love for the world and are expressed through the church. Given that both evangelism and service are central to Newbigin's understanding of the church's mission, how do the two relate to each other?

The relation between service and evangelism "has been a matter of considerable discussion and practical difficulty in the story of the Church's mission."[252] Firstly, evangelism and service cannot be separated because they both are integral to Jesus' mission. Newbigin observes, "Our Lord was sent both to preach and to be the servant of all. Each of these two activities has its proper dignity within the wholeness of the mission."[253] Both are part of the church's total mission and both have the character of witness. Newbigin justifies his argument biblically by appealing to the mission of the apostles and of Jesus himself. Newbigin says, "When [John] the Baptist sent to ask 'Art thou he that is to come?', He [Jesus] answered by pointing both to the works of healing and to the preaching of good news. All these together are the signs of the presence of the Kingdom."[254] Newbigin also describes the practical effect of divorcing service from evangelism. "Preaching which is divorced from deeds of love is without power to evoke belief."[255] Separating evangelism from service is equally disastrous; "Deeds of love which are permanently disconnected from witness to Christ evoke belief in the wrong thing."[256]

249. Newbigin, *A Word in Season*, 34.
250. Ibid.
251. See Newbigin, "The Church As A Servant Community."
252. Newbigin, *A Faith For This One World?*, 91.
253. Newbigin, *One Body*, 22–23.
254. Newbigin, *One Body*, 22–23, see also Luke 17:20–22.
255. Newbigin, *A Faith For This One World?*, 91.
256. Ibid., 91. A further reason why these two cannot be separated is words are, strictly speaking, also deeds: "God's words are deeds which accomplish what they express. It is by the uttering of words that Jesus performed his 'works', and the words of Jesus are still the means by which the Father 'does his works'" (Newbigin, *The Light Has Come*, 183).

Secondly, "if service and evangelism are not to be separated, neither must they be wrongly related"[257] by subordinating one to the other. Service should not be subordinated to evangelism because the church's service is modelled on Jesus. "When our Lord stretched forth his hand to heal a leper, there was no evangelistic strategy attached to the act. It was a pure outflow of the divine love into the world, and needed no further justification. Such should be the Church's deeds of service."[258] If service was subordinated to evangelism then deeds which should be pure acts of love and compassion become suspect as having an ulterior motive.[259] Christian works of love should be, like Christ's, "a spontaneous outflowing of the love of God for men, not a means to something else."[260]

Likewise, evangelism cannot be subordinated to programs of service. When this happens the church displays a lack of "faith in the supernatural power of the living word to bring forth fruit a hundredfold."[261] Where "service which does not explicitly point men to Christ Himself, [it] ultimately mocks men with false securities."[262] What "is certainly wrong," says Newbigin,

> is a policy which deliberately silences explicit evangelism and tries to put service in its place. For that can only mean that we are offering men our work in place of the works of God, inviting them to trust in the flesh instead of in the Spirit. The best of our service can never take the place of the cross of Jesus Christ.[263]

## Can Service Be Missionary and Still Be Pure Service?

His description of service and evangelism as part of God's mission of holy love to the world sounds good, but in what sense is service *missionary*, and if it is then what is meant by *missionary*? Newbigin says that, "Missionary work, from the time of the first apostles, has always included deeds of service. But not all forms of service can be rightly regarded as 'mission' in the narrower sense, though they are part of the total mission of the Church."[264] Newbigin here draws a distinction between a broad and a narrow sense of

---

257. Newbigin, *A Faith For This One World?*, 91.
258. Newbigin, *One Body*, 22–23.
259. Ibid., 22–23.
260. Newbigin, *A Faith For This One World?*, 91.
261. Newbigin, *One Body*, 22–23.
262. Ibid.
263. Newbigin, *A Faith For This One World?*, 91.
264. Newbigin, *One Body*, 43–44.

the word mission. This broad sense is described above. Actions constitute mission in the narrow sense "when they are part of an action of the Church in going out beyond the frontiers of its own life to bear witness to Christ as Lord among those who do not know Him, and when the overall *intention* of that action is that they should be brought from unbelief to faith." Newbigin admits that, "We are here trying to draw a very fine distinction, but I do not think we can avoid doing so if we are to define rightly the proper *differentium* of the missionary task."[265]

Admitting that this is a fine distinction, is it convincing? Newbigin argues that in the narrow sense an action is missionary when it has the intention of bringing non-Christians to faith in Christ. Is this not problematic given that he has just warned us, with good reason, that Christian service should be pure acts of love and compassion without an ulterior motive? In Christian service, then, is it possible to serve with the spontaneous motive of love and with the intention of bringing people to faith, without an ulterior motive? I suggest that Newbigin does not adequately reconcile what appear to be quite opposite statements. This is perhaps why Newbigin occasionally seems to use *mission* (in the narrow sense) and *evangelism* synonymously.[266] Newbigin is right, however, to claim that evangelism and service ought to be held together whilst also being distinguished from each other. Service can be both intentionally missionary (in the narrow sense of the word) and be a pure outflowing of love without ulterior motive because both service and evangelism flow from God's love for the world. To arbitrarily divorce the two, like subordinating one to the other, is to misunderstand God's mission and misrepresent him to the world.

Evangelism and service are both part of the church's mission to the world and need to be rightly related to each other. For Newbigin it is God's design that evangelism and service go hand in hand, so that "the word illuminates the deed, and the deed authenticates the word, and the Spirit takes them both to bear His own witness to the Resurrection."[267] Evangelism and service mutually authenticate and illuminate each other. The source of both evangelism and service is the new life in Christ. As the church's mission participates in the *missio Dei*, so both evangelism and service find their source in God's holy love for the world; one cannot be subordinated to the other. "The true connection between these two things," says Newbigin, "is not logical but ontological; it lies in the fact that both are seen to come out of the one reality, the new being, the community of the Holy Spirit."[268]

265. Ibid., emphasis original.
266. Newbigin, *The Reunion of the Church*, 10–11.
267. Newbigin, "From the Editor," 422.
268. Newbigin, *One Body*, 22–23.

## Part One: The Trinitarian Missiology of Lesslie Newbigin

## THEOLOGY OF RELIGIONS

### General Revelation and Other Religions

As a missionary and bishop working in a religiously pluralist society, Newbigin had profound respect for non-Christian religions. He thought of these religions as seeking "a true vision of God and a true union with him."[269] Speaking of the 'good nonChristian' Newbigin says, "His religion is certainly not one of mere falsehood or mere illusion. It is the response—in many cases a response which has a nobility and seriousness that puts us to shame—to the real witness that God has placed in the heart of every man."[270] Newbigin has no difficulty affirming a degree of general revelation based on the biblical text.[271] He sees as evidence of this every noble quality that is evident in other religions, including atheist secularism.[272] In seeking to be respectful to other religions and true to his own faith, Newbigin holds together particularity and universality, the uniqueness and finality of Christ with God's universal salvific will and general revelation.[273] On the one hand, Newbigin refrains from evaluating this religious response as legitimate or illegitimate. "We have no vantage point from which we have any right to judge that response," he says. On the other hand,

---

269. Newbigin probably had Hinduism and Islam in mind as these were and continue to be the most populous religions in India. He was probably not concerned with Buddhism, alone among the world religions in its doctrinal atheism.

270. Newbigin, *A Faith For This One World?*, 66–67.

271. Newbigin's preferred biblical texts in this regard are John 1:9 and Acts 14:17.

272. Newbigin approvingly quotes from the part of the "Jerusalem Message" addressed to non-Christians, "We rejoice to think that just because in Jesus Christ the light that lighteneth every man shone forth in its full splendour, we find rays of that same light where he is unknown or even is rejected. We welcome every noble quality in nonChristian persons or systems as further proof that the Father, who sent his Son into the world, has nowhere left Himself without witness.

Thus, merely to give illustration, and making no attempt to estimate the spiritual value of other religions to their adherents, we recognize as part of the one Truth that sense of the Majesty of God and the consequent reverence in worship, which are conspicuous in Islam; the deep sympathy for the world's sorrow and unselfish search for the way of escape, which are at the heart of Buddhism; the desire for contact with ultimate reality conceived as spiritual, which is prominent in Hinduism; the belief in a moral order of the universe and consequent insistence on moral conduct, which are inculcated by Confucianism; the disinterested pursuit of truth and of human welfare which are often found in those who stand for secular civilization but do not accept Christ as their Lord and Savior" (World Missionary Conference, Jerusalem 1928, cited in Newbigin, *The Finality of Christ*, 29).

273. John Sanders describes these as the two theological axioms that guide Christian thinking of those outside the Church. Sanders, *No Other Name*, 25.

the coming of the gospel means quite simply and seriously the end of it. That which all religions seek, namely a true vision of God and a true union with him, can only be the gift of God; and that gift is given in Jesus Christ. Christ is the end of religion in the same sense that he is the end of the law.[274]

Despite affirming many positive qualities of non-Christian religions, the coming of Jesus Christ means an end to all religion, all human seeking after God, because God has become human.

During Newbigin's mission to India, there were two opposing and dominant movements in Christian missions concerning the theology of religions: a triumphalistic over-confidence in the gospel on the one hand and a crisis of confidence in that same gospel on the other. Born one year before the Edinburgh Missionary Conference of 1910, Newbigin does not display the triumphalism of that conference, associated with missionary activity during the colonial period. By the time Newbigin went to India there were signs that the colonial era was coming to an end, and with it, colonial attitudes. The former colonized countries, after independence, experienced a self-determination expressed in nationalism and a revival of the non-Christian religions, which was especially true of India. Meanwhile, there was in Europe a crisis of confidence in Christianity as manifested in declining church attendance from the 1960s and the death-of-God and secular theology movements associated with names such as William Hamilton, John Robinson and Harvey Cox. Christendom was visibly crumbling; however, Newbigin does not display any evidence of his own lack of confidence in the gospel. Shaped by his deeply held faith and his Reformed theological heritage, with its high doctrine of God's sovereignty, Newbigin successfully walked a path between over-confidence and crisis. His attitude toward other religions is respectful and generous whilst his confidence in the gospel remained unshakable.

## *Mission and Other Religions*[275]

As a missionary, Newbigin believed in communicating the gospel to all those outside of the Christian faith, with the confident hope that they will become God's reconciled reconcilers. He despised the cultural imperialism of proselytism which created an 'us and them' division, where members of

---

274. Newbigin, *A Faith For This One World?*, 66–67.

275. For several recent engagements on this see Jacob, *Religious Pluralism and the Finality of Christ*; George, *The Gospel as Public Truth*; Adams, *Christ and the Other*; Goheen, "The Finality of Christ;" Thomas, *Christ and the World of Religions*.

other religions communities were asked to forsake all to join the Christian community. He says,

> Christ is the light that lightens every *man*. My point is that the Christian missionary is not going out to enroll men under the banner of a tribal deity. We are not inviting strangers to come into our house. We are asking all men to come to their own home where they have as much right as we have . . . Christ belongs now as truly to the Hindu and the Muslim as he does to us. He is now their true light. He is not the head of religion, but the head and King of the human race.[276]

For Newbigin all humans are made in the *imago Dei* and this image is restored in Jesus Christ, so, "in bringing Christ to men, we are restoring to them their true nature."[277]

To this end, Newbigin issued a call to the church's theologians and theological educators and a wider call to the church in general. Taking the latter first, Newbigin was convinced of the "*need for much bolder experiment in entering into the spiritual wrestlings of the nonChristian faiths today . . . This calls for a much greater openness in our encounter with the nonChristian faiths than has been common in recent years.*"[278] Newbigin envisioned Christians engaging in serious friendships with Hindus, Muslims and other members of non-Christian faiths, honestly engaging in spiritual matters. No doubt aware of the potential danger of this openness, Newbigin desired

> that there shall be distributed throughout the whole membership of the Church a deep, and strong, and experimentally verified conviction about the sufficiency and finality of Christ for the whole world. I say experimentally verified, because you cannot really stake everything on a belief that you have not tested and found true.[279]

Newbigin modelled this himself when he jointly led weekly scriptural studies with the leader of the Hindu Ramakrishna Mission in Kanchi, although he later reflected on the ineffectiveness of this method.[280]

---

276. Newbigin, *A Faith For This One World?*, 65.

277. Ibid., 66–67.

278. Newbigin, "The Work of the Holy Spirit," 32, emphasis original. See also Newbigin, *The Mission and Unity of the Church*.

279. Newbigin, "The Pattern of Partnership," 44, emphasis original.

280. Decades later, whilst Bishop of Madras, Newbigin was involved in the Community Service Center which sometimes organized inter-faith meetings, the purpose of which was to address problems which faced all in the public life on the young nation. Newbigin found these inter-faith experiences far more productive than the weekly

Regarding the church's theology, Newbigin observes that "our systems of dogmatics are not directed towards the nonChristian systems of thought, but against rival statements of the Christian faith."[281] For him this has led to a "failure to penetrate boldly and deeply into the thoughtforms of the nonChristian faiths in order to state our Gospel in their terms."[282] In Newbigin's experience the majority of new converts were from low caste Hindu backgrounds; high-caste well educated Hindus were generally less responsive to the gospel. Since it is the church's missionary responsibility to effectively communicate the gospel to them, Newbigin argues that the whole theological curriculum ought to be re-conceived in missionary terms beginning with a change in ecclesiology, recognizing the fundamental *missionary* nature of the church. To this end Newbigin worked hard to found the Christian Institute for the Study of Religion and Society in October 1957 in Bangalore, for the purpose of equipping the church to engage with the issues posed by traditional Hinduism and by the contemporary Indian political climate.

When the WCC merged with the IMC, the missionary nature of the church was formally acknowledged by member churches, although a change in ecclesial missionary consciousness would take time. Speaking from my own experience of studying at leading theological institutions in three different continents, it is my observation that Newbigin's call has gone largely unheeded. Within Christian theology faculties, courses on non-Christian religions make up a tiny percentage within the curriculum. Furthermore, courses on non-Christian religions are often taught by religious studies rather than theology departments. The rise of religious studies in Western universities has largely compartmentalized the study of non-Christian religions to these faculties which adopt a methodology that differs significantly from the Christian missionary and theological approach that Newbigin called for. Furthermore, the increased specialization of theological and biblical studies makes it even harder for these academics to also become competent scholars of another religion. Even so, Newbigin's challenge to theological educators remains most pertinent more than fifty years after

---

discussions with the Ramakrishna monks in Kanchi because in Madras all participants were reaching beyond their standard formulas to seek answers to the problems with which God was confronting them all. Newbigin, *Unfinished Agenda*, 228. Elsewhere Newbigin says, "The real point of contact between Christian and nonChristian is not in the *religion* of the nonChristian but in his *humanity*" (Newbigin, *A Faith For This One World?*, 65). That is why the Madras discussions concerning human needs were more beneficial than the purely religious discussions in Kanchi.

281. Newbigin, *The Mission and Unity of the Church*, 8.
282. Newbigin, "The Work of the Holy Spirit," 29.

it was issued, and no doubt theologians and biblical scholars will respond to it to the degree that their self-understanding as theological educators is pervaded by a missionary consciousness.

## SUMMARY

In this chapter I have surveyed the key themes from Newbigin's missiology, which can be characterized as biblically rooted, church-centered, and prophetic in the sense of calling the church back to its missional responsibility, back to missional church-structures, and back to biblical missionary methods. This prophetic element reveals a radical streak in Newbigin's missiology. He was unafraid to challenge unbiblical church structures that had stood for fifteen-hundred years. He called for nothing less than organic church unity as the revealed will of God for all churches, in opposition to almost the entire Protestant ecclesiological edifice. He resisted attempts to reduce mission to inter-church aid and uncompromisingly proclaimed the kerygmatic responsibility of the church, when doing so aroused stiff opposition.[283] Newbigin was a radical but he was not a maverick; his radical streak was borne out of loyalty to the gospel. As already said, he was biblically rooted and historically grounded in the traditions of the church. What I have interpreted as radical could also be rightly understood as faithfulness to the unchanging Word of God and mission of God amidst the turbulent ideological currents of the world; unchanging steadfastness within a sea of change. Indeed, the designation radical can either reveal much about the person to whom it is ascribed, or about the context in which that person is being described.[284] No doubt his unwavering nature made Newbigin an

283. I refer here to the divergence between Newbigin's ecumenical and missionary vision and the direction the WCC took from its 1968 meeting in Uppsala, encapsulated in his ongoing disagreement with Konrad Raiser, who was the WCC General Secretary from 1993 to 2003. See Newbigin, "Ecumenical Amnesia"; Wainwright, *Lesslie Newbigin*, 128–34.

284. Being called a radical is akin to being called an extremist, but neither designation is inherently negative. It is worthwhile recalling Martin Luther King Jr's reply to the charge of being an extremist in his famous "Letter from a Birmingham Jail." He writes: "At first I was rather disappointed that fellow clergymen would see my nonviolent efforts as those of an extremist." Further on in the letter he continues, "But though I was initially disappointed at being categorized as an extremist, as I continued to think about the matter I gradually gained a measure of satisfaction from the label. Was not Jesus an extremist for love: 'Love your enemies, bless them that curse you, do good to them that hate you, and pray for them which despitefully use you, and persecute you.' Was not Amos an extremist for justice: 'Let justice roll down like waters and righteousness like an ever flowing stream.' Was not Paul an extremist for the Christian gospel: 'I bear in my body the marks of the Lord Jesus.' Was not Martin Luther an extremist: 'Here I

asset and a challenge to the ecumenical movement during his many decades of participation. Newbigin's missiology is steadfast, biblical, radical and prophetic, but to what extent is it trinitarian?

---

stand; I cannot do otherwise, so help me God.' And John Bunyan: 'I will stay in jail to the end of my days before I make a butchery of my conscience.' And Abraham Lincoln: 'This nation cannot survive half slave and half free.' And Thomas Jefferson: 'We hold these truths to be self evident, that all men are created equal.' So the question is not whether we will be extremists, but what kind of extremists we will be." "Letter from a Birmingham Jail." With this in mind perhaps it is right to understand Newbigin as an extremist for the gospel?

CHAPTER 2

# Newbigin's Theology of the Trinity

## INTRODUCTION

THE WRITING IN 1962 of *The Mission of the Triune God*[1] represents a substantial shift in Newbigin's thinking. Until the appearance of that book, republished in 1963 under the title *The Relevance of Trinitarian Doctrine for Today's Mission*, the doctrine of the Trinity had barely featured in his written work. From 1963 onwards, however, it became a major concern. This chapter will consider the reasons for that shift, noting in particular the influence of Charles Cochrane, and trace its development in *Trinitarian Doctrine* and in subsequent writings, particularly *The Open Secret*. I will argue that it is in *Trinitarian Doctrine* itself that there exists Newbigin's most substantial articulation of the importance of the Trinity for our understanding of God's mission. The chapter will conclude with a summary assessment of Newbigin's trinitarian missiology and by noting a number of areas that require further development.

## THE HISTORY AND DEVELOPMENT OF NEWBIGIN'S TRINITARIAN THEOLOGY

Newbigin did not always regard the doctrine of the Trinity as centrally important. He explains: "In my own theological training, the doctrine of the Trinity played a very minor part. Of course it was not denied or questioned, but it had no central place." He writes further: "In the *magnum opus*

---

1. Newbigin, *The Mission of the Triune God*, n.p.

of my revered theological teacher, John Oman, there is no reference to the Trinity."[2] No doubt neglect of the doctrine of the Trinity by Newbigin's theological teacher reflected the wider neglect in the Western theological world prior to the trinitarian resurgence instigated by Karl Barth. However, Newbigin did learn from Oman the importance of the personhood of God, a theme that would eventually feature significantly in Newbigin's understanding of the doctrine of the Trinity.[3] As a careful student of Scripture, Newbigin noticed that the New Testament is full of references to Father, Son and Spirit, and he found that if one looks below the surface of Paul's letters one will find these references over and over again.[4] However, it appears that during Newbigin's studies at Westminster College, Cambridge, these trinitarian observations remained largely un-interpreted and unappreciated. Newbigin's relative ignorance of the importance of the doctrine of the Trinity extended to his study of the patristic era, the principal period of trinitarian development. He recalls,

> I always regretted that when I was a theological student and had to study all the heresy of the first four centuries, nobody really explained to me that it was all part of the struggle to express the new reality that had come into the world with Jesus, using the old language which was already saturated with Greek philosophical thought and with the strict monotheism of the Old Testament.[5]

For two and a half decades following Newbigin's departure for India in 1936, the subject of the Trinity hardly features in his writings. Newbigin's Christian faith was always directed toward the Triune God, but prior to 1962, the subject of God's Triunity was not significant for him. His writing from this period focuses on other subjects, notably the church (*The Reunion*

---

2. Newbigin, "The Trinity," 2.

3. Hunsberger, "The Church," 101. An early expression of Newbigin's trinitarianism that reveals Oman's influence is found in *Sin and Salvation*, where Newbigin says, "When God created man He did not create an individual; He created man-and-woman. For God is not an individual; God is personal but He is not a person. He is a Trinity, Father, Son and Holy Spirit, one God; one personal being in whom love is perfect and complete because love is both given and received" (*Sin and Salvation*, 17–18). For further reading on Oman's doctrine of God, see Bevans, *John Oman*.

4. Similarly, Kelly, in his *Early Christian Creeds*, says of the tripartite pattern in the New Testament that "the Trinitarian ground-plan obtrudes itself obstinately throughout, and its presence is all the more striking because more often than not there is nothing in the context to necessitate it. The impression inevitably conveyed is that the conception of the threefold manifestation of the Godhead was embedded deeply in Christian thinking from the start" (23).

5. Newbigin, *Living Hope*, 11.

of the Church and *The Household of God*), salvation (*Sin and Salvation*), and mission (*A South India Diary*; *One Body, One Gospel, One World*; and *A Faith For This One World?*). In these writings the occasional mention of the Trinity reveals an instinctive, and sometimes profound, but largely unexamined sense of its importance for missiology.[6] Then, in approximately 1962 something happened that forever changed Newbigin's theology.[7] "In my own experience," he recollects, "trinitarian doctrine came alive when I read classical scholar Charles Norris Cochrane's book *Christianity and Classical Culture* (1940)."[8]

Newbigin's reading of Cochrane was the catalyst for the subject of the Trinity becoming significant, even decisive, for Newbigin's theology. Soon after reading Cochrane Newbigin attempted to formulate the importance of the doctrine of the Trinity for that to which he had given his life, the mission of the church. In 1962 Newbigin wrote *The Mission of the Triune God*, which he redrafted and published in 1963 as *The Relevance of Trinitarian Doctrine for Today's Mission* (the title was later shortened to *Trinitarian Doctrine for Today's Mission*)[9] in which he claims the doctrine of the Trinity is *absolutely indispensable* for a true missiology. This is quite a turnaround from his previous theological position. Then, after this publication, there follows fifteen

---

6. Wainwright locates Newbigin's discovery of the importance of the doctrine of the Trinity in his writing of *The Household of God*, published a decade before *Trinitarian Doctrine*, when his increased attention to the third Person of the Godhead led him to give the book a trinitarian structure. Wainwright says, "the reality of the Trinity, never of course absent from his earlier writings, gained a new prominence that was thereafter maintained in his thought and shaped it powerfully" (Wainwright, *Lesslie Newbigin*, 98). Although there are some profound reflections on the doctrine of the Trinity and important developments in Newbigin's Pneumatology, the evidence suggests Wainwright has overemphasized his case. I suggest that Newbigin first expressed this discovery in writing in *The Mission of the Triune God*.

7. It is most likely that Newbigin read Cochrane in 1962. However, in a 1990 GOCN article Newbigin recalls that *Christianity and Classical Culture* "made a deep impression on me when I read it 50 years ago" ("The Threat and the Promise," 2). That would date his reading of Cochrane to its year of publication, 1940. If this recollection is correct then it is highly unusual that for over twenty years after reading the work he largely ignored its contents, only to then dramatically discover its significance in the early 1960s. I hypothesize that there are two possible scenarios. One, Newbigin did in fact read Cochrane in 1940 but its significance largely escapes him until his re-reading of it in approximately 1962 when it forever impacts his thinking. Or, two, Newbigin mistakenly confused the date of his reading of Cochrane with the date of Cochrane's publication.

8. Newbigin, "The Trinity," 2. From the context it is almost certain that what Newbigin here refers to as 'trinitarian doctrine' is 'the doctrine of the Trinity' rather than 'a trinitarian construal of Christian doctrine,' although for Newbigin the latter does follow the former. Newbigin adopted this imprecise phrase from Cochrane, *Christianity and Classical Culture*, 361.

9. I engage with *Trinitarian Doctrine for Today's Mission* unless otherwise stated.

years of almost complete silence concerning the Trinity. This is surprising because if his trinitarian theological discovery was as momentous as he claimed, then one would have expected him to develop his trinitarian theology and express his thoughts in writing. Instead, all one finds is a one-page article on "Trinitarianism" in the 1971 *Concise Dictionary of Christian World Mission* which is too short to contain any notable progress in thought. In it he simply mentions the importance of Cochrane's study and condenses some of his previous trinitarian material.[10] This strange period of silence, I contend, is not due to a change in Newbigin's mind about the importance of the doctrine of the Trinity but to the historical circumstances in which he found himself. Two considerations are especially noteworthy.

First, Newbigin wrote *Trinitarian Doctrine* with the hope "that it would provide the basis for a [WCC–IMC] post-integration sequel to *One Body*—a manifesto, in fact, for the new Division of World Mission and Evangelism. But this was not to be. Wim [Visser 't Hooft—WCC General Secretary]," he continues, "disapproved of its theology, and . . . its impact was limited. It was nearly twenty years later that I had the opportunity to develop its argument in a full-length book, *The Open Secret*."[11] Newbigin was discouraged from further developing and reflecting upon trinitarian missiology by his friend and WCC superior Visser 't Hooft. Second, Newbigin did not have the opportunity to develop his trinitarian missiology. The reason for this was the impact of 'the secular decade' of the 1960s, which was beginning to be felt in the church.[12] Newbigin says that "the theological earthquake which was shaking the world of English-speaking Christians was a much more serious affair than the debate about missiology."[13] Issues that are briefly mentioned in *Trinitarian Doctrine* such as secularization, and the relation of the Gospel to non-Christian religions, become the focus of full length books (*Honest Religion For Secular Man* [1966] and *The Finality of Christ* [1969] respectively). The intellectual currents of the world had moved on. As a church leader rather than a professional theologian, Newbigin did not have the time in his busy schedule to reflect further upon the importance

---

10. In this brief article Newbigin says that the importance of the doctrine of the Trinity "for mission may be suggested in the following points. (1) Jesus Christ cannot be introduced to those of another religion simply as 'God.' He can only be introduced as the Son of the Father. (2) The sovereign freedom of the Holy Spirit over as well as within the church is the starting point of missionary renewal. (3) The church's mission is the clue to world history, but is subject to the Father who over-rules all things according to his will" ("Trinitarianism").

11. Newbigin, *Unfinished Agenda*, 199.

12. See, for example, Robinson, *Honest to God*; Cox, *The Secular City*.

13. Newbigin, *Unfinished Agenda*, 199.

of a *trinitarian* missiology and, in service of the church, his incisive intellect was required elsewhere. Only after the theological impact of the secular decade began to subside, after retirement from India, and upon taking up a lecturing position at Selly Oak Colleges, did the opportunity to develop the trinitarian arguments in *Trinitarian Doctrine* present itself. He took up this opportunity in 1978 with the publication of *The Open Secret: An Introduction to the Theology Of Mission*.[14] I will return to a consideration of this work in due course.

In *The Light Has Come: An Exposition of the Fourth Gospel*, published in 1982, Newbigin further reflected on the trinitarian material in John's gospel, particularly the crucial Johannine motif of Jesus' relationship to his Father, and the prominence of the Holy Spirit in the Farewell or Upper Room Discourses (John 13:31—16:33). In 1987 Yale University Press published Jesuit Michael Buckley's *The Roots of Modern Atheism* in which he traces the effect of Thomas Aquinas' synthesis of classical and Christian thought. He emphasizes the necessity of the revelation of God as Trinity as the starting point for theological thought, as opposed to all forms of natural theology. In Newbigin's words, Buckley's thesis is that "theology runs into the sand when it seeks some grounds supposedly more reliable than God's revelation of himself in Jesus Christ."[15] Buckley's book exercised considerable influence upon Newbigin, who had read the work by 1991, and perhaps a year earlier.[16] Regardless of precisely *when* Newbigin read Buckley's book, it remains

---

14. A second edition was published in 1995 and it is this edition which I draw upon.

15. Newbigin, "Theism and Atheism," 2. In a later article Newbigin expands on this theme: "In the first part of his [Thomas'] great work he sets out to demonstrate by rational proofs the existence of God, and he does so without reference to Jesus Christ. Then in the third part he says that we know God through Jesus Christ. I realize, of course, that Aquinas is more nuanced than that, but we see in Aquinas what a great shift has occurred from Augustine's 'I believe in order to know' to Aristotelian philosophy, which is not dependent on faith. This I believe has been the fatal flaw of apologetics in the last 300 years" (Newbigin, "Way Out West," 22). However, drawing on Walsh and Middleton, *The Transforming Vision*, 110–22 and Chaplin, *Introduction to a Christian Worldview*, 101–5, Goheen contends that this problematic dualism in Western culture goes back to Augustine's acceptance of neo-platonism. He says "Newbigin has simply highlighted the positive stream within Augustine. While Newbigin sees the turning point at Aquinas' appropriation of Aristotle, he does not sufficiently recognize that the Augustinian synthesis with neo-Platonic rationalism paved the way for Aquinas" (Goheen, "As the Father Has Sent Me," 383).

16. I hypothesize that Newbigin read Buckley's book in 1990 for two reasons. First, in 1991 he mentions that he has recently read it. Newbigin, "Theism and Atheism," 1. Second, in 1990 Newbigin wrote the one-page article "What Do We Mean By 'God'?," 7, in which he contrasts Christian trinitarian thinking with natural theology, emphasizing the necessity of God's triune self-revelation as the starting point for thought; both classic Buckleyian themes.

an important influence on his later trinitarian theology, for he incorporates prominent Buckleyian themes into his subsequent exposition of the Trinity. It may well have been around this time that Newbigin preached a Trinity Sunday sermon (on the Trinity) in which Buckley's themes of revelation versus speculation appear to underlie his thought.[17]

Upon publication of the BCC Study Commission's *The Forgotten Trinity* in 1991, drafted by Colin Gunton, Newbigin wrote a letter to all his fellow URC ministers commending this book because it could help to recover confidence "in that most central of all Christian teachings, in the teaching of what it means to say 'God.'"[18] Although Gunton was one of the most prolific British trinitarian theologians of the twentieth century, he is not a significant influence on Newbigin's trinitarian theology simply because Gunton's trinitarian publications do not appear until near the end of Newbigin's life.[19] However, through their interaction at Kings College, London, they developed a strong friendship, and in Gunton's work Newbigin found a systematic treatment of his own theological commitments.[20] Accordingly, in Part Two of this book I will draw quite heavily from Gunton's main works of systematic trinitarian theology *The Promise of Trinitarian Theology* and *Father, Son, and Holy Spirit*.[21]

In 1993 Newbigin presented his paper "The Trinity as Public Truth" at the Fifth Edinburgh Dogmatics Conference on *The Trinity in a Pluralistic Age*, the proceedings of which were published in 1997.[22] In this presentation he acknowledges the influence of Buckley's *The Roots of Modern Atheism* and Jürgen Moltmann's *The Trinity and the Kingdom of God*. Newbigin utilized Moltmann's contrast between trinitarianism and 'monotheism' used in a pejorative sense, because he connects the latter with the Western tendency to modalism and Unitarianism. On 6 March 1995 Newbigin wrote a letter to Wm. B. Eerdmans, Jr. of Eerdmans Publishing Company.[23] In this

17. Newbigin, *A Trinity Sunday Sermon*.
18. Newbigin, "Letter to URC Ministers."
19. The beginnings of Gunton's trinitarian theology can be seen in his *Enlightenment and Alienation* for which Newbigin wrote the Foreword. When Newbigin refers to Gunton he primarily refers to this work, which is concerned with critically engaging modern Western culture more than articulating a trinitarian theology. Gunton was also a member of the British Council of Churches Commission on Trinitarian Doctrine Today, which published three volumes under the title *The Forgotten Trinity* (1989–1991).
20. I owe this insight to Murray Rae from personal conversation. Rae met regularly with Newbigin when he was a student at Kings and attended a number of conferences with both Newbigin and Gunton together.
21. Gunton, *The Promise*, and idem, *Father, Son and Holy Spirit*.
22. Newbigin, "The Trinity as Public Truth."
23. Newbigin, "Letter to Wm. B. Eerdmans, Jr."

letter he relates that he is due to give a series of six talks at Holy Trinity Brompton, London, on a broad introduction to Christian faith and practice. Significantly, Newbigin's first talk was entitled "God, the Holy Trinity," which was later published as chapter 1 of *Living Hope in a Changing World*. This was to be Newbigin's last recorded discussion on the doctrine of the Trinity both in speaking (1995) and published material (published 2003).

The last major influence on Newbigin's trinitarianism thus far unmentioned is Karl Barth. Although Newbigin read Barth as part of his theological training at Cambridge, and met him several times under the auspices of the WCC, it was only in 1974 that Newbigin was strongly impacted by Barth's theology. In the summer following his return from India to Britain, Newbigin read through the entirety of Barth's *Church Dogmatics* and later described it as "an immensely rewarding experience," "enthralling," and "a needed preparation for the much more difficult missionary experience which . . . lay ahead."[24] Barth begins his *magnum opus* with the doctrine of the Trinity, intentionally reversing the order and priority given to the doctrine by his theological forebear Friedrich Schleiermacher. By giving it such a place, Barth explains, its content will be "decisive and controlling for the whole of dogmatics."[25] Newbigin found a trinitarian theology in Barth that is profoundly cohesive and in accord with his own theological convictions. Consequently, in Part Two as I seek to develop a trinitarian missiology in the tradition of Lesslie Newbigin, Barth too will be a key resource.[26]

This brief overview of the historical development of Newbigin's trinitarian theology highlighted the decisive impact of Cochrane's *Christianity and Classical Culture*. An examination of Newbigin's theology of the Trinity must begin with understanding this impact.

## Charles Cochrane's *Christianity and Classical Culture*

*Christianity and Classical Culture* is a historical work in which Cochrane traces the development of classical thought from its restoration under

---

24. Newbigin, *Unfinished Agenda*, 241–42.

25. Barth, *CD* I/1, 303.

26. Given that "An overwhelming perception exists that Barth and mission are like oil and water," this decision may seem strange. Flett, *The Witness of God*, 164. For example, Waldron Scott maintains that "within the more than eight thousand pages of his systematic theology Karl Barth devotes a mere four and one-half pages to the specific topic of foreign missions" (Scott, *Karl Barth's Theology of Mission*, 9). Against this perception, the doctrines of Trinity *and mission* are both major themes in Barth's theology, which Part Two will demonstrate. Flett has also demonstrated this in *The Witness of God*.

Emperor Augustus to its disintegration in the fifth century. Cochrane's thesis is: "The fall of Rome was the fall of an idea, or rather of a system of life based upon a complex of ideas which may be described broadly as those of Classicism; and the deficiencies of Classicism, already exposed in the third century, were destined sooner or later to involve the system in ruin."[27] In developing his thesis Cochrane sought "to bring out the salient points of Christian thinking in relation to the classical background, as the central feature of the historical revolution,"[28] that is, the uprising and succession of Christian thought from the classical period. Cochrane examines 'cross-sections' of Christian thought that reveal the central elements and conceptual foundations of the historical revolution. He locates the origin and cause of this revolution in thought in the development of the doctrine of the Trinity, as formulated by Athanasius and founded upon his understanding of Jesus as *homoousios* with God the Father.

Classicism, in its Platonist form, involved the division of reality into the two worlds of thought and sense, the intelligible and sensible realms (the *cosmos noetos* and the *cosmos aisthetos*). A consequence of this dualistic cosmology was the classical disjunction of being and becoming. Classical thought also taught that the universe could be explained in terms of chance and necessity, and that history was the product of the unending struggle of virtue against fortune, human skill against fate. These doctrines formed a key part of the conceptual framework through which human experience was understood. Cochrane argues that there were 'radical deficiencies' in this conceptual framework that led to its downfall and replacement by a wholly different worldview.[29]

In the midst of this classical world, Christianity, with its basis in a different, Hebraic, way of thought, was growing. The early Christian leaders and thinkers sought to articulate and explain the gospel using the dominant language and concepts of their classical world. Cochrane shows how Arius sought to articulate his Christology within the classical framework, whereas Athanasius, as he developed his Christology, felt compelled to abandon altogether the classical axioms of thought. Athanasius believed that classical thought was a dead end, had issued in insoluble puzzles, and that "this was the inevitable result of its having accepted a vicious or defective starting-point."[30]

---

27. Cochrane, *Christianity and Classical Culture*, 355.
28. Ibid., 360.
29. Ibid.
30. Ibid., 361.

Classical cosmology understood the cosmos to be made up of formless matter and motionless forms. Rejecting this starting point, Christians pointed to "the Trinity as the creative and moving principle."[31] Athanasius pointed to the Triune God as the *arché*, the cause of all causes.[32] "The doctrine of the Trinity," Cochrane avers, "provided the basis for a radically new and unclassical account of the structure and content of experience."[33] As a starting point for thought, the doctrine of the Trinity is "a basic principle broad and inclusive enough to bear the weight of the conclusions derived from it and to sustain, rather than stifle, the life of religion and philosophy."[34] As a result of Athanasius' claim that the Triune God is the *arché* of reality, including thought, no attempt was made to demonstrate this truth in terms acceptable to classical thought; instead it was propounded as a matter of faith.[35] Rather than justifying this new starting point on other grounds, Cochrane explains, "faith in the God of revelation was proposed as indispensable to full understanding."[36]

For Cochrane this is the kernel of the historical revolution that led to the demise of Classicism and the emerging dominance of Christian thought based on its trinitarian starting point. Describing the heart of this revolution, Newbigin explains

> The long and often arcane theological battles of the patristic period were, at heart, battles about the question whether Jesus is Lord in this absolute sense. For Greek philosophy to accept the full meaning of the apostolic message that the logos was identical with the man Jesus of Nazareth required nothing less than a complete abandonment of fundamental dualisms of matter and spirit, of time and eternity, of visible and invisible. One could, without a total break with traditional philosophy, accept the idea that Jesus was like God (*homoiousios*) but not that he was one in being with God (*homoousios*). The historian Gibbon mocked at the spectacle of Christians fighting over a diphthong, but that apparently minute difference concealed the whole difference between surrender to an ultimate pluralism and acknowledgement that God has actually made himself known by presence in the stuff of human history. It if is [sic.] true that God has done this, then this has to be the starting point of all fundamental

---

31. Ibid., 244.
32. Ibid., 362.
33. Ibid., 237.
34. Ibid., 361–62. See also Newbigin, *Truth to Tell*, 17–18.
35. Cochrane, *Christianity and Classical Culture*, 237.
36. Ibid., 238.

thinking and the criterion by which all ultimate truth-claims are judged. The whole existence of the Christian faith hung on that diphthong.[37]

## The Significance of Christianity and Classical Culture for Newbigin

As noted above, the doctrine of the Trinity 'came alive' for Newbigin when he read *Christianity and Classical Culture*. The big idea that Newbigin took from Cochrane was the missional potency of the doctrine of the Trinity as the starting point for human thought. In its infancy the early church was small, persecuted, and surrounded by a self-confident, hostile and dominant culture. It was to the people of this culture that the early church sought to commend the gospel of Jesus Christ, and the key battleground was in the world of thought. Cochrane's analysis taught Newbigin that the early church succeeded in this missional challenge because of the doctrine of the Trinity. The early church's struggle to formulate the doctrine of the Trinity was, contends Newbigin, "an essential part of the battle to master the pagan world view at the height of its power and self-confidence."[38] From its trinitarian starting point the early church out-thought the decaying classical civilization and made possible the healing of dualisms inherent in classical thought.[39] Classicism was supplanted by a Christian framework of thought that subsequently shaped European public discourse and thought for over a millennium. This commanded Newbigin's attention as a missionary success par excellence.

Newbigin learned from Cochrane the significance of the doctrine of the Trinity as *arché*. He was insistent that the doctrine of the Trinity form the starting point and paradigm for thought;[40] a conviction that was later reinforced by his reading of Michael Buckley's *The Roots of Modern Atheism*.[41] The doctrine of the Trinity is the new *arché*, the fresh starting point of a new plausibility structure for the realm of human thought, including theology. Consequently, in both *Trinitarian Doctrine* and *The Open Secret* Newbigin expounds the importance of the doctrine of the Trinity for mission, and

---

37. Newbigin, "Religious Pluralism," 228–29. Patently, therefore, Brunner is wrong to state that "the doctrine of the Trinity" has not "ever been a central article of faith in the religious life of the Christian Church as a whole, at any period of its history" (Brunner, *Dogmatics*, 1:205).

38. Newbigin, *Trinitarian Doctrine*, 34.

39. Newbigin, "The Trinity," 2.

40. Ibid., 3.

41. Newbigin, "Theism and Atheism," 2.

then turns to address specific missiological questions from this trinitarian perspective. In the preface of *Trinitarian Doctrine* Newbigin explains that it "is not written to advocate any particular line of action, but rather as an effort to understand . . . We must see before we can act rightly. If the vision is right, we shall know how to act."[42] Newbigin's conviction concerning the doctrine of the Trinity as *arché* gave rise to two key themes in his thought.

The doctrine of the Trinity is the *arché* for understanding and interpreting the structure and content of human experience and so cannot by definition be explained or justified on other grounds; it must be accepted by faith. Newbigin learned from Cochrane's presentation of Athanasius and Augustine that faith is the first step towards knowledge. Later, Newbigin combined this insight with Polanyi's argument that there can be no knowing without personal commitment.[43] Recognition of the doctrine of the Trinity as *arché* led to the conviction that it is futile to attempt to justify any aspect of the Christian faith, including the doctrine of the Trinity, in terms dictated by plausibility structures that do not have the gospel as their starting point. Accordingly, one commonly finds in Newbigin's work assertions such as: "It has never at any time been possible to fit the resurrection of Jesus into any world view except a world view of which it is the basis."[44] This conviction led Newbigin to repudiate much of what is known today as apologetics,[45] that is, the (misguided) attempt to explain the gospel in terms determined by the present reigning plausibility structure. Newbigin turns this approach on its head and instead asks, regarding the mission to modernity, "What would it mean if, instead of trying to understand the Gospel from the point of view of our culture, we tried to understand our culture from the point of view of the Gospel?"[46] This pivotal methodological decision, the importance of which is difficult to overestimate,[47] Newbigin learned from Cochrane's portrayal of Athanasius' development of the doctrine of the Trinity.

A second theme emerging from Newbigin's consideration of Cochrane's work is that the doctrine of the Trinity ought to be the starting point for missiological thought. Newbigin became convinced that God's Triunity is intrinsic to the gospel and its communication.[48] Consequently, he developed the thesis that the doctrine of the Trinity comes to the fore

---

42. Newbigin, *Trinitarian Doctrine*, 9.
43. Newbigin, *Proper Confidence*, 50.
44. Newbigin, *Honest Religion for Secular Man*, 53.
45. For a consideration of this subject, see chapter 3 footnote 45 [x-ref].
46. Newbigin, "Can the West be Converted?," 32.
47. Weston remarks "His [Newbigin's] call to interpret culture in the light of revelation rather than vice versa remains one of primary importance to evangelical thinking on the whole issue of contemporary mission" ("Gospel, Mission and Culture," 54).
48. Newbigin, *Trinitarian Doctrine*, 34–35.

in a missionary situation and recedes in a non-missional context. Geoffrey Wainwright observes that "Newbigin found a historical precedent and a substantive norm in the early Church's articulation of a fully trinitarian doctrine of the God it proclaimed in the Gospel amid the struggle with the pagan world."[49] Having lived for over two decades in India, Newbigin knew of the enormous missional challenge the church faced as it sought to evangelize amongst people conditioned and shaped by what Newbigin repeatedly called 'Indian thought'. He would later find, on returning to Britain, that the culture of modernity was similarly inhospitable to the Gospel.

Newbigin read Cochrane at the start of the 'secular decade', the 1960s, by which time he had already recognized the threat posed by secularism, and once again, the battleground was in the world of thought. The parallels between classicism and the emergent secularism are striking. Cochrane observes that Cicero accepted and propounded the principle of 'philosophic doubt', and that in his system of thought, "there was nothing in the universe superior to reason."[50] These themes re-emerge in the Enlightenment and have contributed to the development of secularism in Western culture. The principle of philosophic doubt was central, for example, to the method of Descartes who significantly shaped the philosophical foundations of Enlightenment thought.[51] As the early church's trinitarian starting point led to missional success over Classicism, so Newbigin believed that the modern church needed to return to the doctrine of the Trinity as the first step towards a missional engagement with modern culture. Hence Newbigin says the purpose of *Trinitarian Doctrine* is "to invite the missionary movement to bind to itself afresh the strong Name of the Trinity."[52] In what is arguably his most fully developed treatise in his mission to modernity, *Foolishness to the Greeks*, he insists that "The twin dogmas of the Incarnation and Trinity . . . form the starting point for a way of understanding reality as a whole."[53]

Cochrane's work provided Newbigin with an important *historical* perspective for his mission to modernity. It revealed how a sophisticated system of thought that had been dominant for centuries could be overcome by the message of the gospel. Armed with this perspective, Newbigin remained undaunted before the brilliant achievements of modernist thought and its

49. Wainwright, *Lesslie Newbigin*, 179.

50. Cochrane, *Christianity and Classical Culture*, 41, 42.

51. As Thielicke eloquently remarks, "Cartesian doubt is an opening chord that calls for quiet, and the concert of the modern age begins" (Thielicke, *Modern Faith and Thought*, 57).

52. Newbigin, *Trinitarian Doctrine*, 33. This appears to intentionally use the language of the famous prayer attributed to St. Patrick known as St. Patrick's Breastplate, and translated into English by Cecil Frances Alexander.

53. Newbigin, *Foolishness To The Greeks*, 90.

apparent dominance over the Western church. This historical perspective strengthened Newbigin's confidence in the gospel in the face of the modernist claims and gave additional impetus to his mission to modernity. This is not insignificant given that in the 1960s and the decades that followed, Christianity in Europe was in full scale retreat before the confident and advancing forces of secularism. Core to Newbigin's mission to modernity was his eagerness to help restore to the Western church a 'proper confidence' in the gospel. Crucial to this endeavor was Newbigin's reading of another historical work; Paul Hazard's *The European Mind: 1680 to 1715*. In this work Hazard identified the Enlightenment as the birth of modern Europe and the crucial point at which Europe turned its back on the gospel. This identification gave to Newbigin a focus and a starting point for his mission to modernity. Hazard's account of the Enlightenment, Newbigin reflects, "seemed to provide the perspective I was looking for."[54]

## *Newbigin's Trinitarian Claims*

After discovering the importance of the doctrine of the Trinity, Newbigin proceeds to make a number of bold trinitarian claims. Standing in the tradition of the twentieth-century trinitarian renaissance, Newbigin considers "the most fundamental of all Christian doctrines [to be] the doctrine of the Triune being of God."[55] His understanding of the gospel was intrinsically trinitarian; indeed, he could not explicate the gospel except in trinitarian terms.

> The gospel [af]firms that in the happenings which the New Testament records at a particular time and place ('under Pontius Pilate') God was present in the fullness of his being in the man Jesus; that this Jesus understood himself to be the Son of his Father 'who is in heaven' and whose rule embraces all creation; and that the Spirit by whom Jesus was conceived, led and sustained would, through his final act of loving obedience to the Father, be communicated to all who would give their lives to him.[56]

In *The Gospel in a Pluralist Society*, the pinnacle of Newbigin's mature theological reflections, he states, "The mission of the church is to be

54. Newbigin, *Unfinished Agenda: An Updated Autobiography*, 251. Unless otherwise stated, references to *Unfinished Agenda* will be to the original 1985 edition. See also Newbigin, "A Mission to Modern," 163.

55. Newbigin, "Lay Presidency," 181.

56. Newbigin, "What Do We Mean by 'God'?," 7, emphasis original.

understood, can only be rightly understood, in terms of the trinitarian model."[57] Elsewhere he claims that divine revelation is trinitarian in character, and that "we need a Trinitarian understanding of God if we are to understand the cross."[58] He describes the Christian life as "a sharing in the life of the Blessed Trinity itself" and thus the church is "an extension to creatures of the life of the Trinity."[59] Speaking of church unity, Newbigin writes, "the true nature of the Church's union [is] a union in Christ and in the Father through the Spirit."[60] He claims further that the Trinity provides the grammar for inter-faith dialogue[61] and he also states that "the doctrine of the Trinity . . . is the necessary starting point of preaching."[62]

These far-reaching claims receive extended consideration in *Trinitarian Doctrine for Today's Mission* (1963) and *The Open Secret* (1978); each will be studied in turn. Newbigin himself advises that in *The Open Secret* he further develops the arguments in *Trinitarian Doctrine*.[63] In what follows, therefore, I will consider these two works in sequence. While Colin Greene and Timothy Tennent suggest that *The Open Secret* is the best starting point for examining Newbigin's trinitarian missiology,[64] my own view is that *Trinitarian Doctrine* provides the most substantive account. Of course, other works of Newbigin augment *Trinitarian Doctrine* in places and provide further insight into his thought. As I examine *Trinitarian Doctrine*, therefore, I will draw on these other works as appropriate.

## INTRODUCING TRINITARIAN DOCTRINE FOR TODAY'S MISSION

In *Trinitarian Doctrine for Today's Mission* Newbigin invites "the missionary movement to bind to itself afresh the strong Name of the Trinity."[65] The book was written, however, primarily to examine the hesitancy of the Chris-

57. Newbigin, *The Gospel in a Pluralist Society*, 118.
58. Newbigin, *Living Hope*, 35.
59. Newbigin, *The Reunion of the Church*, 48, 71.
60. Ibid., 109.
61. Newbigin, *The Open Secret*, 183.
62. Newbigin, *Trinitarian Doctrine*, 35. I will examine this claim in 'The Trinitarian Gospel' in chapter 6.
63. Newbigin, *Unfinished Agenda*, 199.
64. Greene, "Trinitarian Tradition," 68. Tennent, *Invitation to World Missions*, 68. However, Tennent does recognize that "Newbigin's project was never worked out. *The Open Secret* . . . never attempted anything more than the broad outlines of a Trinitarian theology of mission" (ibid., 68).
65. Newbigin, *Trinitarian Doctrine*, 33.

tian missionary movement at that time. His deliberations on the doctrine of Trinity are shaped by that prior concern. *Trinitarian Doctrine* belongs to the context of the 1950s and 60s, a time in which, as Wilbert Shenk notes, "a spate of books appeared on the 'crisis' facing missions."[66] David Bosch remarks that in one year alone, 1964, four books appeared, all written by missiologists or mission executives, which strongly criticize the church's missionary activity.[67] Goheen comments that "The collapse of colonialism, global westernization, resurgent secularism, and a revolutionary optimism provided a volatile mix."[68] Newbigin writes as a missionary concerned with the doubt, uncertainty and decreasing momentum of the contemporary missionary movement. He aims to address the underlying issues with a view to restoring confidence in the church's mission. Hence, *Trinitarian Doctrine* is primarily a work of missiology. Following Japanese theologian K. Koyama, Bosch notes that, "The Japanese character for 'crisis' is a combination of the characters for 'danger' and 'opportunity.'"[69] Newbigin felt this crisis at a personal level. He recalls, in the early 1960s, "I was being challenged at every point to re-examine my most basic Christian beliefs. It was not easy."[70] He took the occasion of crisis as the opportunity to develop his thesis on the cruciality of the doctrine of the Trinity for missiology.

In *Trinitarian Doctrine* Newbigin contends that "a faithful dealing with the issues which press upon us in the missionary work of the Church requires an understanding of the work in terms of the whole Christian doctrine of God as Father, Son and Spirit."[71] He also affirms that "we can begin to understand the coherence and the relevance of the trinitarian faith as it illuminates the [missiological] questions we are asking."[72] A two-way movement is evident here. Newbigin moves from the missiological questions to highlight the importance of the doctrine of the Trinity while the doctrine of the Trinity, in turn, informs his missiology. His argument proceeds in two steps: first, by an examination of the church's tentativeness toward mission, and second, by addressing this tentativeness from a trinitarian perspective. He aims to shine light onto the shadows of doubt that were falling over the

---

66. Shenk, *Write the Vision*, 51. This crisis in missions paralleled world developments, especially the end of colonial era. In 1960 alone, eighteen African countries declared their independence from Europe.

67. Bosch, *Transforming Mission*, 2.

68. Goheen, "As the Father Has Sent Me," 66.

69. Bosch, *Transforming Mission*, 3.

70. Newbigin, *Unfinished Agenda*, 198.

71. Newbigin, *Trinitarian Doctrine*, 82.

72. Ibid., 51.

church's mission, and at the same time to elucidate the logic and significance of the doctrine of the Trinity for the theology of mission.

In the conclusion of this book Newbigin says, "I have given three illustrations [in chapters 5, 6, and 7 respectively] of the way in which, as it seems to me, the doctrine of the triune nature of God helps us to understand and fulfil our missionary task in the face of issues which perplex us. Doubtless other examples will come to the mind of the reader."[73] Accordingly, it is clear that Newbigin intends this book to be indicative rather than comprehensive, and he acknowledges that the work lacks "depth and solidity;" it is a "small essay" offered "as an invitation to discussion rather than as the announcement of conclusions."[74] This comment is both modest and descriptive, for *Trinitarian Doctrine* presents not the careful research of a scholarly monograph but the work of a missionary and missiologist 'on the ground', theologizing as he lives out his missionary vocation. As such, *Trinitarian Doctrine* is a work not of systematic missiology but of pioneering and exploratory missiology, written to provide theological direction after the integration of the IMC with the WCC. Thus, *Trinitarian Doctrine* was a highly contextual work intended to invite discussion concerning real missionary problems that Newbigin claimed could be adequately addressed only by drawing on trinitarian resources within the Christian tradition.

In the introduction I noted that Newbigin's theology is best understood as strategic and prophetic rather than systematic, and this is true of *Trinitarian Doctrine*. In it he offers a series of insightful indications of the importance of the doctrine of the Trinity for the theology of mission, but due to the exploratory and occasional nature of the work, these indications are largely undeveloped. There is a need, therefore, for systematic theologians and missiologists, following in Newbigin's wake, to develop them further. While the remainder of this chapter is devoted to a consideration of Newbigin's trinitarian missiology, especially as articulated in *Trinitarian Doctrine*, in Part Two I will attempt the more challenging task of developing a systematic trinitarian missiology in the tradition of Newbigin. To that end, as I explore Newbigin's trinitarian missiology in this chapter I will note its strengths and suggest areas that need to be developed further. This will help form the platform for my work in Part Two.

73. Ibid., 82.
74. Ibid., 9.

## THE TRINITARIAN MISSIOLOGY OF TRINITARIAN DOCTRINE FOR TODAY'S MISSION

### *Introduction*

Newbigin begins *Trinitarian Doctrine* by describing the contemporary ecumenical and missionary landscape and does not begin to develop a trinitarian missiology as such until the fourth chapter. Prior to that, he considers missions in an ecumenical perspective (chapter 1), the limits of ecumenicity, including a discussion concerning the theology of religions (chapter 2), and questions concerning the contemporary state of missions (chapter 3). Newbigin ends chapter three by asking, "How is His [God's] work in the world related to His work in the Church?" He then begins chapter 4 with, "The thesis here presented is that a satisfying answer to this question can be reached only along lines which take the full trinitarian doctrine of God as the starting point for systematic thinking."[75] It is in this fourth chapter, "The Relevance of Trinitarian Doctrine," that he presents the outline of his trinitarian missiology.

The missiological context for this work is the post-Tambaram[76] dominance of ecclesiocentric missiology, embodied in Newbigin's *One Body, One Gospel, One World*, which Newbigin believes was founded too exclusively on Christ's person and work. Supplementing this, Newbigin acknowledges that there have been calls for missiology "to make a large place for the work of the Holy Spirit" and he concurs with such requests.[77] Newbigin strives for a theology that is Christ-centered and ecclesially located, giving due attention to the Father and that has a well-developed pneumatology. Accordingly, he perceives *Trinitarian Doctrine* to be both a corrective, and a constructive contribution to missiology.

Newbigin's trinitarian missiology takes its point of departure from the trinitarian logic of the New Testament witness. While it is widely recognized that the New Testament has no doctrine of the Trinity as such, Newbigin observes that a trinitarian pattern underlies the language and theology of the apostle Paul,[78] and is evident in the gospels as well. Since *Trinitarian Doctrine* was addressed to "those who are concerned with and committed to the missionary task,"[79] he probably takes for granted his readers' familiarity

---

75. Newbigin, *The Mission of the Triune God.*

76. Following the 1910 Edinburgh and 1928 Jerusalem meetings, the third world mission conference was held in Tambaram, near Madras, India, in 1938.

77. Newbigin, *Trinitarian Doctrine*, 33. Newbigin undoubtedly has Roland Allen in mind here.

78. Ibid., 34.

79. Ibid., 9.

with the trinitarian substructure of the Pauline corpus. Newbigin's reflection on the biblical roots of the doctrine of the Trinity is disseminated throughout *Trinitarian Doctrine* and other works. For example, in the next chapter Newbigin points out that at Jesus' baptism the Father's communication to the Son was not without the presence and activity of the Spirit descending in the form of a dove. The Spirit, Newbigin continues, anointed Jesus in the synagogue at Capernaum. The Spirit enabled the disciples to also be witnesses, and it is by the Spirit's work that they receive the gift of sonship and are enabled to continue the Son's mission. The Spirit is also at work in the disciples as "the instalment and proof of the glorious end to which history is being brought by the Father."[80] Taken together, Newbigin's presentation of the biblical roots of the doctrine of the Trinity is significant, but its dispersed presentation lessens its impact and lucidity.

From the Bible Newbigin turns to history, specifically to the significance of the doctrine of the Trinity in the early church's missionary endeavors. In its missionary encounter with Greco-Roman culture the church found itself compelled to articulate the gospel in trinitarian terms for several reasons. The early church found in the doctrine of the Trinity the foundation for a framework of thought that enabled the solving of questions insoluble within a classical framework of thought. Far from being "a troublesome piece of theological baggage," the doctrine of the Trinity had a unique missionary utility.[81] Newbigin says that the early church's struggle to articulate the doctrine of the Trinity was "indeed an essential part of the battle to master the pagan world view at the height of its power and self-confidence."[82] Here Newbigin is clearly indebted to Cochrane's analysis of the *history* of mission in *Christianity and Classical Culture*, which Newbigin transforms into a *theology* of mission. According to this theology, the doctrine of the Trinity has a unique missionary utility everywhere and always. This raises the question: does the doctrine of the Trinity have a missionary utility with other religio-philosophical beliefs? This question is highly relevant because scholars such as Aasulv Lande maintain that the doctrine of the Trinity is culture-bound to the Christian contextualization of the gospel in Greco-Roman culture, that it should remain in its socio-cultural past, and that for our purposes in the twenty-first century it is irrelevant.[83] Newbigin's further argument regarding the early church's trinitarian articulation of the gospel answers Lande's objections and takes us to the heart of his trinitarian missiology.

80. Ibid., 40.
81. Ibid., 35.
82. Ibid., 34.
83. Lande, "Trinitarian Missiology." The argument in Part Two of this work constitutes my response and refutation of Lande's contentions.

## The Trinitarian Gospel

Newbigin explains that the early church articulated the gospel in trinitarian terms because the gospel concerns the person and work of Jesus, the only begotten Son of the Father, and one anointed by the Holy Spirit. "He reveals God by showing us the love and obedience of the Son to the Father. No account of the Gospel which does not put this in the center can be accepted."[84] Against Lande's claim, therefore, Newbigin maintains that the person and work of Jesus cannot be accurately communicated except in his relation to the Father and the Holy Spirit. Consequently, 'the relevance of trinitarian doctrine' is coextensive with the relevance of the gospel.

To preach the gospel, Newbigin explains, an evangelist will usually begin with the hearers' own understanding of the great God above all gods, which Newbigin found present in rural South India. Then, in order to relate Jesus to the great God above all gods, the evangelist must somehow explain the Trinity. This is because it is manifestly incorrect to identify Jesus as just one of the gods, but it is also unfaithful to the New Testament to say that Jesus *is* this great high God. Newbigin says that Jesus "does not appear among men as a theophany, in the sense of a temporary manifestation of the Ruler of all things; he appears as the Son who lovingly submits himself to the will of him who rules all things."[85] In *The Open Secret* Newbigin explains that Jesus is not merely *Swamy* (Lord), or *Satguru* (the true teacher), or *Avatar* (incarnation of God), or *Kadaval* (the transcendent God). All of these fit within the Hindu world of ideas so that to call Jesus one of these is to accommodate him within this worldview illegitimately. This would leave Jesus incorrectly identified, the hearers' unchallenged, their worldview uncontested, and the gospel unknown.[86] "The truth is that one cannot preach Jesus even in the simplest terms without preaching him as the Son. His revelation of God is the revelation of 'an only begotten from the Father', and you cannot preach him without speaking of the Father and Son."[87] Furthermore, by listening to the hearers the evangelist typically discovers evidence of the prevenient work of the Holy Spirit, preparing them to receive the gospel without any human planning. Subsequent to their conversion, they will look back and recognize this prevenient pneumatological activity as the work of the same Spirit who spoke to them through the evangelistic preaching and enabled them to receive this message as the word of God.

---

84. Newbigin, *Trinitarian Doctrine*, 39.
85. Ibid., 39.
86. Newbigin, *The Open Secret*, 19–20.
87. Newbigin, *Trinitarian Doctrine*, 36.

Arguing from Scripture, Newbigin avers that "The Gospel records, and the New Testament as a whole, show us Jesus as the Son of the Father, as the 'Beloved Son', as the 'Only begotten from the Father.' It is impossible to think of him [Jesus] or to speak of him truly apart from the Father."[88] To preach Jesus as the revelation of God, Newbigin claims, is to preach the Triune God, because the center of the gospel is the relationship between God the Father and Son. Newbigin himself illustrates the logic of this claim in his early book *Sin and Salvation*. In describing 'The Work of the Savior', Newbigin is compelled by the second page to speak of the Holy Trinity. With respect to the gospel message articulated in John 3:16, "For God so loved the world that he gave his only Son," Newbigin explains, "In order to understand this [giving of the Son] we have to speak briefly about the doctrine of the Holy Trinity."[89] In his argument he permits no separation of Soteriology from Christology. Moreover, his discussion about Christology inevitably progresses, as it did for the Church Fathers, to discussion of God the Holy Trinity.

> Thus even in its most elementary form the preaching of the Gospel must presuppose an understanding of the triune nature of God. It is not, as we have sometimes seemed to say, a kind of intellectual capstone which can be put on to the top of the arch at the very end; it is, on the contrary, what Athanasius called it, the *arché*, the presupposition without which the preaching of the Gospel in a pagan world cannot begin.[90]

Although Newbigin makes no explicit reference to Schleiermacher here, it is likely that he has in mind that father of modern Protestant theology who famously described the doctrine of the Trinity as the capstone (*schlussstein*) of Christian doctrine. According to Schleiermacher, God's real presence in Christ and in the common Spirit of the church is the key element leading to the doctrine of the Trinity. For him this doctrine is the crowning achievement, the finishing stone of the theological structure, holding the doctrines of salvation, the church, Christ and the Spirit together.[91] By contrast, Newbigin, following Athanasius,[92] perceives that the doctrine of the Trinity is the *arché* of Christian doctrine.

Newbigin argues further that in addition to being the *arché* of theology, the doctrine of the Trinity is also the presupposition necessary for

---

88. Ibid., 39.
89. Newbigin, *Sin and Salvation*, 57.
90. Newbigin, *Trinitarian Doctrine*, 36.
91. Schleiermacher, *The Christian Faith*, 738–79.
92. Cochrane, *Christianity and Classical Culture*, 236, 362–63.

gospel preaching. God's self-presentation as Triune necessarily underlies the *missio ecclesiae* and missionary proclamation. Not that an explicit trinitarian theology will be the substance of the evangelist's message or the new converts' understanding. Rather, since the gospel is trinitarian, the communication of that gospel (evangelism) begins by bearing witness to the Triune God. This is no insignificant claim given that a leading theologian and respected contemporary of Newbigin's, Emil Brunner, claims that the "doctrine of the Trinity . . . does not belong to the sphere of the Church's message."[93] Newbigin's twin arguments that the gospel is irreducibly trinitarian and that evangelism begins by bearing witness to the Triune God are essential constituents of a trinitarian missiology. In Part Two I will further explore and substantiate these claims.

Newbigin's exposition of the trinitarian nature of the gospel itself answers the objection raised earlier by Lande. The doctrine of the Trinity has a missionary utility in all cultures because it describes the being and action of the God that the missionary church is called to proclaim and represent. In Newbigin's missiology there is a permanent link between *Trinity* and *mission*; he also argues that the converse is true. The doctrine of the Trinity comes to the fore in a missionary situation and it recedes in a non-missional Christian context. Newbigin supports the first argument with his account of the church's missionary engagement with the Greco-Roman world, and from his own experience of missionary engagement with Hindu India. By contrast, during the era of European Christendom "the doctrine of the Trinity has not occupied a comparable place in the thought of Christians."[94] Though still formally confessed, he laments that the doctrine of the Trinity has become marginalized. Here Newbigin supports the point famously elaborated by Karl Rahner in his 1970 work *The Trinity*: "despite their orthodox confession of the Trinity, Christians are, in their practical life, almost mere 'monotheists' . . . should the doctrine of the Trinity have to be dropped as false, the major part of religious literature could well remain virtually unchanged."[95] Rahner traces the cause of this neglect partly to Thomas Aquinas who made the distinction between the two treatises *De Deo Uno* (On the One God) and *De Deo Trino* (On the Triune God). In later works Newbigin would join Rahner in attributing much of the Western neglect of the doctrine of the Trinity to Thomas.[96] Thus, in *The Open Secret* Newbigin suggests that

---

93. Brunner, *Dogmatics*, 1:206.
94. Newbigin, *Trinitarian Doctrine*, 35.
95. Rahner, *The Trinity*, 10–11.
96. See in particular Newbigin, "The Trinity." There, Newbigin's discussion simply

> The working concept of God for most ordinary Christians is—if one may venture a bold guess—shaped more by the combination of Greek philosophy and Islamic theology that was powerfully injected into the thought of Christendom at the beginning of the High Middle Ages than by the thought of the fathers of the first four centuries.[97]

Newbigin himself does not develop this historical conjecture, but if his insight is correct then this is an instance of Christianity capitulating to culture, a theme which features prominently in his later mission to modernity.

Newbigin does not offer a structured argument for his claim that the doctrine of the Trinity recedes in a non-missional Christian context, but given his argument thus far it is not difficult to see how it might proceed. Missionary activity leads to the proclamation of the Triune God and thus to an increased awareness of the importance of the doctrine of the Trinity. Hence, in a non-missionary setting the doctrine of the Trinity might, over time, simply recede in its perceived importance. Newbigin suggests that in Christendom the doctrine of the Trinity "has usually been regarded as a venerable formulation handed down from the past."[98] The link between Trinity and mission can and must be sustained. Conversely, the connection between 'no mission' and 'no Trinity'[99] is interesting, but of secondary importance and beyond the scope of this study.[100] The relation of Trinity and mission, central to which is the announcement of the gospel, derives from Newbigin's more fundamental point that the gospel is trinitarian.

Since the gospel bears witness to God's Triune self-revelation, Newbigin avers that Christian missiology must be trinitarian. Accordingly, Newbigin offers something of a thesis statement: "a true understanding of the questions which God raises for us in our time, and a true restatement of the meaning of the missionary task will rest, as the New Testament rests, upon the revelation of God as Father, Son and Spirit."[101] The remainder of

---

amounts to an enlargement of this existing theme rather than the emergence of a new theme in his trinitarian missiology.

97. Newbigin, *The Open Secret*, 27–28. One missiology professor agrees: "Twenty years' experience teaching religion to undergraduates in both a state university and a denominational liberal arts college leads me to confirm Newbigin's guess" Zahniser, "The Trinity," 2). Zahniser is Emeritus Professor of Christian Mission at Asbury Theological Seminary and Scholar-in-Residence at Greenville College, Illinois.

98. Newbigin, *Trinitarian Doctrine*, 35.

99. See the article by Simpson, "No Trinity."

100. An investigating of this connection would be the work of historians and sociologists of religion and not systematic theologians.

101. Newbigin, *Trinitarian Doctrine*, 36.

*Trinitarian Doctrine* is an attempt to justify this thesis. After affirming the irreducibly trinitarian nature of the gospel—that it bears witness to the being and action of the Triune God—Newbigin's trinitarian missiology proceeds by describing the actions of the Triune Persons.

## God's Trinitarian Mission

### The Father

In Newbigin's theology, God the Father is almost exclusively related to divine providence. The heart of Jesus' teaching, he says, is "God's fatherly rule of all things . . . God who created all things, also sustains them and directs them according to his will."[102] This means that in the tumult of history no movement is outside of his control. "Neither imperialism nor anti-imperialism is a mere work of the devil. God rules and uses them all."[103] Newbigin ascribes the work of divine providence exclusively to God the Father, who rules over all and cares for all. His argument for this ascription amounts to the claim that he is following Jesus' own depiction of his Father. While accurate, this argument needs to be further substantiated.

Newbigin's trinitarian missiology begins, where the gospels begin, with Jesus proclaiming the kingdom of God. As such, his account of the Father's sending of the Son, and thus the Father as the initiator of mission, is largely implicit. The sending of Jesus is subject to God's providential rule: "The Father alone is in control . . . the coming of the Son is the event by which the Father has chosen to bring all things to the point of decision, to the issue of judgement and salvation."[104] Later Newbigin affirms the eternal procession of the Spirit but does not discuss it.[105] For Newbigin, God *ad intra* rarely comes into direct focus, but when it does his discussion is instructive. The life of God *ad intra* is, for Newbigin, one of dynamic love.

> Within the eternal being of God love is a never-ceasing self-emptying and out-pouring, forever met by the same out-poured love, the love of the Father and the Son in the unity of the Spirit. Eternal life is no motionless serenity, but love meeting love, the rapture of love forever poured out and forever received.[106]

---

102. Ibid., 39.
103. Ibid.
104. Ibid., 40.
105. Ibid., 80.
106. Newbigin, *The Household of God*, 130.

Newbigin repeatedly affirms the doctrine of *perichoresis* vis-à-vis God *ad intra* that leads to the unity of divine action *ad extra*. "The Father and the Son are so perfectly one in their mutual indwelling that when we listen to the works of Jesus and attend to his works, we are coming to see God."[107] In emphasizing divine unity, Newbigin rejects the word *equality* as a descriptor of the Father-Son relation. "The unity of Father and Son is not one of 'equality' but of love and obedience. Jesus is utterly dependent upon the Father."[108] Thus, Newbigin holds to a trinitarian order whose *arché* is God the Father. He describes God the Father as "the source of all being and of all truth,"[109] thus appearing to affirm God the Father as *arché* pertaining to both order and ontology. To the Son and Spirit Newbigin does not make this ascription.

An account of God *ad intra* is essential to a robust trinitarian missiology. As has been seen, Newbigin's presentation of this subject is dispersed throughout his works. I will build on Newbigin and examine in greater detail the intra-trinitarian perichoretic unity, and the eternal processions. Further, I intend to supplement his account with a consideration of the mutual dependence of Father and Son, and offer a modified perspective of God the Father as *arché*.

## The Son

In *Trinitarian Doctrine* Newbigin does not attempt to offer a comprehensive presentation of the mission of the Son.[110] This is likely because he wrote *Trinitarian Doctrine* as a corrective to missiology that he considered to be founded too exclusively on Christ's person and work.[111] He does, however, develop several features of the mission of the Son, including the affirmation that Jesus is the center of the *missio trinitatis Dei*. In the working of God's Fatherly rulership, Jesus Christ is the "visible center and point of reference."[112] The mission of the Son "was not just one of the strands that make up human history, but was the disclosing of the true end of that history."[113] Furthermore, the center and focus of Jesus' saving work, and thus the center

---

107. Newbigin, *The Light Has Come*, 183.

108. Ibid., 66.

109. Ibid., 69.

110. This is also true regarding *The Open Secret*. He has, however, already written an extended examination of the saving work of Christ in the sixth chapter of *Sin and Salvation*, 56–91.

111. Newbigin, *Trinitarian Doctrine*, 33.

112. Ibid., 53.

113. Ibid., 46.

of history, is the cross.[114] Newbigin is convinced of this biblically, and this conviction was reinforced by the impact and enduring influence of his 'conversion' experience in which he saw a vision of the cross.[115] Such was the impact of this vision that Newbigin reflects,

> I was sure that night, in a way I had never been before, that this was the clue that I must follow if I were to make any kind of sense of the world. From that moment I would always know how to take bearings when I was lost. I would know where to begin again when I had come to an end of all my own resources of understanding or courage.[116]

Concerning the person of Jesus Newbigin unhesitatingly speaks of the Son's dependence upon, and submission to, his Father. Jesus is not a temporary manifestation of the Ruler of all things. His revelation of God is that of a Son submitting to, and obeying, his Father. Jesus submits to his Father's ordering of events as the form in which his mission, and that of his followers, is to be carried out.[117] Perhaps unintentionally, Newbigin has opened up the possibility of affirming, with Barth, that "for God it is just as natural to be lowly as it is to be great."[118] In Part Two I will explore this potentially rich insight hinted at by Newbigin.

Central to the mission of the Son, for Newbigin, is his revelation of God: "Jesus is, quite simply, God's revelation of himself. It is God whom we meet when we meet Jesus."[119] This revelation of God, when received and comprehended, is reconciliatory, for "there can be no revelation apart from reconciliation."[120] Furthermore, Newbigin conceives of this reconciling revelation and this revelatory reconciliation in a trinitarian manner. The Father reveals himself in the sending of his Son, and coming to a true knowledge of the Son is the work of the Spirit: "Only the action of the Spirit can reveal

---

114. "Of course the cross must not be isolated from the whole work of Christ. Without His incarnation there could be no cross and no salvation. Without His words and works we should not know who it was that died for us there. Without His resurrection the cross would not be known to us as victory but as defeat. Without His ascension to the Father and the gift of the Spirit, we who live at other times and places could have no share in Christ. All these things are parts of the one complete work of Christ for the salvation of the whole world. But the center and focus of that work is the cross" (Newbigin, *Sin and Salvation*, 61).

115. Newbigin, *Unfinished Agenda*, 11–12.

116. Ibid., 12.

117. Newbigin, *Trinitarian Doctrine*, 39.

118. Barth, *CD* IV/1, 193.

119. Newbigin, *The Light Has Come*, 165.

120. Ibid., 17.

who Jesus is."[121] It is by the sovereign and gracious action of the Holy Spirit, "the Spirit of the Father and the Son . . . [that] my reason and conscience are enabled to acknowledge the Son and through him to join in glorifying the Father."[122] Newbigin's trinitarian account of the saving work of Christ is central to his missiology.

Jesus' saving work included crucially the creation of a community to be the bearer and proclaimer of salvation. In *The Household of God* Newbigin makes the point that it was the church, not a book, creed or system of thought, that was Jesus' primary legacy.[123] The church was the continuation of Jesus' own redeeming mission. It is his representative "having and ministering to the world His own divine power to heal and to forgive."[124] As his representative, the church bears verbal witness to him and "is also itself the bearer of God's redeeming grace, itself a part of the story of redemption which is the burden of its message."[125] Newbigin affirms both that the missionary church acts in Christ's power, and that it is subject to the continuing ministry of the exalted Christ,[126] but he does not delineate their inter-relationship. In Part Two I will develop an account of the mission of the Son that builds on Newbigin's work by offering an examination of the inter-relationship between the missions of the Son, the Spirit, and the church.

## The Holy Spirit

One of the great strengths of Newbigin's missiology is his theology of the Holy Spirit. In *Trinitarian Doctrine* Newbigin's trinitarian missiology begins with the coming of Jesus and so this is where his account of the Spirit also begins. For Newbigin, the Spirit's role in the life of Jesus is not apparent or merely for our sakes; it is central to the Son's mission.[127] The Father's communication to the Son at his baptism was not without the action of the Spirit. "It is as the one anointed by the Spirit that he [Jesus] stands up in Capernaum to announce the year of the Lord's favor."[128] Here Newbigin

121. Ibid., 11.
122. Ibid., 69.
123. Newbigin, *The Household of God*, 27.
124. Ibid., 94.
125. Ibid.
126. Newbigin, *Trinitarian Doctrine*, 53, 54.
127. Contra Badcock's depiction of Cyril of Alexandria's view, that "The Spirit descended upon Jesus at his baptism, not for his sake, but for ours" (Badcock, *Light of Truth*, 41).
128. Newbigin, *Trinitarian Doctrine*, 40.

suggests the Spirit is empowering the Son in his mission (logos-missiology). In the following sentences he suggests that it is the witness of the Spirit that is primary, not only in the church's mission but also in that of the Son.[129] Newbigin makes clear that the Spirit empowers the Son in his mission (logos-missiology) and that the Spirit carries out his mission through the Son (Spirit-missiology), though this inter-relationship is not explained in detail. In Part Two, therefore, I will develop both of these aspects of the *missio Dei* in the complementarian manner suggested by Newbigin. His emphasis here is on a strong unity between the working of the second and third hypostases. He does not explicitly adhere to the trinitarian rule *opera trinitatis ad extra sunt indivisa*, but he does clearly teach the unity of God's actions in the economy. Emphasizing this unity: "the Spirit is one with the Father who rules all things and with the Son in whom all things are to be consummated."[130] This economic unity is both historical and eschatological, resting upon the prior ontological unity already discussed.

The Holy Spirit, for Newbigin, provides the connection and continuity between the Son's mission and the mission of the church. It is by the Spirit's presence that the disciples, and by extension the church, "receive the gift of sonship and are enabled thereby to continue in the world the ministry of the Son." The Spirit gives vitality to the church, and is himself "the instalment and proof of the glorious end to which history is being brought by the Father."[131] The Spirit convicts the world of sin, righteousness and judgement, and he speaks through the persecuted church. In sum: "It is he who is, properly speaking, the missionary."[132] Accordingly, it is the Holy Spirit who advances and leads the missionary church. The Spirit's work is not confined to the church. Instead, "the Spirit goes, so to speak, ahead of the Church. Like Cornelius, men of every age and nation have been miraculously prepared beforehand to receive the message of Christ."[133] Here Newbigin hints at a form of *praeparatio evangelica*,[134] though without developing this concept. For Newbigin this preparation of cultures and persons for the gospel is due to the working of the Spirit, and is not a 'natural' receptivity in creation

---

129. "And it is not blasphemy against the Son, but blasphemy against the Spirit speaking and working in him that becomes the occasion for final condemnation. Likewise, for the disciples also, it is the Spirit who is the witness" (ibid., 40).

130. Ibid., 53.

131. Ibid., 40.

132. Ibid.

133. Ibid., 53.

134. The early church doctrine that God had long been at work in cultures helping prepare them to receive the gospel by infusing into them ideas and themes that would grow to fruition through interpretation in a fully Christian context.

or a natural 'point of contact' between God and humanity. Indeed it became increasingly clear to Newbigin, particularly after returning to his native Britain, that cultures could often be radically inhospitable to the Christian gospel. The work of the Spirit is needed to bring about the transformation of thinking entailed in Christian conversion. This prevenient work of the Spirit prepares the way for the church. "But—because the Spirit and the Father are one—this work of the Spirit is not in any sense an alternative way to God apart from the Church; it is the preparation for the coming of the Church, which means that the Church must be ever ready to follow where the Spirit leads."[135] Accordingly, the Spirit leads the church in her missionary pilgrimage to the ends of the earth and the end of time.

## The Missionary Church

It is with the mission of the *church* that Newbigin is directly concerned in *Trinitarian Doctrine*, and so it is this account which is the most developed. In Jesus, God has disclosed the true end of human history. Through Jesus, God confronts the world with the ultimate decision of judgement or salvation, and so "precipitates a double process of gathering and separating, of consummation and judgement."[136] This is because it is the Father's purpose to sum up all things in Christ (Ephesians 1:10). In the mission of the church God continues to bring the world to this decision, and in that sense the church continues "in the world the ministry of the Son."[137] The church's continuation of the Son's mission is carefully delineated, and so Newbigin refrains from employing the indefinite language of the church's mission as an extension of the Son's mission. He defines the church's mission in the world as "the continuation of that double process [of gathering and separating] till its end. Missions, in the sense of a particular kind of action within the mission of the church, are the means by which new communities are brought within the range of this process."[138] He conceives of the church's mission in a trinitarian manner in which Father, Son, Spirit and the church are all active agents. The Father continues to confront the world with Christ through the church's mission. Jesus continues to come to people "through the missionary work of the Church."[139] The church is the result of the ongoing mission of the Holy Spirit; it is "the outward form of the continuous

135. Newbigin, *Trinitarian Doctrine*, 54.
136. Ibid., 52.
137. Ibid., 40.
138. Ibid., 52.
139. Ibid., 53.

work of the Spirit in re-enacting Christ's coming among men."[140] Newbigin depicts the church as both having a mission and being a participant in the mission of God. She is both active in her loving obedience to the Father and the community through whom the Triune God bears witness to himself. The latter is particularly emphasized by Newbigin, meaning that his theology of the church is trinitarian, missional, teleological, and to a certain extent, instrumental. Elsewhere, however, Newbigin makes clear that the church is not to be conceived in merely instrumental terms. It is not simply a means to an end. In *The Household of God*, for instance, Newbigin makes clear that the church cannot be understood only in terms of her missionary function. "The Church is both a means and an end, because it is a foretaste . . . a real foretaste of heaven."[141] Furthermore, in her mission the church is not rendered a passive object through which God speaks and acts. She remains active, and her actions of bearing witness are concurrent with God's action through her. Nevertheless, "The witness which the Church bears to the world is . . . not something contrived by the Church itself. It is the work of the Triune God."[142]

A further feature of the church's mission is that it is christologically determined: the church shares in Christ's sonship and in his mission. Jesus confronted people with the disclosure of history's true end, and he continues to do so through the church's mission. Accordingly, the church's mission "is the clue to world history . . . in the sense that it is the point at which the meaning of history is understood and at which men are required to make the final decisions about that meaning. It is, so to say, not the motor but the blade, not the driving force but the cutting edge."[143] This relation between the particularity of the church and the universality of world history, based on the uniqueness and universality of Christ's person and work, also explains the necessity of what Newbigin calls 'foreign missions', or better, 'pioneer' missionary work amongst 'unreached' and 'least reached' people groups.[144]

> This readiness to relate the Gospel with constantly new human situations is an essential part of the Church's witness to the character of what God has done for all men in Christ . . . The phrase 'all the nations' has to be taken seriously, and for this

---

140. Ibid.

141. Newbigin, *The Household of God*, 147. Newbigin does speak of this in *Trinitarian Doctrine*, 40, 48, but these comments remain largely unexplained.

142. Newbigin, *Trinitarian Doctrine*, 48.

143. Ibid., 45.

144. Rogers uses these terms in *A Basic Introduction*, 105

reason the phrase 'foreign mission' still has its own propriety and necessity.¹⁴⁵

Reflecting on 'foreign mission' in an earlier work, he acknowledges that

> There is of course, something absurd about this missionary passion to get out to the ends of the earth even while there is a colossal unfinished task at home. But it is part of the absurdity of Christianity, Christianity which claims that these insignificant little churches are not just local societies, but advance posts of a vast colonial power, agents of an imperialism which is destined to control the world. You are a 'colony of heaven'—says St Paul to the Philippians, very conscious of the fact that they were under a foreign power. The Church must always be, in a sense, foreign, and the fact that it insists on crossing every national frontier is an indispensable symbol of its supernatural character and calling.¹⁴⁶

The abiding significance of pioneer missionary work is that it reminds the church of the cosmic nature of the gospel, the *missio ecclesiae*, and the *missio trinitatis Dei*. "The preaching of the Gospel to the whole world is the witness to the cosmic nature of what God has done in Christ."¹⁴⁷ Newbigin's articulation of the cosmic nature of the *missio Dei* is vitally important and will be developed further in chapters 3 and 4 below.

The church is also christologically determined in relation to the Father's providential rule. As the Son did not seek to rule history but accepted his Father's ordering of events, so

> The task of the Church in relation to the events of world history is not to be the governor and controller of them, but to be the suffering servant and witness of the Lord, manifesting in its witness the true meaning of these events. The Church is not the instrument of God's governance of the world, but the witness of his governance both by speaking and by suffering.¹⁴⁸

The church also bears witness to God through its participation in the suffering of Christ. In its persecution, the church can take comfort that the Holy Spirit promises to witness powerfully through it.

145. Newbigin, *Trinitarian Doctrine*, 47

146. Newbigin, "The Pattern of Partnership," 41–42.

147. Newbigin, *Trinitarian Doctrine*, 46. Similarly, in *The Open Secret* Newbigin writes, "Mission is concerned with nothing less than the completion of all that God has begun to do in the creation of the world and of humankind. Its concern is not sectional but total and universal" (Newbigin, *The Open Secret*, 56).

148. Newbigin, *Trinitarian Doctrine*, 41.

The church is completely dependent upon the gracious action of God the Holy Spirit. Newbigin makes the point repeatedly that the actuality and efficacy of the church's witness is entirely reliant on the Holy Spirit, who blows where he wills. "The Spirit is the Spirit of the Father and of the Son. His work is to enable us to participate in Christ's Sonship, to be one with him in his obedience to the Father. And only he can enable us to participate in, and thereby be the occasion of, his witness."[149] The task of the church is to cooperate with the action of the Holy Spirit by being open, in every aspect of her life, to the sovereign rule of the Holy Spirit.[150] In Part Two I build on this and seek to explain what this means practically. As ordained by God, the church's testimony is essential to the *missio Dei*, but it always remains chiefly *God's* mission which the church serves. By the Spirit the church is caught up into the Son's loving response to the Father and also goes forth into the world to bear witness to the Triune God. Through this going forth of the church, through its words and deeds, the Spirit draws yet more people into the church, and into adopted sonship in Christ. For Newbigin the God of the church's mission, the God of the missionary church, is one whose serene repose is mobile.[151] Reflecting on Newbigin's teaching of the church, it is missional, teleological, christocentric, and Pneumatological. In summary, Newbigin says "the Church's mission to all the nations is a participation in the work of the triune God."[152]

## God's Work in the World

The question that frames the fifth chapter of *Trinitarian Doctrine* concerns the relation between God's work in Christ and the church, and God's work in the continuing events of world history. With this question in mind, Newbigin emphasizes that the Spirit bears witness primarily, not to what Jesus has done once and for all, but to what the Father is doing in the events of world history. He describes the church "as the witness people, in whom the Spirit is present to bear witness of the real meaning of the things which happen in the world, so that—*in relation to these things*—men are compelled to make decisions for or against God."[153] The framing question of this chapter provides the context for this emphasis. However, it is more theologically accurate to speak of the Spirit bearing witness to the person and work of

---

149. Ibid., 81.
150. Ibid., 50.
151. I owe this phrase to Professor Ivor Davidson from personal conversation.
152. Newbigin, *Trinitarian Doctrine*, 54.
153. Ibid., 40, emphasis original.

Jesus, and indeed, Newbigin affirms this also. Writing in the early 1960s, Newbigin's focus on God's work in the world is part of what Wainwright has called 'The Secular Flirtation'.[154] His re-reading of the New Testament under the sway of the *zeitgeist* of the secular decade, plus the influence of Arendt van Leeuwen's *Christianity and World History*, led Newbigin to focus on God's work in the world outside of the church. He refers to this as the 'secular interpretation of the Gospel.' Before the end of the 1960s he saw the weaknesses in this approach,[155] and consequently this emphasis is not found in Newbigin's works published after the 1960s. What, then, is the relation between God's work in the world and in the church? "It is not confined to the work of the Church, but it is not detached from it, for its ultimate purpose is to lead men to the acceptance of their true destiny in Christ."[156] Here Newbigin nuances helpfully the relation between the church and God's kingdom. In both refusing a simple identification and refusing to conceive of them as unrelated, he has pointed the way forward. Despite Newbigin's 'secular flirtation' in *Trinitarian Doctrine*, the church still remains central to his conception of the *missio Dei*. That mission "proceeds by the way of election, of choosing; and the Chosen and Beloved is none other than Jesus Christ."[157] Here election is only mentioned in passing, but in later works Newbigin expands on how election fits within the *missio Dei* and the *missio ecclesiae*.[158]

## The Church's Mission of Healing

The church's mission is to follow the example of Jesus by announcing the good news of God's imminent reign, embodying this good news in acts of healing, releasing and quickening, and making disciples.[159] While in agreement with Newbigin, I find his *explanation* of this ministry for the *missio ecclesiae* to be incomplete in two ways. The first concerns his account of the church's healing ministry. Newbigin explains that the church embodies the gospel in its medical institutions and programs of technical aid. Although these are indeed a vital part of the *missio ecclesiae* and signs of God's king-

154. Wainwright, *Lesslie Newbigin*, 341–54.
155. Newbigin, *Unfinished Agenda*, 153, 254.
156. Newbigin, *Trinitarian Doctrine*, 54.
157. Ibid., 51.
158. See especially Newbigin, *The Open Secret*, "Chapter Seven: The Gospel and World History," which shall be discussed in due course, and also *The Gospel In A Pluralist Society*, "Chapter Seven: The Logic of Election."
159. Newbigin, *Trinitarian Doctrine*, 47.

dom, Jesus' own ministry of healing is of a different character.[160] The basis of Jesus' ministry of healing is not human prowess and medical skill, but prayer and the power of God. Ironically, given Newbigin's later criticism of the reductionist features of Modernity, he is himself inclined to a reductionist account of the divine economy at this point and defers to modernist assumptions that obscure the miraculous character of Jesus' healing ministry.

A second limitation in Newbigin's account of the ministry of healing is his claim that "These acts have the character of witness." He continues, "They will be signs rather than instruments," which means "They are not the *means* by which God establishes his Kingdom."[161] It is surely true that these are signs of God's kingdom, and they do have the character of witness, but why can they not also be *instruments* of God's kingdom? Newbigin is here concerned to stress that these signs can be misinterpreted and that this can lead to a human response that opposes God's kingdom. He is also keen to distance the advance of God's kingdom from all colonial associations. Although colonial rule was extended through deeds of power, God's kingdom is not, and at the most these embodiments of the gospel bear witness to God's reign rather than being instrumental in advancing it. Accordingly, Jesus does not appear as a temporary manifestation of the Ruler of all things, and the church is not called to be the governor and controller of history but to bear witness to the meaning of history in Christ.[162] Elsewhere he is also concerned to stress that the kingdom of God is not the product of human achievement, but is a heavenly gift. Summarizing Newbigin's concern, Goheen says,

---

160. Granted, God chooses to heal through medical and non-medical means. However, healing through medical means is a learned skill practiced by trained doctors and other medical practitioners, whereas healing in the ministries of Jesus, the apostles and the Church is qualitatively different. The New Testament writers attest consistently to the *spiritual* cause of healing. Jesus and the apostles healed the sick because they had authority (Matt 10:1) and power (Luke 9:1–2) which could be given instantaneously, unlike medical skill which is learned over years. This authority belongs to Jesus and those on whom He confers it (Acts 3:6–7), and *faith* in Him is often associated with its operation (Matt 13:58; Mark 5:34; 10:52; Acts 3:16). Paul explicitly states that the operation of healing in the church is one of the Holy Spirit's gifts and a manifestation of his working (1 Cor 12:7–11), not human expertise and ability. In agreement with this, Williams states "Gifts of healing are wholly supernatural endowments. They are not natural gifts, nor are they the result of developed skills" (*Renewal Theology*, 2:368). Consequently healing is subject to the Holy Spirit's determination and is not ultimately within human control (Fee, *The First Epistle*, 587–99). For further reading, see Williams, *Renewal Theology*, 2:253–57, 367–74.

161. Newbigin, *Trinitarian Doctrine*, 47, emphasis original.

162. Ibid., 39, 45.

> Our future life is not simply an extension of this life, corrupted as it is by sin. This life is not fit for the kingdom of God and therefore is under the sentence of death. All human achievements will be buried beneath the rubble of history. Our entry into the renewed life of the kingdom comes by resurrection.[163]

Newbigin is right that the kingdom of God is not a human achievement, and the signs of the kingdom can be misinterpreted, but his apparent fear of an over-realized eschatology leads to an overly futurist eschatology. Although the Bible teaches that in the eschaton the kingdom of God will descend from heaven as a gift (Rev 21:2), it also teaches Christians to pray and work for the actual coming of God's kingdom on earth as in heaven; that is, now, albeit in part. While in agreement with Newbigin's concerns, these signs, or mighty acts, should also be understood as instruments by which God advances his kingdom. The kingdom is not endlessly deferred, and in the life, death and resurrection of Jesus, the kingdom of God has been inaugurated. The redemptive transformation of God's fallen creation has begun. The church should expect to see, therefore, the manifestations of God's kingdom in its midst even while the fulfilment of God's kingdom awaits Christ's coming again. This surely is the point of Jesus' response to the enquiry from John the Baptist: "Go and tell John what you hear and see: the blind receive their sight, the lame walk, the lepers are cleansed, the deaf hear, the dead are raised, and the poor have good news brought to them."[164]

Jesus began his ministry by quoting the words of the prophet Isaiah in the Nazareth synagogue: "The Spirit of the Lord is upon me, because he has anointed me to bring good news to the poor. He has sent me to proclaim release to the captives and recovery of sight to the blind, to let the oppressed go free, to proclaim the year of the Lord's favor."[165] Where and when events transpire that accord with this proclamation, God's kingdom advances. Jesus says, "But if it is by the finger of God that I cast out demons, then the kingdom of God has come upon you."[166] Jesus explicitly connects releasing people from demonic oppression with the actual, and not merely indicative, coming of God's kingdom. Speaking specifically of Jesus' exorcisms, Boyd says, "The kingdom of God advances as victims of the kingdom of Satan are freed."[167] Not that God's kingdom is definitively established on earth because of exorcism or healing, but God's kingdom, his dominion and

---

163. Goheen, "As the Father Has Sent Me," 138.
164. Matt 11:4–5.
165. Luke 4: 18–19.
166. Luke 11:20 ESV.
167. Boyd, *God At War*, 199.

rule, has been further realized in the lives of those who are released from demonic, physical and/or psychological oppression. Thus, when God the Holy Spirit acts through the church in exorcism or healing, such events are both a sign and a witness to God's coming kingdom *and instrumental* in the further realization of God's rule in that person or persons. This realization is partial because perfect human submission and obedience to God lies on the other side of the *parousia*. This does not cut the eschatological tension, either through an over-realized eschatology or through consigning God's kingdom to a purely future reality. God's kingdom is both already and not yet, both present and future, both the already-experienced and ontologically and existentially real down-payment and foretaste, and the future totality. It will be appropriate therefore, to develop this aspect of the incarnational nature of the *missio ecclesiae* in my later attempt to build upon and extend Newbigin's trinitarian missiology. I will return to this aspect of the church's mission in 'Parables and Miracles—Words and Wonders' in chapter 4.

## Evangelistic Witness: Planned and Unplanned

In much of *Trinitarian Doctrine*'s fifth chapter Newbigin develops his missiology by reflecting on Mark chapter 13. Considering verse eleven of that chapter[168] he comments, "The Church must therefore not be anxious how or what to say [regarding witness], but be anxious rather that all her life, even in the seemingly unimportant details, is open to the sovereign government of the Holy Spirit of God."[169] Newbigin's teaching on evangelism often emphasizes witness that is demanded in the context of trial—the context of Mark 13:11. A similar theme appears in 1 Peter 3:15—"Always be prepared to give an answer to everyone who asks you to give the reason for the hope that you have" (NIV). Newbigin often contrasts this with humanly planned evangelistic activity, which he speaks of more negatively. He emphasizes the *un*expected ways in which the Spirit bears witness through the church, sometimes to the detriment of the more 'expected' ways. Accordingly, Newbigin gives less attention to biblical passages that speak of human initiative in evangelism (in response to God's initiative and command) such as the 'Great Commission' (Matthew 28:18–20), or Paul's custom of going to the synagogues and reasoning from the Scriptures with those in attendance that Jesus is the Christ (Acts 17:2). Newbigin does this despite the fact that as a

---

168. "When they bring you to trial and hand you over, do not worry beforehand about what you are to say; but say whatever is given you at that time, for it is not you who speak, but the Holy Spirit."

169. Newbigin, *Trinitarian Doctrine*, 50.

young man he personally engaged in intentional, planned evangelism, such as street preaching in south India. Nevertheless, Newbigin chiefly emphasized the 'unplanned' aspect of evangelism for at least four reasons that are contextual, experiential, and biblical-theological.

First, Newbigin is conscious that as a Western missionary and missiologist he is part of a movement and tradition that has always laid enormous emphasis on the 'Great Commission.' This emphasis largely originates with William Carey,[170] commonly called the founder of modern missions, and continued to be emphasized in Newbigin's lifetime through Donald McGavran's Church Growth school.[171] Not content simply to repeat the tradition, Newbigin intended his presentation to be a corrective to Anglo-Saxon missiology's dominant drift. He acknowledged the validity of Christ's command as a motive for mission, but was concerned that it would make mission more of a burden than "a kind of explosion of joy."[172] Furthermore, the missionary imperative can be turned into a law laid upon the Christian conscience, whereas witness is a gracious gift that is promised to Christians as "a spin-off of Pentecost."[173] I aver that Newbigin would agree with Tennent who said, "Missions . . . is never *less* than a command of Christ, but it is certainly far *more* than that."[174] In practical terms, this led to a different conception of missionary success: "Success is not measured by the number of adherents or the range of visible influence upon affairs." This is simply because these effects are not within human capability or responsibility. Rather, Newbigin continues, "The significance of the Church's missionary witness will lie at this point: that it is the place where men are confronted with the reality and power of God's Kingdom. The rest is in the hands of the Father. It is sufficient for the Church that it be faithful."[175] Newbigin's missiology here serves as a useful and necessary corrective to the dominant portrayal of mission in Anglo-Saxon evangelicalism.

---

170. Bosch says, "Although the 'Great Commission' also featured during the Reformation and Protestant Orthodoxy, the person really to be credited with putting it on the map, so to speak, was William Carey in his 1792 tract entitled *An Enquiry into the Obligations of Christians to Use Means for the Conversion of the Heathen* . . . Since Carey, the appeal to Matthew 28:18–20 has always been prominent in Protestant (more especially evangelical Anglo-Saxon) missions" (*Transforming Mission*, 340).

171. Newbigin critiques McGavran's interpretation of Matt 28:18–20 in *The Open Secret*, 122–45.

172. Newbigin, *The Gospel in a Pluralist Society*, 116.

173. Newbigin, "Context and Conversion," 308.

174. Tennent, *Invitation to World Missions*, 99.

175. Newbigin, *Trinitarian Doctrine*, 54.

Second, the Protestant modern missionary movement was closely related to colonial expansion. Accordingly, Western missionaries in Africa, Asia, and the Pacific represented superior wealth, technology and power.[176] In this context the Great Commission could be easily interpreted as the powerful Western church extending its strength and influence over the non-Western world. Aware of this potential stigma Newbigin says, "Missions can hardly claim to be respectable at the present time unless they take pains to disown publicly the patterns of colonialism."[177] These patterns include talk of power and strategy, for that "kind of language, appropriate for a military campaign or a commercial enterprise, is not appropriate here."[178] For Newbigin, mission is not primarily about controlled human planning and strategy but about the free and sovereign work of the Holy Spirit.

Both the first and second reasons are largely contextual, whereas Newbigin's third consideration is experiential in nature. He recounts his missionary experience in India of learning to follow the leading of the Holy Spirit. From this experience Newbigin observed that significant missionary advances have come about when the Holy Spirit worked through a humanly unexpected event, and the church followed his lead rather than devising their own. Newbigin contrasts this with organizing "the work of missions as though the strategy were wholly in our hands," which he likens to being blind to the Spirit's working.[179] Emphasizing this contrast, Newbigin insists that witness to Christ "will occur only if it is, so to say, not the contrived witness of the Church, but the sovereign activity of the Spirit dwelling in the Church."[180] Reaffirming this perspective in *The Open Secret*, Newbigin maintains "My own experience as a missionary has been that the significant advances of the church have not been the result of our own decisions about the mobilizing and allocating of 'resources.'"[181]

---

176. Ibid., 68–69.

177. Ibid., 12. Similarly, in *The Open Secret* he remarks "Mission is not essentially an action by which the church puts forth its own power and wisdom to conquer the world around it" (59–60).

178. Newbigin, *The Open Secret*, 64. This is ironic because elsewhere Newbigin uses precisely the kind of language he here disavows: "We are not sent into battle by a commander who stays behind" (Newbigin, *Mission In Christ's Way*, 29). He also complains that the Church, "unlike a mighty army, often appears to be a sort of perpetual convalescent home in which the patients are invited once a week to take their spiritual temperature and put out their spiritual tongue" (Newbigin, *Christian Freedom*, 27).

179. Newbigin, *Trinitarian Doctrine*, 79.

180. Ibid., 50.

181. Newbigin, *The Open Secret*, 64.

Fourth, Newbigin consistently teaches that "the Holy Spirit of God is himself the missionary."[182] As discussed in 'The *Missio Dei* and the Holy Spirit' in chapter 1, it is the Holy Spirit who bears the essential and primary witness to Christ; the church's role is strictly secondary.[183] Newbigin observes that the most decisive missionary frontier for the primitive church was that between Jew and Gentile. This frontier was first crossed at Antioch, where the first congregation of Gentile believers was born. It was not crossed by the deliberate action of a humanly-planned missionary strategy;

> The first witnesses to the gospel in Antioch were not missionaries but refugees. And so it has happened over and over again and so it continues to happen. 'Unreached peoples' are reached and cultural frontiers are crossed by refugees, fugitives, famine-stricken villagers, conscripted soldiers, traders, professional workers, and many others. A whole history of the 'expansion of Christianity' could be written with very few missionary names in it![184]

This fourth reason is biblical-theological, and is arguably the most important to him. Newbigin believed it was right and proper to highlight the Spirit's work as *the* crucial dimension of evangelism.

Despite these good reasons, Newbigin does not do justice in his theology of mission to the more humanly proactive form of bearing witness that has its proper place within the overarching mission of the Holy Spirit.[185] Nonetheless, a significant strength of Newbigin's missiology is his stress upon the priority of God in his mission conducted through the church.

## *Pneumatology and Missionary Advance*

In his seventh chapter[186] Newbigin asks, under the influence of Roland Allen, why there is so little spontaneous expansion of the church in Asia and

---

182. Newbigin, *Trinitarian Doctrine*, 71. Similarly, in *The Open Secret* Newbigin says, "in the New Testament portrayal of mission the central reality is the active work of the living Holy Spirit himself" (Newbigin, *The Open Secret*, 130).

183. Newbigin, *A Word In Season*, 22. Similarly statements can be found in *Trinitarian Doctrine*, 40, and in *The Open Secret*, 130.

184. Newbigin, "Cross-Currents," 150.

185. Of course, I reserve this proper place only with the following proviso: "Only as God uses the church as an instrument of his own missionary activity can the church's act be properly considered mission" (Flett, *The Witness of God*, 37).

186. I have deliberately omitted an account of *Trinitarian Doctrine's* chapter 6 since its trinitarian missiology does not add to that presented in chapters 5 and 7.

Africa as the New Testament would lead us to expect.[187] Additionally, "Why are the resources of the missionary movement today so largely exhausted in the support of dependent churches and why is so little energy available for fresh advance?"[188] Newbigin adopts Allen's emphasis on the pivotal importance of the Holy Spirit in the theology and practice of mission. He describes the enormous disparity between Paul's missionary methods and those of the modern missionary movement as a whole, and insists that a recovery of biblical missionary methods requires recovering the centrality of the Holy Spirit in both the theory and the practice of missions. Speaking of the Holy Spirit in missions Newbigin says,

> it is not too much to say that the whole 'method' of St. Paul (if that be the right word for something which is far more than a method) rests upon this single point: that the Holy Spirit of God is himself the missionary; that his presence and blessing are given to those who receive the Gospel; that the presence and blessing are recognizable by those who have the Spirit; and that where the Spirit is, there is all the power and all the wisdom and all the grace that man needs or can expect for the life in Christ.[189]

Newbigin recalls Paul's argument in Galatians, in which he appealed to the Galatian Christians' experience of the Holy Spirit as constitutive of their salvation and adoption. As in the first century, one of the problems of the modern missionary movement is legalism. Newbigin points out that Paul's answer was to point to God's grace in the cross and God's gift of the Holy Spirit.[190] "Faithfulness to the New Testament must bring us to give to the Spirit a much more central place not merely in the theory but also in the practice of missions."[191] By way of personal testimony Newbigin explains how the Holy Spirit leads the missionary advance and how he learned to follow his lead, starting with finding out what the Spirit has already done and then building on that.[192] Through experience, Newbigin found that "The things of the Spirit are discerned by the Spirit, and such discernment grows only with use." Conversely, "One can become progressively blind to

---

187. This question was most valid at the time of writing, but since then such 'spontaneous expansion' has indeed occurred, and is continuing. Philip Jenkins has studied this growth and its effects in *The Next Christendom*; and *The New Faces of Christianity*.

188. Newbigin, *Trinitarian Doctrine*, 68.

189. Ibid., 71.

190. Ibid.

191. Ibid., 78.

192. I have discussed this in "Missionary Methods and Roland Allen" in chapter 1.

them."¹⁹³ In his missiology Newbigin's emphasis on the person and work of the Holy Spirit is strengthened by his reading of *Acts of the Apostles*, in which, as John McIntyre observes "there is a scarcely a chapter in which the Holy Spirit is not mentioned, often centrally and strategically and by no means peripherally or tangentially."¹⁹⁴

Newbigin recognizes that as well as an under-emphasis there is a danger of an over-emphasis on the centrality of the Holy Spirit in missions. Seeking to avoid distortion, Newbigin accentuates mission as the mission of the Triune God, Father, Son and Spirit. "The Spirit is the Spirit of the Father and of the Son. His work is to enable us to participate in Christ's Sonship, to be one with him in his obedience to the Father."¹⁹⁵ He further explains:

> The Spirit is the Spirit of Christ. The decisive mark of his presence is the confession Jesus Christ is Lord . . . His coming is the fruit of hearing and believing the Gospel of Jesus Christ crucified and risen. He takes the things of Christ and shows them to us. He leads men to Christ, in whom we are baptized into one body, the body of Christ . . . The Spirit binds men to Jesus, to his historic life and to the fellowship of those who confess him as Lord.¹⁹⁶

Newbigin's Pneumatology is thus closely related to both Christology and ecclesiology. The Spirit is free and sovereign and goes ahead of the church, "but it is (if one may put it so) the church that he goes ahead of."¹⁹⁷ Konrad Raiser is therefore mistaken, I suggest, to claim that Newbigin "can state his basic Christological and ecclesiological affirmations almost without any reference to the pneumatological dimension."¹⁹⁸ It is the Spirit who "binds men to Jesus Christ in the fellowship of his one body." He continues, "The Sprit binds men to Jesus, to his historic life and to the fellowship of those who confess him as Lord."¹⁹⁹ This is critical because, "When this is forgotten, the name of the Spirit may be invoked to justify attitudes and practices which destroy the unity of the body. Mere vitality is not necessarily the mark of the presence of the Holy Spirit. Everything which grows vigorously is not thereby proved to be of God."²⁰⁰ Here Newbigin refers to

193. Newbigin, *Trinitarian Doctrine*, 79.
194. McIntyre, *The Shape of Pneumatology*, 55.
195. Newbigin, *Trinitarian Doctrine*, 81.
196. Ibid., 79–80.
197. Ibid., 80.
198. Raiser, "Is Ecumenical Apologetics," 50.
199. Newbigin, *Trinitarian Doctrine*, 80.
200. Ibid.

political and religious movements that appear to have extraordinary vitality, particularly in the 1960s, which saw the independence of so many former European colonies. He probably also has in mind those who were calling for the Christian ecumenical movement to broaden its embrace to encompass adherents of all religions, as discussed and dismissed in the second chapter of *Trinitarian Doctrine*. Locating his theology of the Holy Spirit between Christology and ecclesiology effectively wards off religious pluralism and relativism, and provides theological justification for the ongoing *missio ecclesiae*.

Describing the relation of the Holy Spirit to the Father Newbigin writes,

> The Spirit is the Spirit of God. He proceeds from the Father. It is by him that we are able to acknowledge God as Father. The characteristic utterance of the Spirit is 'Abba, Father.' By him we are able to believe that the fatherly rule of God governs all the events of human history . . . the Spirit is the assurance of our adoption as children of God (Rom 8:14–24).[201]

Newbigin has carefully related the mission of the Spirit to both Son and Father, and in so doing seeks to emphasize that mission is the work of the Triune God, not the Spirit alone. This emphasis "enables us," says Leonard Hodgson whom Newbigin approvingly quotes, "to keep the right proportion in our faith,"[202] and Newbigin adds, right proportion in the missionary task. It obviates any missiology that is founded too exclusively on any one of the Triune hypostases, thus concurring with one of the aims of *Trinitarian Doctrine*.[203] Nevertheless, it is clear that in Newbigin's missiology it is *the Holy Spirit* who is the leading actor and who is most prominent. It must be acknowledged that in a previous chapter Newbigin teaches that both the Son and the Father direct and act in the *missio Dei*.[204] However, in this chapter it is the Holy Spirit whom he repeatedly singles out, emphasizing that "missions are indeed subject to the mission of the Spirit."[205] Newbigin calls for "a willingness to trust the Holy Spirit to lead us in new paths and create new forms of fellowship for new adventures in obedience. A truly biblical understanding of the triune God must surely furnish these things."[206] I concur with Newbigin's emphasis that, in the mission of the Triune God, it

---

201. Ibid.
202. Quoted in ibid., 82.
203. Ibid., 33.
204. Ibid., 53, 54.
205. Ibid., 79.
206. Ibid., 67.

is especially appropriate to identify the *Holy Spirit* as the Lord over and chief actor in the *missio ecclesiae*. There is scope to develop further the theological rationale for this. In chapter 4 below, I will attempt to support and supplement Newbigin's emphasis on the work of the Spirit and will relate it to the ongoing mission of the exalted Christ.

## Summary

In *Trinitarian Doctrine* Newbigin sought to provide a robust theological foundation and justification for the ongoing missionary enterprise. Key to his success in doing so was his location of mission within the doctrine of the Triune God.

> We [the church] are invited to participate in an activity of God which is the central meaning of creation itself. We are invited to become, through the presence of the Holy Spirit, participants in the Son's loving obedience to the Father. All things have been created that they may be summed up in Christ the Son. All history is directed towards that end.[207]

The *missio trinitatis Dei* is 'the central meaning of creation itself.' Newbigin expounds this in terms of 'the Son's loving obedience of the Father' and all things being 'summed up in Christ.' In an earlier work Newbigin speaks of ecclesial existence as "a sharing in the love of God, the love which is the life of God, which unites the Father and the Son in the Spirit in that ultimate mystery of trinity in unity which is the source and the goal of all created being."[208] God's Triune life, which is love, is thus identified as the origin and *telos* of the cosmos. The scope of the *missio Dei* is all-encompassing. The Triune God freely created the world out of love and for participation in the divine perichoretic love. This was and remains God's purpose for creation; that creation will respond to and participate in the divine nature.

*Trinitarian Doctrine* makes several contributions, the first of which is providing the missionary movement with a secure and truthful theological foundation for its ongoing work. Related to that, this work also puts the doctrine of the Trinity firmly on the missiological map and attempts to establish a trajectory for missiological discussion that is thoroughly trinitarian. This present work attempts to extend this trajectory further. *Trinitarian Doctrine* also offers an outline for how a systematic trinitarian missiology might proceed. The trinitarian missiology Newbigin offers here is sophisticated,

207. Ibid., 83.
208. Newbigin, *The Household Of God*, 126–27.

robust and insightful. That it is not comprehensive or fully developed is understandable given the pressing nature of his responsibilities in the church, but his work does establish contours along which further works of trinitarian missiology might proceed. Having examined *Trinitarian Doctrine* we shall now turn to consider Newbigin's other extended presentation of trinitarian missiology, *The Open Secret*, to see how he adds to and fills out these contours.

## CONSIDERING THE OPEN SECRET

### *The Elements of Newbigin's Trinitarian Foundation*

Published in 1978, the context of *The Open Secret*, set out in its first two chapters, is the church's discovery of itself in a new missionary situation which, above all, requires theological understanding. The pressing question which confronts the church's missionary enterprise is 'What right do you have to preach to us?' Drawing upon the answer given by the apostles, Newbigin claims that the church preaches 'in the name of Jesus.' The authority for the church's proclamation is given by Christ himself. It is in the light of that commission that Newbigin proceeds, in chapters 3 to 6, to develop his trinitarian missiology.

Chapter 3 consists in a twofold expansion of Newbigin's response to the question 'Who is Jesus?' First, reflecting on Mark 1:1–15, Newbigin says that the earliest Christians identified Jesus as the announcer of God's reign, the Son of God the Father, and the one anointed by the Spirit of God.[209] Second, in a missionary setting, answering this question can only be done using the language and system of thought that is shaped by pre-Christian experience. To answer truthfully, to do justice to the ultimacy of who Jesus is, requires straining this thought-system to the point of breaking.[210] Newbigin sketches how this early Christian confession was first received by the Greco-Roman world by summarising part of the story Cochrane tells in *Christianity and Classical Culture*.[211] Following this account, Newbigin argues that articulation of Jesus' identity necessarily leads to an affirmation of God as Father, Son and Spirit; gospel proclamation necessitates trinitarian articulation.[212] This gospel proclamation typically challenges the thought

---

209. Newbigin, *The Open Secret*, 21–24.

210. Ibid., 19–20.

211. Ibid., 24–27.

212. Similarly, Barth notes that the words Father, Son and Spirit in the baptismal formula "occur in the context of the missionary command. Mission is objectively the expansion of the reality and truth of Jesus Christ" (Barth, *CD* IV/4, 96–97).

system of the gospel's hearers and calls for the replacement of that system by a worldview founded upon the self-disclosure of the Triune God. Newbigin's main trinitarian arguments thus far clearly bear the mark of Cochrane's influence.

From this point, Cochrane's historical and analytical thesis becomes the basis of Newbigin's efforts to outline a trinitarian missiology. The doctrine of the Trinity is the trump card, he says, that should not be reverently held back but played again and again. It should not be "treated like a talent for safekeeping," but must be "risked in the commerce of discussion."[213] In its mission the church is not just offering forgiveness of sins in Jesus, the Son of the Father and the One anointed by the Spirit. The missionary offer includes within it a thought-system or worldview, based on the doctrine of the Trinity, that offers a true account of human experience. The missionary challenge is to articulate, in contemporary terms, the truths of trinitarian faith using biblical resources. Based on the trinitarian identification of Jesus from Mark 1:1–15 Newbigin develops a three-article missiology in which Christian mission involves proclamation of the kingdom of the Father (chapter 4), sharing in the life of the Son (chapter 5), and bearing the witness of the Spirit (chapter 6).[214]

Mission involves the proclamation of God's reign over all creation. The Bible is unique because it claims to recount a universal history, the metanarrative of which proceeds by following the path of election. In brief, election for Newbigin represents God's choosing of some to be the bearers of his blessing for all. Over time, the focus of the blessing of election increasingly narrows, although the scope is always universal. From Noah through to Abraham, Jacob, Judah, David, and so on, the narrowing finally arrives at Jesus' proclamation of the kingdom—the beginning of the gospel.[215] Jesus bore witness to the reign of God through words, works of power, and sacrificial suffering in a way that is both open and yet a secret. Emphasizing the cross in paradigmatic fashion, Newbigin insists that faithful witness to God's reign will be borne through enduring opposition and suffering, because God works through death and resurrection. Mission is faith in action. "It is the acting out, by proclamation and by endurance, through all the events of history, of the faith that the kingdom of God has drawn near."[216]

213. Newbigin, *The Open Secret*, 27.

214. Ibid., 29.

215. Later in *The Open Secret* Newbigin spends an entire chapter—7—on election. For more on Newbigin's understanding of election, see "Election in Newbigin's Missiology" in chapter 1.

216. Newbigin, *The Open Secret*, 39.

Jesus' proclamation of the kingdom is the dawning of the 'day of the Lord' and as such God's kingdom is uniquely present in Jesus' person, crucified and risen. Newbigin points to the cross of Christ as the decisive clue concerning the manifestation of God's reign. In the cross, which seemed to be a defeat, God's reign is not manifested and established as people expected. The cross is a particular event at a specific historical and geographic location. Since God's reign concerns the whole of history, those who are far removed from the event by time and space are related to it "by participating in the life of that society which springs from it and is continuous with it."[217] The presence of God's reign continues from Jesus' earthly ministry in history through the church, but not as might be expected. The New Testament routinely and openly presents the church as flawed and sinful. Consequently, the church represents the reign of God in the world, "not in the triumphalistic sense (as the 'successful' cause) and not in the moralistic sense (as the 'righteous' cause), but in the sense that it is the place where the mystery of the kingdom present in the dying and rising of Jesus is made present here and now."[218] Mission is a sharing in the life of the crucified and risen Son.

Mission is also bearing the witness of the Spirit and in chapter 6 Newbigin sketches a third article missiology. He first traces the activity of the Spirit in Jesus' ministry, and then proceeds to describe the Spirit's activity in the church. In the former, Jesus is in the foreground with the Holy Spirit in the background, but these roles are reversed after the ascension. At Pentecost, the disciples receive the same anointing of the Spirit as Jesus did at his baptism. Thereafter the Spirit takes center stage and becomes the primary active agent. Stressing the role of the Spirit in Jesus' mission and in the church's mission provides theological continuity between them. "It is thus by an action of the sovereign Spirit of God that the church is launched on its mission. And it remains the mission of the Spirit. He is central."[219] In the Holy Spirit's mission He is the chief protagonist. It is the Spirit who converts both the world and the church, who goes ahead of the church in its missionary journey, and who is Lord over both the church and her mission, because it is the Spirit's mission.[220] Mission is chiefly the activity of the Holy Spirit; "The church's witness is secondary and derivative. The church is witness insofar as it follows obediently where the Spirit leads."[221] Witness

217. Ibid., 51.
218. Ibid., 54.
219. Ibid., 58.
220. Ibid., 56.
221. Ibid., 61.

is God's gift and not the church's accomplishment. Mission is hope in action because the Holy Spirit has been given to the church, not as its possession, but as the real down-payment of God's reign. This deposit is characterized by the experience of love, joy, and peace, and a hope-filled promise that the inauguration of God's reign has begun.

The church should carry out its mission in Christ's way. This means that the cruciform way in which Jesus carried out his mission becomes normative for his followers. As the church does so it can trust that God the Father, whose reign it proclaims by word and deed and endurance, will make his reign known. Newbigin argues for an ecclesiocentric missiology, since it is in this community which bears Christ's name, despite its evident flaws and habitual failings, that the presence of God's reign is mysteriously present in a cruciform manner. The scandal of the cross as the place where God reigns is extended down through history to include the church, without losing any of its scandal. Finally, the church is the intentional consequence and creation of God through the actions of Jesus and the Spirit. As Jesus was Lord to his disciples in his mission, so the Holy Spirit is Lord over the church's mission.

Newbigin's three-article missiology is rooted in the triune nature of God himself. His proposed missiological framework consists in understanding the church's mission through the lens of the following threefold model: (i) submission to and confident proclamation of the Father's sovereign and cosmic rule; (ii) participation in the life of the Son, especially his death and resurrection; (iii) obedience to the Spirit's leading as Lord over the church's mission. This threefold *model*, which Newbigin intends to use as a framework to discuss contemporary missiological problems, is more akin to a *worldview*.[222] Later Newbigin explains, "The ultimate model, *in terms of which I am to understand what is the case and what is to be done*, is furnished by the biblical story."[223] A worldview provides a framework of interpretation through which a person makes sense of the world. For Newbigin, the doctrine of the Trinity is the foundation of, and provides the contours for, his worldview.

Newbigin's trinitarian worldview clearly underpins his exposition of election in chapter 7. Human being is a being-in-relatedness made in the image of that being-in-relatedness which is the being of God himself. Accordingly, interpersonal relatedness is intrinsic to the method and character of salvation, which is why God, in election, chooses some to be the bearer of blessing for all. Central to God's gift of salvation is the restoration of mutual relatedness, and that is why salvation is communicated by way of election.

---

222. Ibid., 65.
223. Ibid., 117, emphasis added.

"There is no salvation except in a mutual relatedness that reflects that eternal relatedness-in-love which is the being of the triune God."[224] Newbigin's trinitarian foundation becomes evident in a second sense also; in election God the Father chooses people in the Son and assures them of the completion of what he has begun by giving his Spirit.[225]

In chapters 8 and 9 Newbigin discusses several substantial missiological subjects which reaffirm some theological themes first set out in *Trinitarian Doctrine*, especially chapter 7. Though important, these chapters show less dependence upon the trinitarian foundation that Newbigin has laid.

## *Trinitarian Missiology within* The Open Secret

Three of the major themes of this work—the emphasis on *trinitarian* missiology, election, and the hidden and revealed nature of God's reign—are interlinked in Newbigin's thought.[226] The subject of election—God's choosing of some on behalf of all—and the notion of the 'open secret', coalesce in a trinitarian manner. Newbigin's conception of election implicitly describes the Holy Spirit's activity of revealing Jesus to people chosen by the Father to be witnesses to all.[227] To these witnesses the reign of God is open, but to others it remains (provisionally at least) secret. His theology of election also reveals an understanding of the inter-relatedness of all human beings which, in previous works, Newbigin traces back to the Triune God creating humans in his relational image.[228] Similarly, his presentation of the hidden and revealed character of God's kingdom is suggestive of an underlying trinitarian understanding. "The reign of God [the Father] is both revealed and hidden in the words and works of Jesus and supremely in his cross and resurrection. It has to be proclaimed to all the nations by those to whom its secret has been entrusted [by the Holy Spirit]."[229] Newbigin repeatedly locates the presence of God's reign in Christ crucified, although in subsequent chapters I will seek to provide a fuller explanation of the presence of God's reign prior to, during, and following this central event of history. Newbigin's

---

224. Ibid., 77.

225. Ibid., 71.

226. In his review of *The Open Secret* Hoedemaker identifies rightly these themes but he fails to observe the essential connection between them. Hoedemaker, Review of *The Open Secret*, 456.

227. Newbigin, *The Open Secret*, 36.

228. Newbigin, *Sin and Salvation*, 17–18.

229. Newbigin, *The Open Secret*, 37.

account of God's reign, in the Holy Spirit's activity in and through the ministry of Jesus and the apostles, will also be developed further.

Newbigin's trinitarian reasoning is overt in his description of the origin of the church's mission in the mission of Jesus partly because his preferred biblical passage on mission, John 20:21–22,[230] is explicitly trinitarian. In this passage, he explains, "His [Jesus'] mission is to be their [the disciples'] mission. And so also his Spirit is to be theirs."[231] Describing the incorporation of the disciples into Jesus' mission given by the Father, Newbigin writes, "The disciples are now taken up into that saving mission for which Jesus was anointed and sent in the power of the Spirit."[232] Once again a robust pneumatology, influenced by Roland Allen, is the driving force behind both his ecclesial missiology and his missional ecclesiology. In *The Open Secret* Newbigin sketches how the mission of the Holy Spirit is related to the mission of the church, to the ongoing mission of the exalted Christ, and to a broader trinitarian missiology. My task will be to develop this sketch into a more comprehensive painting.

One reviewer of *The Open Secret* said that it "breaks little new ground, mostly consolidating positions expressed by the author in earlier writings."[233] I hold that this is true for the trinitarian missiology within *The Open Secret*. The trinitarian framework underlying Newbigin's exposition of election is a development of equivalent material in *Trinitarian Doctrine*, but consists chiefly in a restatement of material found in *The Household of God*.[234] The apparent new ground of trinitarian inter-faith dialogue, to which I will return presently, might also be regarded as a development on *Trinitarian Doctrine*, but it is also found in earlier works.[235] Newbigin himself claims that in *The Open Secret* he has developed thoughts found in seed-form in *Trinitarian Doctrine*,[236] but this seems to apply to broader missiological questions rather than to his trinitarian missiology per se. After directly examining the doctrine of the Trinity in relation to mission in chapters 3 to

---

230. "Jesus said to them again, 'Peace be with you. As the Father has sent me, so I send you.' When he had said this, he breathed on them and said to them, 'Receive the Holy Spirit.'"

231. Newbigin, *The Open Secret*, 48.

232. Ibid.

233. Scherer, Review of *The Open Secret*, 89.

234. For my discussion of this see "Election in Newbigin's Missiology—Relational Theological Anthropology" in chapter 1.

235. Two earlier versions of this trinitarian inter-faith dialogue can be found in *Christian Witness in a Pluralist Society*, 19–24 and "The Basis, Purpose and Manner," 260–70.

236. Newbigin, *The Open Secret*, vii–viii.

6, the remaining chapters "look at contemporary issues in mission from the point of view of this Trinitarian faith."[237] In chapters 7 to 10 the trinitarian logic behind these chapters is largely 'secret' and only becomes 'open' in the aforementioned account of election, and in one further instance.

## Trinitarian Inter-Faith Dialogue

In 'The Gospel Among the Religions' (chapter 10), Newbigin develops a trinitarian theology of inter-faith dialogue. In my estimation this is *The Open Secret*'s most significant development of trinitarian missiology beyond that contained in *Trinitarian Doctrine*. As with much of Newbigin's theologizing, the trigger for this discussion is a biblical passage, in this case John 16:12–15,[238] which speaks of the Holy Spirit leading the church into all truth. Newbigin says,

> This passage suggests a Trinitarian model that will guide our thinking as we proceed. The Father is the giver of all things. They all belong rightly to the Son. It will be the work of the Spirit to guide the church through the course of history into the truth as a whole by taking all God's manifold gifts given to all humankind and declaring their true meaning to the church as that which belongs to the Son.[239]

This quotation is really a condensed summary which he then works out with regard to interfaith dialogue, saying "it is the doctrine of the Trinity that provides the true grammar of dialogue."[240]

First, Christians and their dialogue partners meet as children of one Father, sharing a common patrimony as created human beings, regardless of whether the partners have accepted their sonship. This means that Christians are eager to listen to and learn from their partners what God has shown to them. Both parties meet in a shared context of the one common world, and they meet in a specific, shared historical context in the ongoing history of the world, under the providential rule of God. Second, Christians

---

237. Ibid., 29.

238. "I still have many things to say to you, but you cannot bear them now. When the Spirit of truth comes, he will guide you into all the truth; for he will not speak on his own, but will speak whatever he hears, and he will declare to you the things that are to come. He will glorify me, because he will take what is mine and declare it to you. All that the Father has is mine. For this reason I said that he will take what is mine and declare it to you."

239. Newbigin, *The Open Secret*, 179.

240. Ibid., 183.

participate in the dialogue as members of Christ's body, sent in the world by the Father to continue Jesus' mission. Consequently, Christians are vulnerable to the temptation of feeling the power of a different religion's worldview such that the other's way of viewing the world becomes a real possibility. For both dialogue partners, "The meeting place is at the cross, at the place where the Christian bears witness to Jesus as the Judge and Savior of both of them."[241] Christians participate in the dialogue as those who are deeply rooted in Christ and in the life of his body. This is necessary since real dialogue requires vulnerability as a precondition; and since "The world of the religions is the world of the demonic;"[242] the Christian goes not in their own strength but as deeply rooted in Christ. Third, Christians participate in this dialogue in the faith and expectation that the Holy Spirit will glorify Jesus by converting both partners in the dialogue. Like Peter in his meeting with Cornelius, Christians must be prepared to be changed themselves as a result of the dialogue, because, "Dialogue means exposure to the shattering and upbuilding power of God the Spirit."[243] Additionally, the Christian enters the dialogue expectant that the Holy Spirit may radically convert the partner as well as the Christian. Finally, the Christian engages in the dialogue knowing that whilst the Holy Spirit is at work glorifying Christ, other spirits are also at work but to nefarious ends, thus rendering the gift of discernment essential and irreplaceable.[244]

Newbigin's trinitarian inter-faith dialogue is commendable for several reasons. He advocates a theology of inter-faith dialogue that upholds the importance of conversion, as traditionally understood, while avoiding the charges of religious imperialism that a post-colonial world is sensitive to. He does justice to the reality of the demonic in the world of religions, and thus to the need for discernment while avoiding the simplistic accusation that non-Christian religions are the work of devils. Further strengths of Newbigin's approach are readily apparent. Both parties in the dialogue do engage in the discussion under the providential rule of God the Father and in the context of a shared human life. His second point, that Christians engage in this dialogue as members of Christ's body, is developed particularly well, and could no doubt be developed further. His third point relating to the Holy Spirit is both valid and insightful, but also problematic.

Despite the utility of the Peter-Cornelius story for inter-faith dialogue, it may be asked why this particular story should be paradigmatic

241. Ibid., 185.
242. Ibid., 186.
243. Ibid.
244. Ibid., 183–88.

for inter-faith dialogue, rather than for example, Paul's custom of reasoning with the Jews in the synagogue that Jesus is the Messiah (Acts 17:1–9). Selecting the latter as paradigmatic would evidently lead to a different theology of inter-faith dialogue. One might ask also, whether the extension of this narrative into something of an exemplar risks subverting the story's historical uniqueness—the watershed moment in which membership of the people of God is opened to the Gentiles, as Gentiles, because of Jesus.

There is room for debate too about Newbigin's claim that Christians and non-Christians are children of one Father. This claim, based on the doctrine of creation, is both pragmatically useful and theologically problematic. It is useful in inter-faith dialogue because it grounds both parties in the common theological status of children of God and it undergirds theologically the point that both faith-parties can learn from the other. However, this theological claim appears to skim over the fact that the Fatherhood of God in Scripture is predicated upon the particularity of his relationship to the Son and is extended to others by adoption. In other words, God's Fatherhood of people belongs chiefly to the doctrine of salvation. But Newbigin does not address this, nor does he seek to defend his case. Newbigin's trinitarian inter-faith dialogue is a promising and creative development within his trinitarian missiology, but like much of his work it is constructively indicative rather than comprehensive.

It must be acknowledged, however, that Newbigin's claim of God's universal Fatherhood is not without warrant. It is true that God's Fatherhood is chiefly revealed with the coming of Jesus the Son, but this revelation simply makes known that God is Father eternally; Jesus reveals what has always been the case. There is a minor motif in the Old Testament that relates God's Fatherhood of all to his actions as Creator. Picking up on this motif, both Josephus and Philo use the nouns for 'father' and 'creator' as equivalents. In the New Testament there are some biblical passages, such as Ephesians 3:14–15, which appear to teach a cosmic understanding of God as Father. Praying, the author of Ephesians says, "For this reason I bow my knees before the Father, from whom every family in heaven and on earth takes its name." Markus Barth argues that here, and in Ephesians 4:6,[245] the author of Ephesians is teaching a cosmic Patrology, which belongs together with a cosmic Christology (1:4–23) and a cosmic Ecclesiology (2:7, 10; 3:10).[246] This relation between God's Fatherhood and creation has been canonized forever in church tradition in the Nicene and Apostles' Creeds. In both creeds the first article ascribes to God the *Father* the role of 'maker/creator

---

245. "[O]ne God and Father of all, who is above all and through all and in all."
246. Barth, *Ephesians 1–3*, 379–80.

of heaven and earth.' According to Scripture and tradition, there belongs to God's Fatherliness the role of creator. All of God's creatures, therefore, especially those made in the divine image and likeness, are his children.

God's universal Fatherhood can also be developed christocentrically in Barthian fashion. In his theology, Karl Barth made a distinction between our status before God *de jure* and our status *de facto*. He suggested that all people are in fact God's children by virtue of Christ's universal redemption, ontically though not yet epistemically. Consequently, according to Barth, all human beings are in fact God's children by virtue of ontic participation in the sonship of Christ, though not all yet know this or have experienced this. Finally, God's Fatherhood in creation must not be understood to be unrelated to his Fatherhood in salvation. God's actions in creation and salvation are not discrete actions without necessary connection. Creation and salvation are related as the continuous action of the God whose goal in creation and salvation is the same—creaturely participation in the Triune *koinonia*.

## *Summary*

When Newbigin wrote *The Open Secret* it was the most mature expression of his missiological vision to date.[247] In the subject areas of election, and especially inter-faith dialogue, Newbigin's articulation of the importance of the Trinity for understanding the *missio Dei* is a development on *Trinitarian Doctrine*. Yet, the trinitarian missiology found in *The Open Secret* is a less substantial reaffirmation of that found in *Trinitarian Doctrine*. There is a trinitarian logic that underlies *The Open Secret*, but Newbigin rarely articulates this explicitly; this then, will be my task in Part Two. I concur with Hunsberger who notes the scarcity of trinitarian material in *The Open Secret*, observing that the trinitarian basis for mission that Newbigin claims to develop closely resembles an exposition of election.[248] Consequently, I maintain my contention that *Trinitarian Doctrine* is the primary text for understanding Newbigin's trinitarian missiology.[249]

---

247. This was only to be surpassed, eleven years later, by the publication of *The Gospel In A Pluralist Society*.

248. Later in that same work, Hunsberger says "In *The Open Secret* the dynamic of the whole theology is really supplied by the 'inner logic' of election, and the trinitarian chapters seem almost to be forced into the picture" (Hunsberger, *Bearing the Witness of the Spirit*, 67, 241–42).

249. Flett suggests the same in "'Who Is Jesus Christ?,' 260–61.

## THE "ECONOMIC" NATURE OF NEWBIGIN'S TRINITARIANISM

Earlier I observed that Newbigin's doctrine of the Trinity is economic in orientation, for it is chiefly concerned with elucidating God's action in and for the world. Frances Young expresses a similar view, observing that Newbigin's trinitarianism is an 'economic' trinitarianism. She provides little explanation, however, of her further claim that "Newbigin's trinitarianism is not theologically developed."[250] Taken in general terms this claim is supported, I suggest, by the explorations in this chapter. However, if Young means that Newbigin's trinitarianism is *limited* to economic concerns, then I contend that she is mistaken. While acknowledging that Newbigin's trinitarianism is 'practical', by which he presumably means economically focused, Wainwright contends that in Newbigin's theology of the Trinity there is "no *mere* 'economic trinitarianism', for the cooperation of the divine Persons toward the world rests on, and testifies to, their mutual coinherence *in se* and it is in being drawn into their communion that human salvation consists."[251] Concurring with Wainwright, I contend that Newbigin's doctrine of the economic Trinity is undergirded by his theology of the ontological Trinity. Although he does not frequently discuss the matter in detail, I believe there are four reasons why Newbigin holds to a true correspondence of the economic and ontological Trinity.

First, Newbigin's doctrine of revelation makes it clear that Jesus really is God's self-presentation. In a 1977 paper entitled *Christian Witness in a Pluralist Society*, Newbigin says, "in Jesus we see 'God as he really is,'" and he speaks of "The knowledge of 'God as he really is' in the man Jesus."[252] Newbigin reiterates this view in his commentary on John's gospel: "Jesus is, quite simply, God's revelation of himself. It is God whom we meet when we meet Jesus."[253] Furthermore, Newbigin is most explicit in his early work *The Reunion of the Church*, where he says that in the incarnation there is found "the one revelation in time of the ever-living God *as He eternally is*."[254] It is clear for Newbigin that the economic revelation of the Triune God rests upon a prior ontological foundation.

Second, Newbigin does speak directly about God *in se*, and characteristically for him this occurs when prompted by the biblical text itself.

---

250. Young, "The Uncontainable God," 84.
251. Wainwright, *Lesslie Newbigin*, 331.
252. Newbigin, *Christian Witness in a Pluralist Society*, 10, 9.
253. Newbigin, *The Light Has Come*, 165.
254. Newbigin, *The Reunion of the Church*, 79, emphasis added.

## Newbigin's Theology of the Trinity   111

In *The Light Has Come* he says, "The Father and the Son are so perfectly one in their mutual indwelling that when we listen to the words of Jesus and attend to his works, we are coming to see God, and it is therefore futile and irrelevant to look elsewhere."[255] Thus, Wainwright is correct that Newbigin's trinitarian theology testifies to the *perichoresis* of the Triune Persons.[256] Furthermore, Newbigin also speaks of the mutual glorification of the Triune Persons: "For the glory of God is not the self-glorification of a supreme monad; it is the glory of perfect love forever poured out and forever received within the being of the triune God."[257] Intriguingly, he goes on to speak of this mutual trinitarian glorification not only within the being of God but also incorporating the divine missions to the world, which includes the church-in-mission.[258] In this Newbigin anticipates Pannenberg's thought-provoking work on the relation between the eternal processions and the temporal missions, which I discuss at the end of the next chapter. Thus, Newbigin is not afraid to discuss God's being *in se*, but when he does so he typically refers to the "unceasing outpouring of love within the being of the triune God."[259] Suggesting that the joy of the Lord is "the perfection of surrender in love and obedience," Newbigin cautiously says that this is "the very substance—if one may dare to say so—of the Godhead."[260]

Third, in two personal letters to Roy Clouser, author of *The Myth of Religious Neutrality* to which Newbigin often made reference in his later writings, it is clear that Newbigin refused to think and speak of God *pro nobis* apart from God *in se*; that is, he refused to sever the relation between the ontological and economic Trinity. In the first letter, Newbigin finds abhorrent the idea of speaking of God as he really is behind God as revealed in Jesus Christ. "Why can't we trust him to be what he has shown himself to be in Jesus Christ? I'm afraid I can't conceal the deep repugnance that I feel for this kind of speculative metaphysics."[261] Then, in his second letter Newbigin spells out in more detail what he means.

> To raise the question of a distinction between God as he actually is and God as he has revealed himself to us (even if it is only to say that there might be a difference), does two things. (i) it implies that we have access to some knowledge of God apart from

255. Newbigin, *The Light Has Come*, 183.
256. Wainwright, *Lesslie Newbigin*, 331.
257. Newbigin, *The Light Has Come*, 175.
258. Ibid., 183–84.
259. Ibid., 203.
260. Ibid., 201–2.
261. Newbigin, "Letter to Roy Clouser (i)."

what he has made known to us, which is false; and (ii) it is a re-enactment of the primal sin of the Fall, namely the attempt to get behind God's word to what he 'really' has in mind—precisely the point made by the serpent in Genesis 3.4.²⁶²

Newbigin is confident that in Jesus God has truly revealed himself, and for him this Christological affirmation is *the* foundation for all subsequent theology. However, Newbigin does not proceed to offer a detailed discussion of the relation between the economic and immanent Trinity; nor does he comment on the well-known 'Rahner's rule', which states 'the immanent Trinity *is* the economic trinity and the economic Trinity *is* the immanent Trinity'.²⁶³ The purpose of Rahner's rule is to safeguard the reality of God's self-disclosure in the divine economy. That is, in Jesus and the Spirit there really is the *self*-giving of God, and so this divine self-revelation is trustworthy and true. Therefore, in its intent Rahner's rule is certainly in accord with Newbigin's theology.

However, Rahner's rule can also be interpreted as the absolute identification of the economic with the immanent. This strong ontological interpretation of *is* in Rahner's rule has been criticized for its pantheistic (or panentheistic) tendencies, that render creation the correlative of God. Robert Letham's formulation is a case in point: "God is not free, but is bound up with the world in an ongoing mutual history. The Incarnation was not the result of a decision freely made by God, but instead overflowed out of his being."²⁶⁴ Newbigin himself avoids any such danger as is evident, for example, in his claim that it is part of "the paradox of revelation, that it must be both a veiling and an unveiling if it is to be true."²⁶⁵ In other words, God truly gives himself in Jesus so that there is no hidden god behind the incarnate Son; nevertheless, the eternal being of God is not exhaustively disclosed. Newbigin's claim seems to agree with Zizioulas' view, that "although the Economic Trinity is the Immanent Trinity, the Immanent Trinity is not exhausted in the Economic Trinity."²⁶⁶

Fourth, in an unpublished 1997 electronic document entitled "Reflections on the 'Affirmation of Faith' embodied in the Eucharistic Liturgy proposed for use in the Church of South India," Newbigin is concerned that in the proposed liturgy Christ is not adequately related to the one God.

---

262. This unusual notational style is original. Newbigin, "Letter to Roy Clouser (ii)."
263. Rahner, *The Trinity*, 22.
264. Letham, *The Holy Trinity*, 364.
265. Newbigin, *The Light Has Come*, 97.
266. Zizioulas, "The Doctrine of God the Trinity Today," 24.

> The three persons of the triune God are not properly denoted merely by their functions in the economy of salvation, since the one God is at work in all these functions. They are properly described in terms of their relationships. The Father is Father of the Son, and the Son is Son of the Father. It is this mutuality of relationships which is the vital truth in the doctrine of the Trinity but which is absent here.[267]

Here Newbigin affirms the priority, both in importance and in time, of intra-trinitarian relations over the operations of the Triune Persons *pro nobis*. Although Newbigin here omits mention of the immanent Trinity, elsewhere he makes it clear that the intra-trinitarian relations evident in the economy belong to God's eternal being. In *The Open Secret* he speaks of "that eternal relatedness-in-love which is the being of the triune God."[268]

I have attempted in the foregoing discussion to demonstrate the ontological moorings of Newbigin's largely economic trinitarianism, thus supporting Wainwright's contention that in Newbigin's theology of the Trinity one finds 'no *mere* economic trinitarianism.' Newbigin teaches a true correspondence between the ontological and the economic Trinity, which reveals that his trinitarianism is not limited to economic concerns. Nevertheless, since his concerns are largely economic, I will build on his trinitarian missiology by developing a robust account of God's being *ad intra* in Part Two.

## EVALUATING NEWBIGIN'S TRINITARIAN MISSIOLOGY

### Strengths

Newbigin's primary concern is to engage faithfully with the missiological issues confronting the church in his day and this led him to reflect on the doctrine of the Trinity. Newbigin's thoughts on the Trinity constitute only preliminary reflections and insights rather than a magisterial exposition, but nonetheless his achievements in the field of trinitarian missiology are impressive. Newbigin recognized that the doctrine of the Trinity is little understood by the great majority of Christians and makes little impact upon either their lives or their theology. He sought to retrieve this doctrine from the margins of Christian thought and to bring it back to the center where it belongs—for the common Christian understanding of God, for the church at large, and for the missionary movement in particular.

---

267. Newbigin, "Reflections on the 'Affirmation of Faith.'"
268. Newbigin, *The Open Secret*, 77.

Newbigin makes the connection between the doctrine of the Trinity and the church's mission explicit. He rightly identifies the fact that the trinitarian struggles and debates that surround the development of the doctrine of the Trinity are part of the missional context of the church witnessing to pagan culture. He observed that the doctrine of the Trinity comes to the fore in a missionary situation, and recedes in a non-missional context. Following Cochrane, Newbigin claimed that the doctrine of the Trinity was a crucial part of the church mastering the world of classical thought at the height of its power. Furthermore, he notes that the doctrine of the Trinity is related to the church's mission because this doctrine is integral to the church's gospel, the center of which Newbigin identifies as the relationship between Father and Son. Thus, he shows how the Triune God is the starting point and the abiding subject of preaching, and conversely, how the gospel cannot be communicated without reference to God as Triune. In other words, he recognizes that God's action in the economy is irreducibly trinitarian. For him, the doctrine of the Trinity is the *arché* for Christian theology, for theology rests on the revelation of God in Christ, a revelation that is irreducibly trinitarian. Hence, a true understanding of the missionary task will rest on an understanding of God as Trinity. Similarly, Newbigin held that God advances his mission by way of election, the conception of which rested on a trinitarian foundation. In summary, the doctrine of the Trinity is central to the *kerygma* of the church and central to the church's theological task.

Newbigin explored the relation of the church's mission to world history, exposing in the process influential but false philosophies of history. He also explained the relation of God the Father's rule over the world to his work in the church, showing that although God works through whichever socio-political movements he wishes,[269] there is no alternative or supplementary way of salvation outside of Christ. Furthermore, Newbigin describes the doctrine of providence in trinitarian terms; the Father guides history towards its *telos*, the summing up of all things in Christ, and by the Spirit leads people to a decision concerning Christ. He successfully and coherently incorporates the doctrines of creation, election, providence, the church, redemption, and the last things, into the *missio trinitatis Dei*, while retaining its center in the missions of Son and Spirit. Newbigin successfully makes explicit the implicit trinitarian language of the New Testament, especially of the Pauline corpus. In essence, Newbigin concurs with the orthodox trinitarian rule *opera trinitatis ad extra sunt indivisa*, and he particularly succeeds in describing the distinctive roles appropriate to the Triune Persons. One of these roles that receives a heavy emphasis in Newbigin's treatment is his assertion that the Holy Spirit is himself the missionary.

269. Ps 115:3—"Our God is in the heavens; he does whatever he pleases."

Although incomplete by his own admission,[270] Newbigin's achievements in trinitarian missiology were remarkable, especially given his historical context. John Flett's chief complaint against missiology in the era in which Newbigin wrote his major trinitarian works was that "*Missio Dei* claims to provide a Trinitarian framework for concepts that do not draw on that doctrine."[271] Instead, *missio Dei* theology "never escapes an anthropological grounding for missions."[272] If Flett's persuasive historical analysis of the *missio Dei* is to be accepted, even in general terms, then Newbigin's trinitarian missiology stands as an important exception to this. Later Flett lamented that "*Missio Dei*'s 'Trinitarianism' developed at an express distance from Christology."[273] Again, Newbigin's work stands out as a clear exception, which is a remarkable achievement. His account of God's mission is explicitly grounded in the doctrine of the Trinity, centering on the person of Christ. Newbigin's trinitarian missiology succeeded where that of his contemporaries fell short. It is perhaps no coincidence, therefore, that the recently published books on trinitarian missiology, by Timothy Tennent and John Flett in 2010, both draw on Newbigin. Such is the ongoing relevancy of Newbigin's work for theologians and missiologists in the twenty-first century.

Newbigin explains, again in trinitarian terms, the importance of church unity, and the relation of the church's mission to the witness and mission of the Holy Spirit. He also explains how the *missio ecclesiae* is mission in the way of Jesus Christ, based on Jesus' words: "*As* the Father has sent me, so I send you."[274] The church's mission is christologically determined and pneumatologically empowered and pioneered. He relates the universal scope of the *missio Dei* and the atonement to the universal scope of the *missio ecclesiae*, and thus makes clear the necessity of 'foreign missions.' Influenced by Roland Allen, Newbigin maintains that the Holy Spirit is Lord of the church's mission. Also under Allen's influence, he subjects traditional missionary methods to critical scrutiny and endorses proposals by Allen that give a prominent place to the Holy Spirit in both the theory and practice of missions. In missiology, Pneumatology is inextricably tied not only to ecclesiology, but also to Christology and trinitarian theology. Newbigin thus heads off theologies of religious pluralism that would sever these ties.

270. He described *Trinitarian Doctrine* as lacking "depth and solidity" and gave to *The Open Secret* the original subtitle of *Sketches for a Missionary Theology*. Newbigin, *Trinitarian Doctrine*, 9.

271. Flett, *The Witness of God*, 36.

272. Ibid., 77.

273. Ibid., 198.

274. John 20:21, emphasis added.

Newbigin developed an innovative trinitarian theology of inter-faith dialogue. Due to the influence of other scholars he became increasingly hostile towards natural theology, and his resolute Christocentrism meant that he strongly resisted the generic idea of god or the concept of god-in-general. Instead, all accurate knowledge of God comes and can only come from God's self-revelation in the divine economy centering on the person of Christ. Consequently, Newbigin opposes non-trinitarian concepts of God, tracing the history of their entry into the Western mind. This, of course, is none other than a working out of the importance of the Trinity as the starting point for all thought, which Newbigin first learned from Cochrane.

In summary, Newbigin's articulation of the doctrine of the Trinity is closely moored to the biblical text which he seeks to articulate faithfully. Newbigin's chief contribution is not in providing a comprehensive trinitarian missiology—such a task did not prove to be possible for a missiologist 'on the run.' Rather, Newbigin's significance lies in identifying the importance of trinitarian missiology and personally pioneering the way forward. Newbigin was one of the first to apply systematic theological insights regarding the importance of the doctrine of the Trinity to the realms of missiology. He did so in the context of the missiological questions of his day. These missiological questions are not identical to the most pressing missiological questions in the early twenty-first century. However, by insisting that challenges to the church's mission can be rightly understood only by starting with the *arch*é of theology and its abiding subject, the Triune God, Newbigin has shown the way forward.

## *Summary*

In this chapter I have undertaken an examination of Newbigin's trinitarian missiology as presented in both his published and unpublished work. I have also outlined the major influences on his trinitarian thinking, the most notable of which was the work of Charles Cochrane. This chapter has traced the historical development of Newbigin's trinitarian missiology. Newbigin's emphasis on the importance of the Trinity for missiology was both timely and important, but for understandable reasons, he did not develop a full systematic account of such a missiology. I have also argued that despite its early dating, *Trinitarian Doctrine for Today's Mission* remains the key text for understanding Newbigin's deliberations on this topic. I have sought to identify *when* Newbigin discovered the importance of the doctrine of the Trinity and I have attempted to explain why Newbigin wrote nothing further on this topic until fifteen years after he had first recognized the importance of the doctrine of the Trinity. I have summarized the strengths of Newbigin's trinitarian missiology, of which there are many, as well as areas that are omitted or undeveloped. Bringing Part One to a close, let me sketch in brief outline how I propose to build upon Newbigin's work in developing a thorough and systematic trinitarian missiology in the tradition of Lesslie Newbigin.

## BUILDING ON NEWBIGIN'S TRINITARIAN MISSIOLOGY

It is clear that Newbigin recognized the vital importance for missiology of the doctrine of the Trinity. I have argued that he sowed seeds for such a missiology but did not develop it himself in any thorough-going fashion. My purpose in Part Two then, is to develop a trinitarian missiology in a way that is consistent with Newbigin's theological convictions. To that end, I will attempt to provide a more robust account of the doctrine of the Trinity itself, drawing particularly on theologians from Newbigin's own Reformed tradition, especially Karl Barth. I will consider in particular the missiological implications of a robust trinitarian theology. This project will be set out in four chapters: the Triune being of the missionary God (chapter 3), the missions of the Son and Spirit (chapter 4), the *missio ecclesiae* (chapter 5), and a conclusion (chapter 6).

Newbigin was insistent that the doctrine of the Trinity was biblically based and the result of reflecting on God's self-revelation in Christ; that is, Christocentrism leads to trinitarianism. Drawing on Cochrane and Barth, Newbigin contends, as has been seen, that the doctrine of the Trinity is the *arché* of Christian doctrine. I will take up this point and argue that God's Triune self-revelation must become the starting point and abiding context for thought. I will also extend Newbigin's brief considerations of God's being *ad intra*, and will explore features of God's immanent being that do not feature in Newbigin's own writings. This will include, in particular, intra-trinitarian *perichoresis*, the unity of the three Persons, intra-trinitarian origins, the monarchy of God the Father, and the communal divine life. Newbigin comments that Jesus "appears as the Son who lovingly submits himself to the will of him who rules all things,"[275] but he does not explore what this means for the nature of God and for an understanding of incarnational mission. In Part Two I will develop both of these themes. Regarding the Triune being of God *ad extra*, Newbigin observes that the *missio ecclesiae* is cosmic in scope because it is based in the *missio trinitatis Dei*. I will develop and elaborate on the cosmic nature of the *missio Dei* in both its protological and

275. Newbigin, *Trinitarian Doctrine*, 39.

eschatological dimensions. I will also take up and investigate the hint by Newbigin that the mutual trinitarian glorification incorporates the divine missions to the world and includes the church.

In his trinitarian missiology Newbigin rightly observes that Jesus is the center of the *missio Dei*. However, Newbigin's writings omit a detailed account of the Son's mission and so I will develop this account in Part Two, along with the implications for incarnational mission. Newbigin's account of the mission of the Spirit is one of his greatest strengths, but it is indicative in nature and remains under-developed. In Part Two I will elaborate on the mission of the Spirit in relation to Jesus and the church, offering reflections on mission in the way of the Spirit, as well as a theological account of the inter-relation of the missions of Spirit and church.

Next, I will turn to a direct consideration of the *missio ecclesiae* within the mission of the Triune God. Supplementing Newbigin's trinitarian missiology, I will examine how the missionary church is christologically determined. I will elucidate the church's missionary nature in relation to the church's being, her doxological orientation, and the breadth and center of her mission. Lastly, in my concluding chapter I will offer a rigorous theological exposition of the related claims, derived from Newbigin, that the Triune nature of God is irreducibly related to the substance of the gospel and that evangelism begins by bearing witness to the Triune God.

PART TWO

# Constructing a Trinitarian Missiology in the Tradition of Lesslie Newbigin

CHAPTER 3

# Trinitarian Missiology
## The Triune Being of the Missionary God

### TRINITARIAN PROLEGOMENA

*Introducing the Doctrine of the Trinity*

THE DOCTRINE OF THE Trinity is the theological outcome of the conviction that God has uniquely and definitively revealed himself in the person of Jesus of Nazareth. It is rooted in and is a rigorous outworking of the distinctively Christian answer to the question which Jesus puts to every person—"Who do you say that I am?"[1] Consequently, Barth correctly says "The doctrine of the Trinity is what basically distinguishes the Christian doctrine of God as Christian."[2] This doctrine carefully describes who God is, based upon who God has revealed himself to be in Christ and the Spirit. It is therefore rooted in revelation rather than speculation, and this revelation takes shape in the actions of God *ad extra*, in particular the missions or sendings of the Son (incarnation) and the Spirit (Pentecost).

In the life of Jesus, as recorded in the canonical gospels, there are three figures who demand to be understood in distinct personal and divine terms. There is Jesus, the Father to whom he prays and submits, and the Spirit who empowers and leads him. Hence, Moltmann rightly says that "The New Testament talks about God by proclaiming in narrative the relationships of the Father, the Son and the Spirit."[3] In each case the New Testament makes

1. Mark 8:29, NIV.
2. Barth, *CD* I/1, 301.
3. Moltmann, *The Trinity and the Kingdom*, 64, emphasis removed.

it clear that each of these identities is a distinct person and is spoken of in personal terms, but each divine identity is also inextricably related to the other two. For example, Jesus says "The Father and I are one" and "Whoever has seen me has seen the Father," because the Father and Son dwell 'in' each other (John 10:30; 14:9; 10:38). The New Testament clearly bears witness to Father, Son and Spirit not only as distinct and closely related Persons, but also as *divine* Persons. Two most basic confessions in the early church are 'Jesus saves' and 'Jesus is Lord', and these decisively point to the divinity of Jesus, for only God can save and only God is Lord.[4] The early Church Fathers, most notably Athanasius, expressed the divinity of Jesus by saying he is *homoousios* (of the same being) with the Father. As the early church theologians continued to reflect on the mission of the Son and the Spirit they came to understand that the Holy Spirit is also divine. Arguably, the decisive argument was that the functions of the Spirit belong solely to God, particularly sanctifying. Sanctification is part of salvation for it is the process by which a person becomes like God, and God alone can do this. Therefore, the Holy Spirit was understood to be, like Jesus and the Father, fully divine.[5]

The doctrine of the Trinity as a developed doctrine is not formulated in the New Testament, but then few developed doctrines are found there at all. Instead, underlying the New Testament is a pervasive and implicit trinitarian pattern, which sometimes becomes explicit.[6] Apart from the classical trinitarian verses related to the 'great commission' with its command to baptize 'in the name of the Father and of the Son and of the Holy Spirit' (Matt 28:19–20), and the ending of 2 Corinthians commonly known as 'the grace' (13:14), other examples include Ephesians 4:4–6 and Acts 2:32–33.[7]

---

4. The divinity of Jesus was basic to the early Church, for the disciples (the proto-Church) worshiped Jesus during his ministry (Matt 14:33), after his resurrection (Matt 28:9, 17), and understood belief in Him to be decisive for salvation (Rom 10:9). The New Testament authors speak of Jesus being the "image of God" (Col 1:15), "in very nature God" (Phil 2:6), the "exact representation of God's being" (Heb 1:3) in whom "the fullness of God dwells bodily" (Col 1:19; 2:9).

5. Other arguments for the Spirit's divinity include the fact that the Holy Spirit is closely associated with the Father and Son in the baptismal formula, and almost all of the titles of God are applied to the Spirit, especially the word 'holy'. But, according to Basil, "the greatest proof that the Spirit is one with the Father and the Son is that He is said to have the same relationship to God as the spirit within us has to us: 'For what person knows a man's thoughts except the spirit of a man which is in him? So also no one comprehends the thoughts of God except the Spirit of God.' [1 Cor 2:11]" (Basil, *On the Holy Spirit*, 67).

6. This is in direct contradiction of Brunner's contention that "not only the word 'Trinity', but even the explicit idea of the Trinity is absent from the apostolic witness to the faith" (Brunner, *Dogmatics*, 1:205).

7. For further details see Jenson, *Systematic Theology*, 1:91–94.

Trinitarian Missiology    123

The New Testament bears witness to a vibrant trinitarian religion which worships God as Father, Son and Spirit, but has yet to conceptually grasp their interrelation and how this fits with biblical monotheism. For example, Revelation 5:13 speaks of all of creation singing "To the one seated on the throne and to the Lamb," but does not attempt to explain the relation of these two identities. One commentator, George E. Ladd, says

> Here are the raw materials of a trinitarian theology. John, as a Jew, was an inflexible monotheist; there is and can be only one God. Yet the Father is God, and the Son shares equally the divine prerogatives and the worship and adoration which God alone can receive. It is because of this high Christology along with unswerving monotheism that the church later formulated its trinitarian theology: one God existing in three persons. John does not reflect upon it, nor offer any explanation for it. He simply records what he together with the early church experienced.[8]

The New Testament contains the elements of the doctrine of the Trinity, and it was the work of later theologians to bring these strands together. Gregory of Nazianzus pointed to a gradual progress in clarification and understanding of the mystery of God's revelation in the course of time. He said,

> The Old Testament preached the Father openly and the Son more obscurely. The New Testament revealed the Son, and hinted at the divinity of the Holy Spirit. Now the Spirit dwells in us, and is revealed more clearly to us. It was not proper to preach the Son openly, while the divinity of the Father had not yet been admitted. Nor was it proper to accept the Holy Spirit before [the divinity of] the Son had been acknowledged . . . Instead, by gradual advances and . . . partial ascents, we should move forward and increase in clarity, so that the light of the Trinity should shine.[9]

The doctrine of the Trinity teaches that God is three-in-one, or Triune, and we have seen the origins for this belief in *three* divine Persons. However, the early church consistently refused to articulate a belief in three gods (tritheism), due to the overwhelmingly monotheistic context provided primarily by Judaism but also by philosophical monotheism. The central Jewish prayer, known as the Shema, comes from Deuteronomy 6:4 and begins, "Hear O Israel! The Lord our God, the Lord is One" (NASB). The first

---

8. Ladd, *A Commentary on the Revelation of John*, 94.
9. Gregory of Nazianzus, quoted in McGrath, *Christian Theology*, 239.

commandment in the Decalogue is that Israel have no other gods besides YHWH. The belief in one God was never seriously threatened, thus effectively excluding tritheism as a serious theological consideration. Naturally, this led the early church to consider the identities of the Father, Jesus and the Spirit within a monotheistic framework. The doctrine of the Trinity is the outcome of this process, with the Western and Eastern wings of the church respectively articulating that God is three *personae* in one *substantia* or three *hypostases* sharing one *ousia*.

The formulation of the doctrine of the Trinity was a radical reconception of the oneness or unity of God. Robert Jenson says, "The doctrine of the Trinity was the creation, if one will, of a *new ontology* of 'God' on the basis of the gospel."[10] This caused such a fundamental conceptual and linguistic theological earthquake, that "it was a long time before the full implications of this could be worked out because it was such a revolution in thinking as to what the word God meant."[11] During this time, other simpler formulations were offered to describe the being of God. The conceptual tension in believing that God is both three and one led some to remove the tension altogether by over-emphasizing God's oneness, most notably in modalism and subordinationism.

Modalism strongly asserts that the Father is God, the Son is God, and the Spirit is God. It denies the Trinity, however, because modalism understands the Father, Son and Spirit to be identical to each other, three different names for one and the same divine person. According to modalism, there is no difference, save that of appearance, between Father, Son and Spirit. Each is a term for the same one God. It is as if at different points in time, God wears different masks or adopts different personas, revealing himself first as Father, second as Son, and third as Spirit. The early church decisively rejected modalism for two important reasons. First, the Bible does not present Father, Son and Spirit as identical. Rather, the Bible consistently differentiates between the Triune Persons whilst also affirming their extremely close mutual relations. If modalism were true, then when Jesus prays to the Father he would in fact be praying to himself, rendering Jesus' actions misleading and nonsensical. Arguably the clearest indication that the Triune Persons are distinct from each other is the baptism of Jesus. When Jesus is being baptized, the Spirit descends on him in the form of a dove, and the voice of the Father is heard from heaven (Mark 1:9–11). Second, modalism suggests that Father, Son and Spirit are actually *prosopa* or masks adopted by God. If God does not reveal his actual identity but only a mask or an adopted persona, then the relation between God's identity and the adopted persona

10. Jenson, *God After God*, 47.
11. Newbigin, *Living Hope in a Changing World*, 11.

is unclear. Thus, it is not possible to ever actually come to know who God really is because there is a god who remains hidden behind the revealed personas. Modalism renders God unknowable, whereas the doctrine of the Trinity affirms that God the Father has revealed himself by sending the Son and Spirit who share the same divine being (*homoousios*). In Jesus and the Spirit we have to do with none other than God himself.

Like modalism, the trinitarian heresy of subordinationism also prioritizes oneness over threeness, and has two primary roots. First, Leonard Hodgson explains, "Subordinationism . . . attempts to preserve divine unity by making one Person ultimately the real God and the others divine because of their relation to Him."[12] Second, in the New Testament there is a 'trinitarian order' in which the Father sends the Son and the Son submits to the Father. Based on these two factors subordinationism teaches that the Father alone is the one true God, whereas the Son and Spirit are understood to be exalted creatures (possibly angels), semi-divine beings, but not God Almighty. Subordinationism was popular because it adhered to a simple account of divine unity that excluded multiplicity. However, the doctrine of the Trinity, rooted in the revelation of God in Christ and the Spirit, affirms multiplicity within divine unity. In Hodgson's view, both modalism and subordinationism "sprang from the same root. They were attempts to account for the historical facts of the Christian revelation with perfect loyalty to the unrevised conception of unity," and so "surrendered the revelation to the idea of unity."[13] However, subordinationism does not account for the facts of the gospel, which clearly affirm the divinity and distinct identities of Son and Spirit.

Subordinationism does highlight what can be called an order within the Trinity, but this does not entail ontological subordinationism. The Triune Persons share the same divine being and are equally God, but this ontological equality does not exclude distinctions and roles amongst the Persons, to which the New Testament bears witness. The incarnate Son's knowledge is inferior to the Father's (Mark 13:32), and whilst the Father has life in himself, the incarnate Son has the same only because it has been granted to him by the Father (John 5:26).[14] The trinitarian order is clearly depicted in the Garden of Gethsemane where Jesus submits to his Father's will,[15] and in Jesus' stark statement that "the Father is greater than I."[16] The apostle Paul explains that all things are *from* God the Father whereas all

---

12. Hodgson, *The Doctrine of the Trinity*, 100.
13. Ibid., 99, 98.
14. I return to a detailed consideration of this verse later in this chapter.
15. Matt 26:39.
16. John 14:28.

things are *through* God the Son (1 Cor 8:6), and at the end of time all creation will be subjected to God the Son, who will in turn then be subjected to God the Father (1 Cor 15:25–28). The Father eternally begets the Son and spirates the Holy Spirit and not *vice versa*. Irenaeus of Lyon famously portrayed this order by describing the Son and the Spirit's action in the world as the two hands of God the Father. There is a trinitarian order which emphasizes the priority or monarchy of the Father, but this is not to be understood as an ontological hierarchy but a difference in order and function. Furthermore, complementing this trinitarian order is a reciprocity between and among the Triune Persons that points to a mutual dependency, rather than the asymmetrical dependency of Son and Spirit upon the Father. The Son depends upon the Father for his identity because he is eternally begotten of the Father. Likewise, the Father's identity as *Father* depends upon the Son, for the Father cannot be Father without someone to be the Father of, i.e. the Son. Both Father and Son depend upon each other for their identity but they do so in different ways. Similarly, the Spirit is involved in the giving of the Son (Matt 1:18) as the Son is in the giving of the Spirit (Acts 2:32–33). The mission of the Son is different in character from the mission of the Spirit, for in Bruner's words "Jesus is theocentric, and the Spirit is Christocentric," but this difference is not to be understood hierarchically.[17] There is subjection among the Triune Persons, but it is more mutual and reciprocal than simply unidirectional, as clearly indicated by the trinitarian notion of *perichoresis*.

*Perichoresis* is a vital concept which helps explain the unity and interrelations of the Triune Persons. The word *perichoresis* comes from *chorein* meaning both 'to make room' and 'to contain', thus it includes the notions of mutual movement and mutual indwelling.[18] The concept was first used by Gregory of Nazianzus to help explain the hypostatic union of the two natures of Christ,[19] but since John of Damascus, came to be applied to the coinherence (*circumincessio*—passing into one another) of the Triune Persons.[20] This conceptual development was unidirectional and meant that *perichoresis* could no longer be used in Christology without seriously damaging the doctrine of the person of Christ; but Christology's loss was trinitarian theology's gain. Classically this idea is found in John 14:11 where Jesus says, "I am *in* the Father and the Father is *in* me." Father, Son and Holy Spirit mutually dwell in one another in such a mysterious way that God is

---

17. Bruner, "The Son is God," 106.
18. Tan, "A Trinitarian Ontology," 292.
19. Torrance, *The Christian Doctrine of God*, 102.
20. Barth, *CD* I/1, 370.

one. They are a community of being, a Being-in-communion,[21] in which there is genuine difference (the Father is not the Son, the Son is not the Father, and the Spirit is neither the Father nor the Son) yet also complete and indivisible togetherness. God's being is irreducibly relational in himself, for God's being is a communion of three loving Persons who eternally give love to and receive love from each other. Thus Torrance says, "what the doctrine of the Holy Trinity supremely means, that God himself is love."[22] This eternal giving and receiving of love amongst the Triune Persons vividly describes how, eternally, 'God is love', for God is the primary object of God's affections.[23] Without positing some kind of plurality within God, it becomes untenable to contend that from eternity God is love[24] unless one is willing to eternalize creation and opt for a form of pantheism (or panentheism), an option which the church universal has consistently rejected.[25] The communion that is God is so intimate that each Triune Person dwells in and interpenetrates the other two. God's being is constituted in the perichoretic relations between Father, Son and Spirit "who give and receive their reality to and from one another."[26] *Perichoresis* renders God's unity more com-

---

21. See Zizioulas, *Being As Communion*.

22. Torrance, *The Christian Doctrine of God*, 162.

23. Gunton explains "the doctrine of the Trinity is the teaching that God is love, not only towards us, but in his deepest and eternal being" (Gunton, *Father, Son and Holy Spirit*, 18).

24. C. S. Lewis states succinctly "If God was a single person, then before the world was made, he was not love" (*Mere Christianity*, 145). Letham contrasts this with an Islamic view of God and says that according to Islam Allah cannot be, prior to creation, personal or love. Letham, *The Holy Trinity*, 444.

25. Surprisingly, William Barclay in his popular Daily Study Bible series actually advocates this pantheistic or panentheistic view. He says "God's act of creation was a necessity of His divine nature, because, being love, it was necessary for God to have someone whom He might love, and who might love Him" (Barclay, *The Letters of John and Jude*, 117). Refuting this view Barth declares "It is not part of God's being and action that as love it must have an object in another who is different from Him. God is sufficient in Himself as object and therefore as object of His love. He is no less than the One who loves if He loves no object different from Himself." He continues, "In the fact that He determines to love such another, His love overflows. But it is not exhausted in it nor confined or conditioned by it. On the contrary, this overflowing is conditioned by the fact that although it could satisfy itself, it has no satisfaction in this self-satisfaction, but as love for another it can and will be more than that which could satisfy itself. While God is everything for Himself, He wills again not to be everything merely for Himself, but for this other" (Barth, *CD* II/1, 280).

26. Gunton, *The Promise*, 94. I affirm this with Gunton and Pannenberg and against Moltmann who argues that the being of God is constituted by the monarchy of the Father. Ibid., 39; Pannenberg, *Systematic Theology*, 1:325; Moltmann, *The Trinity and the Kingdom*, 165.

prehensible, for by describing the coinherence and interpenetration of the Triune Persons, it is possible to envisage how the threefold God is yet one.

The confession that God is Triune originates from reflecting on God's actions in the divine economy—the space-time administration of God's actions in history. That is, from reflecting on the divine missions of Son and Spirit the early church concluded that in the divine economy, God is Triune. However, the doctrine of the Trinity seeks to describe not only God's actions but also God's eternal being. Thus it is customary to speak of the *economic Trinity* to describe God as revealed in the divine economy, and the *ontological* or *immanent Trinity* to describe the eternal being of God. The doctrine of the ontological Trinity underpins and verifies *God's* self-revelation in time and space by guaranteeing that who God has revealed himself to be (the economic Trinity) is actually who God is in and of himself (the ontological Trinity). The doctrine of the Trinity holds that the ontological and economic Trinity truthfully correspond to one another, so in Pannenberg's words, "as God reveals himself, so he is in his eternal deity."[27] The purpose of the doctrine of the *ontological Trinity* is that God really *is* who God is revealed to be in Jesus Christ and the Holy Spirit. There is no different sort of God potentially hidden behind Jesus and the Spirit, for in the Incarnation and at Pentecost we have to do with the self-giving of God. However, some theologians reject this true correspondence between the economic and ontological Trinity, and suggest that the language of God as Father, Son, and Spirit is metaphorical and should not be pressed too far.

At the *After Newbigin* conference, Perry Schmidt-Leukel suggests that trinitarian formulas are "to be understood as somehow analogical, metaphorical, symbolic, or mythological approximations to a reality that in itself lies completely beyond human comprehension and description?"[28] Similarly, in her contribution on this theme, Frances Young, drawing on Gregory of Nazianzus, says that whilst human beings can in some measure know God in the *oikonomia*, she says "But the subject matter of *theologia* is beyond human conception or speech, and only heretical busybodies attempt to speculate."[29] In other words, it is not possible to know whether the

---

27. Pannenberg, *Systematic Theology*, 300. Many recent accounts of the doctrine of the Trinity have followed Karl Rahner in affirming that the economic Trinity *is* the immanent Trinity, and the immanent Trinity *is* the economic Trinity. Rahner, *The Trinity*, 22. This dictum, sometimes known as Rahner's rule, arguably goes too far by simply identifying God's eternal being with God's being in his self-revelation. For God's self-revelation to be true it must really correspond to God's eternal being, but to completely identify the two is to confuse the order of knowing with the order of being. Gunton, *Father, Son and Holy Spirit*, 43.

28. Schmidt-Leukel, "Mission and Trinitarian Theology," 63.

29. Young, "The Uncontainable God," 87.

economic and ontological Trinity truly correspond, and the subject of God's being *in se* belongs solely to apophatic theology. In Heather Ward's response to Schmidt-Leukel, she rightly explains that all metaphorical language intends to convey likeness within otherness. Consequently, the doctrine of the Trinity does use analogical and metaphorical language and as such conveys some true likeness which thus rules out Schmidt-Leukel's suggestion that the divine reality 'lies *completely* beyond human comprehension and description.' Ward says, "Christian theology has . . . never been entirely apophatic. The scandal of the incarnation makes possible and necessary a kataphatic theology; the human word does, at some level, participate in the truth of the Word."[30] Hence, contra to Young, the subject matter of *theologia* is not *completely* beyond human conception or speech. More seriously, Schmidt-Leukel's proposal that trinitarian language is "symbolic, or mythological approximations to a reality that in itself lies completely beyond human comprehension and description" is a betrayal of the incarnation and Pentecost, the two definitive acts of divine self-revelation in which God has given himself to be partially but nevertheless truly known. Whilst Young is rightly concerned to articulate "God's essential otherness,"[31] that even in God's self-revelation God remains hidden, she is wrong to say that God *in se* is 'beyond human conception or speech.' One can speak accurately of God *in se* because the ontological and economic Trinity truly correspond. In God's self-presentation in Christ and the Spirit, God has truly given himself, and so exclusively apophatic language for God is irrevocably forbidden.

The doctrine of the Trinity is important essentially because it seeks to truthfully describe the being of God.[32] In describing the being of God, the doctrine of the Trinity articulates a mystery, and in the person of Christ and in his person alone, comprehensibility prevails over incomprehensibility.[33] Thus, Jürgen Moltmann explains "The intention and consequence of the doctrine of the Trinity is not only the deification of Christ; it is even more the Christianization of the concept of God. God cannot be comprehended without Christ, and Christ cannot be understood without God."[34] The doctrine of the Trinity teaches that accurate, truthful and reliable knowledge of God is possible because God has disclosed and introduced himself in the person of Jesus Christ. Right knowledge of God is vital not only in itself,

---

30. Ward, "The Use and Misuse," 74, emphasis added.

31. Young, "The Uncontainable God," 88.

32. Jenson says "The primal function of trinitarian teaching is to *identify* the *theos* in 'theology'" (Jenson, *Systematic Theology*, 1:60, emphasis original).

33. Dalferth, "The Eschatological Roots," 170.

34. Moltmann, *The Trinity and the Kingdom*, 131–32.

but also, because God is the source and origin of all creation, the being and character of God determines everything else and so has enormous practical consequences. Schwöbel argues, "That this is the case is not a matter of theological principle but of historical observation."[35] The doctrine of the Triune God is crucial, therefore, for rightly shaping one's view of reality. Gunton suggests that "the value of the theology of the Trinity lies more in enabling a rethinking of the topics of theology and culture than in offering a privileged view of the being of God."[36] This is why he speaks of "doing theology from the Trinity" because "everything looks—and indeed is—different in the light of the Trinity."[37]

## *Newbigin's Call for a Trinitarian Missiology*

Newbigin believes it is vital that missiology is decisively trinitarian for numerous reasons, the first of which is contained in his bold assertion that "the doctrine of the Trinity . . . is the necessary starting point of preaching."[38] I discuss this claim in detail in chapter 6, but simply put, he claims that a missiology that is not thoroughly trinitarian is a betrayal of the gospel, which reveals and bears witness to the Triune God. Second, Newbigin contends that to think through missiological questions in a theological manner requires understanding the *missio ecclesiae* in terms of the doctrine of God as Father, Son and Spirit.[39] To locate the church's mission apart from the mission of the Triune God is to misunderstand it. Furthermore, these missiological questions in turn throw light on the doctrine of the Trinity, for Newbigin argues, "we can begin to understand the coherence and the relevance of the trinitarian faith as it illuminates the [missiological] questions we are asking."[40] Third, locating the church's mission within the historical trinitarian mission of God is to find a permanent theological justification and motivation for it. In the past the Christian missionary enterprise has been tied with colonialism and with the belief that world history was moving towards a more just, human and peaceful world order, so when these beliefs were brought into question, confidence in the church's mission was

---

35. Schwöbel, "The Renaissance of Trinitarian Theology," 9–10. He does acknowledge, however, that "the relationship between our views of God and our views on the order of personal and social relationships is complex" (ibid., 11).
36. Gunton, *The Promise*, xxix.
37. Ibid., xxix, 4–5.
38. Newbigin, *Trinitarian Doctrine*, 35.
39. Ibid., 82.
40. Ibid., 51.

shattered.⁴¹ It is in this context that Newbigin wrote *Trinitarian Doctrine for Today's Mission* and he reminds his readers that the church's mission is not merely a human effort about which one can be optimistic or pessimistic.⁴² He says,

> We are not engaged in an enterprise of our own choosing or devising. We are invited to participate in an activity of God which is the central meaning of creation itself. We are invited to become, through the presence of the Holy Spirit, participants in the Son's loving obedience to the Father.⁴³

Fourth, since the church's mission is a participation in the mission of God, a trinitarian missiology reminds the church that it is God who is the primary missionary. It is comforting for the church to know that the burden does not primarily rest on her shoulders, but that she is called to work for and with God for the accomplishment of his mission. Practically, this is of enormous consequence, and drawing from the writings of Roland Allen, Newbigin argues that the apostle Paul's missionary success was chiefly down to his 'method' which "rests on this single point: that the Holy Spirit of God is himself the missionary."⁴⁴ Fifth, a trinitarian missiology is also vital because Newbigin observed how missiology goes astray when it overemphasizes either the Holy Spirit or the person of Christ. A fully trinitarian missiology thus enables theology to keep a right proportion to the missionary task.⁴⁵ The doctrine of the Trinity is the uniquely Christian description of the being of God, and the church's mission is to bear witness, to the ends of the earth, to this God who was in Christ reconciling the world to himself. Missiology must therefore be trinitarian for it to be Christian.

## *Divine Revelation as the Epistemology of the Doctrine of the Trinity*

The subject of revelation is crucial to missiology because it investigates theological epistemology, that is, the origin and content of our knowledge of God. As Western society transitions from modernity towards late/

---

41. Ibid., 22–23.
42. Ibid., 21–22.
43. Ibid., 83.
44. Ibid., 71. Similarly, Pope John Paul II called the Holy Spirit "the principal agent of mission" (Encyclical Letter *Redemptoris missio*, quoted in Bevans, "God Inside Out," 103).
45. Newbigin, *Trinitarian Doctrine*, 82.

post-modernity, satisfactorily addressing epistemological questions is becoming increasingly urgent for the mission of the Western church to its own culture. The origin of revelation is the Triune God, and the doctrine of the Trinity itself, like all other doctrines, is grounded in revelation, in God's self-disclosure. The heart of the church's message is bearing faithful witness to the Triune God, and from many quarters God's identity as Triune has increasingly been challenged. The church's mission includes apologetics,[46] that is, defending the faith, at the heart of which is giving a reasoned account of God's Triune identity. Furthermore, it is essential for a *trinitarian* missiology to first articulate an account of God's Triune identity *before* proceeding to develop other essential features of a theology of mission, otherwise it will drift away from its theological moorings.

The Triune God's self-revelation in Christ and the Spirit is the starting point for both Christian faith and all branches of Christian theology, including missiology. Since God's Triune self-revelation is the starting point, the truth of the doctrine of the Trinity cannot be demonstrated or verified on other grounds. Such an attempt "would be just as fallacious as attempting to justify ultimates in terms of what is not ultimate."[47] T. F. Torrance explains,

> Christians found that the supreme truth of God's incarnate self-revelation in salvation history could not be known on the strength of anything other than itself, but only through a primary act of cognitive assent to its compelling claims and saving impact. That is to say, the God and Father of our Lord Jesus Christ is to be known through faith creatively called forth from people in response to the thrust of its intrinsic truth upon them, and in sharp antithesis to what they had believed about God before.[48]

---

46. Newbigin's attitude towards apologetics can be understood both as extremely positive, and as a disavowal of the whole enterprise, depending upon how "apologetics" is defined. Newbigin had no time for the kind of apologetics that sought to use rational means to persuade unbelievers, within their existing plausibility structures, that faith in Christ is reasonable. He did not attempt to provide 'evidence that demands a verdict' (see Josh McDowell). However, much of Newbigin's work is rightly understood as apologetics because he sought to defend and explain the Christian faith as reasonable, based on a distinctly Christian plausibility structure. Newbigin's intellectual and spiritual biographer Geoffrey Wainwright entitles the tenth chapter of his *Lesslie Newbigin*, "The Christian Apologist." Newbigin's apologetics consisted of challenging modern Western notions of what is considered 'reasonable' by critiquing the questionable assumptions of their underlying plausibility structures, in the light of the gospel. This became the focus of his life's work after returning from India, and Wainright suggests "It is as an apologist to the doubting and to the unbelieving that he now became chiefly known" (*Lesslie Newbigin*, 335).

47. Torrance, *The Christian Doctrine of God*, 28.

48. Ibid., 19.

What Torrance is ruling out is any kind of epistemological foundationalism by which one can test the claim of the Triune God's self-revelation on the basis of external criteria. This opposes Kant's view that God's self-revelation could be incorporated into another category, that of being or ontology.[49] On the contrary, being or ontology is understood by first understanding who God is, because he is the ground of all being and the Being from whom all being derives. Consequently, Karl Barth says,

> According to Holy Scripture God's revelation is a ground which has no higher or deeper ground above or below it but is an absolute ground in itself, and therefore a court from which there can be no possible appeal to a higher court. Its reality and its truth do not rest on a superior reality and truth. They do not have to be actualized or validated as reality from this or any other standpoint. They are not measured by the reality and truth found at this other point.[50]

If it is indeed true, as Christian faith claims, that the everlasting God was, is and forever will be Father, Son and Holy Spirit, that all that is comes from him who is the Creator of all, and that this God has revealed himself in the life of Jesus, then this revelation is ultimate and therefore defines, qualifies and relativizes all other knowledge. Hence, Barth says, "One can either obey or disobey, either believe or not believe, what is called revelation in the Bible—both are possible—but from no other standpoint can one get into a position to see whether it has really happened and its content is true."[51]

To take revelation seriously as *God's* revelation, "then in any doctrine of revelation we must deal expressly with the point that constitutes the mystery of revelation, the starting-point of all thought and language about it."[52] Barth unambiguously identifies this point as the incarnation of God in Christ, and this explains the christocentric nature of his theology. Barth says,

> A church dogmatics must, of course, be christologically determined as a whole and in all its parts . . . If dogmatics cannot regard itself and cause itself to be regarded as fundamentally Christology, it has assuredly succumbed to some alien sway and is already on the verge of losing its character as church dogmatics.[53]

49. Barth, *CD* II/1, 311.
50. Barth, *CD* I/1, 305.
51. Ibid., 305.
52. Barth, *CD* I/2, 124.
53. Ibid., 123.

Whilst Christology must be central, Christology cannot be rightly comprehended apart from trinitarian theology. God's self-revelation in the person of Christ is a revelation of the Son who submits to and loves his Father, and who is conceived, empowered, led, and resurrected by the Holy Spirit. Therefore, Barth says that the doctrines of the Trinity and Christology must be placed at the head of all theological pronouncements, and treated as the foundation for all these pronouncements.[54] Following Athanasius, Augustine, and Barth, Newbigin says, "The twin dogmas of the Incarnation and Trinity thus form the starting point for a way of understanding reality as a whole."[55] For Newbigin, these doctrines provide the twin foundations for the understanding of reality.[56] Following Barth's lead T. F. Torrance says, "The doctrines of the Trinity and of the incarnation thus form together the nucleus at the heart of the Christian conception of God and constitute the ontological and epistemological basis for the formulation of every Christian doctrine."[57] For this reason one cannot write a prolegomenon to the theology of the Trinity "because no prolegomenon to theology can avoid substantive theological content, if not explicit, then certainly implicit."[58] This theological content must follow and derive from a theology of the Trinity, and therefore it is more fitting to speak of "a *post*legomenon, a word in response to revelation that is enabled by God himself."[59] All branches of Christian theology, including the theology of mission, must therefore be christologically and trinitarianly determined. In developing a *trinitarian* missiology, therefore, I am simply articulating a *Christian* missiology that is *by definition trinitarian*.

## *The Special Dogmatic Status of the Doctrine of the Trinity*

Schleiermacher and Barth both recognized the special status of the doctrine of the Trinity. In fact, according to Schwöbel this is about the only aspect of theology they agree upon. This "led both not to attempt finding a place for the doctrine within the framework of dogmatic *loci* but to develop its significance in the epilogomena in Schleiermacher's case and in the prolegomena in Barth's."[60] Although the substance of their trinitarian theologies was

54. Ibid., 124.
55. Newbigin, *Foolishness To The Greeks*, 90, see also 133.
56. Newbigin, *The Other Side of 1984*, 24, 62.
57. Torrance, *The Christian Doctrine of God*, 30.
58. Rae, "Prolegomena," 9.
59. Ibid., 10.
60. Schwöbel, "The Renaissance of Trinitarian Theology," 2.

widely divergent, according to Schwöbel they both agreed that this doctrine "relates to the shape and structure of the whole framework of Christian doctrine and therefore cannot be presented as one doctrine within that framework."[61] Earlier he writes that Barth and Schleiermacher agreed on the doctrine's 'peculiar status', and he is right that neither sought to include the doctrine within the dogmatic framework. However, it is a mistake to say that Schleiermacher believes the doctrine of the Trinity 'relates to the shape and structure of the whole framework of Christian doctrine' as Barth certainly does; for Schleiermacher the opposite is true. Schleiermacher tucked the doctrine of the Trinity away at the end of his *The Christian Faith* precisely because he did not believe it should influence the substance of his theology.

For Schleiermacher the doctrine of the Trinity was a means to an end, to underpin God's redemption of humanity. For him the essential elements of the Trinity are God's real presence in Christ and "in the common Spirit of the Church" because for Jesus to be redeemer and for the church "to be the Bearer and Perpetuator of the redemption through Christ,"[62] God's presence in each must be real. Schleiermacher is clear that "the main pivots of the ecclesiastical doctrine—the being of God in Christ and in the Christian Church—are independent of the doctrine of the Trinity."[63] The doctrine of the Trinity for him simply strengthens rather than ensures the fact of redemption through Christ and his church. Logically, Schleiermacher concludes, "In virtue of this connexion, we rightly regard the doctrine of the Trinity, in so far as it is a deposit of these elements, as the coping-stone of Christian doctrine."[64] The German word translated into 'coping-stone' is *schlussstein* which can also be translated capstone or key stone. Schleiermacher's use of *schlussstein* is in accordance with understanding the doctrine of the Trinity as the crowning achievement, the finishing stone of the theological structure, binding the other doctrines of soteriology, ecclesiology, Christology and Pneumatology together. In colloquial terms, the doctrine of the Trinity was for Schleiermacher the icing on the theological cake. It was precisely this approach to the doctrine of the Trinity that Newbigin was most critical of. Newbigin emphatically states,

> It is not, as we have sometimes seemed to say, a kind of intellectual capstone which can be put on to the top of the arch at the very end; it is, on the contrary, what Athanasius called it, the

---

61. Ibid., 2.
62. Schleiermacher, *The Christian Faith*, 738–39.
63. Ibid., 741.
64. Ibid., 739.

*arché*, the presupposition without which the preaching of the Gospel in a pagan world cannot begin.[65]

In the framing of Schleiermacher's dogmatics, the doctrine of the Trinity formed the conclusion because he did not believe it was important and so did not want it to impinge upon anything else. Barth, in his *Church Dogmatics*, intentionally reversed this ordering by making the doctrine of the Trinity the *arché* of dogmatics, as Newbigin also has done for missiology.

Methodologically, Schwöbel explains the decision to discuss the doctrine of the Trinity at the start of dogmatics meant that it "must be conceived as the gateway through which the theological exposition of all that can be said about God in Christian theology must pass."[66] Anatolios makes the same point in asserting that the "Trinitarian doctrine is the hermeneutical key to Christian faith."[67] Jenson concurs, and volume one of his two-volume systematic theology is entitled *The Triune God*. Explaining this methodological decision Jenson says,

> The primal systematic function of trinitarian teaching is to *identify* the *theos* in 'theology.' Under most circumstances, such teaching must therefore appear at the very beginning of a theological system. For if a systematically developed discourse about God precedes the exposition of Trinity, there is a danger that a nontrinitarian identification of God may be hidden in that discourse, to confuse all that follows.[68]

Jenson argues that the doctrine of the Trinity must precede all other doctrines within a theological architectonic because one's doctrine of God determines and affects all other doctrines. One cannot understand and articulate any doctrine such as creation, salvation, or anthropology, without working on the basis of an assumption of who God is, and these doctrinal formulations will be reliable or faulty depending upon the accuracy of this

---

65. Newbigin, *Trinitarian Doctrine*, 36. Newbigin draws here on Cochrane, *Christianity and Classical Culture*, 362.

66. Schwöbel, "The Renaissance of Trinitarian Theology," 6. Pannenberg concurs, saying "under the sign of the unity of the immanent and economic Trinity the rest of dogmatics in the doctrine of creation, christology, soteriology, ecclesiology, and eschatology will be part of the exposition of the doctrine of the Trinity" (Pannenberg, *Systematic Theology*, 1:335).

67. Anatolios, "The Immediately Triune God," 166.

68. Jenson, *Systematic Theology*, 1:60, emphasis original. Similarly, Schwöbel says trinitarian theology "effects all aspects of the enterprise of doing theology in its various disciplines. Because of that it is difficult to point to any one area of theological reflection that is not potentially affected by being viewed from a trinitarian perspective" (Schwöbel, "The Renaissance of Trinitarian Theology," 1–2).

assumption. Likewise, for a Christian missiology that is necessarily *trinitarian*, God's Triune identity must be elucidated before describing salvation in Christ, the mission of the church, inter-faith dialogue and so on. Instead of building a missiological superstructure on unexamined and potentially inaccurate assumptions concerning the doctrine of God, it is wiser to explicitly exposit a doctrine of the Trinity as both the prolegomenon and foundation for a Christian missiology. As T. F. Torrance rightly states, "God's distinctive self-revelation as Holy Trinity, One Being, Three Persons, creates the overall framework within which all Christian theology is to be formulated."[69] For all areas of Christian theology, including missiology, the doctrine of the Trinity uniquely provides this framework, not because it offers a unique concept of God, but because it "insists on the fundamental and irrevocable difference between God and all our models, ideas and concepts of God."[70]

The doctrine of the Trinity is accorded primacy not only because it affects and determines all areas of Christian doctrine, but as T. F. Torrance explains, because

> properly understood it is the nerve and center of them all, configures them all, and is so deeply integrated with them that when they are held apart from the doctrine of the Trinity they are seriously defective in truth and become malformed. Moreover, if the Christian conception of God and of all his activity toward us in creation and redemption is essentially trinitarian, then the trinitarian perspective must be allowed to pervade all Christian worship and practice, all interpretation of the Holy Scriptures, and all proclamation of the Gospel, and must be given a regulative role in the dynamic structure of all Christian thought and action.[71]

Unless all Christian doctrine is regulated by the doctrine of the Trinity it will go astray and no longer be *Christian* theology. It is for this reason that Pannenberg states "the doctrine of the Trinity is an anticipatory sum of the whole content of Christian dogmatics."[72] Missiology concerns the saving actions of God, and so in articulating a trinitarian missiology the first task is to describe the being and life of the Triune God, Father, Son and Spirit.

---

69. Torrance, *The Christian Doctrine of God*, 2.
70. Dalferth, "The Eschatological Roots," 169.
71. Torrance, *The Christian Doctrine of God*, 31.
72. Pannenberg, *Systematic Theology*, 1:335.

## GOD'S BEING AD INTRA

### Intra-Trinitarian Origins: The Eternal Processions

#### Introduction

Traditionally the distinctions between the divine *hypostases* have been explained with recourse to relations of origin, and they stand in dissimilar relations of origin to one another.[73] The Eastern Orthodox Church distinguished between the generation of the Son and the procession of the Spirit, following Johannine language. Latin theology in the Middle Ages spoke of the procession of both Son and Spirit, but the procession of the Son was begetting, and the Spirit was breathing. Thus to distinguish the Persons of the Godhead by relations of origin, the Father actively begets, the Son is passively begotten, and the Spirit is passively breathed.[74]

#### The Eternally Begotten Son

The Nicene Creed confesses the faith of the church when it affirms, 'We believe in one Lord, Jesus Christ, the only Son of God, *eternally begotten of the Father . . . begotten, not made*, of one Being with the Father.' The concept of the Son as eternally begotten was first described by Origen. For Origen there was no time when the Son was not, as Athanasius was later to argue.[75] Jenson explains that Origen's concept of the Son's eternal generation denies "the generally presumed equivalents between having a beginning and having a temporal beginning."[76] The Son's begetting was eternal, that is, in eternity. Hodgson credits Origen with freeing "trinitarian theology from one element in subordinationism, *i.e.* temporal secondariness, yet other elements remained."[77] The image of generation safeguards the direct

---

73. Barth, *CD* I/1, 363.

74. Pannenberg, *Systematic Theology*, 1:305.

75. Ibid., 275. Pannenberg notes Maurice Wiles' objection that in Origen the eternal generation does not here apply to the Son alone but to all spiritual creatures. In other words, Origen's formulation does not necessarily lead to orthodox trinitarian doctrine. Nevertheless, he is important for introducing this concept to theology.

76. Jenson, *Systematic Theology*, 1:99.

77. Hodgson, *The Doctrine of the Trinity*, 100. Origen's Christology is not without fault, as Schleiermacher explains that for Origen, "the Father is God absolutely, while the Son and Spirit are God only by participation in the Divine Essence—an idea which is positively rejected by orthodox Church teachers, but secretly underlies their whole procedure" (Schleiermacher, *The Christian Faith*, 747).

continuity between the being of the Father and that of the Son, thus ruling out all improper talk of an exalted creature or a descended divine being.[78]

The eternal generation or begetting of the Son differs from common uses of the term generate/beget, for it describes the bringing forth of God by God. It is thus set apart from creaturely begetting, which describes the generation of one creature by another, and the act of creating, in which God creates a creature.[79] It also differs from "intellectual generation (e.g., in the teacher-pupil relation) and that of spiritual generation (as in believers when they become children of God)."[80] Schleiermacher believes that although the begetting of the Son is as different as possible from any form of temporal generation, nevertheless, "the term itself, if it means anything at all, must at least indicate a relationship of dependence."[81] This insight cannot be denied, though the consequences he draws from it can be. He says this undeniably suggests that the power and glory of the Father is greater than that of the Son, which is a road that ends in Arianism or another variant of subordinationism; a road that the Nicene theologians established led outside of *Christian* theology. However, Schleiermacher is right that the Son is indeed dependent on the Father for his generation, but this dependency is not unidirectional. There was never a 'time' when God was not God, Father, Son and Spirit. Therefore, there was never a 'time' when the Son was not yet begotten, because there was never a 'time' when the Son was not. Nor was there ever a 'time' when the Father was without his Son, for then he would not be Father. Hence, the Father's begetting of the Son was an *eternal* begetting, without beginning or end.

Rather than seeing the language of begetting as a threat to the Son's divinity, Barth positively sees in his begetting "the real becoming of Jesus Christ, His eternal becoming appropriate to Him as God, His relation of origin and dependence as God in His distinctive mode of being."[82] Luther explains that the Son is *homoousios* with the Father and is equal to him in all things, "except that He is from the Father and not the Father from Him, like as radiance is from brightness of the divine essence and not the brightness of the divine essence from the radiance."[83] Granting the asymmetry of this language, it is nevertheless the case that the Father is not Father without Son, even if the order is from Father to Son and not *vice versa*.

78. Barth, *The Göttingen Dogmatics*, 122.
79. Barth, *CD* I/1, 433.
80. Ibid., 431.
81. Schleiermacher, *The Christian Faith*, 743.
82. Barth, *CD* I/1, 430.
83. Quoted in ibid., 441.

### The *Logos Asarkos*

In the light of the incarnation the Son is known to be Jesus of Nazareth, but prior to the incarnation it is necessary to posit the *logos asarkos*, the Word without flesh. In asserting the necessity of positing the *logos asarkos* I am aware that this is not without contention. Contemporary theologians hold a variety of views on this matter, and it is in the context of this ongoing dialogue that I seek to articulate and substantiate this assertion. The positing of the *logos asarkos* is necessary to ensure that the incarnation, for the Son, was genuinely a novel and free divine act and that Jesus is none other than the eternal divine Son or Word of God. God's act of love for humanity in the incarnation was a free act in that God the Son did not have to become human. Positing the *logos asarkos* means the Son was not enfleshed until being conceived in Mary's womb by the Holy Spirit, thus paying attention to the historical density of God's economic actions. Some theologians, such as Robert Jenson, are very nervous about *logos asarkos* language. He says,

> Thus despite what may at first seem the obvious reading of the prologue, we may not, if we follow the Gospel it introduces, conceive the pre-existence of the Son as the existence of a divine entity that has simply not yet become the created personality of the Gospels.[84]

The chief problem in postulating the *logos asarkos* is that it can quickly lead to the unknowability of God. It can suggest that there is a divine figure lurking behind God's self-revelation in Jesus, thus questioning the authenticity of this self-revelation. If Jesus is not identical to the eternal Son of God, this *logos asarkos*, then this raises questions about the identity of Jesus and the identity of God. In order to ensure that which is most important in all theology, that God really *was* in Christ, that Jesus really is *homoousios* with the Father, one cannot permit a sundering of Jesus from the eternal Word of God. However, one does not have to make these foundational theological errors when affirming the *logos asarkos*.

There was never a time when the Son was not, but there was a time when the Son was without human flesh. To suggest that the Son always had human flesh is theologically and scripturally unwarranted and it also undermines the authenticity, actuality and radicality of the incarnation. According to the Scriptures God sent his Son, which must mean the pre-incarnate Logos, to be born of a woman.[85] There is complete continuity between Jesus and the eternal Logos, with the exception of Jesus' humanity. In the event

---

84. Jenson, *Systematic Theology*, 1:139.
85. Gal 4:4.

of the incarnation, the *logos asarkos* irreversibly becomes the *logos ensarkos*. However, this event was preceded by the eternal decrees of election which include the decrees of creation and incarnation. Since these decrees all precede the creation of time and space, God's decision to create cannot be separated from his decision to exist *for us* in the sending his Son in human flesh. It is not possible to prise open a 'sequence' within God's eternal decrees of election, because such temporal language does not apply to pre-temporal decrees. Confessing the *logos asarkos* prior to the divine decrees stresses the free and gracious nature of the divine decision of the incarnation of the Son. Those who reject this are left with the alternative of suggesting that the Son is eternally the *incarnandus*, on the way to becoming incarnate. This unacceptably compromises God's freedom because the incarnation would become a necessary act. Furthermore, this view is in danger of panentheism for it eternally requires a creation to which the Son is sent, thus eternalizing creation.

Since the eternal decrees of election the Son of God was *incarnandus* and after the incarnation the Son is and forever will be *incarnatus*, so there is no longer a *logos asarkos*. The eternal Son was the *logos asarkos* (God apart from us), who in the eternal decrees became the *incarnandus* (God for us), and who two thousand years ago became incarnate as the person of Jesus (God with us). So, now there is no 'hidden Son' or *logos asarkos* 'behind' the person of Jesus for the eternal Son is forever the God-man associated with Galilee and Golgotha. George Hunsinger explains that since pre-temporal election begins with the *logos asarkos* and ends with the *logos ensarkos*, "this makes any human access to the *logos asarkos* of no practical or theoretical consequence."[86] This ensures that Jesus is truly *homoousios* with the Father and guarantees the authenticity of divine self-revelation and the efficacy of divine reconciliation. God's intention in Christ to become human and live amongst the creatures made in his image and likeness is the beating heart of the eternal divine decrees, in which the *logos asarkos* became the *incarnandus*, and thus testifying to God's loving intentions, literally, from the beginning. It speaks therefore of God's unwavering resolve for his creatures to share in the blessedness of the communion that is the divine life.

## Filioque

Turning our attention to the eternal procession of the Spirit, there is an approximately millennium-old dispute over whether the Spirit proceeds from the Father alone—the Eastern Orthodox view and original wording of the

---

86. Hunsinger, "Election and the Trinity," 188.

Nicene Creed—or from the Father and the Son (*filioque*)—the Western Roman Catholic and Protestant view and wording of the modified Nicene Creed. For the purposes of articulating a trinitarian missiology it is not necessary to enter into a sustained discussion of the *filioque*, but it is worth mentioning three areas that are potentially at stake in the debate that directly bear upon a trinitarian missiology.

First, numerous scholars blame the *filioque* and its underlying Augustinian Pneumatology for the Western tradition's under-developed theology of the Holy Spirit.[87] This includes the historic Western tendency to deny that there is a proper mission of the Holy Spirit by rendering him to be *merely* an agent in the Son's ongoing mission, applying Christ's work to believers.[88] There are self-evident parallels between the *filioque* and the tendency to subject the person and work of the Spirit to God the Son, although the former does necessitate the latter. Furthermore, Gunton states that "the neglect of the Holy Spirit and the underplaying of the human life and ministry of Jesus . . . are simply two sides of the same coin."[89] Historically, Jesus' miracles are often attributed to his divine nature rather than to the empowering of the Spirit, with the ontologically focused Logos Christology crowding out the more functionally oriented Spirit Christology.[90] For missiology it is essential that there is a disavowal of all docetic tendencies. It is also essential that there is a fully developed Pneumatology, including a Spirit Christology which emphasizes the reciprocal relation of Son and Spirit, and an affirmation of the proper mission of the Holy Spirit because, as Newbigin says, "It is he who is, properly speaking, the missionary."[91]

Second, theologians on both sides of the *filioque* debate have said that what is at stake therein is the veracity of God's self-revelation. For Barth, since the Spirit is the Spirit of Father and Son in the economy and eternally, "then in the one case as in the other the Holy Spirit is the Spirit of the love of the Father and the Son, and so *procedens ex Patre Filioque*."[92] Barth says that to deny this is to deny that God's self-revelation truly corresponds to God's eternal being, thus compromising God's self-revelation. On the other side, Gunton believes that the *filioque* is to blame for Western tendencies towards

---

87. Schreiter says "Certainly one consequence of the addition of the *filioque* in the Nicene Creed has been to keep the theology of the Holy Spirit underdeveloped" (Schreiter, "Jesus Christ and Mission," 435). See also Gunton, *The Promise*, 131.

88. Coffey, "A Proper Mission."

89. Gunton, *Father, Son and Holy Spirit*, 54.

90. However, this is a feature of the whole Christian tradition and not only the Western Church. Badcock, *Light of Truth*, 41.

91. Newbigin, *Trinitarian Doctrine*, 40.

92. Barth, *CD* I/1, 483.

modalism.[93] For him, the teaching that the Spirit proceeds from Father and Son invites speculation concerning their underlying unity, suggesting there is a god behind the God revealed in the gospel. He says "while there remain two apparently ultimate principles, however unified in communion, discontented minds will seek that which underlies them."[94] I believe neither argument is incontrovertible, but both share the justified and important concern that God really *is* who he has revealed himself to be in Christ by the Spirit.

Third, an account of the doctrine of the Trinity must preserve the distinctions between the Triune Persons in order to represent faithfully the God of the gospel to which the *missio ecclesiae* bears witness. If the *filioque* is affirmed then, positively, there is an implied reciprocity between Father and Son. However, since to the Son is attributed a source of divinity, it is important to stress that the Son is not a fount or source *in the same way* as the Father, "obscuring the unique direction of 'sending' within the communion of God."[95] In other words, the trinitarian order must be maintained. Gunton believes that affirming the *filioque* smudges the hypostatic distinctives particularly between Son and Spirit, leading to a more hierarchical rather than a reciprocal conception of their interrelation. If the Spirit's eternal origin is in the Father *filioque*, then it is important to prevent a quasi-hierarchical concept of the Son-Spirit interrelation from eclipsing the mutuality between Son and Spirit. In the New Testament Jesus is a gift of the Spirit through his miraculous conception, he receives the Spirit at his baptism, and he gives the Spirit at Pentecost.[96] A trinitarian missiology needs to be faithful to God's self-presentation as recorded in Scripture by paying attention to the intra-trinitarian distinctives, including the priority of the Father and the reciprocity between both Father and Son and Son and Spirit.

Regardless of whether a theologian or missiologist affirms or denies the *filioque*, he/she must take care to be robust theologically in at least these three areas. A sound trinitarian missiology will include a developed (as opposed to an under-developed) Pneumatology, will underscore and not undermine the fact that in divine self-revelation God really and truly gives himself, and will carefully attend to the Triune hypostatic particularities,

---

93. Whether Western theology has modalistic tendencies is debatable, but the non-trinitarian nature of much of the Western tradition has been well documented by theologians including Karl Rahner, Jürgen Moltmann, Michael Buckley, S. J., James B. Torrance and Vladimir Lossky.

94. Gunton, *Father, Son and Holy Spirit*, 55–56.

95. For this reason Fiddes rejects the *filioque*, though of course this inherent potential danger does not necessarily need to be realized. Fiddes, *Participating in God*, 80.

96. Gunton says as well as the Son being an agent of the pouring out of the Spirit, "the incarnate Son is equally the gift of the Spirit. We have to speak of the Spirit's Jesus as much as of Jesus' Spirit" (Gunton, *The Promise*, 132–33).

including the reciprocity between the Triune Persons and the revealed trinitarian order.

## The Monarchy of God

### Introduction

The identity of Jesus is central to the gospel, which is at the heart of the church's mission. Rather than simply equating Jesus with God, Newbigin explains that in the gospels Jesus "does not appear among men as a theophany, in the sense of a temporary manifestation of the Ruler of all things; he appears as the Son who lovingly submits himself to the will of him who rules all things."[97] The New Testament describes God as Father, Son, and Spirit, and each is described in different and distinct ways, yet within a specific order. Drawing particularly on Pannenberg, I shall discuss the order amongst the Triune Persons and its important implications for missiology.

John Calvin describes the economically revealed trinitarian order, in which

> to the Father is attributed the beginning of activity, and the fountain and wellspring of all things; to the Son, wisdom, counsel, and the ordered disposition of all things; but to the Spirit is assigned the power and efficacy of that activity. Indeed, although the eternity of the Father is also the eternity of the Son and the Spirit, since God could never exist apart from his wisdom and power, and we must not seek in eternity a *before* or an *after*, nevertheless the observance of an order is not meaningless or superfluous, when the Father is thought of as first, then from him the Son, and finally from both the Spirit.[98]

Thus it is quite natural at some level to speak of an inherent and loving submission of the Son and Spirit to the Father, although the word submission needs to be carefully qualified.[99] In seeking to convey knowledge of God revealed in Jesus and the Spirit, as the missionary church does, there are two opposite extremes to be avoided. Over-emphasizing the priority of the Father tends to lead towards subordinationism, thus undermining the full divinity of Son and Spirit, and strongly affirming the co-equality of the Triune Persons can lead to overlooking the trinitarian order and hypostatic distinctives. Care must be taken to avoid both because they fail to accurately

---

97. Newbigin, *Trinitarian Doctrine*, 39.
98. Calvin, *Institutes*, I.xiii.18, 142–43, emphasis original.
99. BCC Study Commission, *The Forgotten Trinity Vol. 1*, 33.

reflect God's self-revelation in the divine economy, in which Jesus and the Spirit are truly God, *homoousios* with the Father by whom they are sent to accomplish his will. Therefore, it is important to establish the boundary-markers for trinitarian discourse between which lies the captivating and yet mysterious land that trinitarian theology seeks to chart.

## Trinitarian Order: God the Father as *Anarchos* and *Arché*

Logically, description of the trinitarian order described in the New Testament begins with the priority of the Father, for within both the Catholic and Protestant West and the Orthodox East there is an emphasis on the Father as the fount or source or cause of the Trinity.[100] Pannenberg explains that "Tradition has it that the Father alone is without origin (*anarchos*) among the three persons of the Trinity, that he is the origin and fount of deity for the Son and Spirit."[101] The term *arché* has often been used to describe the role of God the Father, meaning that the Father is the beginning, cause of being, origin, source or fount of the Son and Spirit. Regarding the monarchy of the Father, an equivalent term to *arché* is *aition* which means to cause or author. This was a dominant view in the early church, and according to Gunton, theologians such as Tertullian and Basil, and the council of Nicaea all affirmed that "the *substratum* of God is the Father."[102] The concepts *anarchos* and *arché* attributed to God the Father are theological twins. However, to say that the Father is *arché* in a strong sense can easily lead to an erroneous understanding, suggesting that the Father has a higher degree of deity than the Son and Spirit. Nevertheless, the priority of the Father also enjoys strong support from both Scripture and tradition.

Offering a modern restatement of the traditional understanding of God the Father as both the *arché* of the Trinity and *anarchos*, Moltmann asserts that the Son and Spirit are constituted in their relations of origin to the Father, whereas the Father is constituted through himself, and so is *anarchos*. "He being himself without origin, is the origin of the divine persons of the Son and the Spirit." The Son and the Spirit are constituted through their processions from the Father, but the "Father must be constituted through

---

100. Gunton, *The Promise*, 197.

101. Pannenberg, *Systematic Theology*, 1:311. Olin Curtis, speaking of the personal peculiarity of each Person in the Trinity, identifies the peculiarity of the Father as *that of origination*. Curtis, *The Christian Faith*, 502, referenced in Zahniser, "The Trinity," 11–12.

102. Gunton, *The Promise*, 54.

himself."[103] However, Moltmann is also careful to insist upon the co-divinity of the Triune Persons, saying "We have to distinguish between the constitution of the Trinity and the Trinity's inner life."[104] He argues that at the level of the Trinity's inner constitution the Father is *arché*, which he carefully qualifies,[105] but regarding the inner-trinitarian life the divine Persons are consubstantial and co-eternal, perichoretically inter-penetrating each other. He simultaneously affirms that the Father is the 'origin' of Son and Spirit, and that the Triune Persons are 'equally primordial'.[106]

Despite Moltmann's careful exposition of what is the dominant view in the Christian tradition on this subject, other voices in the tradition are even more cautious. Gregory of Nazianzus says "I should like to call the Father greater, because from him flows both the equality and being of the equals, but I am afraid to use the word origin (*arché*) lest I should make him the origin of inferiors."[107] When using the terms *arché* and *anarchos* I believe it is crucial to distinguish between trinitarian order among the Triune Persons who mutually share the same divine being (*homoousios*), and a quasi-ontological hierarchy within the Trinity.

To suggest that the Father is *arché* and *anarchos*, as Moltmann has done, is to assert that in some sense the divine substance is originally proper to the Father alone, and by derivation for Son and Spirit. Since the intra-trinitarian relations of origin are constitutive for the Son and Spirit only, and not the Father, the Father is the origin or cause of deity.[108] Pannenberg believes this is problematic for two reasons. First, it constitutes a relapse into pre-Nicene subordinationism because "If the Father, unlike the Son and Spirit, were to be equated with the divine substance, then the Son and Spirit would necessarily be hypostases that are subordinate to the supreme God."[109] Second, to hold that the Father alone is *anarchos* is to "rule out genuine mutuality in the relations of the trinitarian persons."[110] Furthermore, any ontological prioritizing of the Father over the Son and Spirit would mean that the latter derive from the former. Pannenberg says this "leads into the problems of

103. Moltmann, *The Trinity and the Kingdom*, 165.

104. Ibid., 183.

105. Firstly he says that the term derives from cosmology and therefore can only be haltingly applied to the Trinity. Secondly he says that in using it one must resist "the logical compulsion to monarchical reduction and the non-trinitarian notion of a single origin (both of which are inherent in it)" (ibid., 166).

106. Ibid.

107. Quoted in Gunton, *The Promise*, 198.

108. Pannenberg, *Systematic Theology*, 1:280.

109. Ibid., 283.

110. Ibid., 311–12.

either modalism on the one hand or subordinationism on the other. Neither then, can be true to the intentions of trinitarian dogma."[111] Both of these alternatives amount to theological and missiological disasters. Instead, he points to Athanasius' teaching to demonstrate that there is genuine mutuality between the divine Persons. "Athanasius . . . argued forcibly against the Arians that the Father would not be the Father without the Son."[112] There is therefore a relation of mutual 'dependence' between Father and Son, although they are not dependent on each other in the same way, for the Father begets and sends the Son and not vice versa. Despite Augustine's opinion that this is 'absurd', the relations between Father and Son are irreversible but the dependence is mutual.[113]

Continuing to draw on Athanasius, Pannenberg states that "the Father would not be the Father without the Son . . . therefore . . . he was never without the Son."[114] Spelling this out even further, Pannenberg says that because "the Father is not the Father without the Son . . . he does not have his Godhead without him."[115] This is quite contrary to classical Father-as-*anarchos* language such as that found in Thomas who, speaking of God the Father, says he "does not presuppose any person."[116] In making this bold move Pannenberg does away with the theology of God the Father as *anarchos* altogether. For this view then, John 5:26 is potentially theologically problematic. Jesus says "For just as the Father has life in himself, so he has granted the Son also to have life in himself." Despite first appearances, however, I do not think that Jesus' words here are contradictory to the view developed by Pannenberg drawing on Athanasius.

Interlude—John 5:26

John 5:26 cannot be rightly understood apart from John's framework of the Father-Son and the Father-Son-world relationship. John's presentation of the Father-Son relationship has an intrinsic order to it, such that the Father is greater than the Son (14:28). It is the Father that sends Jesus and not *vice versa* (John 6:39; 8:29; 9:4), and likewise it is the Son who does the Father's

111. Ibid., 298.
112. Ibid., 311–12.
113. Augustine, *De Trinitate* 7.2, see also 5.3, quoted in Jenson, *Systematic Theology*, 1:112.
114. Pannenberg, *Systematic Theology*, 1:273.
115. Ibid., 322.
116. *Tractatus de Trinitate*, Question 39, viii in Part One of *Summa Theologica*, quoted in Hodgson, *The Doctrine of the Trinity*, 159.

will (John 5:30; 17:4), and not the other way around. Complementing this order is John's presentation of the Father and Son/Word as inseparable and equally divine.[117] The Word who became flesh (1:14) was both with God in the beginning and indeed was God (1:1-2). Jesus says "The Father and I are one" (John 10:30). For this his hearers took up stones to stone him for blasphemy for he, a mere human being, was claiming to be God. John 1:4 declares of the eternal Word that "in him was life," and this is repeated and elaborated in John 5:26. Thus, Köstenberger concludes that "the Son's possession of life in himself [makes him] equal to the Father (v. 26)."[118] Summarizing these two elements of Johannine theology, Köstenberger says "Jesus is everywhere in John's gospel presented as equal yet obedient to God the Father."[119] Nevertheless, this description of the Johannine account of the Father-Son relation is incomplete apart from the world to which the Father sent the Son.

For John, the Father sent the Son so that the world might have eternal life, and repeatedly for John, it is faith in Jesus that is determinative of eternal life (John 3:16; 11:26). Speaking more broadly, John's gospel teaches that for humanity the locus of eternal life is the Son (John 5:21, 24; 6:63, 68; 14:6). Like God, Jesus is also the 'fount of life' (Ps 36:9), for in Jesus is life itself (1:4; 14:6). The larger Johannine corpus concurs, calling Jesus 'the living one' (Rev 1:18), and speaking of "the eternal life that was with the Father and was revealed to us [in the Son]" (1 John 1:2). The Johannine teaching that the Son is the locus of eternal life for humanity is perhaps most clearly taught in 1 John 5:11–12—"And this is the testimony: God gave us eternal life, and this life is in his Son. Whoever has the Son has life; whoever does not have the Son of God does not have life." Beasley-Murray says that for human beings, life "means life in the Son."[120] So, the Father has granted that the *incarnate* Son has life in himself *for* humanity, because by having life-in-himself he can also be the giver of life. The incarnate Son has life in himself (John 5:26) so that he has authority to judge humanity and dispense both eternal life and judgement (v. 27–29). Thus, the incarnate Son's reception of

---

117. It is only right to point out that Newbigin, whilst holding to an orthodox trinitarian theology, preferred not to use the language of equality when speaking of the Triune Persons. In commenting on John 5:18–24 Newbigin notes that the word equal is used by the Jews and that in his reply Jesus bypasses it altogether, emphasizing unity not equality. Newbigin says, "The unity of the Father and Son is not one of 'equality' but of love and obedience" (*The Light Has Come*, 66). Although this statement by itself inadequately conveys trinitarian truths, it is faithful to this biblical passage and rightly conveys something of the trinitarian order that is so clear in John's gospel.

118. Köstenberger, *A Theology*, 209.

119. Ibid., 543.

120. Beasley-Murray, *John*, 80.

life-in-himself is tied specifically to his role as Mediator as both Son of God (v. 25) and Son of Man (v. 27).

Despite some interpreters seeing here teaching on the eternal begetting of the Son,[121] and although John 5:26 was used as an anti-Arian argument, Brown says "'life' here does not refer primarily to the internal life of the Trinity, but to a creative life-giving power exercised towards men."[122] Thus, the statement being considered concerns the Father-Son-world relation, rather than the eternal intra-trinitarian processions. Consequently, I concur with Calvin's commentary on this verse. He explains that whilst God the Father remains transcendent, in Jesus God the Son has drawn near, so that he is Emmanuel, God with us. By sending his Son, "God did not choose to have life hidden, and, as it were, buried within himself," rather, "he poured it into his Son, that it might flow to us." Calvin thus concludes that the Father's granting the Son to have life-in-himself "is strictly applied to Christ, so far as he was manifested in the flesh."[123] In conclusion, from its immediate context and the broader context of Johannine theology, John 5:26 applies specifically to the Son's temporal role as mediator rather than the Son's eternal being, and thus does not contradict Pannenberg and Athanasius' argument that the Father and Son are mutually dependent.

## Trinitarian Order: The Triune God as *Anarchos* and *Arché*

Noting the theological interrelation of Father as *anarchos* and *arché*, it is instructive to note what Pannenberg does concerning the Father as *arché*, and again he takes his cue from Athanasius.

> Athanasius, too, could call the Father the 'fount' of wisdom, and therefore of the Son, but only in the sense that one cannot call the Father the 'fount' without the Son who issues forth from it. If, however, we call the Father the fount or principle of the deity of the Son and Spirit in the sense that they are dependent on him for deity but not he on them, then the reciprocity of the self-distinction, and therefore of the trinitarian persons, along with their equal deity, is not upheld.[124]

Pannenberg is able to hold together intra-trinitarian distinctiveness, equality in deity among and mutual reciprocity between the Triune Persons,

---

121. Westcott, *The Gospel*, 87; Carson, *The Gospel*, 257.
122. Brown, *The Gospel*, 215.
123. Calvin, *Commentary on John*.
124. Pannenberg, *Systematic Theology*, 1:322.

while simultaneously affirming the Father as *arché* of the Godhead. Pannenberg also maintains the ordering of the Triune Persons as revealed in the divine economy, since his description of the Father as *arché* reflects this order. The Son and the Spirit serve the Father but the Father does not have his kingdom without Son or Spirit. "The monarchy of the Father is not the presupposition but the result of the common operation of the three persons. It is thus the seal of their unity."[125] Here Pannenberg disagrees with Moltmann who distinguishes between a constitutional and a relational level in the Trinity. For Pannenberg, the relational level *is* constitutional, as it is also for Gunton who clearly spells this out.

> The persons are what they are by virtue of what they give to and receive from each other. As such, they constitute the being of God, for there is no being of God underlying what the persons are to and from each other. God's being is a being in relation, without remainder relational.[126]

As distinct *hypostases* the Triune Persons are *autotheos*, that is, God in themselves through mutual inter-communion and not God by derivation from either the Father or a non-personal divine substance. T. F. Torrance describes the distinctiveness of the Triune Persons by saying they are "distinguished by position and not status, by form and not being, by sequence and not power, for they are fully and perfectly equal."[127]

Following Pannenberg I would abandon the use of *anarchos* for the Father alone, and following Pannenberg and Gunton affirm that Father, Son and Spirit co-constitute each other, so that the Triune Godhead is understood as *anarchos*. Then, there are no conceptual hurdles to jump in affirming the ontological co-equality of the Triune Persons as creedally enshrined in the *homoousion*. Likewise, I would disavow describing the intra-trinitarian *arché* of the Father in an ontological sense, because despite careful and repeated qualification, this language necessarily suggests subordinationism. For the *being* of God this is problematic, for as Gunton explains, "I do not believe that it allows for an adequate theology of the mutual constitution of Father, Son and Spirit."[128] However, I propose that *arché* refers both to God the Father and to the Triune God, but in distinctive ways. First, the Father is the *arché* of the Triune God vis-à-vis the intra-trinitarian order. This order entails that within the Triune Godhead there is both submission

---

125. Ibid., 325.
126. Gunton, *The Promise*, 143.
127. Torrance, *The Christian Doctrine of God*, 175–76.
128. Gunton, *The Promise*, 196.

and being submitted to, but there is not a hierarchy of power. Thus the Son is eternally begotten and the Spirit eternally proceeds from the Father, and not *vice versa*. However, it is insufficient to suggest that the language of *arché* conveys *no* ontological content. Therefore, as well as speaking of the *arché* of the Father relating to order, it is also proper to affirm the *arché* of the Triune Godhead in relation to ontology. T. F. Torrance, following Gregory of Nazianzus, believes that "the monarchy is that of the whole Trinity, not just the Father."[129] This is because, as Gunton has said, Father, Son and Holy Spirit constitute each other in their mutual relations. Arguing that the doctrine of perichoresis strengthens this conclusion, Gunton says "One implication of the threefold community that is God is its dynamism: the being of God is a community of energies, of perichoretic interaction. As such, it is difficult to conceive its consistency with any static hierarchy."[130] As the entire Godhead is *anarchos*, so the Triune God is also *arché*, and within this ontological *arché* is the *arché* of the Father pertaining to order. This double usage of the term *arché* is faithful to the biblical picture of the priority of the Father and at the same time, the unity and full divinity of the Triune Persons. This avoids the two extremes of ontological subordinationism on the one side, and over-stressing the equality of the Triune Persons on the other.[131]

Theologically safeguarding the full divinity of God the Son and Spirit is an essential foundation to Christian missiology. Likewise, accurately representing the trinitarian order is also essential to missiology since it faithfully reflects the nature of the gospel of Jesus Christ, sent by the Father in the power of the Spirit. Describing the nature of God as fundamentally intra-personal rather than in terms of substance characterizes the personal nature of Christian mission. The gospel speaks of a divine Person—God the Father, who sends his only Son to reconcile and redeem humanity, and then, by the Person of the Holy Spirit and through the personal invitation of the church invites all to personally respond in repentance and faith. Indeed, the gospel itself is about how human persons may personally participate in the *koinonia* of divine Persons, thus also becoming brothers and sisters within the communion of saints, the church. By establishing that the Triune Persons are themselves and together both *arché* and *anarchos*, the nature of *being* is understood to be both relational and personal. This is profoundly important for the missionary doctrine of election, the nature of the church,

---

129. Quoted in Letham, *The Holy Trinity*, 366. Elsewhere Gregory also said the monarchy "is not limited to one Person. The Father is the Begetter and the Emitter. The Son the Begotten, and the Holy Spirit the Emission" (Orations 29.2, quoted in Tan, "A Trinitarian Ontology," 283).

130. Gunton, *The Promise*, 72.

131. Ibid., xxiv.

and what it means to be human. This latter point is particularly good news for contemporary Western culture that prizes an individualism that isolates and alienates. In the cultural West the perceived value of community has decreased as hyper-individualism has become normalized. As James White observes, "The names say it all: Youtube. MySpace. And, of course, the 'i' in iPod, iMac, and iPhone."[132] In this context, the teaching that all of life is inter-connected and that human beings are in fact relational and inter-personal beings is profoundly counter-cultural and greatly needed, but more of this in chapters 4 and 5.

The critic of the interpretation of *arché* of the Father as order could still argue that since there is subordination within the Godhead this must therefore have ontological consequences. To deny the Son's submission to the Father would be to deny God's self-revelation in Christ. Therefore, some element of submission within the economic Trinity must be affirmed, although the heresy of ontological subordination(ism) can and must be avoided, for "subordination cannot be used to describe persons who share the same nature."[133] How can the Son's subordination to the Father be clearly affirmed alongside the *homoousios*? In recent times, as with much trinitarian theology, Barth has shown the way forward.

## *The Humility of God*

Thinking through the Christological and theological implications of the earliest Christian confession 'Jesus is Lord', Barth says, "If then, God is in Christ, if what the man Jesus does is God's own work, this aspect of the self-emptying and self-humbling of Jesus Christ as an act of obedience cannot be alien to God."[134] Explaining this further, Barth says "The mystery [of the incarnation] reveals to us that for God it is just as natural to be lowly as it is to be great, to be abroad as to be at home."[135] Since both Father and Son are fully God, *homoousios*, then both submission and being submitted to are not alien to God. Therefore,

> It does not follow that a 'subordination', an 'ordering below' entails an inferiority of personhood, dignity or being . . . Jesus' humiliation, whether we see that demonstrated in his birth, his

---

132. White, *Christ among the Dragons*, 160.

133. Basil, *On the Holy Spirit*, 75. In context Basil is referring to ontology and not order.

134. Barth, *CD* IV/1, 193.

135. Ibid., 192.

washing of the disciples' feet or his sacrificial death, is a mark of his divinity and glory, not of his inferiority.[136]

Objectors to the doctrine of the incarnation, ancient and modern alike, in unison affirm that it stands to reason that God cannot become human, suffer and die because God is self-evidently not human, passible or mortal. The theologian might respond to this objection with three questions: On what basis do you know that God cannot become human? What is your source of knowledge and how do you know this is correct? Who are you to imprison God within his deity and limit his freedom? Indeed, "God's deity is thus no prison in which He can exist only in and for Himself."[137] Following a truly orthodox methodology Barth says, "Who God is and what it is to be divine is something we have to *learn* where God has revealed Himself and His nature, the essence of the divine."[138] The center of divine revelation is the person of Jesus Christ. Reflecting on this astonishing and unanticipatable act of the Word becoming flesh, Barth says, "By doing this God proves to us that He can do it, that to do it is within His nature. And He shows Himself to be more great and rich and sovereign than we had ever imagined. And our ideas of His nature must be guided by this, and not *vice versa*."[139]

Consequently, rather than saying that God cannot become human, almost the opposite is true. Barth asks, "Is it not true that in Jesus Christ, as He is attested in the Holy Scripture, genuine deity includes in itself genuine humanity?"[140] To suggest that the divine being cannot suffer, a virtual axiom of patristic thought due to Hellenistic influence, is also mistaken. Fiddes says that since "God chooses to be humble and even to suffer with his creation, it is not for us to pay God metaphysical compliments by protesting that the divine being will not allow it."[141] Subordination within the Godhead, then, is to be embraced and affirmed rather than hesitantly admitted, for it further reveals the nature of God without entailing ontological subordinationism. Barth saw that by choosing to be lowly, God does not undermine his divinity (if that were possible) but actually demonstrates it. Therefore, as it is God-like to be lowly, so it is God-like to be obedient, for "He Himself is also able and free to render obedience."[142] Barth is saying that not only in the incarnation within the divine economy, but from eternity,

---

136. BCC Study Commission, *The Forgotten Trinity*, 1:33.
137. Barth, *The Humanity of God*, 46.
138. Barth, *CD* IV/1, 186, emphasis added.
139. Ibid., 186.
140. Barth, *The Humanity of God*, 48.
141. Fiddes, *Participating in God*, 13.
142. Barth, *CD* IV/1, 193.

God the Son *in se* is obedient to the Father. This is because, as Augustine says, the Son is sent *before* he becomes incarnate, thus his incarnation points to the eternal origin and nature of the sending and reveals something of the eternal intra-trinitarian relations.[143]

Barth was right in his brilliant insight that in Christ, humanity finds a God who is humble. God does not need to fear losing his Godhead in the incarnation, in the condescension of his becoming human.

> God shows Himself to be the great and true God in the fact that He can and will let His grace bear this cost, that He is capable and willing and ready for this condescension, this act of extravagance, this far journey. What marks out God above all false gods is that they are not capable and ready for this. In their otherworldliness and supernaturalness and otherness, etc., the gods are a reflection of the human pride which will not unbend, which will not stoop to that which is beneath it. God is not proud. In His high majesty He is humble. It is in this high humility that He speaks and acts as the God who reconciles the world to Himself.[144]

Barth has shown that the distinction of Persons is part of the glory of God. The fact that humility belongs to the nature of God means that it is a feature of the mission of God, seen most clearly in the incarnation of Christ. Since the *missio Dei* defines and shapes the *missio ecclesiae*, so humility must characterize the church's mission in the way of the Son and Spirit, within the mission of God.

## *The Eternal Life of the Triune God*

### Trinitarian Life

Christian theology does not affirm belief in God and then seek to understand what it means for God to be Triune. Rather, "When Christian communities speak about God, by definition they have to speak about Father, Son and Holy Spirit. There is simply no other God."[145] What does it mean for God, the Triune God, to be God in eternity, prior to creation? How can the trinitarian divine life be described? Since God is Father, Son and Holy Spirit, how is God's unity to be understood? What relevance does all this

---

143. Augustine, *De Trinitate* 2.5.7–9, quoted in Letham, *The Holy Trinity*, 494.
144. Barth, *CD* IV/1, 159.
145. Kirk, *What Is Mission?*, 27.

# Trinitarian Missiology 155

have to living an authentically human life? And finally, how can one know the answers to these questions?

Robert Jenson says that "Father, Son, and Spirit are persons whose communal life is God."[146] Thus, when asking the question 'What kind of being does the Triune God have?' Jenson indicates that God's being involves a kind of communality. In bold language, John Zizioulas asserts that "The substance of 'God', has no ontological content, no true being, apart from communion.'"[147] That is, God's being is Father, Son and Holy Spirit in eternal mutual fellowship, trinity in unity and unity in trinity. This theological insight comprised something of an intellectual revolution with regards to ontology, and the breakthrough came from reflecting on the Nicene doctrine of Jesus being *homoousios* with God the Father.

When Athanasius and the Nicene theologians championed the word *homoousion*, that Jesus was of one substance with the Father, this terminological innovation brought with it "a new ontological principle: that there can be a sharing in being."[148] To understand the magnitude of this it must be appreciated that *all* forms of ancient Greek philosophy from the pre-Socratic era to Neo-Platonism gave priority to the 'one' over the 'many'; unitary substance enjoyed ontological priority.[149] The *homoousion*, and the philosophy it implies, overturns this long-standing and revered tradition. Neither the 'one' nor the 'many' have priority over each other for the entire framework is reconstructed in which the 'one' and 'many' mutually and simultaneously coexist.

> By insisting . . . that God is eternally Son as well as Father, the Nicene theologians introduced a note of relationality into the being of God: God's being is defined as being in relation. Such is the impact of the doctrine of the incarnation on conceptions of what it is to be.[150]

In God's being there is no need to priorities either the 'one' or the 'many' because true being is to be found not in created existence, but in God's uncreated being which combines both the 'one' and the 'many.' God's being consists of Father, Son, and Holy Spirit in mutual and reciprocal communion, or as Alan Torrance puts it, *Persons in Communion*.[151]

---

146. Jenson, *Systematic Theology*, 1:226.
147. Zizioulas, *Being As Communion*, 17.
148. Gunton, *The Promise*, 9.
149. Zizioulas, "The Doctrine of the Holy Trinity," 52.
150. Gunton, *The Promise*, 9.
151. Torrance, *Persons in Communion*.

The ontology derived from God's self-revelation in Christ and the Spirit amounts to a serious philosophical innovation. "In Aristotle, and certainly in logic until the time of Kant, relation is subordinate to substance . . . something first exists and then enters or finds itself in relation to other things."[152] For Aristotle, and for philosophy in general, *being* is not inherently relational but is related to *substance*, both for God and humans. By contrast, speaking on behalf of Christian theology, "Communion is for Basil an ontological category. The *nature* of God is communion."[153] There is not only relationality but also plurality and diversity *within* the being of God, for the *being* of God is none other than the Triune Persons in communion. The concept of person is consequently recognized to be "*an ontological concept in the ultimate sense*," so Zizioulas concludes that "Nothing is more sacred than the person since it constitutes the 'way of being' of God Himself."[154] For the 'way of being' that is God is not simply 'person', but *Persons in communion*, and therefore to the ontologically ultimate concept of person must be added further ontological content. Zizioulas explains that "The person cannot exist in isolation. God is not alone; He is *communion* . . . Love is a *relationship*, it is the free coming out of one's self, the breaking of one's will, a *free* submission to the will of another."[155] This statement concerning God is of momentous importance because in Christian theology the doctrine of God wholly determines all other doctrines.[156] Hence, Gunton is clearly right in asserting that "the doctrine of the Trinity *is* crucial to ontology."[157]

## God's Being Is in Communion: God Is Love

I have touched on the importance of the categories person and communion, but what does communion mean? Gunton points out that "At the heart of the doctrine that being is communion are four central concepts: person, relation, otherness and freedom."[158] To attempt to define any of these four key concepts in isolation is both difficult and mistaken because they mutually

---

152. Gunton, *The Promise*, 151.
153. Ibid., 71, emphasis original.
154. Zizioulas, "The Doctrine of the Holy Trinity," 56, emphasis original.
155. Ibid., emphasis original.
156. Gunton rightly observes that "it is only through an understanding of the kind of being that God is that we can come to learn what kind of beings we are and what kind of world we inhabit" (Gunton, *The Promise*, xi).
157. Ibid., xi. As I continue to follow Gunton's work it is important to acknowledge that Gunton develops "what can be called a social rather than a psychological approach" (ibid., 195).
158. Ibid., 11.

## Trinitarian Missiology

define and require each other. Therefore, the descriptions that follow use the three other concepts in describing the one in question.

The concept of *person* is perhaps the hardest to describe because of the ever-present danger of anthropological projection onto God of what it means to be human. However, as the Genesis narrative makes clear, humans are made in God's image and *not* vice versa. Gunton builds on the Cappadocian insights in saying that person is logically and ontologically primitive. He explains that

> the personal is both that from which other realities take their meaning and that which is irreducible to other (less than personal) entities . . . a person is different from an individual, in the sense that the latter is defined in terms of *separation from* other individuals, the person in terms of *relations with* other persons.[159]

A *relation* is the way which persons connect or associate or interact with one another that is constitutive of whom the persons are. T. F. Torrance coins the term *onto-relations* to convey that the relations within the Godhead are ontologically constitutive.[160] In Pannenberg's words, "the relations between the persons are constitutive not merely for their distinctions but also for their deity."[161] This description of a relation presupposes that the Persons in question, Father, Son and Holy Spirit, are *other* than each other; that is, distinct and in some way dissimilar to each other. "Personal relations are those which constitute the other person as other, as truly particular."[162] Father, Son and Holy Spirit are not separate individuals but distinct Persons "whose reality can only be understood in terms of their relations to each other, relations by virtue of which they together constitute the being (*ousia*) of the one God. The persons are therefore not relations, but concrete particulars in relation to one another."[163] This clearly distinguishes between the oneness and threeness of God and it explains this new ontological understanding of God's being as communion. *Hypostases* (persons) and *ousia* (being) remain ontologically distinct and inseparably connected.[164] Lastly, the intra-trinitarian relations are *free* relations in that the Triune Persons

---

159. Ibid., emphasis original.
160. Torrance, *The Christian Doctrine of God*, 157.
161. Pannenberg, *Systematic Theology*, 1:323.
162. Gunton, *The Promise*, 11.
163. Ibid., 39. This is contra Paul Fiddes who argues that the divine persons themselves *are* relationships, rather than persons *in* relationship. Fiddes, *Participating in God*, 50.
164. Gunton, *The Promise*, 39.

exist in freedom, not from but *for* each other, and so are relations of love.[165] "There is accordingly an orientation to the other within the eternal structure of God's being."[166] In these free relations the Triune Persons are constituted in a way which upholds each Person's distinct particularity as a kind of 'personal space' that is both received and conferred.[167] Love of the other is central to God's eternal being. God's Being is "inherently altruistic, *Being for others, Being who loves.*"[168]

What does it mean for God to be Father, Son and Holy Spirit in communion? How are each of the distinct divine *hypostases* to be described? Each Triune identity can only be described in relation to the other two, by what each gives to and receives from the other two.[169] "He [God] is both the One who loves and the One who is loved even though there were no creature for Him to love and to love Him in return. God loves, and the purpose of His being is to do this. As He loves, He fulfils His purpose."[170] God's being is irreducibly relational as each Triune Person lives for the other two in relations of love. For Barth, love is not a divine state, nor is loving one of God's many activities, but love is *the* life-act of God.[171] In Newbigin's words, "God is love in action—the love of the Father and the Son in the unity of the Spirit."[172] As Father, Son and Holy Spirit give themselves to each other and receive from each other, God is. Interpreting the biblical affirmation 'God is love', Newbigin says,

> Within the eternal being of God love is a never-ceasing self-emptying and out-pouring, forever met by the same out-poured love, the love of the Father and the Son in the unity of the Spirit. Eternal life is no motionless serenity, but love meeting love, the rapture of love forever poured out and forever received.[173]

This description of God as love points to a dynamic understanding of the being of God and has ontological implications. 'God is love' should no longer refer primarily an outlook or disposition of God's being. Rather this affirmation, says Schwöbel, "can now be understood as an

---

165. Ibid., 143.
166. Gunton, *The Christian Faith*, 187.
167. Gunton, *The Promise*, 128.
168. Torrance, *The Christian Doctrine of God*, 131, emphasis original.
169. I will discuss intra-trinitarian distinctions in more detail in due course.
170. Barth, *CD* IV/2, 755.
171. Ibid., 772, emphasis original.
172. Newbigin, *The Light Has Come*, 43.
173. Newbigin, *The Household of God*, 130.

ontological statement about the mode of God's personal being in relation, and in this way love, interpreted on strictly relational terms, can be understood ontologically."[174] God is love is a description of God's being, for as Barth says, "The statements 'God is' and 'God loves' are synonymous."[175] God is love also means that God is also the source of all true love and that all God's actions are loving actions,[176] including creation, revelation and reconciliation.

In God's action *ad extra* we see God "does not keep to Himself His being and nature as Father, Son and Holy Spirit—the eternal love which He Himself is. He is not the prisoner of His own Godhead. He has and exercises the freedom to be our God."[177] It is in the cross of Christ that God definitively demonstrates and displays his Being as love, and it is in the cross of Christ that God has irrevocably committed himself to relationship with humanity.[178] Commenting on John 3:16-21, Newbigin says "God is known in this action [the incarnation] because God is action—the action of love reaching out to the unlovely and the unlovable."[179] In the giving of himself in the person of Jesus and the Holy Spirit we see a God who "has not withheld Himself from us, but given us Himself. Therefore his love for us is His eternal love, and our being loved by Him is our being taken up unto the fellowship of His eternal love, in which He is Himself for ever and ever."[180] God freely gives himself to humanity and in doing so freely gives his love, so that humanity might participate in the love that God is. God's unconditional love is in no way is merited by the recipients of his love, and yet as loved by God people acquire inestimable worth. God's love for people is purifying in relation to the distortion of human nature. It is also a creative love whereby those who are loved participate in God's eternal love and so are caused to love.[181]

The theological affirmation that God is love in his innermost eternal being, prior to God being love towards creation, is of enormous missiological significance. All facets of the gospel, from creation to crucifixion to consummation, are expressions of God's love. The doctrine of the Trinity roots this loving action, seen supremely in the incarnation, within the

174. Schwöbel, "Christology," 132.
175. Barth, *CD* IV/2, 755.
176. Stott, *Epistles of John*, 160.
177. Barth, *CD* IV/2, 759.
178. Torrance, *The Christian Doctrine of God*, 5.
179. Newbigin, *The Light Has Come*, 42.
180. Barth, *Church Dogmatics* II/1, 280.
181. Barth, *Church Dogmatics* IV/2, 766-76.

eternal being of God, and this is immensely attractive. Daud Rahbar, who earned his doctorate from Cambridge on the ethical doctrine of the Qur'an, was the Pakistani delegate to the International Islamic Colloquium. He wrote "unqualified Divine love for mankind is an idea completely alien to the Quran . . . nowhere do we find the idea that God loves mankind. God's love is conditional."[182] The comparison between the two faiths' doctrine of God at this point could not be more divergent.[183] While chair of Urdu and Pakistan Studies at the Ankara University Rahbar left Islam and became a Christ-follower and was baptized.

God's loving nature is also missiologically significant in that it provides a coherent explanation for what could be termed the 'numerical problem' or the problem of divine unity, that God is simultaneously three and one. Since God is communal, relational, and personal, the one God is 'not a solitary God'.[184] Each divine *hypostasis* is not an individual, for that would be tritheism, nor is each *hypostasis* separate from each other, but, in Cornelius Plantinga's words, "Father, Son, and Spirit are 'members one of another' to a superlative and exemplary degree."[185] Historically, what led to a breakthrough in conceiving of divine unity was the "desynonymising of *ousia* and *hypostasis*, which previously had meant the same—being or substance."[186] This made possible the holding together of distinction within unity, thus at once affirming the unity and multiplicity of God. Describing this Triune *perichoresis*, Barth says the "divine modes of being mutually condition and permeate one another so completely that one is always in the other two and the other two in the one."[187] The doctrine of *perichoresis* has missiological significance particularly in terms of its helpfulness towards conceptually attempting to explain divine unity. Despite the attempts of the Church Fathers, there are no vestiges or analogies of the Trinity that adequately reflect God's unique ontology. *Perichoresis* teaches that three distinct persons mu-

182. Daud Rahbar, *God of Justice*, quoted in Power, "A Volf," 5.

183. The medieval Muslim theologian Abu Hamid al-Ghazzali professed that "Love is to sense a need of the beloved and since Allah cannot be said to have a need or an experience of a need, it is therefore impossible that Allah should love" (quoted in Power, "A Volf," 4). See also Bernie Power, "Do We Worship the Same God?" (unpublished, 2012), http://www.biblesociety.org.au/news/do-we-worship-the-same-god. For opposing views on this subject see Durie, *Which God?*; George, *Is the Father of Jesus the God of Muhammad?*; and Volf, *Allah*. For my own contribution to this subject see Dodds, "The Abrahamic Faiths?"

184. Wilken, "Not a Solitary God," 63–93.

185. Plantinga, "The Threeness/Oneness," 50.

186. Gunton, *The Promise*, 10.

187. Barth, CD I/1, 370. Barth prefers to speak of the Triune Persons as 'modes of being'.

tually share the one divine being by interpenetrating and passing into one another, thus helping to explain how the three in God can be one without losing either the threeness or oneness. Hence Moltmann says, "The unity of the triunity lies in the eternal perichoresis of the Trinitarian persons."[188]

## God's Triune Being: Missiological Implications

The doctrine of the Trinity is commonly ridiculed for doctrinally embodying a self-evident contradiction, and among adversaries of the church's mission, both historical and contemporary, it is seen as something of a soft target. Thomas Jefferson ridiculed the doctrine of the Trinity as "metaphysical insanities,"[189] and the target of this ridicule is most often God being simultaneously both three and one. Thus, Bishop David Jenkins says, "Three does not mean three, one does not mean one, and person does not mean person."[190] Arguably this view is also imbibed by members of the church, so it is "among practical Christians—reverently ignored."[191] Likewise, in the church's mission the doctrine of the Trinity is commonly seen, in Newbigin's words, as "a troublesome piece of theological baggage which is best kept out of sight when trying to convey the gospel to unbelievers."[192] This perspective also undermines Christian confidence in the gospel, for the doctrine of the Trinity is so commonly misunderstood within the church, that it is often said, "Try to explain the Trinity and you'll lose your mind."[193] Missiologically therefore, it is of great importance to offer a coherent explanation of the theo-logic of the doctrine of the Trinity. Whilst appeals to divine mystery are appropriate, they do not supply understanding or confidence in this doctrine, and here the notion of *perichoresis* can help.

The Church-in-mission can point to the explanatory power of *perichoresis* to conceptually hold together threeness and oneness in God. This removes the element of apparent logical contradiction and bears witness to the perichoretic God whose being is in communion. However, by itself this is still an incomplete explanation and will meet with only limited success. In his book *Participating in God* Paul Fiddes argues that one can only understand this personal and relational God through being, not a spectator, but a participant. He espouses "an epistemology of participation . . . We

---

188. Moltmann, *The Trinity and the Kingdom*, 175.
189. Cited in McGrath, *Christian Theology*, 243.
190. Cited in O'Collins, *The Tripersonal God*, 1.
191. Newbigin, "Trinitarianism," 607.
192. Newbigin, *Trinitarian Doctrine*, 35.
193. Pinnock, *Flame of Love*, 22.

cannot observe, even in our mind's eye, being which is relationship; it can only be known through the mode of participation."[194] God's being consists of the Triune Persons in communion, and one comes to know God through redemptive and revelatory participation by the Spirit in the Son's loving relationship with the Father. From the church's understanding of God as three Persons in mutual perichoretic relations, there issues an invitation for others to come to understand this Triune God by themselves personally participating in these relations.[195]

The church cannot adequately explain the doctrine of the Trinity to those outside it because it does not fit into a pre-existing ontology other than that of which it is the basis.[196] The doctrine itself is the product of *dianoia* in theological thinking. T. F. Torrance explains "*Dianoia* is not the forcing of objective reality into a concept but the letting of the mind assume conceptual forms under the pressure of the objective reality or being of God."[197] Ontological conceptions of God based on the incarnation and Pentecost did not fit the pre-existing and dominant Hellenistic philosophical outlook. Rather than seeking to force God's self-revelation into a pre-existing mold (*epinoia*), which resulted in the various Christological and trinitarian heresies,[198] it was vital for ontology to be reconceived *a posteriori* from God's self-disclosure.[199] God's self-revelation does not fit into prior concepts of unity and so it should not be made to conform to the straight jacket of a pre-existing ontology. Rather, the new wine requires new wineskins,[200] and these wineskins can only be constructed *a posteriori* to God's self-disclosure.

194. Fiddes, *Participating in God*, 38.

195. This has been famously portrayed in Rublev's icon.

196. See Newbigin's comment that "It has never at any time been possible to fit the resurrection of Jesus into any world view except a world view of which it is the basis" (*Honest Religion for Secular Man*, 53).

197. Torrance, *Theology in Reconstruction*, 49.

198. Hodgson explains, "The views which came ultimately to be rejected as heretical were those which surrendered the revelation to the idea of unity. Orthodoxy clung to the revelation even at the cost of apparent self-contradiction which was eased, but never completely resolved, by the adoption of an agreed terminology . . . Both kinds of monarchianism, adoptionist and modalistic, sprang from the same root. They were attempts to account for the historical facts of the Christian revelation with perfect loyalty to the unrevized conception of unity. The adoptionist kept this essential unity by denying essential godhood to the Son, the modalist by reducing the incarnation to a theophany. The adoptionist position persisted in Arius, the modalistic in Sabellius and Marcellus" (*The Doctrine of the Trinity*, 99).

199. God's self-introduction in Jesus and the Spirit "demanded not only a revision of the theological idea of God but also a revision of the philosophical idea of unity"(ibid., 98).

200. Polkinghorne, *Belief in God*, 36.

By way of *dianoia*, by the impressing of God's self-revelation in Christ and the Spirit onto philosophical ontology, there arose, to quote a letter usually attributed to Basil of Caesarea, "a new and paradoxical conception of united separation and separated unity" such that God was understood to be "a sort of continuous and indivisible community."[201] *Dianoia* as evident in the development of the doctrine of the Trinity has vital missiological implications.

The missionary church seeks to convey knowledge of God to those outside of the community of Jesus Christ in a manner that is both challenging and relevant. The task of 'challenging relevance'[202] is to communicate the nature and action of God in terms understandable by the recipient community, by using words and concepts belonging to the thought-world of that community. Missionaries spend long years learning new languages, cultures and belief-systems in order to clearly communicate the gospel so that it is both comprehensible and understood as relevant. However, gospel communication must also challenge the hearers to think in new ways that do not entirely fit the old structures of language, belief and thought, because such communication introduces Jesus who does not fit into any pattern of belief or thought, except that on which he is the foundation. As George Hunsberger says, "Embodiment without challenge would lead to syncretism; challenge without embodiment would be irrelevant."[203] In its missionary task the church must be careful to preserve the 'challenging relevance' dynamic of gospel communication, whilst looking to the Holy Spirit to effect a conversion and paradigm shift of belief, thought and affections in the recipient community.

As the development of the doctrine of the Trinity led to philosophical innovations and new theological terminology in the early church, so the missionary church can expect this process to continue as new people and cultures are converted to Christ and seek to articulate their understanding of him in new and culturally-specific ways. For example, Newbigin mentions that A. G. Hogg wrote a series of essays entitled *Karma and Redemption* in which he proposed "an interpretation of Jesus as the one in whom the author of the law of *karma* himself bears the *karma* of humanity."[204] The church's task of communicating the nature and works of God in a way that is challenging and relevant also stands as an ongoing challenge of translation; the challenge to re-conceive and re-describe God in the thought and

---

201. *Letters* 38, quoted in Gunton, *The Promise*, 94.

202. Newbigin takes this term from his fellow missionary to India A. G. Hogg. Newbigin, "Christ and the Cultures," 11–12.

203. Hunsberger, "The Newbigin Gauntlet," 395.

204. Newbigin, "Christ and the Cultures," 11–12.

language of another culture. The ongoing challenge of indigenization and contextualization remain central to the cross-cultural missionary task.

Having discussed God *ad intra* it is now appropriate to turn to a consideration of God *ad extra*.

## GOD *AD EXTRA*

### *Missio Dei*

The concept of *missio Dei* has been the subject of disagreement and debate, but it must be understood to be a reaction against the dominant anthropocentric conception of missions in the modern missionary movement, whose anthropocentrism "severed the . . . strong link between mission . . . and the doctrine of the Trinity."[205] This anthropocentric missiology was historically expressed in the strong link between the modern missionary movement and European colonialism. *Missio Dei* began to surface in the 1950s during a time when many countries that had been European colonies were declaring their independence. Since the modern missionary movement 'from the West to the rest' often went hand in glove with colonialism, the collapse of the latter raised questions about the ongoing validity of the former. The concept of *missio Dei* served to legitimize the ongoing mission of the church by locating mission in the being of God rather than in the failed colonial project, and thus originally served the important critical function of distancing the justification of mission from colonialism. In effect *missio Dei* theology enabled missions to continue with 'business as usual', while it "did not require the church to think through the implications of God's triune being for mission."[206] *Missio Dei* was primarily a reactionary term rather than being a carefully articulated theological concept, with unambiguously identifiable content. Thus, it is not altogether surprising that *missio Dei* has historically functioned as an empty term that has been filled with a variety of different and often incompatible meanings. Hoedemaker says, "the flag of *missio Dei* has been flown on ships carrying a broad range of cargoes," and so he concludes the term is actually unhelpful.[207] Historically, Richebächer

---

205. Jan Jongeneel, *Philosophy, Science, and Theology of Mission in the 19th and 20th Centuries Part II*, quoted in Goheen, "As the Father Has Sent Me," 116.

206. Flett, *The Witness of God*, 45. This underscores the intended value of this present work, in which I attempt to think through the implications of God's triune being for mission.

207. Hoedemaker, "The People of God," 164, 171. By contrast Eddie Arthur, while acknowledging the problematic history of the term, nevertheless argues for its ongoing usefulness. Arthur, "*Missio Dei*," 49–66.

states the term has been predominantly used in two mutually-contradictory ways. *Missio Dei* has been used to justify Christ-centered descriptions of the *missio ecclesiae*, and has also been used to refer to a deity that bears witness to itself in all religious traditions thereby countering the absolute exclusivity of christocentric claims.[208] John Flett argues persuasively that even this estimation is an over-simplification of what is a complex and confusing matter. The debate over the theological meaning of *missio Dei* has been carefully articulated elsewhere,[209] most thoroughly and satisfactorily by Flett,[210] so will not be repeated here.

What is pertinent to this project is Newbigin's usage and conception of *missio Dei*. One of Flett's main concerns is "*Missio Dei* claims to provide a Trinitarian framework for concepts that do not draw on that doctrine."[211] While I concede this is generally true historically, Newbigin's usage of *missio Dei*, at least from *Trinitarian Doctrine* onwards, constitutes an important exception.[212] In that work, and those which follow, he utilizes the *missio Dei* concept in an explicitly and intentionally trinitarian manner, as my account of his trinitarian missiology in chapter 2 makes clear. Newbigin is critical of those who use the doctrine of the *missio Dei* "to support concepts of mission which bypass the Church and even bypass the name of Jesus." He says "That is a radical misuse of the concept,"[213] because

> a Trinitarian perspective can be only an enlargement and development of a Christo-centric one and not an alternative set over against it, for the doctrine of the Trinity is the theological articulation of what it means to say that Jesus is the unique Word of God incarnate in world history.[214]

---

208. Richebächer, "Editorial," 465.

209. See, for example, Hoedemaker, "The People of God"; Bosch, *Transforming Mission*, 389–93.

210. Flett, "*Missio Dei*"; idem, *The Witness of God*.

211. Flett, *The Witness of God*, 36.

212. Flett comes close to acknowledging this exception of Newbigin's usage of *missio Dei*. He identifies Newbigin as the chief author of the Willingen statement, which although he finds to be problematic in numerous ways, nevertheless "remains close to a complete definition of *missio Dei*" (*The Witness of God*, 161).

213. Newbigin, *The Gospel in a Pluralist Society*, 135.

214. Newbigin said this in critical response to Raiser. "Ecumenical Amnesia," 2. Regarding Raiser's trinitarian concept of the *missio Dei*, Wainwright says, "Raiser's trinitarian invocations, it may be observed, amount to no more than airy references to 'Trinity'—materially undefined—as a form of Godhead and a 'model of unity'" (Wainwright, *Lesslie Newbigin*, 131).

Newbigin's usage of *missio Dei*,[215] which I now take up, draws on the doctrine of the Trinity and is determined by that doctrine. Accordingly, *missio Dei* is here understood as helpful shorthand to describe the temporal mission of the Triune God who sends his Son and Spirit in revelation and reconciliation to the world which he loves, and so is thoroughly christocentric and trinitarian. Central to the missions of Son and Spirit is the church, and so the *missio Dei* creates, commissions, and contains the *missio ecclesiae*. I also use *missio Dei* in agreement with Kirk, who says "When Christian communities speak about God, by definition they have to speak about Father, Son and Holy Spirit. There is simply no other God. Therefore to speak about the *missio Dei* is to indicate, without any qualification, the *missio Trinitatis*."[216]

## Why Did God Create the World?

To understand the mission of God in and for creation one must ask the question 'Why did God create the world?' This question can only be answered theologically by looking at Jesus Christ, for it is there and nowhere else that God's purpose and mission for creation is disclosed. Protestant theologian Moltmann offers the answer, "The mission of Christ achieves its purpose when men and creation are united with God. In this union God is glorified through men and in it they partake of the glory of God himself."[217] Ion Bria's representation of Orthodox views is remarkably similar. He says "God's involvement in history aims at drawing humanity and creation in general into this communion with God's very life."[218] Taking a slightly different but complementary approach, the Roman Catholic Church's First Vatican Council pronounced that God created the world "out of his goodness" and "to manifest his perfection."[219] Summarizing these views, one could say that God created the world to manifest his perfection and to draw humanity and all creation into union with the divine life. Offering a slightly more de-

---

215. I refer here chiefly to the substance of the *missio Dei* rather than the language. Flett notes that Newbigin's actual usage of *missio Dei* language is sparse, due to, from his perspective, its historical misuse. Flett, "'Who is Jesus Christ?,'" 262–63.

216. Kirk, *What Is Mission?*, 27. Flett criticizes this statement as indicating and perpetuating "the popular notion that Trinity doctrine underlies *missio Dei* theology" (*The Witness of God*, 47). While this is a fair criticism based on Kirk's further discussion of this in his endnotes (page 239), Kirk's statement can also be read as a factual theological statement, and as such, remains valid. It is this latter sense that I draw on for my work.

217. Moltmann, *The Church*, 59.

218. Bria, *Go Forth In Peace*, 3.

219. Quoted in Jenson, *Systematic Theology*, 2:17.

tailed answer to this question, Johann Baier says "The final end of creation is the glory of God's wisdom, goodness and divine power; an intermediate end is the good of humanity."[220] The relationship between these final and intermediate ends is of crucial importance for understanding theological anthropology and the *missio Dei*, but one must begin with the final end of creation.

Regarding God's purpose in and for creation, Jonathan Edwards' *Concerning the End for Which God Created the World* has been influential. Edwards says, "The great end of God's works, which is so variously expressed in Scripture, is indeed but ONE; and this *one* end is most properly and comprehensively called, THE GLORY OF GOD."[221] Offering further explanation of the purpose of creation, Jenson, drawing on Edwards, says God "must be the final purpose of all his own acts, since he is the source of all good and therefore is the proper and final object of any person's 'regard', and so also of his own."[222] Hence, a major theme in Edwards' theology is God's passion for his own glory, as taught throughout Scripture and notably prominent in Isaiah 48:9-11—

> For *my name's sake* I defer my anger, *for the sake of my praise* I restrain it for you, so that I may not cut you off. See, I have refined you, but not like silver; I have tested you in the furnace of adversity. *For my own sake, for my own sake,* I do it, for why should *my name* be profaned? *My glory* I will not give to another.

It is out of God's passion for his own glory that he creates the world. Following in the tradition of Edwards, John Piper, drawing on the Westminster Confession, believes that not only is the chief end of man to glorify God and enjoy him forever, but also "the chief end of *God* is to glorify God and enjoy himself forever."[223] Piper rightly identifies this as a major theme within Scripture but his articulation of this theme sounds a faintly narcissistic note because he fails to represent the plurality within the divine life. Since God is love it is clearly not possible for God to be narcissistic; indeed such a proposal is preposterous, but Piper's formulation remains unsatisfactory. Put briefly, Piper's language of God's self-glorification is insufficiently trinitarian and is inadequately related to God's love for creation.

---

220. *Compedium theologicae positivae* (1693), i.ii.23, quoted in Jenson, *Systematic Theology*, 2:18.

221. Jonathan Edwards, *The Works of Jonathan Edwards* 1, quoted in Piper, *Let the Nations Be Glad!*, 21-22, emphasis original.

222. Jenson, *Systematic Theology*, 2:18.

223. Piper, *Let the Nations Be Glad!*, 22, emphasis added.

To glorify God is to delight in, love and adore him. Father, Son and Spirit have been mutually loving and glorifying each other from all eternity. Out of God's desire to further glorify himself God freely created others before whom the Father would glorify the Son, and the Son glorify the Father, and the Spirit glorify the Father through the Son. Additionally, God would be glorified in the creation not only by his own actions but also by the creation itself glorifying the Father with the Son and with the Spirit. Explaining that the existence of creation and its glorifying of God does not add to or enhance God in any way, Kathryn Tanner says, "Without hopes of any advance on God's own goodness thereby, God's gifts to the creature are a kind of love-filled non-purposive or gratuitous trinitarian overflow."[224]

The God whose being is communion created the world to participate in his glorious, Triune, loving communion. God's passion for his own glory and his loving intentions for his creatures are not in opposition but are elements of God's one creative purpose, as Brunner explains.

> As the Holy God He wills to glorify Himself in His Creation; as the loving God He wills to give himself to others. His self-glorification, however, is in the last resort the same as His self-communication. He wills to glorify Himself that that which He gives is received in freedom, and rendered back to Him again: His love. Hence the revelation of this love of His is at the same time the revelation of the purpose of His Creation.[225]

Brunner goes on to say that God's love is the final cause of creation, and in Jesus this has been revealed. Furthermore, as the one by whom and for whom the world was created, Jesus is also the goal of creation because in him God has united earth with heaven, humanity with divinity. Consequently, Brunner says "It is indeed for this end alone that God has created the world; that in it He should manifest His glory and give Himself to His Creation; this is the meaning of the world, and this is its goal."[226] God's love and glory are indivisible because, says Moltmann, "God is glorified through

---

224. Tanner, *Jesus, Humanity and the Trinity*, 68.

225. Brunner, *Dogmatics*, 2:13. Along similar lines Karl Barth says "God's loving is an end in itself... Certainly in loving us God wills His own glory and our salvation. But He does not love us because He wills this. He wills it for the sake of His love. God loves in realizing these purposes. But God loves because He loves; because this act is His being, His essence and His nature. He loves without and before realizing these purposes. He loves to eternity" (Barth, *CD* II/1, 279).

226. Brunner, *Dogmatics*, 2:14. In Tanner's language, "God gives simply so that there might be a non-divine reflection of what God is" (Tanner, *Jesus, Humanity and the Trinity*, 68).

the liberation and healing of creation, and that he does not desire to be glorified without his liberated creation."[227]

Drawing these strands together I suggest with Simon Chan that the mission of the Triune God is *communion* and not merely redemption, for the latter's goal is the former.[228] The mission of the Triune God precedes creation making creation, providence and redemption all aspects of the one *missio Trinitatis Dei*. To suggest that communion is God's mission is fitting because it identifies the *telos* of creation with its origin, for "The world and all in it takes its creation and recreation from the trinitarian relatedness of Father, Son and Spirit."[229] Communion is also a helpful category because it has divine and anthropological currency, for God's being is in communion, and humans, created in the divine image, are consequently also relational and communal beings. Jenson's interpretation of Edwards is far more helpful than Piper's. Drawing on Edwards, Jenson says, "And the final goal of creation is thus at once God and his creature united in Christ, the *totus Christus*." He then quotes Edwards directly: "There was, [as] it were, an eternal society or family in the Godhead, in the Trinity of persons. It seems to be God's design to admit the church into the divine family as his son's wife."[230] Edwards' depiction of God's rationale for creation holds together Baier's final and intermediate ends, and holds together God's glory and love, all through the proposed category of communion. Creation's participation in the Triune *koinonia* is chiefly how God is glorified and is the *raison d'être* of creation.

## Why Did God Create Humanity?

God created the world, particularly humans with their uniquely bestowed relational capacity, to participate in the Triune loving. Reflecting on the incarnation as the decisive clue as to why God created humanity, Tanner says "The Son is sent by the Father in the power of the Spirit to bring us into the gift-giving relations enjoyed among members of the Trinity."[231] This understanding of the *telos* of humanity completely depends on the

---

227. Moltmann, *The Church*, 60. Elsewhere Moltmann writes, "in the Old and New Testaments . . . the glorification of God is related to the redemption of human history and the consummation of creation, and the inner-trinitarian glorification of the Father and the Son through the Holy Spirit is seen in precisely this happening" (Moltmann, "The World," 39).

228. Chan, "The Mission," 48.

229. Gunton, *The Promise*, 99.

230. Edwards, quoted in Jenson, *Systematic Theology*, 2:19.

231. Tanner, *Jesus, Humanity and the Trinity*, 68.

concept of difference-within-unity found in doctrine of the Trinity, and can be clearly seen in contrast to a different conception of divine unity. In his book *The Doctrine of the Trinity* Leonard Hodgson contrasts the trinitarian understanding of human union with God, with a monistic conception represented by 'an Indian philosopher.' This philosopher understands divine unity as an undifferentiated unity that is "the complete absence of internal multiplicity."[232] This understanding of the unity of God leads to a completely different conception of the *telos* of creation vis-à-vis divine-human communion. On this view, human union with God is understood in terms of "absorption into the being of God in which we shall at last be rid of our individual self-consciousness . . . the incorporation of a man into that unity would involve the loss of his individual selfhood."[233] In contrast to this decisively non-trinitarian account, a trinitarian description of the divine life and of the *missio Dei* is one

> in which the divine love eternally unites and yet keeps distinct the Persons of the Trinity, therefore we, when we are taken up to share in that life, may hope each to be united with God, and with his fellows in God, in a life of love which shall preserve eternally our personal distinctness.[234]

The purpose of creation, at least vis-à-vis humans,[235] is the fashioning of unique personalities who shall freely glorify God by loving neighbor and by participating in the love that is the Triune divine life. It therefore makes no sense for these distinct human personalities to be absorbed and individually dissipate into the one divine reality, like water droplets returning to the ocean. Creaturely participation in the communal divine Triune being is the purpose and goal both of redemption and of creation itself. Relating this painting of the *missio Dei* in broad brushstrokes to trinitarian theology, how do God's temporal missions relate to the eternal processions?

## *God's Eternal Processions and Temporal Missions*

Trinitarian theology speaks of the eternal begetting of the Son and the eternal proceeding of the Spirit because there is a begetting of the Son and a

---

232. Hodgson, *The Doctrine of the Trinity*, 188.
233. Ibid., 187.
234. Ibid., 187–88.
235. From the Scriptures it is clear that humans are central to the *missio Dei*, but it would be overly anthropocentric to suggest that God's purpose for humanity amounts to God's total purpose for all (human and non-human) creation.

proceeding of the Spirit in the divine economy. Now, for God's revelation to be *God's* revelation he must reveal himself *as* he is. There cannot therefore be a discrepancy between the economic Trinity and ontological Trinity, but rather a true correspondence. Therefore, as there is a begetting of the Son and a procession of the Spirit in the economy of salvation, so this must reflect an antecedent eternal begetting and proceeding.[236]

Describing the relation between the eternal processions and the temporal missions[237] of the Son and Spirit, Gilles Emery says, "The temporal procession is an embassy of the eternal, bringing a part of its home country into our history."[238] That is, the temporal missions are grounded in and are expressions of the eternal processions. The eternal and temporal processions are so called not because of their origin but due to their end point. The end of the sendings/missions of Son and Spirit is temporal, the reconciliation and redemption of all creation, whereas the end of the intra-trinitarian processions is eternal.[239] The eternal processions concern the divine *hypostases* in eternity whereas the divine missions, the sending of the Son and the Spirit, are temporal because they "are defined specifically with regard to the creaturely recipients."[240] To confuse the eternal and temporal divine processions is to risk blurring the biblical distinction between Creator and creation. The eternal divine processions describe happenings within the being of God, whereas the divine missions to creation are volitional and free.

Schwöbel believes that the eternal processions "were in traditional dogmatics insufficiently related to the missions of the Son and the Spirit expressing the role of the Trinity in the economy of salvation."[241] Seeking to correct this oversight, Fiddes states that "This story [the gospel] of sending at a particular time and place in history has its roots in an eternal sending within God . . . The two missions in the world, of the Word and the Spirit, were based in two 'processions' in the inner being of God."[242] Moltmann explains in detail the inter-relation of the eternal and temporal processions.

> As God appears in history as the sending Father and the sent Son, so he must earlier have been in himself. The relation of the one who sends to the one sent as it appears in the history of

---

236. Moltmann, *The Church*, 55.

237. I regard temporal missions and temporal processions as synonyms, but find the former to be clearer and therefore preferred.

238. Emery, *The Trinitarian Theology*, 368.

239. Ibid.

240. Tan, "A Trinitarian Ontology," 285.

241. Schwöbel, "The Renaissance," 6.

242. Fiddes, *Participating in God*, 7.

Jesus thus includes in itself an order of origin within the Trinity, and must be understood as that order's correspondence. Otherwise there would be no certainty that in the messianic mission of Jesus we have to do with God himself. The relations between the discernible and visible history of Jesus and the God whom he called 'my Father' corresponds to the relation of the Son to the Father in eternity. The *missio ad extra* reveals the *missio ad intra*. The *missio ad intra* is the foundation for the *missio ad extra*. Thus theological reflection moves inevitably from the contemplation of the sending of Jesus from the Father to God Himself. 'These movements or *processiones* in the Trinity are the deepest ground for the sendings or *missiones* of the Son and the Spirit.' [A. M. Aargaard] From the Trinity of the sending of Jesus we can reason back to the Trinity in the origin, in God himself, so that—conversely—we may understand the history of Jesus as the revelation of the living nature of God.[243]

Thus it is from God's actions in history that we learn of God's eternal being, bringing the eternal processions and the temporal missions into close proximity to one another. Increasingly in trinitarian theology, the eternal processions and temporal missions are being seen as inseparable, with scholars such as Schwöbel noting that there has been a shift to abandon the absolute distinction between the two. This is of great significance for the theology of mission. Schwöbel states that, for some, this distinction has been "replaced by a description of the trinitarian relations which integrates both the personal distinction and personal communion of Father, Son and Spirit."[244] The move to set aside the absolute distinction between the eternal processions and temporal missions has potentially negative and positive consequences. Positively, this re-description of trinitarian relations crucially includes reviewing sole dependence upon origins of relation for accounting for intra-trinitarian hypostatic distinctions, as we shall see with Pannenbeg's help shortly. Negatively, such a move could compromise divine freedom and undermine the affirmation that God is an eternal communion of love *in se*.

### Flett on the Eternal Begetting of the Son

Flett's articulation of the relation between the eternal processions and temporal missions centers of the eternal begetting of the Son and God's turn

---

243. Moltmann, *The Church*, 54, emphasis original.
244. Schwöbel, "Christology," 140.

## Trinitarian Missiology

to the economy, all expressed through affirming the unity of being and act. Central to Flett's *The Witness of God* is the resolute holding together of being and act—first, in God, and second, in the church. Flett's thesis begins by arguing that God is a missionary God *in se*.[245] Flett argues thus because he rejects the notion that God's action in the economy is only epistemologically significant; for him it is "ontologically substantive for God's life *in se*."[246] God's deliberate movement in the economy is not secondary to God's being or his otherwise defined perfection. Instead, "In his economy, in his movement toward humanity, God lives his own eternal life."[247] In this movement nothing accrues to the being of God, for as Father and Son God already has an 'above' and a 'below' within himself. "It belongs to the very nature of God's perfection that it takes this economic form of witness: God is a missionary God."[248]

Flett is trying to avoid the position in which God's movement in the economy is secondary, ancillary, and perhaps even arbitrary.[249] This position undergirds an ecclesiology in which the church's being is established *in se* and her missionary acts, should she wish to conduct any, are secondary, voluntary, and unrelated to her being. Opposing this, Flett argues that there is no cleavage in God or in the church between being and act. Concerning God's turn to the economy, Flett categorically rejects a conception of this as purely secondary and voluntary, which would separate being from act. I share Flett's rejection of the being-act dichotomy, and the undermining of the church's nature as missionary. However, in places he appears to go too far, such as when he locates the divine turning to the economy *in* the eternal begetting of the Son. "The Father's act in begetting the Son establishes both the deliberate nature of his turning to humanity and the fact that this act belongs to God's perfect being in and for himself from and to all eternity."[250] This is partly why Flett argues that God is missionary *in se*, from and to eternity. With Flett, I agree that the eternal begetting does establish in God a first and second, an above and below, but I do not concur with Flett's conflation of God's self-determination as Father, Son, and Spirit with God's

---

245. "The economic 'sendings' of the Son and the Spirit reveal a God who is missionary in his life *in se*" (Flett, *The Witness of God*, 36–37).

246. Ibid., 206.

247. Ibid., 197.

248. Ibid., 247.

249. His complaint is "God's immanent life becomes his most basic existence, with this movement in the economy already secondary to this being. God's *in se* Trinitarian being-in-act is a first complete step alongside which God's movement toward the world in creating, reconciling, and redeeming is a second step" (ibid., 205–6).

250. Ibid., 209.

turning towards the creature in the divine economy. Such a conflation runs the risk of making God's self-determination as the Triune God an expedient for the sake of the creation and thus undermining the claim that God is in himself an eternal communion of love.

I suspect that behind Flett's repeated insistence that there is no being-act dichotomy is what George Hunsinger calls the 'revisionist' position on Barth, the Trinity and election most associated with Bruce McCormack.[251] This position, according to Hunsinger, maintains that "God's pre-temporal decision of election actually gave rise to the Trinity."[252] I examined the problems with this position in my earlier discussion of the *logos asarkos*. To review it briefly, Flett's argument seems to make God's move to the economy *necessary*, replacing the *logos asarkos* with the *incarnandus*, and threatening divine freedom. I agree with Hunsinger who asserts that

> The eternal Son becomes *incarnandus* by virtue of his own free decision. He does not become *incarnandus* by being generated eternally by the Father. Becoming *incarnandus* is not a necessity that he passively undergoes. On the contrary, it is a matter of his own free decision in obedience to the Father's will.[253]

According to Paul Molnar, the line of thinking developed by McCormack and espoused by Flett is a product of confusing ontology with epistemology, a distinction that he evidently is keen to make.[254] Hunsinger agrees with McCormack, and Flett, that for Barth God's being and act are inseparable, but he rejects the claim that for Barth God's being is *constituted* by his act.

> Act for Barth is no more prior to or constitutive of God's being than the reverse. Barth does not teach, and nowhere states, that act is a consequence of being (*operari sequitur esse*), or that being is a consequence of act (*esse sequitur operari*). They are equally and primordially basic.[255]

Which Barthian school of interpretation is more or less accurate is relevant and important but is not my immediate concern. Flett's legitimate

---

251. McCormack writes, "The event in which God constitutes himself as triune is identical with the event in which he chooses to be God for the human race. Thus the 'gap' between 'the eternal Son' and 'Jesus Christ' is overcome, the distinction between them eliminated" (McCormack, *Orthodox and Modern*, 218).

252. Hunsinger, "Election and the Trinity," 179.

253. Ibid., 182–83.

254. Molnar, "Can Jesus' Divinity," 2.

255. Hunsinger, "Election and the Trinity," 180.

argument that there can be no being-act dichotomy in God, and consequently in the church, appears to me to have gone too far in the direction of compromising divine freedom.

While mission originates in the Triune being of God, who is, eternally, love *in se*, God is not a missionary God from and to eternity. Rather, God's Triune being is constituted in a *self-sufficient* perichoretic communion of loving relations between Father, Son and Spirit *ad intra*. God's Triune love is complete in itself and has no need of an external other. Accordingly, God's mission in creation and redemption is entirely a matter of grace and not of necessity. As love is not incidental but intrinsic to who God is, so mission *ad extra* flows freely out of God's trinitarian being. God is a missionary God. I can agree with Flett, therefore, in affirming that "In his economy, in his movement toward humanity, God lives his own eternal life."[256] With Flett, I also agree that God's turn to the economy is not arbitrary, incidental, or ancillary. The turn to economy is an utterly consistent expression and outworking of the being of God as love, but the suggestion must be avoided that it is necessary to God's Triune being. God's turn to the economy is predicated upon the eternal begetting of the Son which resulted in an above and a below in God *in se*, but against Flett, it does not necessarily *establish* or determine this divine turning. I hold that God's Triune being is perfect in itself and his movement toward humanity is, in John Webster's words, "not the first but a second movement" of God's being.[257] To anticipate some of the argument in chapter 5, the church is constituted by this divine missionary movement and so receives her determination from that mission. This Christological and pneumatological determination means that the church is missionary in nature. Therefore, there is no being-act separation in the church.

For God and the church, mission, as I have defined it, is temporal and not eternal. Mission does indeed come to an end, but loving fellowship does not. Accordingly, I reject Flett's claim that conceiving of mission as 'temporal' and 'provisional' entails that it is "unreal."[258] And I reject Stephen Holmes' assertion, which Flett approvingly quotes, that "the divine mission cannot ever come to an end. There must, therefore, be an eschatological continuation of God's mission. For all eternity, the Father will continue to send his Son and Spirit to bring peace and joy to creation."[259] This reading

256. Flett, *The Witness of God*, 197.

257. John Webster, *Confessing God: Essays in Christian Dogmatics II*, quoted in Hunsinger, "Election and the Trinity," 196.

258. Flett, *The Witness of God*, 266.

259. Holmes, "Trinitarian Missiology," quoted in Flett, *The Witness of God*, 76.

seems unnecessarily forced. The sending of the Son and the Spirit in the New Testament witness presupposes that humanity is estranged and separated from God, whereas according to the loud voice from the heavenly throne, in the eschaton this separation will be done away with: "God's dwelling place is now among the people, and he will dwell with them. They will be his people, and God himself will be with them and be their God."[260] Loving fellowship, not mission, is eternal; for creation will by grace participate in the loving fellowship that God is. The contention that mission is eternal, and the conflation of the eternal begetting of the Son with the God's turning to humanity as supremely expressed in the mission of the Son, compromises the absolute distinction between the eternal processions and temporal missions.

## Pannenberg on the Triune Hypostatic Distinctions

In his *Systematic Theology*, Pannenberg has pioneered the dogmatic exploration of the intra-trinitarian hypostatic distinctions that go beyond and are not restricted to intra-trinitarian relations of origin. He argues that Eastern and Western trinitarian theological language is defective because it sees "the relations among Father, Son, and Spirit exclusively as relations of origin." The chief problem of this approach is it does an injustice "to the reciprocity in the relations," which although it is incorporated into trinitarian theology via the concept of *perichoresis*, has only "a limited impact because of the one-sided viewing of the intratrinitarian relations as relations of origin."[261] Without stopping to evaluate how justified this verdict is on the tradition, his main contention is surely correct, and with important consequences for trinitarian missiology.

Pannenberg clearly and more fully describes the inner relations between the Triune Persons. God the Father is not only related to the Son by way of eternal begetting,

> He also hands over his kingdom to him and receives it back from him. The Son is not merely begotten of the Father. He is also obedient to him and he thereby glorifies him as the one God. The Spirit is not just breathed. He also fills the Son and glorifies him in his obedience to the Father, thereby glorifying the Father himself.[262]

---

260. Rev 21:3 (NIV). See also 1 Cor 13:12; 1 John 3:2.
261. Pannenberg, *Systematic Theology*, 1:319.
262. Ibid., 320.

Relations of origin are not abandoned or superseded but merely supplemented by the mutual relations between the Father, Jesus and the Holy Spirit in history. This provides a richer and more detailed account of God's being which reveals a greater depth of mutual hypostatic relations and perichoretic unity. In one sense, Pannenberg is picking up on his teacher Karl Barth's exposition of the humility of the Son in the divine economy, which he then reads 'back' into the ontological Trinity. Thus, the hypostatic relations that had previously focused on relations of origin were expanded to include the historical obedience of Son to Father. Pannenberg takes this further by incorporating with the protological and historical the eschatological. He states the traditional view that the eternal relation of origin between Father and Son is inferred from the mutual historical relations between Father and Son. This is also true for Barth's account of the Son's humility and obedience to the Father. So, Pannenberg says, "The handing over of the power and rule of the Father to the Son is then to be seen also as a defining of the intratrinitarian relations between the two, as is also their handing back by the Son to the Father."[263] This reveals mutuality in their relationship that could not be attained by simply attending to the Son's relation of origin. It also, however, raises a raft of questions concerning God's relation to time and space, and potentially reveals the specter of panentheism lurking in the background.

Pannenberg says that "By handing over lordship to the Son the Father makes his kingship dependent on whether the Son glorifies him and fulfils his lordship by fulfilling his mission."[264] Claiming support from Barth and Athanasius, he then argues that the Father's kingship is actually the same as his deity or essence, for "lordship goes hand in hand with the deity of God."[265] Therefore, the Father is related to the Son in that he begets the Son *and* he hands over the kingdom to the Son. In this latter act, the Father not only makes his kingdom dependent upon the Son but in doing so actually makes his own being, his own deity, dependent upon the Son. There is therefore not only mutual reciprocity but also mutual subjection, though not in the same way. Pannenberg characterizes the incarnation and the entire mission of the Son as "for the glory of the Father and his lordship."[266] The Son vindicates his Father's confidence in him by faithfully living out in history his loving subjection to the Father, and in so doing confirms his own identity as the Son.[267] The culmination of the incarnate Son's mission,

263. Ibid., 312–13.
264. Ibid., 313.
265. Ibid.
266. Ibid., 309.
267. Ibid., 315.

the crucifixion, therefore marks something of a crisis in the being of God for it questions the success of the Son's mission, which in turn brings into question the Father's kingdom and his very being. Hence Pannenberg says "In the death of Jesus the deity of his God and Father was at issue."[268]

Pannenberg's redescription of the perichoretic intra-trinitarian relations has opened them up to incorporate the historical and eschatological relations between the Triune Persons. By making the Father's deity dependent upon the success of the Son's historical mission Pannenberg has depicted God as making himself dependent upon historical events. Speaking of God the Father he says, "Even in his deity, by the creation of the world and the sending of his Son and Spirit to work in it, he has made himself dependent upon the course of history."[269] Pannenberg believes he is following insights first made by two of Barth's pre-eminent students, Jüngel and Moltmann.[270] Although this could easily collapse into pantheism or panentheism it does not need to, for God the Father has staked his identity not upon history itself, but upon the work of the Son and Spirit in history. Specifically, God the Father has made himself dependent upon the success of the missions of Son and Spirit. Thus the Father's risk is not a reckless one but rather an 'infallible risk', since the Son and Spirit are wholly dependable in glorifying the Father by carrying out their missions. In other words, the Father's identity is wrapped up in the *perichoresis* of the Triune Persons that has been broadened out from the relations of origin to include the temporal missions of the Son and Spirit. This sheds new light on the statement that God is constituted in the perichoretic relations among the Triune Persons and brings missiology into the heart of theology.

The crisis point of the Son's historical mission was his crucifixion, which called the deity of God the Father into question, but just prior to this Jesus prays to his Father. Pannenberg writes, "The prayer of Jesus to the Father that the Father will glorify him is thus answered by the sending and work of the Spirit."[271] Although there is a sense in which Jesus' mission was completed in the nexus of events between crucifixion and Pentecost, it is also the case that that which Jesus inaugurated, namely the kingdom of God and the disciple-making called-out community (*ecclesia*), was entrusted to the Holy Spirit to bring to completion. Naturally, the Spirit's carrying out and completion of this is not separate from the ongoing mission of the

268. Ibid., 314.

269. Ibid., 320.

270. Eberhard Jüngel, "Vom Tod des lebendigen Gottes"; idem., *God As the Mystery of the World*; Jürgen Moltmann, *The Crucified God*, referenced in Pannenberg, *Systematic Theology*, 1:329.

271. Pannenberg, *Systematic Theology*, 1:315.

exalted and glorified Christ and the Father. Jesus entrusted his immediate mission, atonement and reconciliation, and his long-term mission, to the Father, according to whose will he lived in constant submission, and to the Holy Spirit. In the moment on Good Friday at which Jesus' mission and the Father's identity hung in the balance, and then through the agonizing silence of Holy Saturday, creation waited. Then, on the first day of the week marking the beginning of new creation "the Father asserts himself against death by raising up the Crucified"[272] by the Holy Spirit.[273] The incarnate Son had entrusted his very life to his Father and the Holy Spirit by whom he lived and in whose relation his own identity is constituted. By raising him from the dead the Father and Spirit glorify the Son, and this marks the beginning of the Father's glorifying of the Son through the post-Pentecost mission of the Spirit. "Glorifying the Son, the Spirit also glorifies the Father and their indissoluble fellowship."[274]

Moving from the historical to the eschatological, the reciprocal relations between Father, Son and Spirit are not yet completely described. Although the historical mission of the Son was completed at his ascension, the apostle Paul makes it clear that in some sense the Son's mission is also incomplete, for Christ must reign until he has put all his enemies under his feet.[275] Since Christ is at the right hand of the Father in heaven, he will accomplish his ongoing mission by means of the missions of the Spirit and the church. First, the ascended Son receives the Spirit from the Father and pours him out on the day of Pentecost. Thus the mission of the Spirit has its origin firstly in the Father from whom he proceeds, and then also in the Son through whom he proceeds. It is uniquely the Spirit's role to bring honor and glory to the Son as seen on the day of Pentecost when he inspired the apostle Peter to preach about Christ, resulting in three thousand being baptized in the name of Jesus. By not glorifying himself or speaking of himself, but glorifying and speaking of the Son (John 16:13), by bearing witness to him (John 15:26) and reminding the church of Jesus' teaching (John 14:26),

272. Ibid., 329.

273. It is at this point that Colin Greene criticizes Newbigin's exegesis of the New Testament's answer to the question of 'Who is Jesus?' For Greene, Newbigin "doesn't sufficiently underscore the importance of the resurrection as God's answer to that same question. Consequently, as Pannenberg recognizes, 'Only by his resurrection from the dead did the Crucified attain to the dignity of the Kyrios (Phil 2:9–11). Only thus was he appointed the Son of God in power (Rom 1:4). Only in the light of the resurrection as God's answer is he the pre-existent Son'" (Greene, "Trinitarian Tradition," 68). Pannenberg quotation from *Systematic Theology*, 2:283.

274. Pannenberg, *Systematic Theology*, 1:315.

275. See 1 Cor 15:25. See chapter 4 where I discuss the relation between the historical and ongoing parts of the one mission of the Son.

the Spirit shows himself to be the Spirit of truth (John 16:13).[276] It is the mission of the Spirit to glorify the Son and bring all into loyal and loving subjection to him, but more on this in chapter 4. Second, the Son's ongoing mission is accomplished through the mission of the church, which cannot be considered apart from the mission of the Spirit.[277] By the enabling of the Spirit, no doubt related to the ongoing intercession by Jesus for his church, the body of Christ reaches out in word and deed making known repentance for the forgiveness of sins in Jesus' name. The church's mission will not be complete until the good news of Jesus has been communicated to all people (Matt 24:14; Rev 5:9) so that representatives of every tribe and tongue will be found worshipping the Lamb (Rev 7:9). Once Christ's reign over all is complete, he will then hand the kingdom over to God the Father so that God may be all in all.[278] Spelling out the full mutual reciprocity of Triune Persons Pannenberg says,

> in their intratrinitarian relations the persons depend on one another in respect of their deity as well as their personal being, and that this mutual interdependence affects not only the relations of the Son and the Spirit to the Father but also those of the Father to them.[279]

This adds far more depth to the statement that God is constituted in his perichoretic relations. Whilst affirming complete mutual reciprocity between the Triune Persons, Pannenberg does not compromise the trinitarian order that is from the Father through the Son in the Spirit, and the doxological order in which the church's worship of God is in and by the Spirit through and with the Son to the Father. Mutuality and distinctiveness are maintained without collapsing into a simple and unbiblical egalitarianism. What is extraordinary in this account is the increased significance of the church's mission both for herself and for her Lord.

### The Eternal Processions and Temporal Missions: Missiological Implications

The Son and Spirit, by faithfully carrying out their missions to honor the Father, they confirm their own identities as Son and Spirit. Similarly, as the church faithfully carries out her self-effacing mission to glorify the Son who

---

276. Pannenberg, *Systematic Theology*, 1:315.
277. See chapter 4 for an in depth discussion of this inter-relation.
278. 1 Cor 15:24–28. See extended discussion of this passage in chapter 4.
279. Pannenberg, *Systematic Theology*, 1:329.

is the image of his Father, by the Holy Spirit, the church confirms her own identity as adopted children of God, called to declare the praises of him who called her out of darkness and into his marvelous light (1 Pet 2:9). The church's being is located in God's trinitarian missions to the world, and so as the church carries out her mission of participating in the *missio Dei*, her very being is made manifest. This is not to say that as the church carries out her mission she gains or earns her relation with God, for good works do not save her, but rather the good works give expression to God's gracious salvation (Eph 2:8–10). As the church comforts the suffering, heals the sick, feeds the hungry, frees the oppressed, and declares the good news of Jesus and forgiveness of sins in his name thereby advancing God's kingdom, God's very nature is revealed in her, thus confirming her identity as belonging to God. The church's role in contributing towards establishing the kingdom of God and thus God's very being is truly astonishing.

The Father had entrusted his kingship and thus his very self to his Son, who in turn entrusted the carrying out and completion of this kingship to the missions of the Spirit and church. This elevates the importance of the already significant *missio ecclesiae* exponentially. Arriving at the same destination via a slightly different route, Moltmann links, according to Pannenberg, "the consummation of salvation history in eschatology with the consummation of the trinitarian life of God in itself."[280] The danger here is compromising the Creator–creaturely distinction by suggesting that by carrying out her mission the church contributes to the trinitarian life of God, thus making creation's subjection to God constitutive of his identity. This would make the *missio ecclesiae* carry a burden infinitely too heavy to bear. However, in reality, the linking of the eschatological consummation of salvation history with the eschatological consummation of the trinitarian life of God is simply a working out of the premise that the Father's lordship is identical to his deity.

By freely choosing to create the world, God made his own deity dependent upon his rule over creation. When creation rebelled, his own deity was indeed called into question, which is not unrelated to the New Testament statements that Satan is the 'god of this age' who controls 'the whole world.'[281] By asserting himself in raising Jesus from the dead the Father overcame and forever defeated his enemies of sin, death and the devil who had dared to question his deity, and inaugurated the incorruptible kingdom that is the

280. Pannenberg, *Systematic Theology*, 1:330. See Moltmann, *The Trinity*, 126, 160–61. Moltmann says, "The economic Trinity completes and perfects itself to immanent Trinity when the history and experience of salvation are completed and perfected" (*The Trinity*, 161).

281. 2 Cor 4:4 and 1 John 5:19 NIV.

new creation. The 'already' of this historical victory over death anticipates the 'not yet' of Christ's eschatological victory over death (1 Cor 15:25–26). In this time in-between the 'already' and 'not yet' the church carries out her mission by communicating by deed and word the crucifixion and resurrection of Jesus. Thus the church does not contribute to the trinitarian life of God, for this was historically established by the Triune God at the resurrection of Jesus. Rather, in her mission the church actively seeks, by the enabling of the Holy Spirit, to be the means by which Christ *implements* his victory of the empty tomb to and among all peoples. God's being as God is not somehow dependent on the mission of the church, which history shows is a fickle and flimsy thing indeed. On the contrary, God in his grace has grafted the church into the *missio Dei* by adopting her into the sonship of Christ through the Spirit. God in his wisdom has graciously and freely chosen to make the church's mission an important part of the *missio Dei* so that through her God's wisdom should be made known to the principalities and powers (Eph 3:10). The church therefore does not so much presumptuously contribute to the divine nature as graciously and generously participate in the divine nature. Thus the church's mission is embedded "not only within the meta-narrative of God's historicity, but in his very being as Father, Son and Holy Spirit."[282] The *missio ecclesiae* is thus not asked to illegitimately carry more than it can bear, but God still freely confers on the missionary church an unanticipatable, unique and remarkable dignity.

---

282. Tan, "A Trinitarian Ontology," 280.

CHAPTER 4

# The Mission of the Son and Spirit

FRANCES YOUNG POINTS OUT that Newbigin's trinitarianism operates like that of Irenaeus, who calls the Word and Spirit the two hands of God.[1] In this chapter I shall continue to develop a trinitarian missiology beyond Newbigin by discussing, in turn, the two hands of God, that is, the mission of the Son and the mission of the Holy Spirit. Before embarking on this missiological journey it is important to first, briefly, map out the dogmatic landscape; specifically, the interrelation between the missions of Son and Spirit.

## THE INTERRELATION OF THE MISSIONS OF SON AND SPIRIT

The Son's mission cannot be understood apart from the mission of the Spirit, and vice versa, because the missions of the Son and Spirit are inextricably and perichoretically related. Furthermore, these two missions are dogmatically located in immediate proximity to each other. From the perspective of Spirit Christology, the historical mission of the Son (from incarnation to ascension) is part of the mission of the Spirit, which precedes, accompanies and follows the Son's historical mission. After all, the Spirit shares in the sending of the Son, since Jesus was miraculously conceived by the Spirit, and the climax of the Son's historical mission, his atoning death and resurrection, were both accomplished in and by the Holy Spirit.[2] Schwöbel contends that "the theological traditions of the New Testament see the

---

1. *Adversus haereses* 5.1.3; 6.1, referenced in Young, "The Uncontainable God," 84.
2. See Heb 9:14 and Rom 8:11.

Spirit as much as [sic.] constitutive for the Christ-event, as they describe the presence of the Spirit for the believers as a consequence of the Christ-event."[3] The eternal perichoretic relation of Son and Sprit is reflected in the coinherent missions of Son and Spirit. Describing this mutuality between Son and Spirit in Jesus' historical mission, Gregory of Nazianzus says,

> Consider the following, Christ is born, the Spirit is his forerunner (Luke 1:35); Christ is baptized, the Spirit bears witness (Luke 3:21–22); Christ is tempted, the Spirit leads him up (Luke 4:2, 14); [Christ] works miracles, the Spirit accompanies him (Matt 12:22, 28); Christ ascends, the Spirit takes his place (Acts 1:8–9).[4]

From one perspective the Son is the agent of his own mission, as commissioned by the Father, and yet it is also true that the Spirit actively works in and through the Son's mission. However, the Spirit is not subject to his own, proper sending, until the Day of Pentecost when the roles are reversed as the exalted Son inaugurates his ongoing mission by sharing with the Father in the sending of the Spirit. H. B. Swete says, "Without the mission of the Spirit the mission of the Son would have been fruitless; without the mission of the Son the Spirit could not have been sent."[5] The work of Son and Spirit are perichoretically related because their work substantially constitutes the one *missio trinitatis Dei* and because the Triune Persons are constituted in and by their perichoretic mutual relations. Nevertheless, in their unity the work of Son and the work of the Spirit are distinct, corresponding to the intra-trinitarian relations of the Triune Persons who are distinct within their unity of being and purpose. Hence Clark Pinnock is right to rule out language of subordination between the missions of Son and Spirit; rather "there is a mutual and reciprocal relationship between them. Neither Son nor Spirit ought to be subordinated to the other. Each can be viewed in terms of the mission of the other."[6]

---

3. Schwöbel, "Christology," 125. There has been some excellent work on Spirit Christology but this needs to be incorporated into an all-embracing mission of the Spirit in which it comprises a crucial chapter.

4. *Oratio* 31.29, quoted in Wilken, *Remembering the Christian Past*, 84.

5. H. B. Swete, *The Holy Spirit in the New Testament*, quoted in Fee, *Paul, the Spirit*, 85.

6. Pinnock, *Flame of Love*, 92.

## The Ongoing Mission of Christ and the Proper Mission of the Spirit

There is an especially close relation between the ongoing mission of Christ and the post-Pentecost mission of the Spirit. I contend that the sending or mission of the Spirit is not a *replacement* of the mission of Christ as the Eastern Orthodox conceive of it.[7] Nor is the mission of the Spirit merely a function of Christ's ongoing mission, thus subjecting Pneumatology to Christology. Neither is the Spirit's mission merely a continuation of Christ's historical mission, although in certain ways the Spirit does continue Jesus' work, such as teaching truth to the disciples (John 16:12–14). Rather, with David Coffey I affirm "there *is* a proper mission of the Holy Spirit,"[8] but since the Holy Spirit is the Spirit of Jesus (Acts 16:7; Phil 1:19) there is an inextricable, deep, mysterious and extraordinarily close relationship between the ongoing mission of Christ and the post-Pentecost mission of the Spirit, as there was between the work of the Spirit in the life of the Son from incarnation to ascension. Jesus mediates the Spirit to humanity because it was he who pours out the Spirit,[9] baptizes in the Spirit,[10] and gives the Spirit without measure.[11] But the Spirit also mediates Jesus to humanity, for no one can confess 'Jesus is Lord' except by the Spirit,[12] for he enables and causes believers to be united to and participate in the risen Christ.

The ongoing mission of Christ and the post-Pentecost mission of the Spirit so overlap that it is difficult to distinguish between them, and this is further complicated by the fact that the Spirit is the chief agent of the Son's ongoing mission. One possible resolution is to affirm the unity of all divine action, and by following the 'Augustinian' rule *opera trinitatis ad extra sunt indivisa*,[13] affirm that the Son and Spirit are chief agents of the one *missio trinitatis Dei*. Positively, this rule rightly affirms the unity of all divine action. Since the Triune Persons coinhere one another, unity in divine action *ad extra* logically follows. However, this rule can be taken in a stronger sense to mean that the divine Triune operations are *indivisible* such that "no characteristic and distinctive forms of action can be ascribed to Father, Son

---

7. C.f. John 14. Coffey explains that "the Eastern Orthodox position is that there *is* a proper mission of the Holy Spirit, that it began at Pentecost, and that in a real sense it replaced the mission of Christ, which ended at that point" ("A Proper Mission," 227).

8. Ibid., 227, emphasis original.

9. Acts 2:33.

10. Matt 3:11; Mark 1:8; Luke 3:16; John 1:33.

11. John 3:34.

12. 1 Cor 12:3. See Torrance, *Theology in Reconstruction*, 245–47.

13. Barth, *CD* I/1, 375.

and Spirit, there appears to be no point in distinguishing between them."[14] Jenson believes Augustine to be guilty of undermining the distinctiveness of the work of the Triune hypostases *ad extra*. He contends that in Augustine's account of the baptism of Jesus in *De Trinitate* 1.8, a chief text of original trinitarianism, the voice that speaks to Jesus "is indifferently specifiable as the Father or the Son or the Spirit of the whole Trinity."[15] If so, then this clearly undermines the integrity and distinctive identity of the operations of the Triune hypostases *ad extra*, and comes dangerously close to modalism. Whether Jenson treats Augustine fairly, is for my purposes, secondary, but it is clear that to speak of the *indivisibility* of the divine operations *ad extra* is to risk suggesting that these operations are also indistinguishable.

A preferred approach is that of Cappadocian trinitarian theology as represented by Gregory of Nyssa, who says "All action that impacts the creature from God . . . begins with the Father and is actual through the Son and is perfected in the Holy Spirit."[16] Thus it is uniquely the Holy Spirit who perfects, completes and executes the divine will. Similarly, Puritan John Owen says "The Holy Ghost . . . is the *immediate, peculiar, efficient* cause of all external divine operations: for God worketh by his Spirit, or in him immediately applies the power and efficacy of the divine excellencies unto their operation."[17] I believe that concerning the Spirit this is true not only of all divine operations, but particularly of certain functions such as prophecy, revelation, sanctification, and mission. Hence, Fiddes says that "we associate some functions in a particular, but non-exclusive way with particular persons . . . because we find one movement in God takes the 'leading edge' in a particular context."[18] In this age of mission between the time of the incarnation and Christ's *parousia*, it is the Holy Spirit who takes this 'leading edge' among the Triune Persons for it is he who is the chief agent implementing and accomplishing God's mission, though not without nor apart from Son or Father. Consequently, Newbigin rightly and appropriately says of the Holy Spirit "It is he who is, properly speaking, the missionary."[19]

---

14. Gunton, *The Promise*, 4. Pannenberg has similar concerns, in *Systematic Theology*, 1:271–80.

15. Jenson, *Systematic Theology*, 1:111.

16. *Ad Ablabius, ut non sint tres dii*, 125, quoted in Jenson, *Systematic Theology*, 1:110.

17. John Owen, *Pneumatologia*, quoted in Gunton, *The Promise*, 69.

18. Fiddes, *Participating in God*, 103. By 'movements in God' Fiddes means the Triune Persons.

19. Newbigin, *Trinitarian Doctrine*, 40.

With the trinitarian dogmatic framework for the divine missions now sketched, let us first turn to elucidate a thoroughly trinitarian theological account of the mission of the Son.

## THE MISSION OF THE SON

### *Introduction*

The center of the *missio Dei* is the sending or mission of the Son. No theological or missiological account can be accepted that is not hermeneutically controlled by the Father's sending of the Son by the Spirit. The mission of the Son is central to creation and to human history, for "The absolute future has occurred in history before the end of time, so every historical present is decisively qualified by that event."[20] I have already said that the *missio Dei* is to glorify God through giving the gift of life to creation that it might participate in the Triune *koinonia*. From the 'bookends' of Scripture (Genesis 1–3 and Revelation 21–22) it is clear that God's intentions in creation and the new creation are to dwell with his creatures made in his image. The Fall of humanity and its disastrous consequences for the rest of creation set the world on a path unintended by God. In order to realize his creative purposes, his mission, God freely chose to save and reconcile his creation. God's action in the incarnation of the Son was one of unanticipatable mercy and grace, and remains both astonishing and overwhelming. Capturing the reason for this awe and wonder, Barth says, "In Him [Jesus Christ] the fact is once for all established that God does not exist without man."[21]

The four canonical gospels form the center of the biblical witness to Jesus Christ, and Moltmann observes that they "present the history of Jesus in the light of his sending, his mission."[22] Thus, mission is the framework provided by the gospels for understanding and interpreting the life of Jesus. Mission is not only the hermeneutical key for interpreting Jesus' life, but also central to his life. Jenson describes Jesus' life as "a life lived utterly for his mission, that is, for the Father and for those to whom the Father sends him."[23] The Father sent the Son by the Spirit into the world to be the bearer of the trinitarian life in history. However, Moltmann observes that as well as understanding Christ from the perspective of the past, his sending ought also to be understood vis-à-vis the future. Thus, the mission of the Son is

---

20. Braaten, *The Flaming Center*, 76.
21. Barth, *The Humanity of God*, 47.
22. Moltmann, *The Church*, 53.
23. Jenson, *Systematic Theology*, 1:219.

also to be understood from the point of view of its goal and his glorification.[24] Describing this goal, Bria says "Christ was sent for no lesser purpose than to bring the world into the life of God. Christ's mission is, therefore, essentially the self-giving of the Trinity so that the world may become a participant in the divine life."[25]

In the context of this chapter on the missions of the Son and Spirit, I make no attempt to develop or elucidate a thoroughgoing Christology and soteriology, but rather seek to outline the missions of the Son and Spirit in the context of the *missio trinitatis Dei*. In the center of that mission, Jesus "is the means by which human failure to achieve the end for which the human race was created—its movement backwards—is reversed into a movement towards proper perfection."[26] God does not permit humanity's rebellion to be the sole ontological and eschatological determinant. God's love does not permit wayward humanity to be the sole author of its story. Rather, the creator God who providentially rules over his creation once again intervenes, not this time by the sending of prophets, but by the incarnation of the eternal Son of God. The entire mission of the Son is to redirect creation back onto its divinely-intended course, and God's manner of restoring us, becoming human, is consonant with his ends, *koinonia*. The destiny of humanity in Christ is to participate in the divine nature by means of the Spirit, taking us up into the sonship of Jesus. This human and divine togetherness, which is the telos of creation and thus the *missio Dei*, is achieved by means of the unrepeatable and mysterious divine and human togetherness that exists in the incarnate Son, in the hypostatic union of his divinity and humanity. Reflecting on the incarnation, Barth says God has shown that "In His deity there is enough room for communion with man."[27]

## The Reconciling Life of Christ

### Revelation

Jesus' mission of redeeming humanity included definitively revealing who God is. Jesus is our great high priest, "He represents God to us and He represents us to God. In this way He is God's revelation to us and our

---

24. Moltmann, *The Church*, 56.

25. Bria, *Go Forth In Peace*, 5. Similarly, Moltmann says "God experiences history in order to effect history. He goes out of himself in order to gather into himself" (*The Church*, 64).

26. Gunton, *Father, Son and Holy Spirit*, 142.

27. Barth, *The Humanity of God*, 47.

reconciliation with God."[28] He reveals God in his teaching, his action, and in his interaction with other persons as recorded in the gospels. Elsewhere Barth expands on this further, explaining that

> Jesus Christ, as this Mediator and Reconciler between God and man, is also the *Revealer* of them both. We do not need to engage in a free-ranging investigation to seek out and construct who and what God truly is, and who and what man truly is, but only to read the truth about both where it resides, namely, in the fullness of their togetherness, their covenant which proclaims itself in Jesus Christ.[29]

Jesus is the perfect revelation of God, for in him the fullness of God dwells bodily (Col 2:9). "He is the image of the invisible God" (Col 1:15) and "the exact imprint of God's very being" (Heb 1:3). The incarnate Word is the self-communication of God, because although God "dwells in unapproachable light" (1 Tim 6:16), he has chosen to not remain aloof, but in Jesus has introduced himself, to such an extent that Jesus can say that "Whoever has seen me has seen the Father" (John 14:9). Thus, it is clear that human knowledge of God is not something humanly attainable through honed skill, moral striving or intellectual effort. True knowledge of God is *revealed*, that is, given by God as a gift. The center and definitive act of God's self-revelation, towards which all the Old Testament Scriptures point (John 5:39–40), is the person of Jesus the Messiah. That is why Calvin accurately says "God is comprehended in Christ alone."[30] The God of the Torah who dwells above the terrified Israelites on Mt. Sinai has drawn near in Jesus, such that he is Emmanuel, God with us (Matt 1:23, see Isa 7:14). In Jesus, God has not revealed merely theological truths or moral standards, but himself, in person; hence, Newbigin says "Jesus is, quite simply, God's revelation of himself. It is God whom we meet when we meet Jesus."[31]

## Training the Twelve

Arguably, Jesus spent the majority of his short ministry years training his small band of twelve disciples, so it was primarily to them that Jesus revealed who God is and what authentic human being looks like. To the twelve, he also personally modelled a fully human life lived entirely in obedience to the

---

28. Barth, *CD* I/2, 151.
29. Barth, *The Humanity of God*, 44, emphasis original.
30. Calvin, *Institutes*, II.6.4, 347.
31. Newbigin, *The Light Has Come*, 165.

Father by complete dependence upon the Spirit. This modelling includes illustrating authentic and true humanity through his teaching and demonstrating the character of God through the breadth of his actions, including the miraculous and the merciful. Central to the mission of the Son is his highly symbolic choice of "twelve to represent the first nucleus of the community of a renewed covenant," which Kirk says "would hardly be lost on any Jew of the first century."[32] N. T. Wright observes that Israel had not existed as twelve tribes since the Assyrian invasion of 734 BC, and so the twelve disciples represent the eschatological restoration and reconstitution of Israel.[33] It is with these twelve that Jesus shares the last supper, which signifies the new covenant in his blood. This new covenant, which Ezekiel (36:26–27) and Jeremiah (31:31–34) foresaw, is characterized by the giving of new hearts which have the Torah written upon them, knowing God, being forgiven of sin, having the indwelling presence of God's Spirit, and being divinely-enabled for obedience. In this new covenant explained to the twelve, God was in the process of rescuing and re-directing human history.

Jesus' training of the disciples was preparation for entrusting and committing his ongoing mission to them, for they were his primary legacy. As Newbigin famously said, "what our Lord left behind Him was not a book, nor a creed, nor a system of thought, nor a rule of life, but a visible community . . . He committed the entire work of salvation to that community."[34] The secret of Jesus' confidence in his disciples is exactly the same secret Roland Allen identified as the apostolic missionary method, that led to the spontaneous expansion of the church. Jesus had full trust and confidence in the Holy Spirit to indwell, empower, vivify, sanctify and guide his disciples. Jesus knew from first-hand experience that he could completely entrust his disciples to the Holy Spirit. Allen argues that the secret of the apostle Paul's missionary success, in contrast to much of the modern missionary movement, is that he similarly entrusts his converts and his churches to the Holy Spirit.[35] Jesus demonstrated this missiological principle by committing 'the entire work of salvation to that community', because he knew that community was under the sovereignty of the Holy Spirit. Jesus the Rabbi was even content to leave his disciples' instruction unfinished, because he knew that the Holy Spirit would complete the task (John 16:12–15).

---

32. Kirk, *What Is Mission?*, 208.
33. Wright, *Jesus and the Victory of God*, quoted in Kirk, *What Is Mission?*, 208.
34. Newbigin, *The Household of God*, 27.
35. Allen, *Missionary Methods*.

## Vicarious Obedience

The locus of God's re-direction of creation is at precisely the point at which creation went astray—human sinfulness consisting of unbelief and disobedience. In becoming flesh the Son took to himself sinful human flesh, for there is no other kind, but in doing so "He does not come into conflict with Himself. He does not sin when in the unity with the man Jesus He mingles with sinners and takes their place . . . He frees the creature in becoming a creature. He overcomes the flesh in becoming flesh."[36] In the hypostatic union of the Son of God with corrupt human nature, there was no danger that the latter would somehow communicate sin and infect the former. T. F. Torrance explains that the opposite is in fact the case: "The hypostatic union could not have been actualized within the conditions of our fallen humanity without the removal of sin and guilt through atonement and the sanctification of human nature assumed into union with the divine."[37] The doctrine of total depravity reflects the truth that sinning has literally become second nature for humans, so that all have sinned and none are righteous before God. God became human, Khaled Anatolios explains, "because sin had taken root in us and had to be eradicated by the divine presence from within."[38] This eradication took place by way of the incarnate Son's hypostatic union, which "took on the form of a dynamic atoning union which steadily worked itself out within the structures of human existence all through the course of our Lord's vicarious earthly life."[39] The incarnation of the Son of God eliminates human sin from within the Son's human nature for the purpose of humanity's reconciliation with God.

The incarnate Son is not simply God, but "as Son of the Father, is a Godward God."[40] As such, the Son's entire identity or hypostasis is *for* the Father, which is an aspect of the Son's eternal perichoretic relation with the Father. Anatolios explains that the Son's Godward stance "is constituted in full and immediate possession of the term of its orientation (the Godwardness of the Son always fully and immediately attains its goal—that is what it means in this context to say that the Son is 'one in being' with the Father)."[41] The Son's goal is to exist for his Father, and because he perfectly achieves this and lives in an unbroken relation with his Father, the Son's goal is always

---

36. Barth, *CD* IV/1, 185.
37. Torrance, *The Mediation of Christ*, 76.
38. Anatolios, "The Immediately Triune God," 171.
39. Torrance, *The Mediation of Christ*, 76.
40. Anatolios, "The Immediately Triune God," 173.
41. Ibid.

realized. In the incarnation this relation is realized in created time and space as the Son implements his filial relationship with the Father as the last Adam on humanity's behalf.[42] Thus, Newbigin suggests the meaning of the whole of Christ's life is "that the Father's glory may be manifested in the loving obedience of the Son."[43] This unbroken relation and perfect obedience is enacted and carried out from within human nature, as the obedient last Adam. Hence, the Godward God, in sharing our humanity, "perfects humanity's Godward stance by being himself a divine exemplar of that stance."[44] Jesus not only exemplifies Godwardness in his obedient humanity, but he is the one who recapitulates humanity, and both effects and secures its obedience. "So by the obedience, whereby He obeyed unto death, hanging on the tree," Irenaeus explains, "He undid the old disobedience wrought in the tree."[45] Jesus further effected the reversal of humanity's disobedience by constantly distinguishing himself from and submitting to the Father. By not grasping for equality with God (Phil 2:6) Jesus reversed Adam's sin of wanting himself to be God (Genesis 3:5).[46] As the last Adam, Christ's obedience reversed the disobedience of Adam, and for this obedience to be efficacious it had to be voluntary. Speaking of Christ's obedient life that culminated in his death, Calvin says, "He had to submit to death of His own free will to destroy the willful disobedience of men by His own obedience."[47] In Gethsemane, Jesus' free and loving submission to the Father's will to go to Golgotha is the ultimate act of faith in the trustworthiness of God (Matt 26:36–44), overcoming Adam's lack of faith in God's trustworthiness (Gen 3:5–6). Jesus was, in words of the apostle Paul, "obedient to the point of death" (Phil 2:8). Drawing on Lohmeyer, Martin observes, "only a divine being can accept death as *obedience*; for ordinary men it is a necessity. He alone as the obedient Son of His Father could choose death as His destiny; and He did so because of His love."[48] His vicarious obedience complete, Jesus fulfilled the righteous requirements of the law on humanity's behalf (Rom 8:4), so that "Christ

42. Pinnock, *Flame of Love*, 97.

43. Newbigin, *The Light Has Come*, 158.

44. Anatolios, "The Immediately Triune God," 173.

45. Irenaeus, *Epideixis* 34 quoted in Anatolios, "The Immediately Triune God," 171.

46. Pannenberg, *Systematic Theology*, 1:310.

47. Calvin, quoted in Peterson Sr, *Calvin and the Atonement*, 67. Similarly, Marion Conditt says "Until he surrendered Himself willingly His death could not atone for the purposeful rebellion of Adam" Marion W. Conditt, *More Acceptable Than Sacrifice: Ethics and Election as Obedience to God's Will in the Theology of Calvin*, quoted in Peterson, *Calvin and the Atonement*, 68.

48. Martin, *The Epistle of Paul to the Philippians*, 102.

is the end of the law . . . for everyone who believes" (Rom 10:4). By Jesus' obedience "the many will be made righteous" (Rom 5:19). The hypostatic union of the incarnate Son is the instrument of Christ's reconstituting of human nature. Drawing on Gregory of Palamas, Jenson explains,

> Jesus as a man 'receives in himself the fullness of perfect and full deity', so that his creaturely actuality, his 'flesh', is itself 'the infinite fountain of holiness.' Jesus' human action and presence is without mitigation God's action and presence, with whatever that must do to and for creatures.[49]

This vicarious obedience of Christ includes his constant reliance upon the enabling Spirit of God to accomplish the will of the Father, for which he ever-lives. Similarly, Christ's reconciling of humanity by his vicarious obedience and atoning death is incomplete without the Holy Spirit subjectively incorporating human persons into Christ's work. Those who are united by the Holy Spirit with the Incarnate Godward God are, by virtue of the fact that the Son's Godwardness instantaneously reaches its goal, also united into immediate union with the Father, who is *homoousios* with the Son.

## Teaching and Healing Ministry

Jesus' redemptive activity prior to Golgotha is most evident in his teaching and healing ministry. In a religiously and politically oppressive context, Jesus' teaching was aimed at challenging religious traditions that were burdensome or an excuse for sin (Mark 7:9–13). He describes his own mission as setting the captives free and binding up the broken hearted (see Luke 4:16–21). In stories and sermons Jesus' teaching described what God's multifaceted reign was like, and he also outlined in broad brush-strokes the kind of people whose lives reflect God's reign and who enjoy the blessings of that reign (Matt 5:1–12). By his teaching and in his person he made known the truth that sets free (John 8:32), and in his healing and deliverance ministry he enacted this truth. Thus, John Taylor puts it well in saying "The Mission of Jesus Christ was quite simply both to proclaim, and to be, the inauguration of the new age."[50] This was supremely realized in Christ's resurrection, but was also anticipated in the 'mighty acts' and 'signs and wonders' that Jesus performed.

Central to the miracles of Jesus were his acts of healing the sick and demon oppressed. Newbigin observes "The fact that Jesus habitually healed

---

49. Jenson, *Systematic Theology*, 1:144. Quotations from Gregory of Palamas.
50. Taylor, *For All The World*, 22.

sick people is one of the most prominent elements in the tradition. One-fifth of all the material in the four Gospels is concerned with the healing of physical disease."[51] Healing is important because sickness represents parts of God's creation in slavery to forces that spoil creation and oppose God's kingdom rule. Jesus' healings of the sick are instances of the inbreaking of God's kingdom, and are partial anticipations of the fullness of the coming of that kingdom.[52] Jesus' demonstrated authority over sickness and the demonic represent the assault of God's reign upon evil in its many manifestations. Bosch observes that Jesus' contemporaries believed that the demon-possessed were evidence that Satan was lord of this world. Thus, it is significant that in Luke 11:20 Jesus explains that his driving out demons by 'the finger of God' means that 'the kingdom of God has come to you', because "the very pillars on which Satan's supposed reign rests are under assault."[53]

In much theology since the Enlightenment, it has been common practice to under-emphasize the significance of Satan, demons and angels. On the one hand, theologians cannot ignore the angelic realm due to its prominence particularly in the gospels, but on the other, theologians do not quite know how interpret this biblical reality. Consider, for example, Jenson, who says "Jesus' mission had throughout his life set him against the *demons, however we are to stipulate their ontological status*."[54] In contrast McKnight's bluntness is refreshing: "Even if many in our world don't see it or if they demean the idea, the Bible teaches us that there is right now a cosmic battle going on between good and evil," ultimately caused by the devil.[55] Drawing in 1 John 3:8 and Hebrews 2:14 Boyd claims that "the ultimate reason why Jesus became a man . . . was to destroy the devil and place under his foot all his cosmic enemies. The incarnation, then, was an ultimate act of war," which in contrast to modern theology, "the early church saw consistently."[56] From this perspective, Jesus' whole ministry was set against Satan and the

---

51. Newbigin, *The Light Has Come*, 63. He then adds in brackets "The virtual ignoring of this work of healing during most of Christian history is one of the astonishing facts which the theologian and the historian must try to explain" (*ibid*). This is an important and fascinating subject for any missiology that seeks to seriously reflect on 'mission in Christ's way', but for reasons of space cannot be dealt with here. For further reading, see Williams, "Excursus: On the Cessation of Miracles," in *Renewal Theology*, 158–68.

52. Gunton, *Father, Son and Holy Spirit*, 117.

53. Bosch, *Transforming Mission*, 33.

54. Jenson, *Systematic Theology*, 1:193, emphasis added.

55. McKnight, *The Heaven Promise*, 72.

56. Boyd, *God At War*, 201.

demonic. This conflict, which began even while Jesus was still an infant, reached its dramatic conclusion at Golgotha and the empty tomb.[57] Although this is not the only biblical perspective on Jesus' mission, it is a valid and important one, despite some late-modern sensibilities to the contrary.

The holistic nature of God's kingdom embodied in Jesus and his ministry is in marked contrast to the various dualisms of the Western world, which artificially carve up reality into psychological, physical/material and spiritual dimensions. In Jesus' ministry there is no tension between healing the physically sick and healing those oppressed by demons. Disease, illness, and demon oppression all spoil God's good creation, and by their healing Jesus demonstrates that they have no place in God's new creation, in which sin, sickness and the demonic are altogether absent. Sin also spoils the integrity of humans made in the *imago Dei*, and Jesus confronts sin by exposing it (Mark 10:15–18; John 4:16–19), forgiving it (Mark 2:5; Luke 23:34), and telling the sinner "Go your way, and from now on do not sin again" (John 8:11; John 5:14). He forgives sin because in himself he makes atonement for the sins of the world, and then he commissions his disciples to be his ambassadors proclaiming the forgiveness of sins in his name to all nations (Luke 24:47). The evangelists' use of *sozein*—to save—reveals the holistic nature of Jesus' identity as Savior. Their normal use of *sozein* is in reference to saving from sin, but in at least eighteen cases the evangelists use *sozein* to refer to Jesus saving people from sickness. Bosch explains "Thus there is, in Jesus' ministry, no tension between saving from sin and saving from physical ailment, between the spiritual and the social."[58] Forgiveness of sin and healing the sick and demon oppressed are all important works of God's liberating kingdom. Drawing on Mark 2:1–12 Newbigin observes that healing belongs together with forgiveness, because "the work of Jesus is an attack upon the whole power of evil which manifests itself both in sickness and in sin."[59] In the gospels the evangelists' make clear that Jesus' healing and mighty works are apiece with his profound and liberating teaching, such that even to speak separately of the works and words of Jesus is potentially misleading. God's words are performative utterances or speech-acts; "God's words are deeds which accomplish what they express." Newbigin continues, "It is by the uttering of words that Jesus performed his 'works', and the words of

---

57. Luther makes the point that Jesus' opposition to the demonic continues in and through the Church. He says that as Christ defeated the demonic powers on the cross, so "He still constantly gives them a beating" because "Christ is the Lord Sabbaoth, that is, a God of hosts or of the armies, who constantly wages war and takes up his battle position within us" (quoted in Althaus, *The Theology of Martin Luther*, 215).

58. Bosch, *Transforming Mission*, 33.

59. Newbigin, *The Light Has Come*, 64.

Jesus are still the means by which the Father 'does his works', the works of setting all people and all creation free from their bondage to decay (Rom 8:21)."[60] The parables and teaching of Jesus speak of God's kingdom, and the mighty works are signs which point to God's kingdom. Jenson refers to these mighty works as "acted-out parables, of the Kingdom's immediacy. Moreover, as *acted* signs, the miracles 'contain the grace they signify'; they are instances of the *immediacy* of the Kingdom."[61] However, it is in the crucifixion of Jesus and his resurrection from the dead that the kingdom of God is ontologically established and irreversibly inaugurated.

## The Reconciling Death and Resurrection of Christ

Understanding the saving work of Christ that particularly focuses on the events celebrated every Easter has always, in the Christian tradition, been something variegated and multifaceted. In contrast to tight theological definitions, such as the Chalcedonian formula for Christology, soteriology has always defied such singular precision, with John McIntyre identifying thirteen soteriological models, most of which have their origins in the New Testament itself.[62] The New Testament itself draws on a variety of images and uses numerous metaphors to describe and interpret the saving work of Christ, including the battlefield, the law court, and family life. Reflecting on this varied imagery, soteriological models or theories of the atonement are conceptual constructs expressing humanity's sin and God's salvation. Maurice Wiles notes that the variety of soteriological metaphors in the New Testament carries over into the patristic period. He comments that "The teaching of the Fathers on this theme has its faults, but its unsystematic character and its many-sidedness are not to be classed among them."[63] This plurality is, in general, positively understood to be the product of the many-sided nature of Christ's salvation. It is rather like looking through different windows, each with different but complementary perspectives that enrich our understanding of the events of Easter.[64] Due to limitations of space I shall discuss the reconciling death and resurrection of Christ utilizing three soteriological models which themselves draw heavily upon New Testament language and imagery.[65]

60. Newbigin, *The Light Has Come*, 183.
61. Jenson, *Systematic Theology*, 1:177. Quotation source unknown.
62. McIntyre, *The Shape of Soteriology*, 26–52.
63. Wiles, *The Christian Fathers*, 107.
64. This is the analogy used by Tom Smail in his book *Windows on the Cross*.
65. Needless to say a more comprehensive account would discuss all of the soteriological models, but such an analysis is beyond the scope of this present work.

## Christus Victor

In continuation with Jesus' struggle and conflict with demonic powers during his ministry, this conflict comes to a climax in the crucifixion. The New Testament presents sin, death, demons and the devil as Christ's enemies which he overcomes in his life, death and resurrection. This is especially prominent in the synoptic gospels and Pauline corpus, but it is also taught in the Johannine writings, in which the "work of Christ is to vanquish this power and dethrone the devil (cf. John 12:31)."[66] For Aulén and many advocates of this view, the background to the Christus Victor theory of salvation is the divine will which struggles against forces that oppose it. Although this is clearly depicted in the Scriptures, it is opposed by much of the Christian tradition that would agree with Augustine, who says "the will of the omnipotent is always undefeated."[67] By contrast, Aulén portrays what he calls *dualism*, but is better termed limited *dualism*,[68] which reflects the biblical depiction of the "opposition between God and that which in His own created world resists His will."[69] Taking the struggle between God and the forces of evil at face value, this conflict comes to a focus at Christ's crucifixion, where it appears that evil has triumphed. In his song "Jesus is Alive," Christian musician Ron Kenoly encapsulates the dramatic narrative of this moment:

> Satan gleamed with pleasure that day at Calvary
> For he thought he has won a mighty victory
> And like him all of the demons of hell began to cheer
> But little did they know that their end was drawing near.[70]

Like humanity, God engages in warfare, for as Moses says "The Lord is a warrior; the Lord is his name" (Exod 15:3), but unlike humanity Christ's weapons are quite different. Aulén says "Divine love is victorious in self-giving and sacrifice."[71] Satan is said to be the god of this age (2 Cor 4:4) and the

---

66. Aulén, *The Faith of the Christian Church*, 200.

67. *Enchiridion* XXVI. 102. It is truly remarkable that the Christian theological tradition can be so divided on such a fundamental issue. To put the matter bluntly, the tradition is divided into those who, with Berkouwer, believe "Scripture nowhere suggests that God's work is limited by human activity," and those who agree with Bruce Reichenbach that "God's *immediate* purposes and plans are not always realized, for he has entrusted them to human hands" (Berkouwer, *The Providence of God*, 127). Reichenbach, "God Limits His Power," 118, emphasis added.

68. As used by Boyd, *God At War*, 185, and Aune, "Apocalypticism," 25–53.

69. Aulén, *Christus Victor*, 21.

70. Ron Kenoly, "Jesus is Alive."

71. Aulén, *The Faith of the Christian Church*, 201.

ruler of the world (John 12:31; 14:30; 16:11; 1 John 5:19). Smalley helpfully defines the 'world' as "human society, temporarily controlled by the power of evil, organized in opposition to God."[72] Although God is the 'Lord of lords and King of kings' (Rev 17:14), the divine will is not perfectly carried out on earth because of creaturely rebellion. Hence, Pannenberg contends that "To establish the lordship of God is the chief content and primary goal of the mission of Jesus."[73] Jesus carried out his mission, not in a spiritual vacuum, but in what both C. S. Lewis and David Bosch have described as 'enemy-occupied territory'.[74] When humans sinned they passed into the devil's dominion and were subject to the power of death, but by Jesus' atoning death he paid the penalty for human sin, propitiated God's wrath and expiated human guilt. With all sin and guilt paid for, and by Jesus perfectly fulfilling the Torah, he "cancelled out the certificate of debt consisting of decrees against us, which was hostile to us; and He has taken it out of the way, having nailed it to the cross."[75]

Jesus' death marks his greatest conflict of all—his conflict with death itself. Jüngel comments,

> In the event of the death of Jesus, the being of God and the being of death so strike against each other, that the being of one puts into question the being of the other . . . this reciprocal putting of each other into question ends with the rising of Jesus from the dead.[76]

Furthermore, the author of Hebrews explains that through Jesus' death (and resurrection) he destroyed "the one who has the power of death, that is, the devil, and free[d] those who all their lives were held in slavery by the fear of death" (Heb 2:14–15). The Father's raising of Jesus from the dead by the Spirit marks the inauguration of the death of death, which shall be consummated in the eschaton when the old order of things shall pass away. Christ's resurrection is the first-fruits of the resurrection of all those in Christ (1 Cor 15:20), and carries the promise that "all shall be made alive" (1 Cor 15:22). Christ's resurrection constitutes undying evidence that sinful humanity is

---

72. Smalley, *1, 2, 3 John*, 77. Similarly, Longenecker says "In a sense the power of Sin has managed to set up a system, a society, a world, in which things have an almost natural way of running contrary to the will of God" (Longenecker, *The Triumph of Abraham's God*, 41).

73. Pannenberg, *Systematic Theology*, 1:309.

74. Bosch, *Transforming Mission*, 506. Lewis, *Mere Christianity*, 37.

75. Col 2:14 NASB. "[H]aving canceled the charge of our legal indebtedness, which stood against us and condemned us; he has taken it away, nailing it to the cross" (NIV).

76. Eberhard Jüngel quoted in Fiddes, *Participating in God*, 236.

not beyond redemption, and "is a new affirmation of God's first decision that Adam should live."[77] God becomes the last Adam and reverses the first Adam's choice of death, so that in the last Adam the first is rescued. In this rescue, God demonstrates that "The deviance of his [humanity's] will, with its fateful leaning towards death, has not been allowed to uncreate what God has created."[78] God has inaugurated his new creation in which death will finally have no place, and like other aspects of the old order, will pass away. Christ's victory over sin, death, and the devil, gives the church great confidence as exemplified by the apostle Paul who, when discussing the resurrection of the dead, can say audaciously, "'Where, O death, is your victory? Where, O death, is your sting?'" (1 Cor 15:55)

Aulén, whose significance for the soteriological emphasis of *victory* is well known, argues that the cross of Christ represents God's victory, once and for all, over evil powers. He says "The cross is the chief Christian symbol because it is a symbol of victory. It is a crucifix of triumph."[79] This perspective on the Son's mission is of enduring significance because it is not overly anthropocentric, it holds together the objective and subjective dimensions of the atonement, it relates the Son's historical mission to his ongoing mission, and it gives due importance to the church's mission. Boyd explains "The cross and resurrection are anthropologically significant only because they are first of all cosmologically significant."[80] Christ defeated all cosmic powers of evil and thus freed creation from its slavery to corruption (Rom 8:21). Christ had to first tie up the strong man (the devil), before those in his domain of darkness (sinful humanity) could be released.[81] The historical mission of the Son defeated the evil powers that held humanity captive, so that humanity is, *de jure*, free from the power of sin, death and the devil. This is held together with the ongoing mission of the Son and the proper mission of the Spirit, which through the church, invites all people to subjectively appropriate and thus participate in Christ's victory.

## Atoning Sacrifice

Christ's death, which is central to the mission of the Son, is often interpreted and understood in terms of *sacrifice*. In the Old Testament, sacrifice had

77. O'Donovan, *Resurrection and Moral Order*, 14.
78. Ibid., 14.
79. Aulén, *The Faith of the Christian Church*, 201.
80. Boyd, *God At War*, 251.
81. Drawing on Matt 12:29 and Heb 2:14–15. Boyd, *God At War*, 260. For further reading see Kovacs, "'Now Shall the Ruler.'"

many functions including purifying the worshipper from unrighteousness, sealing a covenant, and cleansing from sin. The New Testament explicitly draws on Old Testament sacrificial imagery and expectations in its presentation of Christ's death as a sacrifice. This is especially clear in the letter to the Hebrews, where Jesus the Mediator is both the high priest who offers the sacrifice, and he is the sacrificial Lamb as well. As the High Priest and sacrificial Lamb, Jesus offered himself to God as a sacrifice for sin, thereby sealing a new covenant and procuring righteousness. McIntyre explains that Christ's offering of himself to God is one "in which subsequently the worshipper may also participate; to establish communion between God and those who worshipped him."[82]

The central event of redemption in the Old Testament is the deliverance and exodus from slavery in Egypt, celebrated above all in the Passover. There, a Lamb without stain or blemish is sacrificed, and the blood then spread on the doorframe of the house to protect the Hebrews from the tenth plague of Egypt. In Exodus 12:13 God says, "when I see the blood, I will pass over you, and no plague shall destroy you when I strike the land of Egypt." The Passover meal is central to the church in the form of the Eucharist because the synopticists show that when Jesus celebrated the Passover meal with his disciples, he reinterpreted its meaning, saying "this is my blood of the covenant, which is poured out for many for the forgiveness of sins" (Matt 26:28). John structures his gospel chronology so that Jesus' death occurs at the time of Passover when the animals were being sacrificed in the temple, pointing to Jesus' death as the true Passover sacrifice.[83] Continuing in this tradition the apostle Paul says that "For our Christ, our Passover lamb, has been sacrificed."[84] By Jesus' death, those in Christ are redeemed and delivered from the powerful enemies of sin and death. Those in Christ are no longer enslaved to sin and are rescued from their powerful enemy, death. In this light, Jesus' words in John 11:25-26 are particularly significant: "Those who believe in me, even though they die, will live, and everyone who lives and believes in me will never die."

The New Testament describes Christ's death not simply as a sacrifice but as an *atoning* sacrifice. The Hebrew word for atone, *kpr*, originally meant 'to cover', and referred to covering a person and their guilt from the eyes, and the judgement, of the holy God, thus producing forgiveness.[85] Atonement implies that divine human relationship can be repaired only through a spe-

---

82. McIntyre, *The Shape of Soteriology*, 34–35.
83. Morris, *The Atonement*, 104.
84. 1 Cor 5:7 NIV.
85. McIntyre, *The Shape of Soteriology*, 39–40.

cific act or event, and the English word 'at-one-ment' spells out this 'making one.' In ancient Israel this occurred in the ritual of sacrifice, especially on Yom Kippur (Lev 16), and for Christians atonement happens in the Roman execution of Jesus one Friday afternoon. The apostle John explains that by Jesus' death on the cross he made atonement for the sins of the world (1 John 2:2). In both the Old and New Testaments the atoning efficacy is found in the blood of the sacrifice, for "it is the blood that makes atonement" (Lev 17:11), and "without the shedding of blood there is no forgiveness of sins" (Heb 9:22). Explaining the atoning virtue of shed blood, Brunner says that for restoration of divine-human communion, "Blood must actually flow, for man has forfeited his life by his rebellion against His Creator and Lord."[86] Shed blood means the loss of life and represents God's just punishment on human sin (see Gen 2:17; Rom 6:23). It is for this reason that Gunton observes that the New Testament teaches, for example in Colossians 1:20–22, "that the redirection of creation to its end finally takes shape only in so far as Jesus Christ makes 'peace by the blood of his cross.'"[87]

In Christ, God judged sinful humanity as guilty, and pronounced his 'No' against sin by punishing it with death. The death that Jesus died is substitutionary, for he died for humanity's sin, vicariously bearing and carrying away humanity's guilt and punishment, so that humanity might become righteous in Christ. Describing the wondrous exchange of the cross, Luther says, "This is the mystery of the riches of divine grace for sinners; for by a wonderful exchange our sins are not ours but Christ's, and Christ's righteousness is not Christ's but ours."[88] However, Christ was judged not simply so that humanity might be acquitted. Rather, each person is called to participate in the dying of Christ so that they might also share in his rising from the dead. The Christian does not escape the judgement of the cross but voluntarily, by the Holy Spirit, chooses to enter the waters of baptism, which Newbigin reminds us "is the tomb which is also the womb, the place of dying and of being born."[89] Christians do not make atonement for their sins, for Christ has done this once and for all (1 Pet 3:18), but they do participate in the death of Christ when at baptism they die to their sinful selves and subjectively appropriate their objective death in Christ's death (2 Cor 5:14). Barrett says, although potentially all people died in Christ's death (2 Cor 5:14), "it is no forgone conclusion that all will cease to live to themselves and live henceforth for Christ (v. 15). If they fail to do this, as far as they

---

86. Brunner, *Dogmatics*, 2:284.
87. Gunton, *The Promise*, 183.
88. Quoted in Bloesch, *Essentials of Evangelical Theology*, 1:148.
89. Newbigin, *Unfaith and Other Faiths*.

are concerned God's free favor will have been bestowed upon them in vain. [2 Cor 6:1]"[90] For those who by the Holy Spirit do subjectively participate in Christ's death, Christians, their life is marked by a continual identification with Christ's death (Phil 3:10) by daily denying oneself, taking up one's cross and following Jesus (Luke 9:23). Thus, the apostle Paul can say "it is no longer I who live, but it is Christ who lives in me" (Gal 2:20). Describing this universal death of sinful humanity in Christ, Barth says "in his person he has made an end of us as sinners and therefore of sin itself by going to death as the One who took our place. In his person, he delivered up us sinners and sin itself to destruction. He took this present evil world and buried it in his tomb."[91] In Jesus' vicarious death the life of sin has been brought to its proper end. In its place and, in his person, Christ has made the way so that those in him might be righteous and live for him by participating by the Holy Spirit in his obedient humanity.

### *The Abolition of God-Forsakenness*

On the cross, Jesus' agony is most clearly heard in his cry of dereliction: "My God, my God, why have you forsaken me?"[92] Reflecting on this cry, Jürgen Moltmann insightfully teaches that Jesus vicariously experienced not only death, but also God-forsakenness. On the cross, Jesus cried out his God-forsakenness in the words of Psalm 22 and in doing so profoundly identified with those who also experience this God-forsakenness. Jesus does this "in order that he might suffer with the Godforsakenness of the godless and so vicariously abolish it."[93] He abolishes God-forsakenness because he, the God-man Jesus, has fellowship with the God-forsaken so that they are forsaken no longer. Commenting on Moltmann's insight, Tom Smail says Jesus' togetherness with the God-forsaken "in their distance from God, is a foretaste and promise of their restoration to fellowship with God and an expression of God's seeking, liberating, love for them."[94] On Easter Saturday Jesus experiences God-abandonment so that that experience is itself abandoned, because Jesus now fellowships with those in that existential situation.

90. Barrett, *The Second Epistle*, 183.

91. Barth, *CD* IV/1, 253–54.

92. Matt 27:46 and Ps 22:1.

93. Moltmann, *The Church*, 61–62. Moltmann's distinctive contribution here is not unproblematic. Pastorally, it presents a serious challenge to suggest that the hour of Jesus' greatest need, the Father abandoned Him. This is heightened by the fact that God repeatedly promises to his people that He will never to leave or forsake them (Deut 31:6, 8; Josh 1:5; 1 Kgs 8:57; Heb 13:5).

94. Smail, "Trinitarian Atonement," 46.

Moltmann's distinctive interpretation requires some important qualification. It is inconceivable that the eternal Father-Son relation could ever be ontologically ruptured because God is constituted in the perichoretic relations of the Triune Persons. It is also inconceivable that at his moment of greatest need, the Son was literally abandoned by the Father. Therefore, Jesus' experience of God-forsakenness is real existentially, but not ontologically. On the cross Jesus not only bore the sins of the world, but was made to 'be sin' (2 Cor 5:21), and in that experience Jesus travelled to the distant horizon of the far country of being at enmity with and alienated from God. However, there is nowhere in all of creation that a person can go to completely flee from God's presence. In Psalm 139 King David says "if I make my bed in *Sheol*, you are there . . . If I say, 'Surely the darkness shall cover me, and the light around me become night', even the darkness is not dark to you; the night is as bright as the day, for darkness is as light to you." Even in the darkest experiences, such as the darkness that descended at noon for three hours as Jesus hung on the cross (Matt 27:45), as allegedly reported by the historian Thallus,[95] God is somehow present; for in Jesus, God has once and for all demonstrated that he will not abandon his wayward creation. When a person is enslaved and abandoned to sin, and engulfed by it, even then God in his forbearance graciously preserves and sustains them in Christ (Col 1:17) with a view to their redemption. God's gracious love for humanity, seen in his irrevocable giving of himself in Christ and the Spirit, entails that, for humanity prior to the eschaton, literal God-abandonment is an ontological impossibility.[96] Jesus bore witness to this in quoting Psalm 22, which although it begins with the cry of dereliction, ends in a declaration of confidence in God. So it is that, when a person *feels* alienated from and abandoned by God, God has also experienced this and so is present with them, and by this presence points to the fact that God-forsakenness is a possibility rejected by God the loving shepherd who continues to pursue his lost sheep.

---

95. Thallus was an obscure historian who wrote a three-volume history in the mid-first century. Although this has not survived, the third century Christian historian Julius Africanus, when discussing the prolonged darkness that occurred on the day Jesus died, notes that ". . . in the third book of his history Thallus calls this darkness an eclipse of the sun—wrongly in my opinion" (Boyd and Eddy, *Lord or Legend?*, 122).

96. This comment does not intend to resolve the question of the final destiny of those who have not consciously responded to Christ in repentance and faith.

## Part Two: Constructing a Trinitarian Missiology

### The Historical and Ongoing Mission of the Son

The New Testament clearly presents Jesus as having completed his mission given from the Father (John 17:4; 19:30), but it is also clear that after his ascension Jesus' mission continues. Thus, Jesus' mission falls neatly into two related parts; the historical mission in which he is the sent one who savingly reveals God in history, culminating in the crucifixion and resurrection and ending at the ascension. In this historical mission Jesus acted immediately in history, with the ascension marking his departure from history and the completion of this mission (see John 17:4). The ongoing mission begins at the ascension and will continue until Jesus has put all of his enemies under his feet (1 Cor 15:25–27).[97] Jesus' ongoing mission is still historical because Jesus acts in history, but no longer dwells within history, and is seated at the right hand of the Father (Acts 2:33; Eph 1:20). Even when Jesus seems to act 'directly', such as confronting Saul of Tarsus on the road to Damascus, Jesus' acts, although taking place in history, are not of the same order as his historical mission in Galilee and Judea. This second stage of Jesus' mission, his ongoing mission, needs to be qualified because Jesus is no longer the object of the sending. His ongoing mission is focused first in his person as the great intercessory high priest (Heb 7:25) who is preparing a place for his disciples (John 14:2). Second, Jesus' ongoing mission continues through the mediation of the Spirit whom he poured out at Pentecost, and through his church who are his hands and feet. In Jesus' historical mission, the Father and Spirit are the subject of the sending, and Jesus its object. In Jesus' ongoing mission he is the subject of the sending, and the objects are both the Spirit and the church. From one perspective, therefore, the missions of Spirit and church are both part of the ongoing mission of the exalted Christ.

That the two parts of Jesus' mission are closely related can readily be seen in relation to the church and the atonement. Central to Jesus' historical mission was the training and forming of his disciples as the proto-church, not as an end in itself but as preparation for the time when he would send them forth as his apostles, witnesses to his atoning death and the dawning of new creation in his resurrection. This sending forth by Jesus of the church straddles Jesus' historical and ongoing mission; he sends them as the last act of his historical mission just prior to his ascension, but also tells them to wait for the Spirit whom he will send from the Father as the first act of his ongoing mission. The close relation between the ongoing and historical aspects of Jesus' mission can also be seen in the culmination of the latter in his atoning death and resurrection. The events of Easter were so central to Jesus'

---

97. Barth's preferred language is of Jesus' complete and ongoing mission. Barth, *CD* IV/3.2, 606.

mission that if one were to ask Anselm's question *Cur Deus Homo?*, a crucial part of the answer would be "to give His life as a ransom for many."[98] At the climax of Jesus' historical mission he definitively dealt with human sin and decisively conquered the devil and death itself. Jesus' ongoing mission through the missions of Spirit and church communicates and implements the victories of the atonement to all people to the ends of the earth. Barth is right in saying that Jesus "is not content with what He did once and for all," that is, in his completed historical mission. "He also imparts Himself as the One who has done it. He also tells the world that it is the world reconciled in Him. He also declares to men that they are justified before God and sanctified for Him in and by Him."[99] In conclusion, there are two parts to the one mission of the Son, each with its own distinctive character, and together they form an integrated whole and so cannot be considered separately.

## The Completion of the Son's Mission

In the most extended biblical passage on the resurrection, 1 Corinthians 15, the apostle Paul uniquely describes the completion of the mission of the Son. In his last and final saving act, Jesus will return in triumph and glory and will bring history to a close by defeating death through the resurrection of the dead.[100] After this Paul writes, "Then comes the end, when he [Christ] hands over the kingdom to God the Father, after he has destroyed every ruler and every authority and power" (15:24). After identifying that the last enemy to be destroyed is death (15:26), Paul concludes the pericope: "When all things are subjected to him, then the Son himself will also be subjected to the one who put all things in subjection under him, so that God may be all in all" (15:28). The Son, whose mission is forever defined by the incarnation, completes the final act of his redeeming mission by destroying death and handing over the kingdom to God the Father.

### *God's Kingdom*

Moltmann points out that Paul's use of the word 'kingdom' here is significant, because it is a word central to the gospels, but one that Paul usually

---

98. Mark 10:45 and Matt 20:28.
99. Barth, *CD* IV/3.2, 606.
100. Gordon Fee argues that Paul does not *here* have the general resurrection of the dead in view, but the resurrection of believers in Christ. This, however, is a subject beyond the scope of the discussion here. Fee, *The First Epistle*, 750, emphasis original.

avoids.¹⁰¹ Kingdom here represents God's rule or lordship over creation, which is challenged by people, principalities and powers, and which was irrevocably re-established in the incarnation, with its culmination in the events of Easter. In fact, Pannenberg summarizes the Son's historical mission by saying "the whole sending of Jesus is for the glory of the Father and his lordship."¹⁰² The Father committed the rule of God, the kingdom, to his Son, who in the incarnation humbled himself and became an obedient servant. Jesus, this 'man for others', begins his ministry by declaring that the kingdom of God is at hand and spends his life advancing God's kingdom by teaching the truth about God and his reign, healing people from sickness and demonic oppression, and confronting economic injustice, religious hypocrisy, and social exclusion. Throughout his perfectly obedient life that culminated in his atoning death, Jesus glorified the Father as enabled by the Spirit (Luke 3:22; 4:1, 14). The Father responds to the Son's completion of his historical mission by raising him from the dead by the Spirit (Rom 1:4; 8:11), and restoring to him the eternal primordial glory which he had with the Father. Jesus' triumphant death on the cross and his victorious resurrection unequivocally establishes God's kingdom over the fraudulent jurisdiction of death and the devil. After his ascension, the risen Son continues his mission of extending God's kingdom on earth by the Pentecostal sending of the Holy Spirit, which is also called the proper mission of the Spirit. "The Paraclete, for his part, will then glorify Christ, the Son, by spreading his knowledge and his love."¹⁰³ The Spirit's completion of his mission of glorifying the Son on earth will be followed by the *parousia* of Christ. Then, Christ will finally destroy death and will have thus subdued every ruler, authority and power (1 Cor 15:24–26), completing God's kingdom rule.

## *Paul's Use of Christ and Son*

It is theologically significant that early in the pericope Paul speaks of *Christ's* handing over of the kingdom to the Father (1 Cor 15:24), but by the end he changes his language to speak of the *Son*. Moltmann suggests that as the kingdom is transferred "from one divine subject to another . . . its form is changed in the process,"¹⁰⁴ and I would argue that this change is embodied in Paul's use of language. The distinction being made is between divine designations *ad intra* and *ad extra*. The phrase 'Father, Son and Holy Spirit' is the

---

101. Moltmann, *The Coming of God*, 335.
102. Pannenberg, *Systematic Theology*, 1:309.
103. Moltmann, *The Coming of God*, 334.
104. Moltmann, *The Trinity*, 93.

personal name for God *ad intra*,[105] though of course this is only knowable for God's creatures by divine revelation *ad extra*. Titles such as Creator, Sustainer, Ruler, Redeemer, Savior, Christ/Messiah, and Lord refer specifically to God *ad extra*, that is, God as he relates to his creation. Explaining this distinction vis-à-vis Christological designations, Moltmann says that "all Jesus' titles of sovereignty—Christ, kyrios, prophet, priest, king, and so forth—are *provisional* titles, which express Jesus' significance for salvation in time. But the name of the Son remains to all eternity."[106] Christ refers specifically to the Son's office of mediator between God the Father and humanity. As mediator, Christ has been given 'all authority in heaven and on earth' (Matt 28:18), and the Father has committed his rule, his kingdom, into his hands. Christ will continue to sit at the Father's right hand until his enemies are subdued beneath him (Acts 2:32–36). After all Christ's enemies are subdued, his lordship will be complete, and Christ will have fulfilled his mediatorial office, and so will cease to be the ambassador of his Father.[107] Moltmann observes that the lordship of Christ is 'provisional' and 'eschatologically limited', for it "serves the greater purpose of making room for the kingdom of glory and of preparing for God's indwelling in the new creation, 'so that God will be all in all.'"[108]

The linguistic change from *Christ* to *Son* not only indicates the provisionality of the office of Christ, but also the enduring sonship of the Son. His rule on behalf of the Father completed, the Son thus hands the kingdom over to the Father. This eschatological transfer of divine rule marks the completion of the Son's ongoing mission, and so marks the fulfilment of the Son's obedience and his sonship.[109] This final perfection of the Son's obedience to the Father, like the Son's obedient incarnate existence in history, vicariously represents all in the kingdom of the beloved Son. Consequently, all in God's kingdom who by the Spirit participate in the sonship of Christ, are included and represented and encompassed by the Son's perfect obedience to and glorifying of the Father.

This transferal of the kingdom marks a change in the kingdom, in how God rules his creation. In the divine economy prior to the *parousia*, God the

---

105. Jenson, *Systematic Theology*, 1:46.

106. Moltmann, *The Trinity*, 92. This does not contradict Hebrews 7:17–25 which speaks of the Son being 'a priest forever', for the context of this passage concerns Christ's salvific and intercessory office which in the new heavens and new earth will no longer be necessary. The Son is a priest forever in that He is a priest to the end of time, but He will not be a priest *beyond* the end of time.

107. Calvin, *Institutes*, II.xiv.3, 485.

108. Moltmann, *The Trinity*, 92.

109. Ibid., 92.

Father remains transcendent above his creation and his rule is mediated by his 'two hands', his Son and Spirit. Once all God's enemies are defeated and the kingdom is transferred to the Father, then the Son will no longer need to be the Christ, the High Priest and mediator of new creation, because God the Father will rule directly *with* his Son and Spirit, rather than *through* them. The sinful human nature will be finally cleansed, judged and healed, such that the barrier between humanity and God will be forever removed. Consequently, human knowledge of God will drastically change, for the apostle Paul says that now we know God "in a mirror, dimly, but then we will see face to face" (1 Cor 13:12). The apostle John suggests a similar transformation will occur so that, when Christ is revealed at his *parousia* "we will be like him, for we will see him as he is" (1 John 3:2).[110] Then, the dwelling of God will be with humanity, "He will dwell with them; they will be his peoples, and God himself will be with them" (Rev 21:3). In his commentary on 1 Corinthians 15, Calvin says that in the eschaton "we may cleave wholly to God . . . because the veil being then removed, we shall openly behold God reigning in his majesty."[111]

## Defeat of Death

It is clear that the eschatological death of death is directly related to the resurrection of Christ that is celebrated every Easter Sunday. With Christ's resurrection, death's stranglehold over humanity was decisively broken, and Paul describes this as the 'firstfruits' (1 Cor 15:23) that constitutes both the evidence and guarantee of the future resurrection of those in Christ. Nevertheless, although Christ has personally broken death's power, this victory is yet to be extended to all humanity, and so people continue to die. Thus, the completion of the Son's mission crucially includes death's final destruction, and this "takes place when Christ's own resurrection as firstfruits culminates in the full harvest of the resurrection of those who are his."[112] Since it is the devil who has the power of death (Heb 2:14), death's final destruction also means that "Christ will thus have brought Satan's tyranny to its conclusion."[113] Fee explains that death is the last enemy (1 Cor 15:26) because, "As long as people die, God's own sovereign purposes are not yet

---

110. Calvin says the rule of Christ "is but for a time, until we enjoy the direct vision of the Godhead" (*Institutes*, II.xiv.3, 485).
111. Calvin, *Commentary on Corinthians*.
112. Fee, *The First Epistle*, 757.
113. Ibid., 756.

fully realized."[114] He continues, "at the death of death the final rupture in the universe will be healed and God alone will rule over all beings, banishing those who have rejected his offer of life and lovingly governing all those who by grace have entered into God's 'rest.'"[115] As the conquering of death is associated with the end of the Son's incarnate mission, so the final defeat of death is the culmination of his ongoing mission, with the former guaranteeing the latter.

This raises the question of why there is such a long period of time between the inbreaking of new creation on that first Easter Sunday and the final defeat of death. In substance, this is the same question that is addressed by the apostle Peter as to why the Lord seems slow in keeping his promise to return. Peter's answer is clear: "The Lord is not slow about his promise, as some think of slowness, but is patient with you, not wanting any to perish, but all to come to repentance" (2 Pet 3:9). The time 'between the times' is the age of mission, when through the church the Holy Spirit proclaims the gospel of Jesus Christ for the forgiveness of sins and knits people into Christ's body. Hence, Newbigin is right to say that this eschatological tension between the first and second coming of Christ "cannot be understood apart from the tension of the missionary obligation."[116] Consequently, elsewhere Newbigin says "the Church's mission to the nations is the clue to the real meaning of world history" because the church-in-mission bears witness to people of "what God is doing and will do, of his kingly power which is hidden now but will in the end be revealed to all in its majesty, glory, and terror."[117]

## Christ's Handing Over of the Kingdom

In the handing over of the kingdom to the Father, Paul's choice to avoid 'Christ' and use 'Son' reveals that the event does not concern the mediatorial role of Christ as such, but points to the fact that the exchange between Father and Son is an inner-trinitarian process which does not exclude but includes the world.[118] During Jesus' ministry he spoke of the mutual glorification of Father and Son that was spacious enough to include all of Christ's

---

114. Ibid., 757.

115. Ibid., 760.

116. Newbigin, *The Household of God*, 141. "The implication of a true eschatological perspective will be missionary obedience, and the eschatology which does not issue in such obedience is a false eschatology" (ibid., 135).

117. Newbigin, *Mission of the Church*.

118. Moltmann, *The Coming of God*, 335.

people (see John 17:21).[119] Thus in this handing over of the kingdom from Son to Father, Moltmann says "all created beings are drawn into the mutual relationships of the divine life, and into the wide space of the God who is sociality."[120] This destiny of creation represents the Creator's commitment to his creation and reveals God's purpose for creation.

In the beginning God made humanity to dwell with him, for he walked and talked with humanity in the cool of the day (Gen 3:8). Reflecting on this, Wenham suggests that a "daily chat between the almighty and his creatures was customary."[121] Similarly, in the incarnation God reveals his will to dwell amongst and with his creatures made in the divine image. Thus, it is unsurprising that the vision of the new heavens and the new earth provided in Revelation 21 also shows the *telos* of the whole of creation—that God will dwell with his people (21:4). In this light, Jenson rightly says "The triune God is too intimately involved with his creation for its final transformation to be founded in anything less than an event of his own life."[122] God's involvement in and commitment to creation is revealed in the difference between God prior to creation and God in the eschaton. In the beginning the Triune God was alone, but in the end God will exist forever with his kingdom. Describing this 'divine eschatology', Moltmann says "in the beginning creation—at the end the kingdom; in the beginning God in himself—at the end God all in all."[123] Creation is given the gift of immortality as it is taken into the divine life and so will dwell with God forever (1 Thess 4:17). Although the distinction between Creator and creature will remain, God will be all in all. Calvin explains that this means "all things will be brought back to God, as their alone beginning and end, that they may be closely bound to him."[124]

## Summarizing the Mission of the Son

Newbigin rightly observes that the Bible, taken as a whole, "is an interpretation of universal history from the creation of the world to its consummation."[125] The mission of the Son is at the center of the *missio Dei* and indeed of all human history, not in the sense of a linear timeline, but as that which discloses the meaning and purpose of history, and as the one

119. Ibid., 334–35.
120. Ibid., 336.
121. Wenham, *Genesis 1–15*, quoted in Rogers, *A Basic Introduction*, 8.
122. Jenson, *Systematic Theology*, 2:338.
123. Moltmann, *The Coming of God*, 335.
124. Calvin, *Commentary on Corinthians*.
125. Newbigin, *The Other Side of 1990*.

event, the Christ event, by which all else is to be understood. (This is why the common system of dating time before and after Christ (whether BC/AD or BCE/CE) is so significant.)[126] In this event the Son recapitulates the human story and reconciles Israel and all humanity by his vicarious obedience to the Father, thus fulfilling the covenant entered into on Mt. Sinai. In this life, lived out of perfect love for his Father and for all humanity, God is definitively revealed. This revelation of God was illustrated, explained and demonstrated in Jesus' teaching and performing of the miraculous signs of the kingdom. Jesus entrusted the knowledge and way of life of God's kingdom to his twelve disciples, whom he had trained and formed to be the foundation of the new covenant people of God. Jesus included them in his unique filial relationship with his Father and thus taught them to relate to God, as Abba, in a radically new way. Jesus also models and teaches the twelve that discipleship is cruciform, that God overcomes evil by suffering love, and that their later mission is to be carried out in the way of Christ. On the cross Jesus abolishes the possibility of God-forsakenness. He also defeats the evil principalities and powers by being the paschal lamb who is the atoning sacrifice for the sins of the world, and by being raised from the dead, which signals the destiny of humanity in Christ. In these events celebrated every Easter, the Son completes the objective reconciliation of all humanity. The ascension marks the end of the Son's historical mission and the inauguration of his ongoing mission. This shall be completed at the *parousia*, when Jesus will return and raise to life all the dead in him, thus marking the final death of death, and then he shall hand over the kingdom to the Father, thus marking the beginning of the kingdom that knows no end. However, the Son's ongoing mission is as yet incomplete, and needs to be understood in relation to both the church's mission (chapter 5) and the post-Pentecost mission of the Holy Spirit. Before turning to examine the mission of the Spirit, we shall first consider how the mission of the Son determines the church's mission.

## Mission in Christ's Way

### Introduction

In January 1986 Newbigin gave a series of lecture-Bible studies to the synod of the Church of South India on the theme 'Mission in Christ's Way.' In

---

126. Consequently, this is also why it is being challenged by an alternative system dating from before and after Muhammad's *hijra* to Medina in the year 622 CE or 1 AH (after Hijra).

those lectures, which were subsequently published, Newbigin argues that "It is the manner in which the Father sent the Son that determines the manner in which the church is sent by Jesus. Its mission is governed by the manner of his."[127] The whole book is an extended reflection and discussion of the implications of Jesus' words in John 20:21—"*As* the Father has sent me, *so* I send you." For Newbigin, the church's missional thinking and praxis must be determined by and modelled on Christ's mission; "We are not authorized to do it in any other way."[128] There is a specificity to *how* Jesus sent the disciples, who represent the church, and so the church needs to pay careful attention to the manner of this sending in order to adequately represent the One who sent them and the One to whom they bear witness. In other words, the decisive issue for mission in Christ's way is *missionary methodology*,[129] which focuses on Jesus because he "is God's missionary *par excellence*."[130] The sender, Jesus, commissions the church to mission, and this commission includes not only certain non-negotiable content but also a mandatory method; it is to be mission in Christ's way.

Central to mission is the communication of the good news of Jesus, and this communication incorporates the manner of speaking, the content that is spoken, and the lifestyle and credibility of the speaker. Hence Yoder explains, "The church is then not simply the bearer of the message of reconciliation, in the way a newspaper or a telephone company can bear any message with which it is entrusted."[131] Rather, says Guder, "the communication of the gospel [must] be appropriate to its content." He continues, "The message, the messenger, and the communication of the message should be seen as a whole, based upon the life, death, and resurrection of Jesus Christ."[132] The gracious saving work of Christ that the church is sent out to proclaim must govern all aspects of the church-in-mission, otherwise it will undermine its own mission and its witness to Christ. Thus, the church is encouraged to prayerfully depend upon the gracious enabling of God such that its life bears witness to the gospel and confirms its verbal testimony.

Hunsberger rightly says the church's "very being is the lens through which people view and comprehend the gospel."[133] The veracity of the

---

127. Newbigin, *Mission in Christ's Way*, 23.
128. Ibid., 1.
129. Guder, "Incarnation," 419.
130. René Padilla, "Bible Studies," quoted in Escobar, *The New Global Mission*, 106.
131. John Howard Yoder, *The Royal Priesthood: Essays Ecumenical and Ecclesiological*, quoted in Cartwright, "Being Sent: Witness," 481.
132. Guder, "Incarnation," 420.
133. Hunsberger, "The Church," 103.

## The Mission of the Son and Spirit

church's witness is proportional to the integrity of its character, and this truth identified by Second Clement[134] is even more imperative in our increasingly late/post-modern era. Kirk comments "If a postmodern age is marked by an endless plurality of discordant beliefs and lifestyles, true life in Jesus Christ is more likely to be recognized visually than aurally."[135] Duraisingh is thus correct that the mission of the church "is a way of being in the Spirit; it is first and foremost a posture of being, a style of life."[136] This underscores the importance of the missionary church being herself the different kind of *polis* that embodies in its own life the renewal of all things that God has already begun in Christ and the Spirit.[137] This distinctive *polis* is a unique social presence through which God is at work for societal transformation.[138]

For incarnational mission, the focus is in particular upon the example of Jesus' life as a *model* for mission, and so despite the similarities, should not be confused with moral influence theories of the atonement associated with figures such as Peter Abelard. The life of Jesus provides a standard by which the church-in-mission can test "its own policies, programs and practices."[139] This prevents the church's mission from becoming a self-legislating independent entity, or a wave of the sea tossed by the ever-changing winds of social and cultural change, and continually brings it back under the lordship of Christ.

### *Incarnational Mission*

In recent decades, mission in Christ's way has led to the coining of a new[140] word, *incarnational* mission, and is the missiological dimension of the *imitatio Christi*. Negatively, incarnational mission does not mean that Christians are called to imitate the once-for-all atoning death of Jesus, and so conveys discontinuity as well as continuity with Jesus' mission. This imitation of Christ's mission ought not to be construed in a Pelagian fashion,

---

134. 2 Clem 13:3–4—"But if we Christians do not live what we say, the preacher warned, the pagans will 'scoff at the name [of Christian]" (Kreider, "*Ressourcement* and Mission," 247).

135. Kirk, "Mission in the West," 127.

136. Duraisingh, "From Church-shaped Mission," 11.

137. Cartwright, "Being Sent: Witness," 483–84.

138. Fitch and Holsclaw, "Mission amid Empire,," 399.

139. Kirk, *What Is Mission?*, 39.

140. Although it should be noted that John Mackay spoke of the 'incarnational principle' of mission back in 1964. Mackay, *Ecumenics*, 173.

for there is no imitation of Christ without new birth.[141] Thus, incarnational mission is not divorced from Christ's crucifixion and resurrection, otherwise it would become "unduly moralistic and ultimately not good news at all."[142] Positively, the incarnational approach becomes an ethic of mission "based upon the humanity of Christ, whose life and actions are as much the norm of obedient Christian living as are his words."[143] Guder argues that incarnational mission helps the church grapple with the unfortunate dichotomy between faith and culture. As Christ identified himself in the closest possible manner with humanity by becoming one of us, so "The indigenization and contextualization of Christian witness are then rightly seen as the necessary consequence of the incarnation of Christ."[144] Furthermore, understanding its mission as incarnational helps the church refuse to separate between the means and ends of gospel proclamation, and to choose between doing evangelism and doing justice.[145] Incarnational mission is holistic because it is based on the holistic way in which the Father sent the Son.

Newbigin exemplified the identification and solidarity dimensions of incarnational mission when, in April 1942, a Japanese invasion of Madras was expected imminently. The Governor of Madras ordered all non-essential personnel to leave and the American authorities had ordered all American missionaries to leave. What followed was what many Indians called the 'Great White Flight' which Newbigin described as "an unedifying spectacle." Although he sent his family inland for safety, Newbigin felt it was his duty to remain with the church, and so he donned Indian clothes and disappeared into one of the village congregations.[146]

### Proclaiming the King and his Kingdom

By the Spirit, the Father sent the Son proclaiming that the kingdom of God is at hand. Drawing on Mark 1:14–18 Newbigin gives six observations as to *how* the Father sent the Son. First, Jesus' proclamation was the announcement of a fact rather than the promotion of a new doctrine, the launching of a program, or the call to moral or spiritual reformation. "Something has

---

141. Escobar, *The New Global Mission*, 110.
142. Guder, "Incarnation," 425.
143. Ibid., 422.
144. Ibid. Similarly, Stott says "incarnational mission . . . demands identification without loss of identity. It means entering other people's worlds as he entered ours . . . " (Stott, *The Contemporary Christian*, 357).
145. Guder, "Incarnation," 423–24.
146. Newbigin, *Unfinished Agenda*, 82.

happened. There is a new fact to be reckoned with. The kingdom, the reign of God, has come near."[147] Second, because this announcement concerns the sovereign rule of God over creation, if it was to be reported in a newspaper it would be in the section marked 'World Affairs' and not in the 'Religion' section tucked between 'Drama' and 'Sport.' To use Newbigin's language elsewhere, this announcement is not private opinion of great moral value, but concerns public truth. Thus the church is called primarily to communicate the fact of the Christ-event, that he was crucified and raised on the third day.[148] This fact, rather than the church's opinions on ethical issues, ought to be the primary message that the church is known for. In addition, since one cannot have an opinion about facts, for they are either accepted or rejected, the Christians can be encouraged to give testimonies of God's work in their lives. As the church testifies to the crucified, risen and living Christ in his past and continuing acts, she must resist all attempts by others to domesticate and privatize her message. This is arguably the greatest missionary challenge for the Western church.

Third, the message is not that God is king, for that is not news at all, but that God's kingship "has come upon you. It is now a present reality confronting you. You have to come to terms with it, to make a decision about it. It confronts you now."[149] In her mission, the church is to lovingly and tactfully present the gospel of Christ "to men and women who must receive it by a willing belief, and who can also withhold that belief and therefore choose death rather than life."[150] The Father's purpose is that the Spirit leads all people to a decision about Christ through the mission of the church.[151] Fourth, Jesus called his hearers to repent because of the imminence of God's kingdom. Newbigin explains that God's kingdom cannot be seen or understood by Jesus' hearers because they are facing the wrong way and so need to turn around by doing a U-turn. Jesus is saying, "You have to go through

---

147. Newbigin, *Mission in Christ's Way*, 1.

148. It is often noticed that whilst Jesus came proclaiming God's kingdom, the early Church primarily proclaimed Jesus, but there is no incongruency here. Jesus not only proclaimed God's kingdom but also Himself: as the one whom people should follow (Luke 9:23–24), as the unique fulfillment of the Hebrew Scriptures (Luke 4:16–21; Matt 5:17), as the forgiver of sins (Mark 2:5), as the only way to God (John 14:6), as the source of eternal life (John 11:25–26), and as the one in whom God is uniquely and decisively revealed (John 14:7). God's kingly rule is not something vague and ethereal but has a name and a face—Jesus Christ, and so mission in Christ's way proclaims his uniqueness, not arrogantly, but faithfully. Newbigin, *Mission in Christ's Way*, 7, and Escobar, *The New Global Mission*, 111.

149. Newbigin, *Mission in Christ's Way*, 2.

150. Newbigin, *The Light Has Come*, 43.

151. Newbigin, *Trinitarian Doctrine*, 49.

a total mental revolution; otherwise the reign of God will be totally hidden from you."[152] Those who have made this U-turn realize that the kingdom is all about Jesus, and so "To go on after this talking about the kingdom rather than about Jesus would simply mean that one had not heard the message. It would mean that one had not done the Uturn."[153]

Fifth, Jesus calls his hearers to *believe* the good news that God's reign has drawn near, for this reign cannot be seen but it can be believed; indeed it has to be believed in order to be seen. Elsewhere Newbigin, by drawing on Augustine, does say that "Faith is . . . the only way to knowledge."[154] Belief and trust that in Jesus God's reign has drawn near is the indispensable starting point for understanding both Jesus and God's reign. But sixth, this belief, and I would add repentance, is not humanly possible apart from the enabling of God's Spirit. Additionally, human repentance and faith cannot be humanly produced or generated but is subject to divine initiative, or as Newbigin puts it, "He calls whom He will."[155] There is undoubtedly mystery involved here, in relation to God's desire that all may be saved (1 Tim 2:4). Jesus' parables bear witness to the nature of God's kingdom as an 'open secret' that is disclosed to the disciples but hidden from everyone else (Mark 4:10–12). The nature of God's reign as simultaneously revealed and hidden means that Jesus' mission, including his teaching in parables and his works of power (Luke 7:18–23; Mark 3:22), is largely misunderstood, by the religious and political elite, by the crowds, and even by Jesus' disciples. The Son's mission is first received with great popularity, but ends with confusion and disillusionment as Jesus is crucified and his frightened followers are dispersed. Central to the church's mission is its calling of people to repentance and faith in Christ, whilst prayerfully trusting and expecting God to use these means to draw people to himself. Since repentance and faith are divine gifts, and faith is the first step to knowledge of God's kingdom, the church should be wary of indulging in certain kinds of apologetics that seek to provide persuasive evidence that will bring people to faith in Christ. Although defending the faith, giving clear reasons for faith in Christ, and even seeking to persuade people of the truth of the Christian faith (Acts 17:2–4) are part of the church's mission, the gifts of repentance and faith are given by the Spirit who blows where he wills. Finally, following in the way of Christ, the church-in-mission can expect that she will be misunderstood and treated

---

152. Newbigin, *Mission in Christ's Way*, 3.
153. Ibid., 7.
154. Newbigin, "Certain Faith," 340.
155. Newbigin, *Mission in Christ's Way*, 3.

with hostility. Certainly Newbigin is right in saying "Mission in Christ's way will not be a success story as the world reckons success."[156]

## Suffering and the Way of the Cross

Newbigin comments that mission in Christ's way requires paying careful attention to *how* Jesus carried out his mission in contradistinction from the various contemporary Jewish groups. He explains,

> Mission in Christ's way will mean for us neither withdrawal from conflict into a purely religious security; that way ends in the crumbling ruins of Qum'ran. Neither will it mean confusing the power of the word of God with political and economic power—the way that ends at Massada. It will mean, I think, that we are deeply identified (not just in cheap words) with all who are oppressed . . . and—in the name and in the power of Jesus—challenging all the powers that rob men and women of their dignity, and bearing in our life the cost of that challenge.[157]

Jesus was crucified because he did not shrink back from challenging the powers of evil in all their spiritual, social, economic, structural and physical dimensions. He challenged and overcame these powers through healing the sick, boldly confronting the religious and political elite, and overcoming violence with suffering love. The church's mission in Christ's way includes the costly social and physical engagement with the evil powers that spoil and degrade life, and so like Christ will involve suffering. Newbigin says "The mission of the Church in the world must follow the pattern of him who is its author and subject. It must bear the marks of the cross."[158] However, the church's "programs for teaching, healing, feeding the hungry, caring for the sick and action for justice and freedom are futile if they do not point beyond themselves to a reality greater than they—to the great healer, the great liberator, the one who is himself the living bread."[159] Newbigin is aware that there are some situations where faithfulness in preaching is easier than faithful action for justice, mercy and peace, and other situations "where the deed is easy and the word is costly."[160] Since "words without

---

156. Ibid., 13.
157. Ibid., 27–28.
158. Newbigin, *The Light Has Come*, 208.
159. Newbigin, *Mission in Christ's Way*, 12.
160. Ibid., 14.

deeds are empty, but deeds without words are dumb,"[161] Newbigin explains that "What is required of us is faithfulness in word and deed, at whatever cost."[162]

Mission in Christ's way will inevitably lead to suffering as the church confronts evil in its various guises and manifestations, and for no one in the New Testament is this clearer than the apostle Paul. Writing from prison to the persecuted church at Philippi, Paul instructs them that God "has graciously granted you the privilege not only of believing in Christ, but of suffering for him as well" (Phil 1:29). However, it is in 2 Corinthians 4:7–12 that Paul describes what Newbigin believes to be "the essential character of the church's mission" and "the classic definition of mission." Paul interprets his apostolate as "the carrying forward through the ongoing life of the world of the vicarious passion of Jesus. It is as he actually participates in the passion of Jesus, that he can be the bearer of the risen life of Jesus . . . for the sake of others. His apostolate is authenticated by the marks of the cross."[163] That suffering belongs to mission in Christ's way is clear from the Johannine account of the Son's commissioning of the proto-church in John 20:20–21. There, Jesus sends the church *as* the Father sent him, and just prior to saying these words Jesus "showed them his hands and his side" (John 20:20). Newbigin comments "It will be those same scars in the corporate life of the church that will authenticate it as indeed the body of Christ, the bearer of his mission, the presence of the kingdom."[164] Mission in Christ's way, in the way of the cross, is a corrective to all forms of triumphalism. Indeed, in following Christ the church is assured of final triumph, and with this knowledge that comes by faith the church's mission is a "participation in the passion of Jesus as he challenges and masters the power of the evil one."[165] The church is called to follow Jesus in "living out the advancing kingdom of God in a world under siege from the kingdom of Satan."[166] Thus, "there is no participation in Christ without participation in this passion and this conflict."[167]

161. Ibid., 11.
162. Ibid., 14.
163. Ibid., 24.
164. Ibid., 23.
165. Newbigin, *The Light Has Come*, 233.
166. Boyd, *God At War*, 283.
167. Newbigin, *The Light Has Come*, 233. For further reflection on the place of persecution and suffering within the *missio Dei*, see chapter 16, "The Suffering, Advancing Church" in Tennent, *Invitation to World Missions*.

## Parables and Miracles—Words and Wonders

Teaching and healing ministries are central to mission in Christ's way. The church's teaching ministry is not an end in itself, but part of the process of making disciples who are also apostles; disciple-apostles of Christ who are themselves sent to make more disciple-apostles (Matt 28:19–20).[168] This teaching centers on the cross, where Jesus took away the sins of the world, and his resurrection which is the inbreaking and inauguration of God's new creation. Furthermore, Jesus commissioned the disciple-apostles to preach repentance for forgiveness of sins in his name (Luke 24:47) and to pronounce God's forgiveness (John 20:23). Newbigin comments "People are not released from the grip of sin by a general theological statement that God is one who forgives. Release from guilt has to be specific and concrete, addressed with authority to each person."[169] Drawing on Barth, Newbigin argues that Jesus is not asking the disciple-apostles to bring forgiveness to some but withhold it from others, but by way of the Hebrew form of emphatic statement, asks them to bear and personally convey reconciliation with God, the release of guilt, and thus peace.[170]

The modern missionary movement 'from the West to the rest' has typically carried out its mission in the way of Christ the healer, primarily by sending out medically trained missionaries. Indeed, medical missionaries were seen as "the heavy artillery of the missionary army" and were used "in the less responsive fields, in Islamic societies, and above all in China."[171] This is a valid and necessary interpretation of mission in the way of Christ the healer, but it would be reductionist to limit the church's ministry of healing to this. Newbigin's Sri Lankan friend and fellow missiologist and ecumenist D. T. Niles says,

> According to the testimony of Acts of the Apostles there were three primary elements in the ministry of the early Church. They preached the Gospel, healed the sick and cast out devils. It will not do, therefore, for us to say, we do preach the Gospel, we run hospitals and devils don't exist. The ministry of healing that Jesus entrusted to His Church does include the work done in hospitals, but it is infinitely more.[172]

---

168. Newbigin says "It is clear in the original Greek that 'disciple the nations' is the main verb, and that 'baptizing and teaching' are adverbial clauses defining what 'discipling' is" (Newbigin, *Mission in Christ's Way*, 36).

169. Ibid., 29.

170. Ibid., 30.

171. Walls, *The Missionary Movement*, 214.

172. Niles, *Upon The Earth*, 87.

Historically, this Western reductionism has been carried via the modern missionary movement to Asia, Africa, Latin America and Oceania with quite harmful consequences. "Western Christianity," according to Walls, "has effectively been disabled from helping in the desolating situation of witchcraft by the fact that its worldview had no real place for the objective reality of witchcraft."[173] Walls' choice of words is accurate, for the Western church's mission is *disabled* by this cultural blind-spot due to the syncretism of the Western church. Hunsberger, the founder of the Gospel and Our Culture Movement in North America, contends that in the ongoing encounter between the gospel and Western culture, "For the churches of the West, this means maintaining the readiness to recognize unwarranted accommodations to their culture in order to disentangle themselves."[174] Concurring with his insight, I suggest that this applies not only to the areas of individualism, materialism, economic injustice, and poor stewardship of the environment, but also to the area of extra-medical healing and spiritual powers. One reason (amongst many) for the early church's missionary growth was the success of Christian exorcism in comparison with the unpredictable results of their contemporaries (see Acts 19:13–16). As Adolf von Harnack observed: "It was as exorcisers that Christians went out into the great world, and exorcism formed one very powerful method of their mission and propaganda."[175] Writing in 1995, Marguerite Kraft asserts that this Western blindspot is perpetuated in the lack of focus on spiritual warfare in both Western and non-Western theological institutions. She says "Activity by evil spirits is found in all but one of the books of the New Testament, yet very little attention is given in seminary and Bible school curricula to evil spirits and the power they wield."[176] Although this blindspot will still be perpetuated for many years to come, in recent decades the Western church has started to increasingly overcome this cultural blindspot concerning the

---

173. Walls, *The Missionary Movement*, 99. Similarly, speaking of the daily issues people face regarding health, healing, spirit possession, visions and dreams, witchcraft, sorcery, ancestor spirits and so on, Kenyan theologian John Mbiti says traditional theology is "largely ignorant of, and often embarrassingly impotent in the face of, human questions in the churches of Africa, Latin America, parts of Asia, and the South Pacific" (in Kraft, *Understanding Spiritual Power*, 35).

174. Hunsberger, *Bearing the Witness of the Spirit*, 279.

175. Adolf von Harnack, *The Mission and Expansion of Christianity in the First Three Centuries*, quoted in Boyd, *Got At War*, 393.

176. She goes on to argue that "'For today's world solid courses in spiritual warfare based on the research of local worldview of spiritual power and biblical teaching should be part of current seminary and Bible-school training" (Kraft, *Understanding Spiritual Power*, 129, 132).

reality of extra-medical healing and spiritual powers[177] through the witness of Christians from the two-thirds world, such as Niles, and from the influence of the charismatic and Pentecostal movements. In the decades to come I suspect that with the benefit of hindsight this will be one of the chief contributions made by Pentecostal and charismatic theology to the wider theological world.

Andrew Lord contends that "Pentecostal/charismatic experience has demonstrated the missionary effectiveness of the gifts of the Spirit."[178] He then cites C. Peter Wagner who says that in Ecuador: "Divine healing was one of the keys to baptizing 1,500 new Christians and planting seven churches in six weeks."[179] Mission is carried out in the name of the One who has all *authority* in heaven and earth, and so is carried out in the power of the resurrection by the gift of the Holy Spirit.[180] This conviction should prevent the church from falling into the danger of resignation and acquiescence because faith in the resurrection is faith that God has begun to intervene in this old creation with the new. Newbigin says "The cross is not abject submission to the power of evil; it is the price paid for a victorious challenge to the powers of evil."[181] When the church is faced with sick people and those who have died after prayer for healing has been offered, acquiescence to what is deemed to be 'God's will' is a strong temptation, but an apophatic approach is to be preferred. This is because routinely assigning sickness to the will of God does not fit well with God's definitive self-revelation in Jesus. Drawing on David S. Cairns' book *The Faith that Rebels*, Newbigin says Cairns

> pointed out that there is no case in the gospels of a man or woman being brought to Jesus for healing, and Jesus saying: "Accept your suffering; it will purify your soul." There is no such case. In every case that is recorded Jesus immediately responds by action to heal the sick, to cast out the evil spirit. His ministry was a ministry of active challenge to all the powers of the devil, whether in the disease that racks the body, the evil spirit that

---

177. A common term to describe these phenomena is the *supernatural*, but following Kraft this is not helpful due to the dualism implied by the term. Kraft, *Understanding Spiritual Power*, 10.

178. Lord, "Mission Eschatology," 117.

179. C. Peter Wagner, *Spiritual Power and Church Growth*, quoted in Lord, "Mission Eschatology," 114.

180. Escobar, *The New Global Mission*, 110.

181. Newbigin, *Mission in Christ's Way*, 25.

torments the soul, or the corruption and hypocrisy that poisons the body of society. It was a faith that rebelled.[182]

Those in the church have responded to Christ by submitting to him, but this submission is simultaneously a commitment to rebelling against every vestige of the old order of things that is passing away (Rev 21:1–4). According to Newbigin, the church is called, like Christ, to "an active and uncompromising challenge to all the powers of evil." which leads not to triumphalism but to suffering because "it is also a totally vulnerable challenge." Finally, like Christ, in the church's uncompromising but vulnerable challenge to evil "the final victory is God's and not ours. In what seems like defeat, the victory of God is actually won."[183] Thus, the success of the church's battle with evil, like the success of the church's evangelistic mission, is not in the church's hands and is not a measure of the church's missional faithfulness.[184] Rather, the church is committed to living and praying, like Jesus, "Your will be done." Newbigin rightly comments that this "is where we learn what is mission in Christ's way."[185]

### *Trinitarian Mission: Living for the Father as Enabled by the Spirit*

Jesus describes his own ministry in terms of servanthood, and the One whom he constantly served was his heavenly Father. According to Robert Jenson, Jesus' life was "a life lived utterly for his mission, that is, for the Father and for those to whom the Father sends him."[186] Jesus embodied and perfectly fulfilled in himself the 'great commandment' of loving God and neighbor, but he did so not by being a wandering altruist who indiscriminately loves all but by specifically carrying out his Father's will of making disciples. Despite the presence of needy people Jesus did not heal *all* of the sick in *every* town and village before he moved to the next location (Luke 4:43) because he had a focus on carrying out his Father's will (John 6:38) as revealed by the Spirit.[187] Wilken rightly says "The Son always acts in conjunction with the Holy Spirit, never on his own. On that point the Scriptures are clear."[188] As

182. Ibid., 25.
183. Ibid., 25–26.
184. Ibid., 14.
185. Ibid., 5.
186. Jenson, *Systematic Theology*, 1:219.
187. Perhaps one reason for this divine strategy is that, by Jesus performing signs of the kingdom in every major populated area in Judea, God was preparing Israel (and her neighbors) for the forthcoming mission of the Church.
188. Wilken, *Remembering the Christian Past*, 86.

enabled and led by the Spirit, Jesus completed the work his Father had given him to do, and so just prior to the cross Jesus prays, "[Father,] I glorified you on earth by finishing the work that you gave me to do" (John 17:4). This reveals something of the focused nature of the historical mission of the Son. All of the poor in Israel were not fed, all of the sick were not healed, all of the demonized people were not set free, and those living outside of Israel had not heard the good news (Matt 15:24), yet Jesus could say he had completed his mission because he had perfectly carried out his Father's will. Similarly, the church's existence for others ought not to be carried out *purely* on the basis of need, but rather the church is to spend and pour out her resources by doing the Father's will, as Jesus did, by the leading of the Spirit. Naturally, this can only be discerned in the context of an ongoing relationship with God in the midst of changing circumstances and cannot be prescribed for all people, places and times. The historical mission of the Son was limited in its immediate scope (although of course universal in its effect), but his ongoing mission is truly universal and it is the latter into which the church has been incorporated. Thus, the scope of the church's mission is vast, for its goal is the coming of God's kingdom in its fullness and so its mission is as broad as this kingdom-vision and includes evangelism, healing, feeding the poor, transforming unjust political and socio-economic structures, the stewardship of creation, relief and development work. To carry out the Father's will and to prevent exhaustion, it is imperative that each church community seeks the guidance of God's Spirit and seeks to keep in step with the Spirit concerning *how* they are to carry out their specific missions as part of the broader *missio ecclesiae*, within the *missio Dei*.

## THE MISSION OF THE SPIRIT[189]

### Introduction

Expounding the mission of the Spirit requires direct engagement with both Pneumatology and missiology, both of which have been largely neglected in theological history. Andrew Walls suggests that at the theological banqueting table "mission studies are roughly the equivalent of after-dinner mints,"[190] while Clark Pinnock comments that "Our language is often revealing—the Spirit is a third person in a third place."[191] Although over two

---

189. I have published an earlier version of some of what follows in Dodds, "The Mission of the Spirit."

190. Walls, *The Cross-Cultural Process*, 273.

191. Pinnock, *Flame of Love*, 10. Pinnock later adds, "Though we speak of the Spirit as a third Person, from the standpoint of experience Spirit is first" (14).

decades have passed since its publication, Bosch's *Transforming Mission* is still the landmark publication in missiology.[192] In that work he does briefly describe the Lucan emphasis on the Spirit of mission, and notes that this subject has been largely neglected for most of theological history and has only been rediscovered in the twentieth century.[193] Kim argues that there is a specific "need to develop Bosch's work through a consideration of the 'mission of the Spirit' and not just the 'Spirit of mission.'"[194] An account of the mission of the Spirit in all its facets should include his mission prior to creation,[195] in the act of creation, in the old covenant, in and through Jesus, and post-Pentecost. Since it is not possible here to detail a comprehensive mission of the Spirit, I will restrict my focus to the proper mission of the Spirit post-Pentecost.

In the broadest terms, the mission of the Spirit can be framed in the cosmic context of trinitarian glorification. According to Moltmann, "the Spirit glorifies the Son and the Father in creation. Together with the Son he glorifies the Father." The Father sends the Spirit through the Son and the Spirit's mission is to glorify Son and Father. To this end, the direct objects of the Spirit's mission are reconciled and unreconciled humanity. God has so freely committed himself to his creation, especially that part which is made in the divine image and likeness, that God's glorification is tied to the reconciliation of creation. Hence Moltmann continues, "This trinitarian history of glorification points beyond itself to the goal of the trinitarian history of God's dealings with the world."[196] Biblically and theologically this glorification has a focus; the mission of the Spirit is to be the agent of the Father's summing up all things in Christ, "to bring history to completion and fulfilment in Christ."[197]

---

192. Pioneers involved in re-establishing the importance of Pneumatology include Roland Allen, Lesslie Newbigin, Hendrikus Berkhof and John V. Taylor.

193. Bosch, *Transforming Mission*, 114–15.

194. Kim, "Post-Modern Mission: A Paradigm Shift in David Bosch's Theology of Mission," quoted in Lord, "The Pentecostal-Moltmann Dialogue," 283.

195. I here refer to an eternal mission as opposed to the Spirit's temporal mission(s), and have in mind Jenson's comment that the Holy Spirit is the One who "liberates Father and Son to love each other." Elsewhere he adds "the Spirit *liberates* the Father for the Son and the Son from and for the Father" (Jenson, *Systematic Theology*, 1:156, 161, emphasis added).

196. Moltmann, *The Church in the Power of the Spirit*, 59.

197. Pinnock, *Flame of Love*, 194.

## The Mission of the Spirit: Communion

Paul's concluding remarks in his second letter to the church in Corinth ends with that trinitarian verse commonly known as 'the grace', in which the Holy Spirit is spoken of as the creator of *koinonia*, fellowship or communion. Creating fellowship in time and space is central to the Spirit's mission and mirrors the eternal nature of the Spirit as the *vinculum caritatis*. Drawing on this Augustinian tradition, Barth suggests that the Spirit's essence is to be thought of as the consubstantial fellowship between Father and Son, which corresponds "as a prototype to the fellowship between God as Father and man as His child the creation of which is the work of the Holy Spirit in revelation."[198] At Pentecost, the Spirit of eternal divine communion becomes the Spirit who unites God's creatures to the divine communion and thus to a creaturely communion in Christ. As Tan notes, this creation of *koinonia* in time and space is bifocal in that "the Holy Spirit brings us into a vertical oneness with God, and into a horizontal communion with other believers."[199] Human entry into the divine *koinonia* in Christ by the Spirit is simultaneously and necessarily ecclesial.

To the extent that the church is the assembly of regenerate people in Christ, the Day of Pentecost described in Acts 2 is the birthday of the church. The church is completely dependent upon the work of the Spirit without which she would not exist. Luke parallels the Spirit's creating of the church near the beginning of Acts with the Spirit's conceiving of Jesus in Mary's womb near the beginning of his gospel. He does this to show continuity of divine action, for in his gospel he describes "all that Jesus *began* to do and teach"[200] and in *Acts* he deals with all that Jesus *continued* to do and teach through the work of the Spirit and the birth and expansion of the church.[201] Luke also does this to show that the church and her mission are in fact a product of God's missionary activity. The church is God's community and since her mission is a part of God's mission it is therefore unstoppable (see Acts 5:34–39).

The first act in the mission of the Spirit is the constitution of the church in Christ. This is significant because as a foretaste of reconciled humanity the church is the goal of the Spirit's mission, and is a central instrument in that mission. Thus, the Spirit creates an ontological and relational communion between the disciples of Jesus and God by including them "within

---

198. Barth, *CD* I/1, 482.
199. Tan, "A Trinitarian Ontology," 290.
200. Acts 1:1 NIV, emphasis added.
201. Marshall, *Acts*, 20.

the scope of Jesus' relation to his Father, thereby gathering them together in *koinonia* with one another."[202] The Spirit incorporates the disciples into the sonship of Jesus, so that by that same Spirit they might share in the Son's relation to the Father and so address God as 'Abba, Father.' Jesus' community of disciples can be understood as the proto-church, but they do not become the church until their reception of the Spirit on Pentecost, for it is by the Spirit that they were baptized into one body, the church (see 1 Cor 12:13). In one divine act the Spirit creates a twofold communion and implements in history an inbreaking and foretaste of eschatological life: a human community living in right relations with God and neighbor. Hence, "Mission can be seen as the work of the Spirit to bring a foretaste of the future kingdom into the world today."[203] When Jesus poured out the Holy Spirit, the gathered disciples were caught up into the Triune *koinonia* and thus in one moment were reconstituted from above and joined together as one supernatural fellowship. This incorporation is necessarily communal, "for the Spirit brings together (*com-*) humanity into the *unity* of Christ."[204] In this adopted sonship the church looks to the Father, and in doing so looks to the world to which the Father sent his Son and Spirit. In that same outpouring, the church was swept up into Spirit's mission, and so his coming had "the effect of directing them outwards, turning them towards the world . . . for it is the role of the Spirit to bear witness to Jesus in the world, and to enable Jesus' followers to do likewise."[205] The Spirit of communion creates a communion between humanity and God and imprints his communion-seeking nature upon the church, thus impelling her outwards to extend and expand this communion to include all peoples. In propelling the church to mission, the Spirit's work mirrors the divine Triune *koinonia*, which is open to the world. Gunton helpfully says "The mission of the Spirit, his sending by the Father through the Son, is to create communion in the Church, and in so doing to prevent the Church from remaining content with its own fellowship."[206]

The Holy Spirit's work in establishing a communion between people and God, enabling them to participate in the divine communion, includes the work of revelation, reconciliation, regeneration, convicting of sin, and giving the gift of faith. It is also associated with the human acts of repentance

202. Watson, "Trinity and Community," quoted in Gunton, *Father, Son and Holy Spirit*, 88.

203. Lord, "Mission Eschatology," 122.

204. Anatolios, "The Immediately Triune God," 176, emphasis original.

205. Watson, "Trinity and Community," quoted in Gunton, *Father, Son and Holy Spirit*, 88.

206. Gunton, *Father, Son and Holy Spirit*, 88.

and conversion. It is the unique role of the Holy Spirit to cross the divide between objective and subjective, in this case Christ's objective atonement for all and that atonement becoming subjectively efficacious for some. The Spirit particularizes the universal salvific work of Christ by applying and appropriating the gift of grace to transform particular lives. Bloesch explains that "The atoning work of Christ on the cross is consummated, but it must be followed by the revealing and regenerating work of the Holy Spirit if man is to be saved de facto (in fact) as well as de jure (in principle)."[207] It is Barth who classically enunciated the principle that only God can reveal God since the finite is not capable of the infinite,[208] or in his words, "God is known by God alone."[209] Thus, divine self-revelation is the work of the Holy Spirit, and it "is more than the communication of information; it is the giving of an invitation."[210] In revelation God discloses himself and invites this creature made in his image into saving fellowship with himself. Revelation goes beyond simply invitation; in revelation God gives himself. This divine self-disclosure and self-giving not only invites, but also establishes a relationship with the creature. Barth explains,

> It is God's reality in that God Himself becomes present to man not just externally, not just from above, but also from within, from below, subjectively. It is thus reality in that He does not merely come to man but encounters Himself from man. God's freedom to be present in this way to man, and therefore to bring about this encounter, is the Spirit of God, the Holy Spirit in God's revelation.[211]

In the one united trinitarian act, divine self-revelation is also reconciliation and regeneration.

The Father reveals himself in the Son who makes atonement for all humanity. The Spirit reveals the Son, who is the image of his Father, and he unites human persons to the saving person and work of Christ to share in his sonship. Tom Smail says, "What Christ has done *for* us on the cross, the Spirit does *in* us, so that we are united with him in such a way that what we are becomes his and what he is becomes ours."[212] The Spirit's work in a person contains both enhypostatic and anhypostatic movements. Enhypostatically the Spirit reveals the identity of the incarnate God, and

---

207. Bloesch, *Essentials of Evangelical Theology*, 1:163.
208. Barth, *The Göttingen Dogmatics*, 117.
209. Barth, *CD* II/1, 179.
210. Newbigin, *Proper Confidence*, 65.
211. Barth, *CD* I/1, 451.
212. Smail, "Trinitarian Atonement," 48, emphasis original.

anhypostatically the Spirit effects a positive response from the person to this divine self-revelation. Barth says, "The Spirit guarantees man what he cannot guarantee himself, his personal participation in revelation. The act of the Holy Ghost in revelation is the Yes to God's Word which is spoken by God Himself for us, yet not just to us, but also in us."[213] The Holy Spirit truly is the 'go-between God' who comes to the creature from without and responds for the creature from within. As the Spirit of Christ, the Holy Spirit adapts the creature into "the single normative stance of the Godward God," Jesus. Thus, for Anatolios the Spirit is "in a certain sense, the humanward God, who precisely as God, immediately effects the humanization of the Son's Godwardness that we may share in it."[214]

This activity of the Spirit possesses the property of being past event and ongoing process. Being born of the Spirit (John 3:3–8), being baptized by the Spirit into Christ's body (1 Cor 12:3), receiving the Spirit of adoption (Rom 8:15), being delivered from the domain of darkness into the kingdom of God's Son (Col 1:13) and turning to serve God rather than idols (1 Thess 1: 9) is clearly an event, a discrete occurrence. Actively participating in and living out the Godward stance of the vicarious obedience of Christ is also a process that begins at conversion and is perfected in the eschaton. Thus, there is a unity between the Holy Spirit's work in reconciliation—both in the work of Christ, in the communication of that work to the creature and his/her response to that work, and his work of sanctification—the enabling of the believer to live a holy life. This pneumatological work is not merely past and present but also relates to the future. Gunton says, "The action of the Sprit is to anticipate, in the present and by means of the finite and contingent, the things of the age to come."[215] Central to God's new creation is redeemed humanity, and so by the ongoing nature of the Spirit's regenerating and sanctifying work that creates and sustains a people in Christ, he implements and anticipates eschatological reality.

## The Spirit's Work in the World

The Spirit's mission activity is not confined to the boundaries of the church, for the Holy Spirit was poured out on *all* flesh and so is omnipresent (Acts 2:17; Joel 2:28). This echoes the universal scope of the Spirit's creative work in the beginning, when he hovered over the waters of creation (Gen 1:2). This Creator Spirit is at work in the physical processes of creation itself, in

---

213. Karl Barth, *CD* I/1, 453.
214. Anatolios, "The Immediately Triune God," 176–77.
215. Gunton, *The Promise*, 67.

## The Mission of the Son and Spirit

both its aspects of nature and history. And it is this Spirit of creation who is also the Spirit of new creation, for "Only the Spirit of creation is strong enough to be the Spirit of resurrection."[216] This Spirit of new creation desires the salvation of all people and so it is reasonable to believe that in his omnipresence the Spirit is redemptively active in all people everywhere. However, like so much of the Spirit's work that reflects his self-effacing personhood, it remains hidden (John 3:8). Since God's concern is for not only the church but the world as a whole, one can reasonably expect to see signs of the Spirit's working in the world that has been created by God and for him. As the Apostle Paul said to his hearers in Lystra, in all the nations God has not left himself without witness (Acts 14:16–17). The world, though fallen away from God has not been abandoned by him, and in Christ and the Spirit it is being redeemed so that, in the eschaton, the kingdom of the world will "become the kingdom of our Lord and of his Messiah, and he will reign for ever and ever" (Rev 11:15). Since the eschatological and Pentecostal pouring out of the Holy Spirit he has been at work, carrying out the will of the Father to guide the world to its God-intended *telos*, that is the summing up of all things in Christ (Eph 1:10). Consequently, it is with confidence that one must confess the activity of the Spirit in the world, but this confidence is not transferrable to epistemically knowing what and where the Spirit is in fact at work. That the Spirit is at work in the world is an example of cataphatic theology, but discerning specific examples of the Spirit's work in the world belongs to the apophatic theological tradition.

There is, for example, a plethora of movements for justice, peace, liberation, and mercy, which resemble the operations of the Spirit mentioned in Jesus' programmatic announcement in Nazareth that inaugurates his ministry. Jesus reiterated Isaiah's proclamation that the work of the Spirit is to preach good news to the poor, release to the captives, bring recovery of sight to the blind and freedom for the oppressed.[217] Although equipped with confidence in the Spirit's work in the world, and with apparent similarities between biblical descriptions of pneumatological operations and contemporary movements, it is still difficult to clearly identify the Spirit's work with any particular movement. For example, every movement is multifaceted, and so whilst elements of one movement can be easily identified with the cause of Christ, such as efforts to relieve extreme poverty, other aspects of that movement may be clearly contrary to that cause. Moreover, how does one know whether the Holy Spirit is at work in certain movements, and who is authorized to make such pronouncements? The South African Dutch

---

216. Pinnock, *Flame of Love*, 63.
217. Luke 4:18–19; see also Isa 61:1–2.

Reformed Church believed that Apartheid was God-ordained, whilst the majority of other Christians believed that working against Apartheid was a work of the Spirit. Martin Luther King, Jr claimed inspiration from God in his work towards establishing equal civil rights for all American citizens whilst he was being opposed by many other Christian ministers.[218] Today the Anglican Communion is divided over the issue of homosexuality, and advocates on both sides of the debate believe they are working for and with God. By faith, Christians confess that the Holy Spirit is active in the world, but attempting to discern in which movements the Spirit is active is a notoriously hazardous undertaking. I suspect that the prophetic discernment of a united church would be more successful in identifying some ways in which the Spirit is at work, than the splintered and fragmented body of Christ that is the current empirical reality. Consequently, whilst a theology of the Spirit's work in the world must be strongly affirmed, it is something of a theological minefield and one I shall not attempt to negotiate here.

As I seek to develop a trinitarian missiology beyond Newbigin's own, it behooves me to discuss the alleged shortfalls in his own trinitarian missiology. Several scholars including Bert Hoedemaker[219] criticize Newbigin's trinitarian missiology as undeveloped. Michael Goheen says that "Newbigin does not work out his insights on the activity of the Father and the Spirit in the world with enough detail."[220] Similarly Richard Gelwick stresses the importance of openness to acts of God outside the church.[221] Although Newbigin would agree with Gelwick here, as I have explained the act of discerning the work of the Holy Spirit in the world is a perilous enterprise.[222] In his response to Gelwick, Hunsberger says,

> Gelwick recommends that Christians 'relate to the Spirit's leading in the global search for peace and justice' and respond to 'the Spirit's calling of humankind to deal pluralistically with the global problems.' Alasdair MacIntyre might be tempted to respond, 'Whose Spirit? Which leading and calling?' How do we discern which among human activities are the Spirit's doings?

218. See King, "Letter From Birmingham Jail."
219. Hoedemaker, Review of *The Open Secret*.
220. Goheen, "As the Father Has Sent Me," 160.
221. Gelwick, "Christian Faith in Pluralist Society," 44.
222. Several recent thinkers, such as Brian D. McLaren and Philip Clayton, have made the attempt. Fitch and Holsclaw criticse their attempts for uncritically identifying "God's work in the Spirit with (a Hegelian/Marxist) generalist justice and peace efforts in the world," and for writing about the work of the Spirit in the world in a way that is undetermined by the person and work of Christ. Fitch and Holsclaw, "Mission amid Empire," 391.

> Which signs are the signs of the Spirit? How do we adjudicate between our different conclusions about what the Spirit is calling and leading us to do? Here there is not one singular way, and no clear singular way to move toward discerning what it might be.[223]

I contend that Hunsberger has correctly represented Newbigin's theologically-informed apophatism in this matter, and it is for this reason that, following Newbigin and Hunsberger, I do not seek to further develop this account of the mission of the Triune God with regards to God's work in the world.

The Spirit's work in the world is intrinsically mysterious, part of those secret and hidden things that belong to God (Deut 29:29), which is what one could expect from the Spirit who blows where he wills (John 3:8). What can be unambiguously affirmed is that according to the New Testament the working of the Spirit has two key coordinates: Jesus and the church. Newbigin explains that "The Sprit binds men to Jesus, to his historic life and to the fellowship of those who confess him as Lord."[224] In this regard, the Spirit is certainly active in all peoples testifying about Jesus (John 15:26), convicting the world of sin, righteousness and judgement (John 16:8–11), thereby preparing people to receive the gospel. It is now a truism to say that the church's missionaries do not take God to a people, but God who is omnipresent is already at work in all people and he brings missionaries to those in whom he is already at work. It has been the experience of countless missionaries that God has been at work in non-Christian peoples and cultures, preparing them for the reception of the gospel often centuries before missionaries arrive.[225] The Holy Spirit goes ahead of the church "preparing men's hearts in ways that no man could have planned, so that the Church has all that it can do [sic.] to follow after to make open and visible what the Spirit has already begun in secret before any churchmen knew of it."[226] The Holy Spirit carries out the will of the Father by going ahead of the church into the world, and

---

223. Hunsberger, "Faith and Pluralism," 28.

224. Newbigin, *Trinitarian Doctrine*, 80.

225. Don Richardson documents many examples in his popular book *Eternity In Their Hearts*. Rather than conceiving of this as natural human receptivity to the gospel it should be conceived of as the work of God the Spirit preparing peoples for faith in Christ.

226. Newbigin, *Unfaith and Other Faiths*. Here Newbigin echoes Barth: "It [the Church] has the freedom to fulfil its duty of mission in the knowledge that its Lord has long since preceded it with His Word with His resurrection, and that He is always well ahead of it, so that in this respect, too, it has only to follow Him" (Barth, *CD* IV.3.2, 305).

prompting the church to follow in order to communicate the gospel of Jesus Christ. Thus, the Spirit's work in the world is directly related to Christ and his church.

## The Spirit's Free Election of the Church

The post-Pentecost mission of the Spirit includes the specific work of regeneration, sanctification, conviction of sin, endowment of gifts, empowerment, instruction, and intercession. It is noticeable that all facets of the Spirit's mission post-Pentecost are directly related to the church. Since the Holy Spirit is the missionary Spirit it quickly becomes apparent that the church is central to his mission post-Pentecost; indeed the church is the main instrument of the Spirit's mission. How the Spirit uses the church in his mission can be understood in terms of the doctrine of election. According to Newbigin, the central theme of the biblical story is election: "God's choosing (election) of a people to be His own people, by whom He purposes to save the world."[227] Thus, election must be understood as missionary in character. In the mission of the Son and Spirit it is the church, represented by the disciple-apostles, who, in Christ, are the elect of God. Newbigin says "The instrument of His choosing [election] is precisely the apostolic mission of the Church. 'I chose you,' says the incarnate Lord to His apostles, 'and appointed you, that ye should go and bear fruit' (John 15:16)."[228] In God's election of Abraham, Israel, Jesus and the church, they are to be conduits of God's blessing, not cul-de-sacs.[229] God's mission is the reconciliation of his wayward creation and is therefore cosmic in scope, and the doctrine of election teaches that, "Thinking globally, God acted locally."[230] God accomplishes his universal mission by means of particular election. The challenge to any doctrine of election is holding together the particular with the universal, and in this Newbigin shows the way forward.

Those elected by God are indeed blessed, but they are elected as "Bearers—not exclusive beneficiaries."[231] David Bosch concurs, asserting that "The purpose of election is service, and when this is withheld, election loses its meaning."[232] Newbigin believed that election provides the framework

227. Newbigin, "Why Study the Old Testament?," 75.
228. Newbigin, *The Household of God*, 102.
229. Piper, *Let the Nations Be Glad!*, 106.
230. Howard Snyder quoted in Escobar, *The New Global Mission*, 62.
231. Newbigin, *The Open Secret*, 32.
232. Bosch, *Transforming Mission*, 18. See also Blauw, *The Missionary Nature of the Church*, 22.

in which to understand ecclesiology. He says the church is "the *pars pro toto* in the sense that it is sent in order that the rest of the world may be converted."[233] God has chosen the church to be the bearer of God's blessing, in order that others might also be chosen through the church to receive God's blessing for themselves, and then themselves become channels of divine blessing for others. Election decisively frames ecclesiology, and both are decidedly missional.[234] Election is God's strategy of choosing some, the church, on behalf of all; choosing some for the sake of all.

The Bible depicts divine wisdom appearing as foolishness to human understanding, and in many ways election is a prime example. "The question arises," says Barth, "indeed whether God and the world would not be far better served by a 'word of reconciliation' (2 Cor 5:19) spoken by Jesus Christ Himself and alone, without any co-operation on the part of Peter and Paul, let alone the rest of us."[235] Why would God elect such indirect, inefficient and unreliable means as the church? Why did God not choose to bless all people directly rather than using the fallible, weak, erring and wayward church? By way of a preliminary answer, God's strategy of election is in accord with God's salvific and revelatory action in Christ. If God were to savingly reveal himself to all people directly, then this would entail an ahistorical account of God and divine revelation that is at odds with the biblical witness. But *why* does God savingly reveal himself through actions in history rather than in an ahistorical manner? Why does God savingly act through the church rather than in more efficient and reliable ways that do not depend on human cooperation? To revert to a human analogy, why would a wise manager choose risky and unreliable means of accomplishing his or her purposes? The decisive clue to the answer lies in ascertaining exactly what these purposes are, and how the means are related to the ends. In addressing these questions one must begin with theological anthropology, understood in the light of the doctrine of the Trinity.

Humans are intrinsically relational beings made in the image of the God whose being is in communion. The intrinsic relatedness of the human person is in particular directed both to God, the creature's maker and Lord, and to fellow humans. Sin primarily consists in humans failing to completely love God and fellow humans, and so has both Godward and humanward dimensions. Hence, the reconciliation that God intends for humanity requires repairing the breach not only between humans and God, but also

---

233. Newbigin, *The Finality of Christ*, 97, emphases original.

234. It is worthwhile noting that the most sustained discussion of election by Newbigin prior to 1978 is in his one volume devoted to expounding ecclesiology, *The Household of God*.

235. Barth, *CD* IV/3.2, 607.

between humans and their fellow humans. If God simply desired the salvation of each individual soul, then election appears to be arbitrary favoritism. However, since election is christocentric and corporate, the salvation that God intends for humanity is also christocentric and corporate. Following the Day of Pentecost when "the Lord added to their number . . . those who were being saved," John Stott observes that God "didn't add them to the church without saving them," neither did God "save them without adding them to the church. Salvation and church membership went together; they still do."[236] God is seeking not a city populated with redeemed individuals, but a bride, a body, what Martin Luther King, Jr used to call the 'beloved community.' Newbigin clearly perceived that election is God's means for salvation because it is commensurate with his ends.

> But a salvation whose very essence is that it is corporate and cosmic, the restoration of the broken harmony between all men and between man and God and man and nature, must be communicated in a different way. It must be communicated in and by the actual development of a community which embodies—if only in foretaste—the restored harmony of which it speaks. A gospel of reconciliation can only be communicated by a reconciled fellowship.[237]

God's purpose is that humans should have concern for their fellow humans, therefore God chooses one to be sent to another, and so on, so that all may be knit together in one redeemed fellowship.

Receiving God's saving revelation requires the humility to receive it from another person, God's appointed messenger.[238] This humility is not simply a means to an end, but is itself part of God's saving purpose of reconciling and uniting humanity in Christ, because one aspect of human unity is simply corporate humility before Christ. Thus, the church becomes "His reconciled and reconciling people."[239] John Thompson rightly says "The Church is, on the one hand, the provisional result of mission but, on the other hand, it is God's agent of it."[240] This statement requires first qualification and then elaboration. The church is God's agent of mission, not in the sense that the church exercises an active agency on behalf of a passive or idle God. Rather, God continues to actively prosecute his own mission through

---

236. John R. W. Stott, *The Living Church*, quoted in White, *Christ Among the Dragons*, 161–62.
237. Newbigin, *The Household of God*, 141.
238. Newbigin, *The Gospel in a Pluralist Society*, 82–83.
239. Newbigin, *The Household of God*, 101.
240. Thompson, *Modern Trinitarian Perspectives*, 75–76.

his Son and Spirit, but in such a way that the church becomes, by divine election, the *sine qua non* of the *missio Dei*. It is with this qualification that agency-language for the church in the *missio Dei* is appropriate. Elaborating on Thompson's assertion, as the reconciled humanity, the church is also the sign and foretaste of the *goal* of God's mission. For Newbigin salvation depicts a making whole, a unifying of all creation whose source and pattern is the love within the life of the Triune God, "the summing up of all things in Christ" (Eph 1:10). Christ reveals that God is like a mother hen seeking to gather her chicks under her wings, so there can therefore be no private salvation. Humans cannot experience salvation in its fullness until all for whom it is intended have it together.[241] That is why God advances the *missio Dei* by way of electing the church. Since as the elect people the church is central to the *missio Dei*, it is no surprise that she is central to the mission of the Spirit.

## The Missionary Church within the Mission of the Spirit

The Holy Spirit primarily advances his mission by advancing the mission of the church, for which he is the *conditio sine qua non*. Hence, the Spirit inaugurates his mission on the day of Pentecost by constituting the church in Christ, and he continues to lead and inspire the church in her mission. McIntyre explains "it was the Holy Spirit who was responsible for the birth, survival, growth and development of the early Church, through his inspiration of, and involvement with, the disciples."[242] The Spirit filled the apostles, who then boldly spoke the word of God (Acts 4: 31), led Philip to explain the gospel to the high-standing Ethiopian official (Acts 8:29), prompted Peter to go to Gentile Cornelius without hesitation (Acts 11:12), and set apart Paul and Barnabas thus instigating the first intentional missionary journeys (Acts 13:2). In these last three instances it is the Spirit who moved the church to cross the great divide in bringing the gospel to the Gentiles, arguably the most significant act of translation in church history.[243] The universal scope and goal of the Spirit's mission is particularized through the mission of the church. However, some scholars are nervous about tying the Spirit's mission too strongly to the church's mission, and they correctly point out that the global reach of the omnipresent Spirit is to be contrasted with the geographical limitation of the church-in-mission. This ecclesial limita-

---

241. Newbigin, *The Household of God*, 140.
242. McIntyre, *The Shape of Pneumatology*, 53.
243. See Walls, "The Translation Principle in Christian History," in *The Missionary Movement*, 26–42, and Sanneh, *Translating the Message*.

tion has been exploited by some scholars in order to drive a wedge between Pneumatology and ecclesiology, and suggest that the Spirit can reach people without the church engaging in mission. This is often further combined with an abandonment of the claim to the uniqueness of Christ, *en route* to religious pluralism, by arguing that the Holy Spirit is salvifically working within non-Christian religions and therefore evangelistic work amongst people of other faiths is inappropriate and unnecessary. In turn, this creates a further dichotomy between Pneumatology and Christology, which is highly problematic because the two cannot be separated since there is no separation *within* God. D. T. Niles' statement, "Jesus Christ is the content of the Gospel . . . [and] The Holy Spirit is the missionary of the Gospel"[244] ought to be affirmed whilst also affirming that Christ proclaims himself through the Spirit. When proponents of this pluralistic view seek biblical support they frequently appeal to the story of Cornelius, for according to S. Wesley Ariarajah, this story shows that "there is no need to channel God to people; God has direct access."[245]

In the New Testament it is clear that the Holy Spirit advances the *missio Dei* by way of the elect people, the church, by means of election, and this is clear in the story of Cornelius. In Acts 10:3–6 the Holy Spirit indeed speaks to non-Christian Cornelius through an angel in a vision, without ecclesial mediation, as Ariarajah has said. However, the Holy Spirit does not reveal the gospel to Cornelius, but rather instructs him to send for Peter who will tell Cornelius what to do. The Spirit is free and sovereign and goes ahead of the church, "but it is (if one may put it so) the *church* that he goes ahead of."[246] Peter arrived and *as* he explains the gospel of Jesus Christ "the Holy Spirit came upon all who heard the message" (Acts 10:44). This is unsurprising given that the dominant New Testament portrayal of the Holy Spirit's working is in relation to either eschatology, or to *the Church*.[247] Ariarajah rightly wants to give priority to *God's* activity in mission, but the Bible makes clear that this does not preclude but includes the church's mission. As Bosch helpfully puts it, "The Christian mission is always Christological and pneumatological, but the New Testament knows of no Christology or Pneumatology which is not ecclesial."[248] In Christ, God has irrevocably bound himself to his covenant people the church. Newbigin makes clear that "this

---

244. Niles, *Upon The Earth*, 67.

245. S. Wesley Ariarajah, *The Bible and People of Other Faiths*, quoted in Newbigin, *The Gospel in a Pluralist Society*, 167.

246. Newbigin, *Trinitarian Doctrine*, 80, emphasis added.

247. Carr, 'Towards a Contemporary.'

248. Bosch, *Transforming Mission*, 385.

work of the Spirit is not in any sense an alternative way to God apart from the Church; it is the preparation for the coming of the Church, which means that the Church must be ever ready to follow where the Spirit leads."[249] On this basis I disagree with scholars such as John McIntyre, Michael Goheen, and indeed Lesslie Newbigin, who suggest that *Acts of the Apostles* might just as easily be called *Acts of the Holy Spirit*.[250] McIntyre's main point, that the Holy Spirit is utterly central to *Acts of the Apostles*, is entirely valid. He says "there is a scarcely a chapter in which the Holy Spirit is not mentioned, often centrally and strategically."[251] Likewise, Newbigin says that in *Acts* "we have the full exposition of the work of the Spirit as the real agent of mission."[252] Nevertheless, I believe that *Acts of the Apostles* is correctly entitled because God has uniquely charged the *church* to proclaim the gospel. Of course the Holy Spirit must always be central, for ecclesial proclamation of the gospel is ineffective without the sovereign regenerating work of the Spirit, but the traditional title given to Luke's sequel to his gospel faithfully bears witness to the honor divinely bestowed upon the church and her distinctive role within the *missio Dei*. There can therefore be no separating of Pneumatology from ecclesiology, but nor can there be a blurring of their distinctive missions.[253] Neither can there be "a severing of the Spirit from Jesus Christ," suggesting that the Spirit's direct access is in itself redemptive apart from faith in Christ as explained by the church. This is simply because "If the Spirit relates created beings to God—thus making them holy, in the sense of finally acceptable to God—he achieves this through the Son, the mediator of creation, for there is no other way."[254] Missiology has good reason to insist that Christ, the Spirit, the church, and mission be held closely together.

The lordship of the Holy Spirit over the church and her mission includes not only creating her and directing her mission, but also the work of human regeneration, which is uniquely a work of the Spirit. The church

---

249. Newbigin, *Trinitarian Doctrine*, 53–54.

250. McIntyre, *The Shape of Pneumatology*, 53; Goheen, "As the Father Has Sent Me," 183; Newbigin, *The Open Secret*, 57.

251. McIntyre, *The Shape of Pneumatology*, 55. There is perhaps greater merit in the suggestion that an additional name for *Acts of the Apostles* is *The Gospel of the Holy Spirit*. Bevans, "God Inside Out," 103.

252. Newbigin, *The Open Secret*, 57. For almost identical wording see Goheen, "As the Father Has Sent Me," 183.

253. In the New Testament there is no Christian who is not a member of a local Church. There are a plethora of extra-biblical accounts of God revealing Himself to those beyond the church's bounds, such as Sheikh, *I Dared To Call Him Father*. Interestingly, in that story the author was directed to find local Christ-followers, as was Cornelius.

254. Gunton, *The Promise*, xxviii.

cannot convert people because they must be born of the Spirit.[255] This realization during the Middle Ages would have prevented grotesque distortions of the church's mission and the torture and loss of life which tragically followed. Regeneration depends upon God's self-revelation and God's chosen instrument for this work is the witness of the church, but the presence of the latter does not guarantee the former. Barth explains, "In His revelation God controls His property, elevating our words to their proper use, giving Himself to be their proper object, and therefore giving them truth."[256] In the work of regeneration the Holy Spirit is always sovereign. Describing this divine self-revelation which is regeneration, Barth says

> The creature needs the Creator to be able to live. It thus needs the relation to Him. But it cannot create this relation. God creates it by His own presence in the creature and therefore as a relation of Himself to Himself. The Spirit of God is God in His freedom to be present to the creature, and therefore to create this relation, and therefore to be the life of the creature. And God's Spirit, the Holy Spirit, especially in revelation, is God Himself to the extent that He can not only come to man but also be in man, and thus open up man and make him capable and ready for Himself, and thus achieve His revelation in him.[257]

Given the sovereignty of the Holy Spirit in regeneration, it is curious to note that in the story of Cornelius, which I take as indicative of the whole New Testament witness, the Spirit chose *not* to communicate the gospel because that is the church's role.[258] In making this assertion I am extending the paradigmatic use of the story of Peter and Cornelius beyond Newbigin's usage.[259] It appears that, ordinarily speaking, in his sovereignty the Spirit will not save without the witness of the church, and yet the church's witness alone does not and cannot convert people. There is something of an interdependency between the missions of Spirit and church, not by necessity, but by the design and purpose of God. This obviates Andrew Kirk's comment that "if God's mission is largely tied to the Church then God's freedom is

---

255. For the purposes of this article I use regeneration and conversion synonymously, for with Emil Brunner, I believe they are different aspects of the same happening. Brunner, *Dogmatics*, 3:281.

256. Barth, *CD* II/1, 230.

257. Barth, *CD* I/1, 450.

258. This is not to take away from the historic significance of Cornelius' reception of the Spirit, which needed apostolic verification, that God had granted to the Gentiles repentance that leads to life (Acts 11:18).

259. Newbigin, *The Open Secret*, 64.

seriously compromised."²⁶⁰ Kirk is right, unless God in his freedom chooses to make the church central to the *missio Dei*. The Holy Spirit is Lord over the church's mission in that he is the agent of revelation and regeneration. This lordship resembles the lordship of Jesus, unusual, unexpected, and overturning our human notions of lordship,²⁶¹ but it is still a lordship nonetheless. Describing the church's relationship to the Holy Spirit Barth says, "There does not belong to it the power of the sending and outpouring and operation of the Holy Spirit. It does not 'possess' Him. It cannot create or control Him. He is promised to it. It can only receive Him and then be obedient to Him."²⁶² The relationship is thoroughly asymmetrical since the Holy Spirit is both the Lord and the giver of life, over, in, and through the church's mission.

## The Delegation of Mission to the Church as Risk

Jesus, the Lord of the church, charges the church to mission, but according to Blauw "He does not *delegate* it to them."²⁶³ By this, Blauw means that Jesus' missionary activity does not end where the church's mission begins. Nonetheless, there is a sense in which Jesus does delegate mission to the church, for within the *missio Dei*, the church's responsibilities such as the communication of the gospel, are unique. Newbigin explains that the chief legacy of Jesus' life is the community of disciples, and *"He committed the entire work of salvation to that community."*²⁶⁴ Since the work of salvation is arguably central to the purpose of creation itself,²⁶⁵ taking Newbigin's statement seriously means that God has taken an enormous risk in entrusting a crucial facet of the *missio Dei* to the flawed and fallible church. This risk can also be construed as voluntary divine dependence upon the church for the completion of the *missio Dei*, but this never displaces God as the primary actor in his mission. Thus Newbigin says, "It is not that the church has a mission and the Spirit helps us in fulfilling it. It is rather that the Spirit is the active missionary, and *the church* (where it is faithful) *is the place where the Spirit is enabled to complete the Spirit's work*."²⁶⁶ This language of the church *enabling* God's Spirit seems to undermine the sovereignty and freedom of

---

260. Kirk, *What Is Mission?*, 206.
261. See Mark 10:42–45.
262. Barth, *CD* IV/2, 655.
263. Blauw, *The Missionary Nature*, 89, emphasis original.
264. Newbigin, *The Household of God*, 27, emphasis added.
265. See Newbigin, *Trinitarian Doctrine*, 83.
266. Newbigin, *Mission in Christ's Way*, 20.

God, and runs contrary to Barth's contention that "Only God Himself acting and speaking in Christ is indispensable to the occurrence of the work of God—none else."[267] Barth's point, in which he is correct, is simply that the mission is *God's* mission in which he is the chief agent, including in Christ's free entrusting of mission to the church. But then Barth goes further, arguing that God's work "is thus free from any need or necessity of a human co-operation or assistance without which it could not occur or reach its goal."[268] Barth is right that there is no *necessity* for human cooperation to achieve God's purposes, for God can do as he pleases, but this overlooks God's *desire* to make the completion of his mission partially dependent upon ecclesial cooperation.[269] Newbigin suggests this when he says, in God's "mysterious wisdom—he has allowed the consummation of His purpose to wait upon our obedience, and entrusted to us the task of making His victory known and effective in every nation and in every sphere of life."[270] In God's providence and wisdom he has limited himself by freely choosing to depend upon ecclesial cooperation to accomplish his mission. John Sanders, who explores the nature of divine risk-taking vis-à-vis the doctrine of providence says, "According to Paul, God has chosen to be somewhat dependent upon us [the church] to accomplish the ministry of reconciliation (2 Cor 5:18–20), for God desires collaboration in this task."[271] Nevertheless, any talk of *divine dependence* requires careful qualification.

First, God's dependence upon the church is freely chosen and wholly gracious, for as Barth makes clear, God does not need anything. Second, this dependence is partial and not total. Third, the notion of divine dependence is not completely novel, for in the incarnation the Son was dependent upon the empowering Holy Spirit, and humanly upon Mary and Joseph, in the same way that all infants depend on their parents. Even in the ontological Trinity dependence, in at least some sense, is not alien to God, for each Triune Person depends upon the other two for his being, since God is constituted in and by his intra-trinitarian perichoretic relations. Fourth, there

---

267. Barth, *CD* IV/3.2, 607.

268. Ibid., 607.

269. Barth is not content to suggest that God *needs* anything, even if God freely chooses this need, but he does concur that God does not will to proclaim the Gospel alone, without the Church. "He alone is competent and authorized to perform it. He alone is the Speaker of the Word of God as well as the Doer of His work. But in the exercise of the prophetic office of His, even though it is He alone who control it, He does not will to be alone. Controlling and exercising it, He calls certain men to His side and commissions them to be His disciples or pupils, i.e., Christians" (ibid., 606).

270. Newbigin, "The Present Crisis," 123.

271. Sanders, *The God Who Risks*, 125.

is a strong argument made by some scholars such as Terence Fretheim that dependence is an intrinsic aspect of divine providence due to the kind of world God freely created.[272] Fifth, however God's dependence upon the church is to be conceived it can never be a total sharing of authority, for the biblical Creator-creature distinction always remains.[273] Fiddes puts it well: "God who does not need dependence freely desires to be dependent on us for the completeness of fellowship, for the joy of the dance."[274] Sixth, this suggestion of Christ's dependence upon the church for the completion of his mission could otherwise be expressed as Christ's decision that his self-proclamation will never be without its own creaturely echo. Having thus qualified God's dependence upon the church, it is nevertheless true that *any* concept of such a dependence is extremely humbling for the church, a theme we shall return to shortly. The question remains, *how* dependent is God upon the church? If the church fails in her mission, does that entail the failure of God's mission? Barth was writing from the perspective that the answer to this latter question must be 'no'.

The enormity of divine risk is dependent upon one's views of predestination, providence and divine foreknowledge with which it is directly related, but a full discussion which those subjects deserve is beyond the scope of this discussion. That this risk has been actualized and is not merely a theoretical possibility is clear from Bosch's rather frank description of the church. He says "Throughout most of the church's history its empirical state has been deplorable. This was already true of Jesus' first circle of disciples and has not really changed since."[275] Some of the darkest chapters of church history include the Crusades, the Spanish inquisition, and the persecution of the Anabaptist Christians by other Christians (Protestant and Catholic). The risk is real; the damage done in Christ's name, deplorable. The disobedience of the church explains why the majority of humanity waited *at least* fifteen-hundred years to hear the gospel.[276] Offering a suggestion as to why

272. Fretheim sees this in Genesis 2:5 and 2:15 "where the presence of a human being to till (*'bd*) the ground is considered indispensable for the development of the creation. Human beings are given responsibility for intra-creational development, bringing the world along toward its fullest possible potential" (Fretheim, "Divine Dependence," 5).

273. Hill, "A Response," 15.

274. Fiddes, *Participating in God*, 108. Similarly, McKnight speaks of "the eternal interlocking dance of the Father, Son, and Spirit" (McKnight, *The Heaven Promise*, 117).

275. Bosch, *Transforming Mission*, 519.

276. This is not to deny that mission occurred within Christendom, such as to the Slavs and to Scandinavia, and outside Christendom to central and eastern Asia, but makes the simple point that the vast majority of humanity had not been brought into contact with the gospel prior to 1493. In that year the papal Bulls of Pope Alexander VI

God might risk making his mission somewhat dependent upon the church, Sanders states "God's project is to develop people who love and trust him in response to his love."[277] The mission of the Spirit includes a reconciled human fellowship, and the church is both a means to God's desired end and part of that end itself, a foretaste and first-fruits of God's mission. In God's wisdom, he has made what might be interpreted as the foolish decision to risk making his mission partially dependent upon the church, but this decision is made by the God who said 'My power is made perfect in weakness."[278] Still, God's risk is real, but it would be irresponsible and unacceptable to suggest that the risk is total. Sanders believes that God's risk is a relative and not an absolute risk, and the final outcome of God's mission is never in question.[279] Similarly, I contend that although the church's mission is marked by failure as well as success, it will nonetheless, by the enabling of the Spirit, certainly complete it.

Jesus committed part of the work of salvation to the church and this confidence is not misplaced because, although human, flawed, and fallible, the church is far more than simply this. The church is not chiefly comprised of sinful humans but of persons regenerated by the Spirit and made holy in Christ. Jesus is confident that the church's mission will succeed because the church is animated by the Holy Spirit, and Jesus can completely trust the work of the Spirit in and through the church. In Matthew 16:17–18 Jesus says that he will build his church on the rock, and that rock is the Father's work of revealing the Son by the Spirit, for as Jesus said to Peter "flesh and blood did not reveal this to you, but my Father who is in heaven."[280] Jesus' confidence is supremely on the work of the Spirit in and through the church, and that is why Blauw says Jesus does not delegate the mission to the church. He continues, "Nothing is left to men, not even to the apostles;

---

instructed the Spanish king to bring the gospel to the inhabitants of the Americas. I say 'at least' because a major force in missionary history, the Protestant missionary movement, was approximately two centuries behind its Roman counterpart, and today there are many peoples who are still yet to hear the gospel. Neill, *A History*, 121.

277. Sanders, *The God Who Risks*, 124.

278. 2 Cor 12:9. It is also clear that the ways of God can often appear to humans as foolishness (see 1 Cor 1:18–31).

279. Sanders, *The God Who Risks*, 229. Boyd, who also espouses this view of providence, explains in greater detail how the risk-taking God can be assured of attaining his overall mission, in chapter 5, "Love & War: Risk and the Sovereignty of God," in *Satan and the Problem of Evil*, 145–77.

280. Matt 16:17 NASB. In this passage Jesus attributes this revelation to the Father, but elsewhere revelation is clearly depicted as a work of the Spirit (John 3:4–8 and 1 Cor 12:3). This simply underlines the truth contained in the trinitarian rule *opera trinitatis ad extra sunt indivisa*.

*that*, however, is why everything *can* be delegated to the Church," because "The Holy Spirit guarantees the power of life in the Church, the presence of God in the world, and the publicizing of the Gospel."[281] It is as much an overstatement to say that 'nothing is left to . . . the apostles', for much is delegated to them, as it is to say, with Newbigin, that 'Jesus committed the *entire* work of salvation' to the church. Jesus has committed an essential role to the church within the *missio Dei*, but it is simultaneously true that this delegation is encompassed and underwritten by the mission of the Spirit. When Jesus commissioned his disciples to be witnesses to the ends of the earth he instructed them to wait in Jerusalem because he had also delegated his ongoing mission to the Spirit who creates, builds, inspires, sanctifies, leads, and is Lord over the church.[282] In this, as in so many other ways, the missions of Spirit and church are intertwined. So, Jesus took a significant risk in partially delegating mission to the church, to which the missteps in church history bear witness, but this delegation and this risk were not absolute because he also entrusted his mission to the Holy Spirit on whom he could absolutely depend.[283]

## Pneumatological Mission—The Church's Mission as Shaped by the Spirit

The church's mission is both Christological and pneumatological and so the *missio ecclesiae* is defined by both the person of the Son and the person of the Spirit. The church's mission is often described as being *in the way of Jesus Christ, in the power of the Spirit, to the glory of the Father*. This is true, and I have already discussed mission in the way of Christ. I aim to supplement this necessary insight by suggesting the relation of the Spirit to the *missio ecclesiae* is not only in the *power* of the Spirit, but also in the *way* of the Spirit. The Spirit is literally the life of the church, or in Schleiermacher's words 'the common Spirit of the church',[284] so it is no accident that aspects of the Spirit's character 'rub off' on the church, for the Spirit imprints his personal nature upon the church. McIntyre suggests this, saying that the Spirit's work in the early church is so all-pervasive "that he might be said

---

281. Blauw, *The Missionary Nature*, 90, emphasis original.

282. It is the Spirit's work "to maintain its [the church's] integrity and its loyalty to the purposes for which God created it" (McIntyre, *The Shape of Pneumatology*, 57).

283. Studying the ground between these two points would be a fascinating and worthwhile enterprise which I believe would show how the missions of Spirit and Church are different and distinct from one another.

284. Schleiermacher, *The Christian Faith*, 738.

to stamp his character upon the Church."[285] In other words, as the church walks by the Spirit and is led by the Spirit she bears the fruit of the Spirit (Gal 5:16–23) which expresses the person of the Spirit. The work of the Spirit is by no means restricted to the work of the church, but the church's work must be pervaded by the Spirit for it to be of any consequence. The task of the church in her mission is not to imitate the work of the Spirit, but to sensitively obey and keep in step with him. Drawing on William Hill, Tan notes three distinctive traits that mark the Holy Spirit's identity and work are interiority, anonymity and community formation.[286] Mission in the way of the Spirit means that missiology needs to be pneumatological as well as Christological, thus avoiding Rodney Petersen's concern that an overly christocentric missiology would lead to a narrow christocentric model for mission.[287] Mission in the way of the Spirit means that, as Tan explains, "The basic posture of the Spirit-filled church and pneumatically empowered missionary must be one of humility, anonymity and other-centeredness."[288] Preferring self-effacement to anonymity, what does it mean to say that the church in her mission ought to be humble, self-effacing and other-centered?

### Humility

The missionary church remains humble as she recognizes that her successes are in fact the work of the Spirit. When churches are successfully established and grow, when the sick and emotionally scarred are healed, when the poor are fed and empowered, when the illiterate are educated, when those afflicted by evil are delivered and protected, when injustices are set to rights, then the church can humbly celebrate her own feeble contribution to these successes which truly belong to the Holy Spirit. The church is humble as she recognizes her place in the *missio Dei*, to be Christ's ambassador through which God reconciles people back to himself. She did not earn this right, for she was saved by grace in order to do the good works that God had prepared for her beforehand (Eph 2:8–10). As the church goes about her mission she is aware, sometimes painfully, that she is "the aroma of Christ

---

285. McIntyre, *The Shape of Pneumatology*, 57.

286. Tan, "A Trinitarian Ontology," 290. Hill, *The Three-Personed God*, 302–3.

287. Petersen, Review of *The Open Secret*, 193.

288. Tan, "A Trinitarian Ontology," 290. Zahniser offers a distinct but complementary attempt to describe 'Characteristics of Mission in the Mode of the Spirit.' These characteristics are "discerning points of contact, exalting the person of Jesus, and empowering persons through increasing their awareness, widening their horizons of choice, and freeing them for self-giving" (Zahniser, "The Trinity," 11).

to God among those who are being saved and among those who are perishing; to the one a fragrance from death to death, to the other a fragrance from life to life. Who is sufficient for these things?" (2 Cor 2:15–16) It is humbling for the church to realize she is the aroma of Christ, charged with embodying and preaching the gospel in a world of sin and death, knowing that as she witnesses to the gospel it is only the work of the Spirit who can actually bring life that conquers sins and death. The church remains humble in her mission by living according to the truth that she can do nothing apart from God (John 15:5), and yet *through him* the she can do all things by his strength (Phil 4:13).

## Self-Effacing

Jesus' ministry stood in the long line of Hebrew prophets and like them he called people back to God, his Father, but unlike these prophets Jesus also called people to himself. "Come to me, all you that are weary and are carrying heavy burdens, and I will give you rest" (Matt 11:28). "I am the way, and the truth, and the life. No one comes to the Father except through me" (John 14:6). Unlike Jesus, the Holy Spirit never draws attention to himself but always leads people to Jesus and through Jesus to the Father. T. F. Torrance explains that "The Holy Spirit does not manifest himself or focus attention upon himself, for it is his mission from the Father to declare the Son and focus attention upon him."[289] Elsewhere Torrance states, "The Spirit does not utter himself but utters the Word . . . He does not show his own Face, but shows us the Father in the Face of the Son."[290] The Spirit is self-effacing in that his working brings attention not to himself but to God, the Son and God the Father, which also helps to explain the neglect of Pneumatology in theological history. It is difficult to give sustained attention to a Person whose job it is to turn your attention to another, namely Jesus.

The church in her mission ought also to have these characteristics of pointing away from herself toward Jesus and the Father. This ought to be especially true of church movements that strongly emphasize the Holy Spirit such as Pentecostalism, and according to Anderson this is precisely what we find.

---

289. Torrance, *The Christian Doctrine of God*, 63.

290. Torrance, *Theology in Reconstruction*, 252. Olin Curtis, speaking of the personal peculiarity of each Person in the Trinity, identifies the peculiarity of the Holy Spirit as *self-effacement*. Curtis, *The Christian Faith*, 502–3, referenced in Zahniser, "The Trinity," 12.

> Most Pentecostals throughout the world have a decidedly Christocentric emphasis in their proclamation and witness. The Spirit bears witness to the presence of Christ in the life of the missionary and the message proclaimed by the power of the Spirit is of the crucified and resurrected Jesus Christ who sends gifts of ministry to humanity.[291]

Thus, Pentecostal Pneumatocentrism leads directly to Christocentrism as the self-effacing Spirit does his work in and through the church. As the church goes about her life and mission she should forever be drawing attention to the One who alone is worthy of all praise. In her works of love and service the church does not seek to be honored or recognized, and to that extent self-effacement should characterize her mission.

However, the self-effacing nature of the *missio ecclesiae* should not lead to complete anonymity, for Jesus said "You are the light of the world . . . let your light shine before others, so that they may see your good works and give glory to your Father in heaven" (Matt 5:14–16). The church is not to seek to bring attention to herself, nor is she to practice righteousness in order to be noticed and thus bringing attention to herself (Matt 6:1–4). Her motive for her good deeds must be love of God and neighbor, and as she goes about her good deeds prepared beforehand by God, she is not to hide them but rather to let others see them in order that God whom she serves may be glorified. For example, in many Western countries[292] the Salvation Army are widely recognized and respected for their humanitarian work, and surely this reputation glorifies God. To this extent, her mission ought not to be completely anonymous, that is, unidentified, nameless and secret, otherwise God will not be fully glorified from the church's good deeds. Jesus commissions his disciples to publicly live out their discipleship as outlined in the beatitudes, so that as they carry out their good works they are "a world-missionary force."[293] The difference between the right (Matt 5:16) and wrong (Matt 6:1–4) kind of public good works is whether God or the disciples will be glorified, but as Bruner says, "The distinction is easy to say but difficult to live."[294] Thus, the church should not focus on herself, but as the church goes about her mission she rightly hopes that she will gain new members. As Bosch says, "We cannot be indifferent to numbers, for God is 'not wishing that any should perish, but that all should reach repentance' (2

---

291. Anderson, *Spreading Fires*, 67.

292. This reputation may well extend beyond the West but I can only speak from personal experience of living in Great Britain, the USA and New Zealand.

293. Bruner, *Matthew*, 191.

294. Ibid., 193.

Pet 3:9). AG [*Ad Gentes*] 6 therefore rightly includes church planting and growth in its definition of the goal of mission."[295] Both church growth and good works belong to the *missio ecclesiae* in their own right, and whilst the latter can and does contribute to the former, this ought not be its primary motivation. To summarize, Tan is correct in saying that anonymity should characterize the church's mission in that she should seek for her God to be made known rather than herself, but in this process she too will be rightly noticed as his ambassadors, and this too will bring glory to the Father.

## *Other-Centeredness*

Hill said that the third distinctive trait of the Spirit's work is community formation, which Tan said corresponds to the church's mission being other-centered. I believe both elements are captured in Taylor's description of the Holy Spirit as the 'go-between God' (John V. Taylor). This description draws on deep wells within the Western theological tradition; specifically it is a development of Augustine's notion of the Spirit as the *vinculum caritatis*, the bond of love. Gunton describes the Spirit as the "one whose distinctive function is to bring persons into relationship while maintaining their otherness, their particular and unique freedom."[296] Tom Smail elaborates on this uniquely pneumatological role, describing the Holy Spirit as "the Spirit of *perichoresis*, the person who eternally established and maintains the fellowship (*koinonia*) in which two become one without losing their twoness. Put in less formal terms, the Spirit is the Spirit of love."[297] Gunton and Smail are describing the Spirit's intratrinitarian work as well as in the economy of salvation, with the latter corresponding to and being rooted in the former.

As the church is both birthed by the Spirit and caught up in his mission, so the Spirit's 'go-between' nature and work both encompasses and incorporates the church and impresses itself upon her. Accordingly, the church is Christ's ambassador to the world, going-between God and the world which He loves. This is the priestly mediatorial role of the church as a whole (1 Pet 2:9), which derives from him who is its High Priest. This 'go-between' role includes being ambassadors for reconciliation with God, and also for human reconciliation between estranged parties, whatever the cause of the estrangement. This can take the form of advocacy on behalf of the oppressed, the poor, the neglected and the disadvantaged who particularly *feel* and experience the force of the estrangement more than those

---

295. Bosch, *Transforming Mission*, 416.
296. Gunton, *The Promise*, 133, emphasis original.
297. Smail, "Trinitarian Atonement," 48.

from whom they are estranged. The church's mission vitally includes peacemaking, an activity characteristic of the children of God (Matt 5:9).[298] In this 'go-between' role the missionary church is other-centered as the focus is both on her Lord whom she serves and those to whom she is sent. Therefore, loving God and loving her neighbor should be the focus and characteristic of the church in mission as these are also the greatest commandments on which the law and prophets depend (Matt 22:37–40).

Within the mission of the Holy Spirit, the mission of the church is carried out in the way of the humble, self-effacing and go-between Spirit. In my description of the post-Pentecost mission of the Spirit it is clear that the church's mission is central, and so it is now appropriate to describe the inter-relation of these two missions.

## The Inter-Relation of the Missions of Spirit and Church

Numerous connections between the Spirit and the church's mission can be articulated. Blauw asserts that "The close connection between call to mission and Holy Spirit cannot be exaggerated."[299] This is evident in the descriptions of the giving of the Spirit in John 20:21–23 and Acts 2, which are both for the purpose of mission. The two missions are related in that both are sent from the Father through the Son. That is, the missions of Spirit and church can only be understood within a trinitarian framework, part of the overarching mission of the Triune God. Acts 2:33 teaches that the Father sends the Spirit to Jesus, whom he receives and then pours out on the disciples. In John 20:21–23 Jesus sends the disciples as the Father sent him and with their sending Jesus breathes the Spirit onto them. The missions of Spirit and church are profoundly related to each other and constitute part of the one mission of the Triune God. The unity of these missions can be seen also in that at Pentecost, the mission of the Spirit *in* Jesus is transferred to the mission of the church. This transferal is not without disruption, namely, the crucifixion and resurrection of Jesus. In fact, Newbigin explains that the disruption of the judgement of the cross was necessary before the Spirit could be poured out. This is because "it is only when the fortress of the self has been broken at the cross that the Spirit can come in and take control . . . It is only when the proud 'I' at the center of all our lives has been crucified with Christ that the Spirit can reign in us."[300] Nevertheless, there is continuity in the Spirit's mission in Jesus and then in the church but the character

---

298. For one interpretation of this, see Christian Peacemaker Teams, http://www.cpt.org/.

299. Blauw, *The Missionary Nature*, 89.

300. Newbigin, *The Holy Spirit*, 10.

of the Spirit's presence in each is somewhat dissimilar. As Young-Gi Hong explains,

> In biblical terminology, Jesus was given the Sprit 'without measure' (John 3:34); in the church, the Spirit operates 'according to the measure of faith (Rom 12:3). In the terminology of later tradition, Jesus was endowed with the Spirit 'by nature'; the church is endowed with the Spirit 'by grace'.[301]

Newbigin was therefore right in saying that one cannot understand the church's mission, and I would add the Spirit's mission, apart from the doctrine of the Triune God.[302]

The mission of the Spirit *creates* the church as he unites people to Jesus to share in his Sonship, thus forming a redeemed and adopted community. The church and her mission are also a central component in the Spirit's mission, for she is God's elect people through whom he will save the world. The church herself is part of the Spirit's mission of uniting people to Jesus, because as Cyprian and Calvin have affirmed, you cannot have God as Father without having the church as Mother.[303] Hence, Moltmann overstates his case when he says of the *missio Dei* that "The real point is not to spread the church but to spread the kingdom."[304] This is not only a false dichotomy but it is also incorrect, for the *missio Dei* as seen in Jesus includes his proclamation of the kingdom and building of the church. Moltmann is right in saying the church "is an element in the history of the kingdom of God," but it is far more central to that kingdom than he suggests.[305] Jesus, the one in whom the kingdom of God has come, not only clearly says "I will build my church,"[306] but spends the majority of his earthly ministry doing just that. As the 'proto-church' the disciples were central to Jesus' historical mission, so the church is central to Jesus' ongoing mission and is thus identified as 'his body.' Likewise, the church is also central to the Holy Spirit's mission. In addition, the Holy Spirit instigates and inspires the church's mission through renewal movements and personal refreshing.

The Holy Spirit is the chief actor in the church's mission; he is the primary missionary. Newbigin says, "We are not sent into battle by a

---

301. Hong, "Church and Mission," 306.

302. Newbigin, *Trinitarian Doctrine*, 82.

303. Drawing on Cyprian, *On the Unity of the Church*, cited in Calvin, *Institutes*, IV.I.1, 1012.

304. Moltmann, *The Church*, 11.

305. Ibid., 11. The relation between church and kingdom is complex and crucial for missiology but cannot be further elucidated here.

306. Matt 16:18.

commander who stays behind."³⁰⁷ The Spirit acts in and through the church's mission. Jesus' words in John 15:26–27 suggest that the witness of Spirit and church occur *alongside* one another, for the Spirit will bear witness to Jesus (v. 26) and the church will also bear witness to Jesus (v. 27). The Spirit also goes alongside the church as she experiences opposition. As the Spirit advances the church in mission into what C. S. Lewis calls "Enemy-occupied territory,"³⁰⁸ opposition is inevitable. Greg Boyd goes as far as saying, "The New Testament tells 'good people' to expect bad things!"³⁰⁹ So, when the church is arrested for carrying out her mission, as is still all too common in many parts of the world, Jesus says "When they bring you to trial and hand you over, do not worry beforehand about what you are to say; but say whatever is given you at that time, for it is not you who speak, but the Holy Spirit."³¹⁰ The missions of Spirit and church are distinct but not separate, for they intertwine with each other.

In addition to describing the missions of Spirit and church as *alongside* one another it is perhaps more accurate to say, with D. T. Niles, "the mission of the Church is a mission *within* the mission of the Holy Spirit."³¹¹ This is not to say that the church's mission is merely one (potentially minor) aspect of the Spirit's mission. I have already established that the church is literally central to the mission of the Spirit. Rather, I believe Niles is seeking to highlight the priority and primacy of the Spirit's mission. The Spirit constitutes the church in Christ and oversees her mission. Therefore, the Spirit's mission is not coextensive with the church's mission but broader in range and scope. Johannes Verkuyl rightly suggests that non-ecclesial human activity, "as long as it counters any type of evil and is purposefully performed in ways that help and heal, is connected either knowingly or unknowingly with the *missio Dei* in the world."³¹² While this might be affirmed one must uphold the centrality of the church to the Spirit's mission in order to avoid the unhealthy speculations that dogged the 1960s and 1970s that God is more at work in the world than in the church.³¹³ As the story of Cornelius and Peter clearly teaches, the Spirit goes ahead of the church and calls the church to follow. Newbigin explains that

---

307. Newbigin, *Mission In Christ's Way*, 29.
308. Lewis, *Mere Christianity*, 37.
309. Boyd, *God At War*, 283.
310. Mark 13:11. Lesslie Newbigin develops this in *The Open Secret*, 61.
311. Niles, *Upon The Earth*, 70, emphasis added.
312. Verkuyl, *Contemporary Missiology*, 4.
313. This theological tendency has been caricatured by the saying *intra ecclesiam nulla salus*.

> Because the Spirit himself is sovereign over the mission, the church can only be the attentive servant. In sober truth the Spirit is himself the witness who goes before the church in its missionary journey. The church's witness is secondary and derivative. The church is witness insofar as it follows obediently where the Spirit leads.[314]

In her mission, the church needs to rely upon the leading of the Spirit in her missional praxis. The Spirit is also Lord over the church-in-mission as he directs it. The Spirit opens certain doors like Paul's vision of the man from Macedonia (Acts 16:9), and closes others such as the Spirit forbidding Paul to enter Asia (Acts 16:6). According to Allen and Newbigin this confidence in the Holy Spirit is *the key* to Paul's missionary method.[315] Furthermore, the Lordship of the Holy Spirit is modelled on the lordship of the incarnate Son, thus overturning prevailing human concepts of lordship. The Spirit freely makes himself somewhat *dependent* upon the church's mission, because evangelistic proclamation has been delegated to the church.[316] This makes both the missions of Spirit and church inter-dependent, though not equally or in the same way. The Holy Spirit remains Lord and God over Christ's church.

Lastly, the missions of Spirit and church have the same overarching purpose; they are instruments of the Father's summing up all things in Christ. This summing up in Christ includes evangelism toward those outside Christ, and movements toward church unity for those already in Christ. Newbigin says, "Mission and unity are two sides of the same reality, or rather two ways of describing the same action of the living Lord who wills that all should be drawn to Himself."[317] In its mission the church is "invited to participate in an activity of God which is the central meaning of creation itself. We are invited to become, through the presence of the Holy Spirit, participants in the Son's loving obedience to the Father."[318] The two missions are again only understood within a framework of God's trinitarian redemptive activity. Having described the missions of the Son and Spirit, and their relation to the church's mission, it is now time to directly examine the mission of the church.

---

314. Newbigin, *The Open Secret*, 61.

315. Newbigin, *Trinitarian Doctrine*, 71. Allen, *Missionary Methods*.

316. It would be interesting, but beyond the scope of this project, to consider further the distinctiveness of the two missions, how the subject of *concursus Dei* bears upon the relation of the two missions, and what other tasks have been delegated to the church.

317. Newbigin, "The Missionary Dimension," 208–9.

318. Newbigin, *Trinitarian Doctrine*, 83.

Chapter 5

# *Missio Ecclesiae*

## INTRODUCTION

THE PURPOSE OF THIS chapter is to complete my development of an explicitly trinitarian missiology that is in continuity with the theology of Lesslie Newbigin. Having examined the Triune being of the missionary God (in chapter 3) and the missions of the Son and Spirit (in chapter 4), this chapter will expound the mission of the church within the trinitarian missions of God. Its purpose is not to outline comprehensively the church's mission, but to offer a robust trinitarian theological foundation for the mission of the church. Once laid, construction of the many important and necessary specifics of the *missio ecclesiae* can begin, such as evangelism, social justice, ecological stewardship, and inter-faith dialogue, but this 'second-level' work is beyond this project's scope. In this chapter I will examine the relation of the mission of the church to the mission of the Triune God, investigate the missionary nature of the church, and discuss the nature of the church's mission. One of Newbigin's concerns about the doctrine of the Trinity was that it was, "among practical Christians—reverently ignored."[1] Hence, as I develop a thoroughly trinitarian account of the *missio ecclesiae* I will intentionally engage with practical theological matters as they arise.

---

1. Newbigin, "Trinitarianism," 607.

## THE TRIUNE GOD AND THE CHURCH

The creation of the church is a result of the missions of the Son and Spirit. The one task to which Jesus devoted the majority of his time was the gathering, forming and training of his disciples to be the reconstituted people of God. However, Jesus made it clear that this community which he had gathered to himself could not be the church, and thus his missionary people, without the Holy Spirit. The proper mission of the Spirit commenced with the Pentecostal outpouring that caught up the waiting disciples into the Spirit's mission. The immediate and inextricably related results were the creation of a reconciled community in Christ, the church, and the participation of that church in the Spirit's mission of reconciling people to God through Jesus. On that occasion, the Holy Spirit inspired Peter to preach and three thousand people were reconciled with God. This reconciliation with God includes being incorporated into the reconciled and reconciling people of God, the church. Thus Bosch rightly says "Its mission (its 'being sent') is not secondary to its being; the church exists in being sent and in building up itself for the sake of its mission . . . Ecclesiology therefore does not precede missiology."[2] Since the church is the intended result of both the missions of Son and Spirit, it is clearly central to the purposes of God and owes its being to the *missio trinitatis Dei*. Mission is not only the mother of theology but also of the church, for the church can only understand its being as one part of the trinitarian history of God's mission to the world.

What is the church? Gunton answers, the church is, "in time and space, a living echo of the communion that God is in eternity."[3] The church originates in the outward actions of the Triune God whose being is in communion. This relational God created humans in his image to live in onto-relations[4] of love with their Creator, each other, and in a different sense with the wider creation. Throughout the biblical story humanity's failure to live up to this high calling is notorious, but God's intentions for humanity remain unchanged. The church owes its being to God's gracious act of reconciliation in Christ and so "belongs to the order of grace established within the order of nature for its restoration and direction."[5] The events witnessed to in the gospel thus create the church, and the church is in turn entrusted with embodying and communicating this gospel. God both uses the gospel

---

2. Bosch, *Transforming Mission*, 372. Similarly, Braaten says "mission is not a program added on to the gospel, but is fundamental to its very nature" (Braaten, *The Flaming Center*, 11).

3. Gunton, *Father, Son and Holy Spirit*, 198.

4. Torrance, *The Christian Doctrine of God*, 157.

5. Barth, *CD* IV/3.2, 743.

to gather people to the church for himself and charges the church to communicate the gospel to the ends of the earth; "'Church' and 'gospel' therefore mutually determine each other."[6] Instituted by Christ and constituted by the Spirit in Christ, the church is the human community which has been enabled to participate by foretaste in the eternal communion that God is, and so reflect this communion in its own life in time and space. Gunton explains, "The church is therefore called to be a being of persons-in-relation which receives its character as communion by virtue of its relation to God, and so is enabled to reflect something of that being in the world."[7]

The church is to be a 'living echo' of God's being-in-communion by participating by the Spirit through Christ in the *koinonia* of the Triune God. This ecclesial participation in the Triune *koinonia* includes participation in God's mission of "drawing humanity and creation in general into this communion with God's very life."[8] Grounding the nature of the church in the doctrine of the Trinity, in this account, leads inexorably to the affirmation that the church is missionary by nature.[9] Therefore, the church's being and her missionary nature cannot be separated because the latter belongs to the former. Participating in God and in his mission are not two things but one, for as God's mission "elicits, awakens, and empowers the church" she participates in the missions of Christ and the Spirit to the world. Hence Oden says "*Missio dei* embraces all that the church is and does in its life in the world."[10] God's being is in communion and the church is called to be in herself a community of persons-in-relation and to be part of God's mission of "the transmission of the life of communion that exists in God."[11] The church's very being, therefore, is missionary because it originates in God's mission in which it is central, by being the sign, instrument, and foretaste of this onto-relational community that reflects God's nature, reveals authentic humanity, and points towards humanity's origin, purpose and destiny. The sign that in Christ God is reconstituting humanity was initially expressed in Jesus' calling of the twelve "to represent the first nucleus of the community

---

6. Jenson, *Systematic Theology*, 1:5.

7. Gunton, *The Promise*, 12.

8. Bria, *Go Forth In Peace*, 3.

9. This is important to emphasize since Flett notes this is not always the case. Commenting on Miroslav Volf's *After Our Likeness*, in which he grounds ecclesiology in the doctrine of the Trinity, Flett writes: "Reference to the Trinity . . . does not make it necessary to understand the nature of the church in terms of her movement into the world; instead, it is normative to think of the church in terms of her *koinonia* defined in internal terms" (Flett, *The Witness of God*, 207).

10. Oden, *Life in the Spirit*, 350.

11. Bria, *Go Forth In Peace*, 3.

of a renewed covenant,"[12] the significance of which would have been self-evident to any first-century Jew. "The very existence of the twelve speaks, of course, of the reconstitution of Israel; Israel had not had twelve visible tribes since the Assyrian invasion in 734 BC."[13] The church is called to be and is God's covenant community; the people of God who have been admitted into fellowship with God, have been entrusted with the secrets of the kingdom and the mystery of Christ (Eph 3:2-6; Col 1:26-27), and are called to make known the mystery of the gospel (Eph 3:7-9; 6:19). In particular, the community of Jesus Christ is called to make known the Christ of the gospel, and it is his person and mission that determines the church and her mission.

## *Does the Church Have Its Own Mission?*

The church is constituted in the mission of the Triune God, or in Carl Braaten's words, "The sending of the church to the world is a continuation of the Father's sending of the Son and the Spirit."[14] But is it best to conceive of this mission or sending of the church as a distinct mission to the mission of the Spirit, or as part of the Spirit's mission and the ongoing mission of Christ? The church (in the form of the disciples) is clearly sent by Jesus as recorded in all four Gospels (extended Markan ending) and *Acts*. But, as is made explicit by Luke in *Luke* 24:46-49 and *Acts* 1:4-8, this sending is 'on hold' until the Spirit is poured out. On the day of Pentecost the church is born as the Father pours out the Spirit through the exalted Son on the one-hundred and twenty disciples. Peter is caught up in the Spirit's outpouring and full of the Holy Spirit preaches to the gathered crowd, and the newly-birthed church grows by three thousand members. Peter's preaching is also the first act in the mission of the church. Thus, it is clear that the missions of Son, Spirit and church overlap, and it is clear that the Son and Spirit in their missions are prior to, Lord over, active through, and encompass the church's mission. Based on the New Testament I contend that the church is both a part of the Son and Spirit's ongoing mission and is subject to its own distinctive sending by God.

The sending of the Son and the sending of the Spirit are the two proper divine missions in which God is both sender and sent one. Does the mission of the church constitute a third distinct mission or sending, or is the church caught up in the two divine missions? Put differently, is it accurate to speak of the church having a mission? Several missiologists have answered with

12. Kirk, *What Is Mission?*, 208.
13. Wright, *Jesus and the Victory of God*, quoted in Kirk, *What Is Mission?*, 208.
14. Braaten, "The Triune God," 425.

a resounding 'no.' Pachau pithily remarks, "It is not the church that has a mission, it is God's mission that has a church."[15] Putting it slightly differently, David Bosch says "It is not the church which 'undertakes' mission; it is the *missio Dei* which constitutes the church."[16] Both comments helpfully assert a correct missional order and priority, for God's mission exists prior to the church, constitutes the church, and includes her within the *missio Dei*. Emphasizing that the church is both contained within and is part of the missions of Son and Spirit stresses the point that God himself is the chief missionary, with the church's mission taking a definite second place. The mission of the church is subject to his activity and agency and is both ineffective and meaningless without him.

However, I suggest both scholars overstate their case, since the church is also subject to its own distinct sending by Jesus (as the proto-church) and with the Holy Spirit. The church has been sent for a particular purpose, which she is duty-bound to undertake: to make disciples of all the nations. The quotations by Pachau and Bosch are helpful corrections to an overly anthropocentric and ecclesiocentric missiology, but they do not adequately convey the whole truth of the matter. I contend that the church does have its own mission, but this claim needs to be carefully qualified. It does not have its own mission that is in any sense separate from or unrelated to God's mission, but *within* the mission of God the church's mission is distinctive. In their missions the Son and Spirit bear witness to Jesus, convict people of sin, and grant them the gift of faith, but they do not do so entirely separate from the church's mission. To the church has been granted the distinctive privilege and responsibility of verbally communicating the gospel and offering a human witness of Jesus to others. Granted this witness is entirely ineffective and even potentially damaging without the gracious work of the Spirit who bears witness to Christ through the church's witness, but it is still a task that God has uniquely summoned the church to undertake.[17] Secondarily, the church's mission contains particular responsibilities that do not belong to any other human society.[18] For example, both the church and non-Christian charitable groups, governmental and non-governmental organizations can do the same work of feeding the poor, challenging unjust economic structures, and carrying out relief and development work. Whilst these activities rightly belong to both the church and these other organiza-

---

15. Pachuau, "Missio Dei," 234.

16. Bosch, *Transforming Mission*, 519, emphasis original.

17. I have already discussed this point under 'The Missionary Church Within the Mission of the Spirit' in chapter 4.

18. By this I do not mean to suggest that the Church is merely a human society.

tions, nevertheless the church still has its own distinctive mission which is not exhausted in these activities alone.

Thus, the church does have its own mission in which her own action is crucial, but even in the church's mission God is still the primary actor and chief missionary, for it is not her *own* mission as if it were independently commissioned or unconnected from God's mission into which she has been incorporated. The church's historical existence uniquely embodies the missions of Son and Spirit, although these missions are not restricted to the church. The Son and Spirit are the *sine qua non* of the mission of the church by necessity. The church is the *sine qua non* of the Son and Spirit's mission, not by necessity, but by the free and gracious divine election. The church's mission cannot succeed without the Son and Spirit, and the Son and Spirit's mission will not succeed without the church. Nuancing the matter more satisfactorily, Thomas Oden says "The church does not merely *have* but *is* a mission, the historical embodiment of the mission of the Son through the Spirit."[19] The church does *have* a mission because the church *is* a mission; the *having* follows on from and is subordinate to *being*, because it is the church itself that is sent.

Thus, there are two trinitarian sendings or missions that are rightly associated with the incarnation and Pentecost. There is also a third sending by God, which Brian Edgar calls "the third act of the divine mission in which the Church is sent to make disciples of all nations."[20] Unlike the previous two sendings, however, God is not both the 'sender' and the 'sent one.' Consequently, the sending of the church cannot be mentioned alongside the sendings of Son and Spirit without qualification. Newbigin says helpfully, "The Church is not so much the agent of mission as the locus of the mission."[21] This construal rightly prioritizes God's activity in the order of mission but, once established, I would add that the church is also, secondarily, the agent of mission. To only speak of the church participating in God's mission might neglect the church's missionary nature and could overlook the distinctive role that God has charged the church with. To only speak of the church's mission might suggest that it has no necessary connection to trinitarian missions of God, and might lead to an overly anthropocentric missionary praxis. Consequently, I will continue to make reference to both the church's mission and the church participating in the *missio trinitatis Dei*, with the former understood to be rooted in and derivative of the latter.

19. Oden, *Life in the Spirit*, 350, emphasis original. Similarly Newbigin says the Church needs to "learn again what it means that the Church *is* a mission" (*One Body*, 17).

20. Edgar, *The Message of the Trinity*, 198.

21. Newbigin, *The Gospel in a Pluralist Society*, 119.

## Part Two: Constructing a Trinitarian Missiology

### *The Church-in-Mission within the Mission of God*

The church's mission participates in the post-Pentecost mission of the Spirit and in the ongoing mission of the exalted Christ, or in Barth's terms, the prophetic office of Christ. This mission involves the changing and transforming of people's hearts and minds and as such is necessarily a divine work in which the church is graced to participate. But how is it possible for the church to participate at all in this mission? Barth explains that

> He [Christ] alone is competent and authorized to perform it. He alone is the Speaker of the Word of God as well as the Doer of His work. But in the exercise of the prophetic office of His, even though it is He alone who controls it, He does not will to be alone. Controlling and exercising it, He calls certain men to His side and commissions them to be His disciples or pupils, i.e., Christians.[22]

In God's grace he has freely made room for the church to work for and with God in the accomplishment of the *missio Dei*. According to Fiddes, God knows the future as neither exhaustively determined nor comprehensively foreknown, but has left "things open, making space for our contribution to the creative project."[23] Fiddes sees evidence for this in the nature of God's promises for the future that do not consist of detailed predictions.[24] This openness of the future creates room, "room for the freedom of God, for God to fulfil promises in unexpected ways; there is also room for the freedom of human beings to contribute in their own way to this fulfilment."[25] Whether Fiddes is right concerning the openness of the future, a subject of much recent discussion and debate,[26] his main point is that God has made room for and has invited humanity genuinely to contribute to the *missio Dei*, to partner with God in the accomplishment of this mission. Genuinely creaturely contribution to God's mission can only come from participating

---

22. Barth, *CD* IV/3.2, 606.

23. Fiddes cites as an example Jeremiah's parable of the potter in Jer 18. Fiddes, *Participating in God*, 142.

24. The exegesis of Fretheim's *The Suffering of God* supports this reading, especially chapter 4.

25. Fiddes, *Participating in God*, 142.

26. See for example Boyd, *The God of the Possible*; idem, *Satan and the Problem of Evil*; Hasker, "Foreknowledge and Necessity"; idem, *God, Time and Knowledge*; idem, *Providence, Evil, and the Openness of God*; Pinnock, *The Openness of God*; idem, *Most Moved Mover*; Polkinghorne, *The Work of Love*; Sanders, *The God Who Risks*; idem, "On Heffalumps and Heresies"; Sanders and Hall, *Does God have a Future?*; Swinburne, *The Coherence of Theism*; Wolterstorff, "Unqualified Divine Temporality."

in the movement of God's grace from heaven to earth. Therefore, although God has summoned the church to cooperate with him in the divine mission, this is not to be envisioned as an equal partnership. The church is not the author of the history of salvation, nor is she the reconciler or co-reconciler, nor an independent promoter of the *missio Dei*. Barth suggests it is better to construe the missional relation between God and the church as the difference between the King and his herald, or between the Lord and his slave.[27] In 2 Corinthians 5 the apostle Paul employs the language of ambassadorship to describe the church's missionary task. Commenting on verse twenty,[28] Barrett says that "The same act that effected reconciliation, committed to Paul the word and ministry of reconciliation. 'With the cross, God instituted the office of reconciliation . . . in other words, the preaching itself also belongs to the event of salvation.'"[29] He explains that this is because God himself preaches through the apostolic proclamation. Christ does not delegate his prophetic office to the church but graciously incorporates the church as a participant in the divine work of reconciliation. As the church obediently cooperates with God, she in her own way does have a genuine role to play in the *missio Dei* that is both important and valuable, but it is encompassed by the missions of the Son and Sprit.

The church can only bear fruit to the extent that she dwells in Christ, for apart from him she can offer and contribute nothing (John 15:5). Explaining the mechanics of this cooperation Ion Bria says, "*Synergia* means that God has chosen to work through us. God calls us to surrender ourselves to Christ in order that God may unite us to God's self and work through us, enhancing our freedom and in no way abolishing our personal subjectivity."[30] The church remains weak and useless without repentance and faith, for they are the two *sine quibus non* of *synergia*. However, through repentance and faith, through dwelling in Christ and surrendering to him, and by the empowering of the Holy Spirit, the church can accomplish much. Here the affirmation that the ontological Trinity truly corresponds to the

27. Barth, *CD* IV/3.2, 599–607.

28. "So we are ambassadors for Christ, since God is making his appeal through us; we entreat you on behalf of Christ, be reconciled to God."

29. Barrett, *The Second Epistle to the Corinthians*, 228.

30. Bria, *Go Forth In Peace*, 7. Bria's notion of *synergia* is more robust than Cronshaw's conception of the God-mission-church relation. He writes that "it is not that the church has a mission to perform, but that mission has a church and God invites the church to cooperate with God's mission." So far so good. But he continues, "The burden of mission is lifted, because it is God's work to enact God's mission. But God offers people the privilege of *being involved*." This is a partial truth that is in danger of subtly decentralizing the church within the *missio Dei*, which plays a greater role than just "being involved" (Cronshaw, "Saving Souls," 248, emphasis added).

economic Trinity guarantees not only that in God's self-revelation he has truly given none other than himself, but also that God is truly at work in and through the church as she graciously participates in the mission of the Son and Spirit.[31] Furthermore, since God is constituted in his perichoretic relations that are described in both the eternal processions and the temporal missions, the church-in-mission graciously participates not only in the mission but also in the relations of the Triune God. As Seng-Kong Tan says, "This allows us to embed the Christian missionary vocation not only within the meta-narrative of God's historicity, but in his very being as Father, Son and Holy Spirit."[32] Newbigin understood that the church's participation in the *missio trinitatis Dei* is a participation in the intra-trinitarian glorification. The church's participation in God's trinitarian mission is an invitation

> to become, through the presence of the Holy Spirit, participants in the Son's loving obedience to the Father. All things have been created that they may be summed up in Christ the Son. All history is directed towards that end. The Spirit of God, who is also the Spirit of the Son, is given as the foretaste of that consummation, as the witness to it, and as the guide of the Church on the road towards it.[33]

Historically, the church has had mixed success in submitting to Christ as she goes about her mission, and so Bosch rightly remarks "Our missionary practice . . . is an altogether ambivalent enterprise executed in the context of tension between divine providence and human confusion."[34] Consequently, the spiritual vitality of God's church in different regions ebbs and flows, and it is the work of the Spirit to vivify and renew the church for its missionary calling.

Church historians commonly testify to the link between the work of the Spirit and mission. In my opinion, one of the greatest works of the Spirit in Great Britain was the eighteenth-century Evangelical Revival. It is no surprise, therefore, Andrew Walls observes that the modern missionary movement "is an autumnal child of the Evangelical Revival."[35] Reflecting on church history more broadly, theologian and missiologist José Míguez Bonino states that all great missionary thrusts are connected with renewals

---

31. Tan, "A Trinitarian Ontology," 284.
32. Ibid., 280.
33. Newbigin, *Trinitarian Doctrine*, 83.
34. Bosch, *Transforming Mission*, 9.
35. Walls, *The Missionary Movement*, 79. This assumption is not made by Walls but is mine.

in spirituality because experiences of God have always motivated missions.[36] In terms of recent mission history, the Pentecostal/charismatic movement is the most numerically significant renewal movement in the past century. With its beginnings in 1906, Pentecostalism now comprises over half a billion adherents,[37] Pentecostal/charismatic Christians comprise the second largest Christian community (after the Roman Catholic Church),[38] and charismatic-driven groups deploy the highest number of missionaries globally.[39] J. Roswell Flower, the first general secretary of the Assemblies of God (the largest Pentecostal denomination) and senior church leader at the embryonic stage of the Pentecostal movement, clearly enunciates the connection between charismatic and Pentecostal Pneumatocentrism and the commitment to mission. He says, "When the Holy Spirit comes into our hearts, the missionary spirit comes in with it; they are inseparable."[40] It is the Holy Spirit who initiates and inspires the mission of the church. The Spirit is christocentric and it is his work to inspire the church to love Christ and make Christ known.[41] Thus, Andrew Lord speaks of the "need for an authentic Christian spirituality to undergird all our attempts at mission." He continues, "Without spirituality our mission will be dry and lacking the presence and power of the Holy Spirit—we may try hard, but achieve little."[42] That the Holy Spirit animates the church's mission with himself, the breath of life, is commonly testified to and needs to be continually the church's living experience.

Despite the church's potential, actual and inevitable future failings in carrying out its mission, God still does not will to act by himself as Prophet and Revealer, even though he might well have done. "Even in His final manifestation He will not appear alone but with all His saints (1 Thess 3:13)."[43] Such is the persistent love of God for his creatures and such is the enormity of the honor graciously bestowed by God upon the church-in-mission. It is astonishing that the unlimited, uncontained, omnipotent, omniscient and

---

36. José Míguez Bonino, "Pentecostal Mission is More Than What It Claims," referenced in Lord, "The Voluntary Principle," 91.

37. Tennent, *Invitation to World Missions*, 420.

38. CWME, "Towards Common Witness," 94.

39. Kalu, "Charismatic Movements," 44.

40. Quoted in Anderson, *Spreading Fires*, 65.

41. Bruner says, "In a word, Jesus is theocentric, and the Spirit is Christocentric" ("The Son is God Inside Out," 106). For more on this, see my earlier discussion on the self-effacing nature of the Spirit in chapter 4.

42. Lord, "Mission Eschatology," 119.

43. Barth, *CD* IV/3.2, 656.

omnipresent God should choose to include the work of the limited, faltering and wayward church within his mission.

## CHRIST AND HIS CHURCH

### Christology and Ecclesiology

The church originates in the trinitarian missions of God, the historical and theological center of which is the life, death, and resurrection of Jesus. Therefore, the church is uniquely grounded in and determined by the person and work of Christ. In all of Christ's uniqueness, in relation to the church he is not an isolated individual but head over his body with all its members. Jesus "constitutes an indissoluble whole with those who are His; because what He is and does in the true sense is in their favor and determines their being and action."[44] A robust Christology is a necessary foundation for a healthy ecclesiology, and consequently a deficient ecclesiology often betrays a faulty Christology. The 1943 Papal encyclical *Mystici Corporis Christi* portrayed an unconditional identification between Christ's body and the empirical Roman Catholic Church.[45] It is often argued that ecclesial infallibility, focused on its head the bishop of Rome, is grounded on Jesus being perfect. In the theological traditions of East and West, Jesus' perfection is usually grounded in his divine nature wielding his human nature rather than his perfect reliance upon the empowering Spirit.[46] Similarly, the divine Word is understood to wield the church in like manner, thus a docetic Christology informs a docetic ecclesiology, with Pneumatology being marginalized in both.[47] For both Christology and ecclesiology, the divine and human aspects of each doctrine need to be fully affirmed. Accordingly, the church is not the *Christus prolongatus*, the continuation of the incarnation,[48] for its

---

44. Barth, *CD* IV/2, 824.

45. Bosch, *Transforming Mission*, 169.

46. Badcock, *Light of Truth*, 41.

47. Gunton, *The Promise*, 69.

48. As suggested inaccurately by the Evangelical missiologist Tennent, *Invitation to World Missions*, 87. Describing the relation between Christ's sending and the Church's sending, Barth says "Its sending is not a repetition, extension or continuation. His own sending does not cease as He sends it. It does not disappear in its sending. It remains its free and independent presupposition. Its sending is simply ordered on its own lower level in relation to His . . . He is sent to precede it on the way into the world. It is sent to follow Him on the same way. These are two things. But the two sendings are comparable because they have the same origin. The one God who sends Him as the Father also sends them through Him the Son. Again, they are comparable because they have the same goal. He and they are both sent into the world, which means very generally that they are directed to the world and exist for it" (Barth, *CD* IV/3.2, 768).

human existence differs from that of the Son of God. Barth believes that this suggestion is not only out of place but also blasphemous. The church's "distinction from the world is not the same as His; it is not that of the Creator from His creature. Its superiority to the world is not the same as His; it is not that of the Lord seated at the right hand of the Father."[49]

In order to comprehend rightly the relation between Christ and his church it is necessary to speak of the Holy Spirit. There is clear continuity between the saving work of Jesus and the missionary work of the church, and Pinnock suggests that this continuity has a name—the Holy Spirit. Re-conceiving traditional Roman Catholic terminology of the church as *Christus prolongatus*, he says "The church is an extension not so much of the incarnation as of the anointing of Jesus."[50] Pinnock suggests that the bestowal of Christ's mission to the church coincides with and derives from the transferal of Christ's anointing to the church, and this seems to have strong exegetical support from both Luke (Luke 24:46–49; and Acts 1:4–5, 8) and John (20:21–23). He says,

> At Pentecost the church received the Spirit and became the historical continuation of Jesus' anointing as the Christ . . . He transferred the Spirit to them so that his actions could continue through their agency. The bearer of the Spirit now baptizes others with the Spirit, that there might be a continuation of his testimony in word and deed and a continuation of his prophetic and charismatic ministry.[51]

This ought to be conceived christocentrically, for the transferal of the anointing from Jesus to the church is in fact the church's participation by the Spirit in Jesus the Christ, the anointed one. Indeed, transferal language though helpful pictorially is theologically misleading, for the church's reception of the Spirit is not separate from Christ's reception of the Spirit. Rather, the church is anointed by the Spirit for mission by participating in the Spirit-filled and anointed vicarious humanity of Christ.[52]

## *The Double Orientation of the Church*

The Christological determination of the church extends to the church's vocation. Jesus and the church have a common outlook, for both exist

---

49. Barth, *CD* IV/3.2, 729.
50. Pinnock, *Flame of Love*, 114.
51. Ibid., 118.
52. Torrance, *The Christian Doctrine of God*, 148.

primarily to do the will of the Father. This is carried out by loving the object of their common interest, the world.[53] Barth explains "That it [the church] exists for the world because for God, follows simply and directly from the fact that it is the community of Jesus Christ and has the basis of its being and nature in Him."[54] In John 20:21[55] Jesus says the way in which the church should carry out its mission is modelled on himself. As Jesus is the obedient, humble, sacrificial, suffering servant, so these must also characterize the church-in-mission.[56]

As the *ecclesia*, the church is literally the 'called out people' for she has heard God's voice and has been invited by the Spirit into fellowship with the Son (1 Cor 1:9). It is out of this fellowship that the church is also firmly oriented towards the world, for it is the object of both God's love and hers. The church's love and attention are drawn in two directions—toward the Lord and Savior and toward the world he loves and died to save. Although mission is utterly central to the church, the first object of her affections and loyalty is God himself, and because this is so the church also loves the world. In this sense the church's missional spirituality actually corresponds, however faintly and partially, to the being and action of the Triune God. Tan explains that in the perichoretic relations of self-giving love among the Triune Persons, the being of the eternal three includes eternal rest and action, residence and journey, *hypostasis* and *ekstasis*. The Triune identities are each hypostases that exist in self-giving love to each other. This duality within God then corresponds to God's actions *ad intra*, the eternal, 'homely', inward motion of loving communion, and *ad extra* in the outward historical trinitarian missions to the world. This duality correlates to the church's spirituality for, "On the one hand, the Father, through/with Christ in their Holy Spirit, invites and receives us from the world. On the other hand, the Father commands and sends us through/with the Son, in their Spirit, to the world."[57] In its double orientation toward God and toward the world, the church is called to live "in the creative tension of, [and] at the same time, being called out of the world and sent into the world."[58]

53. Barth, *CD* IV/3.2, 598.

54. Ibid., 763. Similarly, Flett remarks "Jesus Christ's obedience to the one who sent him consists of his obedience to his mission. Likewise, the obedience of the church consists of her obedience to the one who sent her and thus to his mission" (Flett, *The Witness of God*, 265).

55. "Jesus said to them again, 'Peace be with you. As the Father has sent me, so I send you.'"

56. See my earlier discussion "Mission in Christ's Way" in chapter 4.

57. Tan, "A Trinitarian Ontology," 292.

58. Bosch, *Transforming Mission*, 11.

The church's dual focus is ultimately modelled on Christ the Mediator, whose ministry of mediation involves mediating God to the world and the world to God. In the words of the Commission on World Mission and Evangelism,

> The Church manifests God's love for the world in Christ— through word and deed . . . in loving service and joyful proclamation, the Church in that same identification with all humanity, lifts up to God its pain and suffering, hope and aspiration, joy and thanksgiving in intercessory prayer and eucharistic worship.[59]

Thus, the dual orientation of the church is an aspect of participating in the priesthood of Christ, not in the sense of Christ's unique priesthood, such as his self-offering as an atoning sacrifice to God or being the sole mediator between God and humanity. Rather, as the community of Jesus Christ the church, by grace, is called to be and is a holy nation and a kingdom of priests (1 Pet 2:9), thus fulfilling Israel's original call (Exod 19:4-6). As priests minister to God on behalf of people, so the church both loves God in her prayer and worship and intercedes on behalf of the world, offering prayers of thanksgiving, petition and lament. Priests also minister to people on behalf of God, and the church expresses this through its teaching, evangelistic, prophetic, healing and pastoral ministries. The church's priestly nature, deriving from her participation in Christ the High Priest, describes the church's double orientation. This will be considered further in 'The Church's Vocation of Worship and Mission' below.

## THE MISSIONARY NATURE OF THE CHURCH[60]

As I have examined the relationship, first, between the Triune God and the church, and second, between Christ and his church, the church's missionary nature has become apparent. It is now time to discuss explicitly the missionary nature of the church. I have argued that the church finds its origin in the trinitarian mission of God to the world and is a central and concrete instrument of the continuing mission of Jesus and the proper mission of the Holy Spirit. The mission of God precedes and constitutes the church so that the church's being is missionary in nature, and therefore there is no such thing as an ecclesiology that is not inherently missional. As the community

---

59. CWME, "Mission and Evangelism," 66.

60. I have published an earlier version of some of what follows in Dodds, "The Centrality."

of Jesus Christ, the church exists for others because of its Christological determination, for Christ was, in Bonhoeffer's words (following Barth: CD III/2 §45), the 'man for others'.[61] There are three further considerations regarding the basis of the church's missionary nature.

First, the church's mission is historically based on Israel's conviction that God will inherit all nations (Ps 82:8), that God's salvation will reach the ends of the earth (Isa 49:6), and that Israel would be a light to the Gentiles (Isa 42:6) among whom she is a kingdom of priests (Exod 19:6).[62] Building on this, the church's mission is also historically based in the mission of Jesus, who gathered together a small group of disciples to whom he revealed himself as the only begotten Son of the Father, whom he trained and sent throughout Israel proclaiming the kingdom of God and healing the sick. But this gathering, revealing, training and sending were not ends in themselves but essential preparation for their apostolic sending, their mission to the nations, for which they needed power from on high. The church's mission was rooted in Jesus' sending of his disciples during his historical ministry and after his resurrection, and in the pouring out of the Spirit. It is in these sending narratives recorded in all the Gospels and Acts that the church's missionary nature is made manifest.

Second, from this historical beginning in the career of Jesus in first-century Palestine, the church has been sent to the ends of the earth and the end of the world. The *missio ecclesiae* to the world encompasses both history and geography, for the church-in-mission carries the gospel in an 'apostolic procession'[63] to all the nations to the end of time, until Christ returns. This cross-cultural apostolic procession belongs to the very nature of the church. As she translates the gospel across cultural boundaries, it reflects and bears witness to that great and unrepeatable act of translation—the Incarnation—when God become human.[64] The church is literally *in via* across space and time from God to the world; it is literally "a people on the move."[65] Thus, Barth provocatively says "The true community of Jesus Christ . . . exists *as it actively reaches beyond itself into the world*,"[66] thus suggesting that if a church abdicates its missional responsibility it puts its own ecclesial existence at risk. (We will return to this subject shortly.)

---

61. Bonhoeffer, *Letters and Papers*, 381–82.

62. Jenson, *The Triune Identity*, 29.

63. I owe this term to Moltmann, *The Church*, 312.

64. See Walls, "The Translation Principle in Christian History," in *The Missionary Movement*, 26–42.

65. Kirk, *What Is Mission?*, 230. Similarly, Hong says "the church is understood as a movement of the Spirit sent to the world" (Hong, "Church and Mission," 298).

66. Barth, *CD* IV/3.2, 780, emphasis added.

Third, in response to the gracious gift of God in Christ, mission is the natural consequence of the church's passion and love for Christ. Andrew Walls contends "The conviction that Jesus is Lord and the testimony that Christ is risen cannot mean that much unless they are to be shared."[67] If Christ means everything to the church (see Phil 3:7–11), then it is reasonable to conclude that evangelism (one aspect of mission) is inevitable, for out of the overflow of the heart the mouth speaks (Luke 6:45).[68] Consequently, Newbigin states perceptively that "missions are not an extra; they are the acid test of whether or not the Church believes the Gospel."[69] That a church *believes* the gospel entails that she has received the gift of faith from the Holy Spirit and so has been born of that same Spirit. The church's being is pneumatologically constituted, and so, since it is the work of the Spirit to glorify Jesus, bearing witness to Jesus is an expression of the church's fundamental nature. It is for these reasons that there is an ecumenical consensus that the church is missionary in nature.[70] Therefore, it is inaccurate to speak of both the church *and* mission as if these were two different realities in a mutual but undisclosed relation; it is better to speak of the church-in-mission.[71] In traditional theological and ecclesiastical language, the missionary nature of the church relates to its apostolicity.

## *The Apostolic Church*

The Niceno–Constantinopolitan Creed of 381 affirms the 'four marks' of the church; that is, the church is one, holy, catholic and apostolic. Of these four marks, the missionary nature of the church is most evident, although not exclusively so, in the church's apostolicity. The church is apostolic because

---

67. Walls, *The Missionary Movement*, 255.

68. NIV. Admittedly, this was spoken in quite a different context, but the principle is transferrable.

69. Although this is true for all missions it is particularly so for foreign missions. Newbigin, *Mission of the Church to All the Nations*. Elsewhere, Newbigin expressed this thought more fully: "We are commissioned to bring good news, to tell the story of God's marvellous and mighty acts for the salvation of the world. We must not withhold this story from anyone. To keep it to ourselves, as though it were a private 'in-house' story of the Church, as though Jesus were the lord of Christians but not the lord of all, would be intolerable sectarianism. We have no right to keep silent about it, and if we try to do so we deny its truth" ("Religious Pluralism," 241).

70. Vatican II, *Ad Gentes*, §9; CWME, "Mission and Evangelism"; Bosch, *Transforming Mission*, 372.

71. Similarly, Josef Glazik says one should not speak of the Church *and* mission, but only of the mission *of* the Church. "Das Zweite Vatikanische Konzil und seine Wirkung," quoted in Bosch, *Transforming Mission*, 372.

it has been founded on the apostles and their teaching. Episcopal churches typically emphasize apostolic succession by showing the connection of their current bishops back to the first apostles by a direct lineage of succession. Evangelical churches stress the importance of faithfully preserving apostolic teaching as recorded in Scripture and so the importance of being biblical.[72] In the Reformation this was embodied in the maxim *sola scriptura*; that is, doctrine and practice must conform to the teaching of Scripture. Both temporal church unity embodied in Episcopal continuity down through the centuries, and the need to be thoroughly biblical in theology and praxis, are valid and important interpretations of the church's apostolicity. Its primary meaning, however, like the church's oneness, holiness, and catholicity refers to the Triune God. The thrice holy one is the creator and so is God of all. From eternity, this one, holy, and catholic God *is* love, for among the Triune Persons love is both given and received. God's love for the world can be best expressed as apostolic, for it is in the Father's *sending* of the Son and the Spirit that God's love is definitively made known.

The *missio Dei* centers on Jesus, who Hebrews 3:1 describes as the Apostle, meaning 'sent one.' This reflects the gospels' vivid portrayal of Jesus' awareness of being sent by the Father, no more so than in John's gospel where it is depicted forty times.[73] Jesus named his disciples as apostles (Luke 6:13) and sent them out to preach the kingdom of God and heal the sick (Luke 9:1–2; Matt 10:7–8). Increasingly, Jesus closely associated his own mission with that of the apostles, and after the cross and resurrection he makes this connection explicit. After the resurrection, Jesus sent them out to bear witness to his resurrection from the dead and the good news of forgiveness of sins. Jesus' sending out of the seventy (Luke 10:1), the election of Matthias (Acts 1:26) to replace Judas Iscariot, and the New Testament naming of many others as apostles, including Paul, make it clear that the apostolic community and commission is not limited to the original twelve.[74] The original twelve apostles are the *pars pro toto*, the part which represents the whole. In this fashion the original apostles represent the fact that the entire church is a sent community and thus is apostolic in both her nature and her task.[75] As Moltmann says, "The expression 'apostolic' therefore denotes both the church's foundation and its commission."[76] The apostolate is simply the

---

72. Clearly these two categories of church are by no means mutually exclusive.

73. Yannoulatos, "Rediscovering," 5.

74. Ibid., 5–6.

75. "It [apostleship] is designated as the occupation of the Church. It is the *sine qua non* of its life" (ibid., 9, emphasis original).

76. Moltmann, *The Church*, 358.

community founded by the action of the apostolic Triune God, and sent by the Son as he was sent by the Father in the way and power of the Spirit. This refers to the original apostles who were sent by Jesus, and to the continuing apostolate, for Jesus is still calling and sending people in his name.[77]

The apostolate is historical in nature and is related to the eschaton because the church has been sent to bear witness to Jesus to the ends of the earth and to the end of time. As members of the corporate apostolate, Christians are heralds and forerunners of the coming kingdom of God, which will encompass all. Therefore, the apostolicity of the church is unique in being provisional and temporary in nature, for there shall come a time when the *missio ecclesiae* will cease. This is unlike the church's oneness, holiness and catholicity, which will continue to be marks of the glorified church, world without end. Curiously, Bosch disagrees and contends that "the church's mission *will never come to an end.*" He explains, "There was an age when it was believed in all sincerity that it was only a matter of time before we would actually complete the missionary task. Much nineteenth-century missionary policy was built on this premise. Today we know that we shall never reach the stage where we can say 'mission accomplished!'"[78] Bosch is right in saying that there will never come a time when the church can say 'mission accomplished', but there will come a time when Jesus' coming will put an end to the church's mission. Then, the Lord of the church will retire it from its field of service.[79] Describing how the apostolicity of the church is unique amongst the four marks of the church, Moltmann explains

> the historical church *will be* the one, holy, catholic church through the apostolic witness of Christ, and in carrying out that witness; whereas the church glorified in the kingdom of God *is* the one, holy and catholic church, through the fulfilment of its apostolate. Historically the church has its being in carrying out the apostolate. In eternity the church has its being in the fulfilment of the apostolate, that is, in the seeing face to face.[80]

Mission belongs uniquely to the church 'between the times'[81] after which mission shall be no more. The apostolicity of the church relates to the eschaton like no other aspect of the church's being.

Jewish eschatological expectation dictated that this present evil age would be suddenly, dramatically, and irrevocably interrupted by the coming

77. Oden, *Life in the Spirit*, 349.
78. Bosch, *Transforming Mission*, 465, emphasis original.
79. Braaten, *The Flaming Center*, 116.
80. Moltmann, *The Church*, 358, emphasis original.
81. See Padilla, *Mission Between the Times*.

of the Messiah, which would mark the end of time, the ushering in of the eschaton and, for some Jewish groups, the general resurrection of the dead. However, since Israel was to be a blessing to all the nations who would be gathered together to Israel's God, the arrival of the Messiah would leave no historical 'space' open for this ingathering to occur, thus leaving a central motif of the Old Testament unresolved and unfulfilled. Jenson explains that "By Jesus' Resurrection occurring 'first', a sort of *hole* opens *in* the event of the End, a space for something like what used to be history, for the church and its mission."[82] The resurrection of Jesus introduces a new reality to world history that does not belong to it but rather marks the beginning of new creation within the old.[83] Thus, the church-in-mission is thoroughly and irreducibly eschatological in character since it belongs to this 'hole' within the eschaton created by the time between Jesus' ascension and his triumphal return. This age, the church age, could also be rightly called the age of the Spirit, since it is in this age that the Spirit carries out his mission to glorify Jesus and build his church. One relatively recent Christian movement that has grasped this in its theology and praxis is Pentecostalism, which contains "an implicit ecclesiology that viewed the church as the eschatological community, which has to witness about the kingdom. This eschatological urgency resulted in the missionary and evangelistic fervor of early Pentecostalism."[84]

The church is apostolic in that her being consists in being sent by Christ as part of his ongoing mission to the world. A church could have impeccable credentials with regard to apostolic succession, and could have unimpeachable doctrinal orthodoxy, but these alone do not comprise the church's apostolic nature. The church's apostolicity speaks first of her missionary character, of her origin in the sending of Christ, himself the sent one of the Father, and the post-Pentecost sending of the Spirit.

---

82. Jenson, *Systematic Theology*, 1:85, emphasis original. Newbigin's own perspective on this is remarkably similar: "The extending of the Day [of the Lord] into an age is the work of God's mercy. He holds back the final unveiling in order that there may be time for repentance" (Newbigin, *The Gospel in a Pluralist Society*, 110–11). For a detailed study of the eschatological dimension of Newbigin's theology, see Schuster, *Christian Mission*.

83. See the work of N. T. Wright, such as *Surprised by Hope*.

84. Hong, "Church and Mission," 299. Anderson says that at the birth of the Pentecostal movement in 1906 from Azusa Street and other centers (including in other countries) "'Apostolic Faith', Spirit-filled missionaries were sent out to places as far away and diverse as China, India, Japan, Argentina, Brazil, all over Europe, Palestine, Egypt, Somaliland, Liberia, Angola and South Africa—all within two years" (Anderson, *Spreading Fires*, 68).

## *The Church's Missionary Dimension and Intention*

Having established that the church is missionary, what does this mean for ecclesial praxis? Does this mean that all the church's activities ought to have a missionary goal? Missiologists have often strived for their place with biblical scholars and theologians at the theological banqueting table, and find their discipline is often treated with all the culinary centrality of an after-dinner mint.[85] In their zeal to correct the perceived marginalization of their discipline, some missiologists have over-stated the importance of the church's missionary nature thereby almost reducing the church to its missionary function. For example, in her recent article "Mission Theology of the church" Kim says it is not "possible to separate church and mission in terms of their purpose."[86] Whilst it is indeed not possible to *separate* the two, it is customary in theology to *distinguish* between them. She then continues, "The missionary intention of God is the raison d'être of the church, and to fulfil God's missionary purpose is its aim."[87] Similarly, Laing affirmingly quotes Duraisingh as saying, "apostolate is the singular *raison d'être* of the church."[88] Without wanting to quench this missionary enthusiasm, I contend that it is more accurate to say that carrying out God's missionary purpose is central to the church's existence, but the church also exists 'to glorify God and enjoy Him forever'[89] in ways which are not exhausted by missionary faithfulness. In order to avoid undermining the integrity of other aspects of the church, such as its worshiping life, it is helpful to employ Newbigin's distinction between the entire life of the church having a missionary *dimension*, and certain activities of the church having a specifically missionary *intention*, a distinction that has been mentioned in recent missiological literature but not explored.[90] Newbigin says, "Because the Church *is* the mission there is a missionary dimension of everything that the Church does. But not everything the Church does has a missionary intention."[91] By missionary, Newbigin here means missionary in the *narrower* sense, that is, actions that purposely bear witness to Christ "among those who do not know Him," with the explicit intention "that they should be brought from unbelief to faith."[92] Hence, for clarity it is better to modify

---

85. Walls, *The Cross-Cultural Process*, 273.
86. Kim, "Mission Theology," 42.
87. Ibid., 42.
88. Laing, "Missio Dei," 94, emphasis original.
89. Westminster Shorter Catechism.
90. Laing, "Missio Dei," 91.
91. Newbigin, *One Body*, 43.
92. Ibid., 43.

Newbigin's language here and instead speak of the distinction between an *evangelistic* intention and dimension, which he alludes to elsewhere but does not consistently employ.[93] By contrast, the church's mission is understood more broadly to refer to all that God has sent the church into the world to be and to do.

### The Missionary Dimension of the Church

Essential to church life are its 'inward services', which include the church's teaching, preaching, counselling, worshiping and praying. Moreover, one could argue that the church's chief defining characteristic is her having been called into fellowship with Christ (1 Cor 1:9) in order to proclaim the excellencies of God (1 Pet 2:9). The church is the *ecclesia*, the congregation of those called out by God, "who gather round God as their center."[94] Worship of and fellowship with God are therefore central to the church's being (*esse*), hence it is doxology that chiefly defines the nature and destiny of the church. Therefore it is erroneous to interpret all of the church's non-missional activities as purely instrumental for serving the church's mission. Oden comes close to this in suggesting "The very purpose of the coming together of the community is in order that they may be sent . . . Ekklesia exists for the purpose of the apostolate."[95] Although partially true, Oden here neglects the church's doxological orientation of the church. It is true that worship of the resurrected Christ leads to mission, since "mission begins with an explosion of joy,"[96] but this is not its primary purpose. Rather than reducing the church's doxological vocation to its instrumentality for mission, worship is in fact the end goal of mission and of all creation, and so ultimately the end of mission is worship and not *vice versa*. Thus, the church between the times is irreducibly doxological and missional.

Nevertheless, it is true that "all Christian worship has an evangelistic dimension,"[97] for as the church exalts God in her worship the attention of those present is clearly drawn 'upwards' and focused on him who is being worshipped and adored. In Newbigin's writings he frequently reflects on the

---

93. Newbigin, *The Good Shepherd*, 31.

94. Küng, *The Church*, 82.

95. Oden, *Life in the Spirit*, 350–51. Kirk is also in danger of this when he states "the Church is because mission is: *missio sit ergo ecclesia sit*." This is because he is speaking of the *missio ecclesiae* and not the *missio Dei*. Kirk, *What Is Mission?*, 232, emphasis original.

96. Newbigin, *Mission in Christ's Way*, 33.

97. Newbigin, *The Good Shepherd*, 31.

fact that, when an Indian village congregation does not have its own church building its worship services are conducted outside before the curious villagers, with the effect of witnessing to Christ. The church's other 'inward services' such as teaching, pastoral care, and meeting the needs of its members are also pervaded by an evangelistic dimension. However, like worship they are not intentionally evangelistic activities. Like worship, these other church activities should *not* be viewed as *merely* as means to a missionary end, but unlike worship they should not be understood as ends in themselves. For example, although counselling and healing produce good ends in themselves, healed persons, the healing of a person in mind, soul or body is *both* for their own wholeness *and* so that they may more fully participate in the church's mission (and worship). If one danger is to see everything the church does in purely missionary terms, the opposite danger is for all church activities to be perceived as ends in themselves, in which case the church can become, in Barth's words, "an institution for private satisfaction in concert, or a work of sterile inbreeding."[98] For example, pastoral care and counselling are noble ends in themselves but should also be practiced with a view toward mission. Without the end goal of an outward focus these valuable practices can become insular and introspective, and the church's character of being sent to the world to glorify Jesus can fall out of sight. Having touched on the relation between worship and mission, it is now time to directly address this relation.

## The Church's Vocation of Worship and Mission

Worshipping God is an end in itself, and whilst this cannot be reduced to its instrumentality for mission, nevertheless worship does indeed lead to mission. Newbigin explains that God the Father seeks worshippers and he will draw them to the Son by the Spirit.

> This action of the Father is the Father himself in action, for God is Spirit, and Spirit is action—the mighty action which is 'from above' and which, like the wind, is invisible and yet unmistakable in its presence and its powerful effects. God is not essence but action. His being is action, and the action is the seeking of true worshippers out of Jewry and out of Samaria and out of every nation.[99]

---

98. Barth, *CD* IV/3.2, 833.
99. Newbigin, *The Light Has Come*, 53.

As people are drawn to worship the Triune God, their expressions of worship naturally include missionary work, for as Samuel Escobar says, "The single-minded passion for Christ is still the driving force behind mission."[100] Love for God includes desiring that others might know him (evangelism) and includes sharing in his love for the world, thus leading to mission. The renowned modern missionary to Muslims, Kenneth Cragg, says "We present Christ for the sole sufficient reason that he deserves to be presented."[101] The infinite worthiness of Christ is reason enough for mission in both its broad and narrow sense. Consequently, it stands to reason that where love of Christ decreases there will be a corresponding decrease in missionary obedience. In his work *Key to the Missionary Problem*, Andrew Murray identifies the chief problem as a lack of heart. "The enthusiasm of the kingdom is missing. And that is because there is so little enthusiasm for *the King*."[102] Popular Christian songwriter Matt Redman expresses this doxological spirituality in his song "Mission's Flame."

> Let worship be the fuel for mission's flame
> We're going with a passion for Your name
> We're going for we care about Your praise
> Send us out
> Let worship be the heart of mission's aim
> To see the nations recognize Your fame
> 'Til every tribe and tongue voices Your praise
> Send us out
> You should be the praise of every tongue, Jesus
> You should be the joy of every heart
> But until the fullness of Your kingdom comes
> Until the final revelation dawns
> Send us out
> Every tribe, every tongue
> Every creature in the heavens and the earth
> Every heart, every soul
> Will sing Your praise, will sing Your praise
> Every note, every strain
> Every melody will be for You alone
> Every harmony that flows from every tongue
> We'll sing Your praise, we'll sing Your praise[103]

---

100. Escobar, *The New Global Mission*, 17. For a useful survey of motivations for mission, see Verkuyl, *Contemporary Missiology*, 163–75.

101. Kenneth Cragg quoted in Kirk, *What Is Mission?*, 73.

102. Quoted in Piper, *Let the Nations*, 37, emphasis original.

103. From the album *Facedown* (Six Step, 2004).

This vision of the glory, majesty and infinite worthiness of God imparts faith and strength to work for the growing and inbreaking new creation. Bosch comments, "It is precisely the vision of the coming reality of God's glory that compels us to work patiently and courageously in the present, unredeemed world in a manner dictated by the way of Christ."[104] It is this doxological motivation for mission that is the most fundamental for Newbigin. He says,

> I believe that evangelism is essentially a doxological act—an expression of gratitude to the Savior. The life I have in Christ compels me to seek to share that life with others, not because they are otherwise lost (for I am not authorized to determine the limits of the mercy of God) but in order that he—my Savior—may 'see of the travail of his soul and be satisfied.' Its urgency, its necessity, is the urgency, the necessity of worship, of praise, of thanksgiving.[105]

However, as sinful creatures human beings are not able to generate this passion for Christ, for it is evidently a fruit of the work of the Holy Spirit who is drawing people to worship the Father through the Son. As a result of this *opera trinitatis ad extra*, believers are drawn to worship and volunteer themselves for missionary work. Andrew Lord calls this the 'voluntary principle' in missiology and spells out three implications. First, humanly speaking, the motivation for mission occurs at the grassroots and works, humanly speaking, from the 'bottom-up', rather than being a 'top-down', organizational affair. Second, this pneumatological working is not confined to clergy or some other class of Christians, for the work of the Holy Spirit is unconfined. Third, mission "arises out of an experience of God" rather than simply humanitarian concern.[106] This voluntary principle is far more powerful than a sense of duty and anything that can be organizationally commissioned, for this vibrant spirituality not only motivates but sustains missionaries in persecution and affliction. Christians are motivated for mission by the work of the Holy Spirit who glorifies Jesus and stirs in believers a desire to do the same. It is the glory of the Father to bring honor to the Son, and it is the glory of the Son to honor the Father, and it is by the Spirit that Christians are caught up in this trinitarian glorification.

Worship is the eternal trinitarian activity of God as the Father, Son, and Spirit eternally give love to and receive love from each other. By the Spirit and through the Son the church participates in this Triune loving,

---

104. Bosch, *Transforming Mission*, 154.
105. Newbigin, "Integration," 251–52.
106. Lord, "The Voluntary Principle," 83.

and as she beholds the glory of the Lord she is transformed from one degree of glory to another (2 Cor 3:18). At the heart of this transformation is the Spirit's conforming the church to the image of Christ so that she bears the fruit of the Spirit, the first of which is love. The church's being is transformed such that she finds from within herself a greater love for the Triune God and a greater love for the world which the Father so loved that he sent his Son.[107] As the church is caught up into the Triune love that God is *ad intra* and into the universal scope of God's love *ad extra*, especially for those creatures made in the divine image, both her increased love for God and for the world issue in missionary obedience. In a most natural sense, therefore, worship leads to mission. Furthermore, as Colin Greene rightly says "The true purpose of mission is . . . an acted-out doxology. It is that God may be glorified on earth as in heaven."[108] As worship leads to mission and the purpose of mission is worship, so also mission leads to worship as people experience the love of God through the church's loving actions and verbal witness (see Matt 5:16). The church's priestly nature, through its participation in the priesthood of Christ, is seen as the church is caught up in this cyclical relation of worship which leads to mission, which in turn leads to worship, and so on, to the glory of the Triune God.[109]

## *No Mission, No Church*

Given that mission is fundamental to the church's historical being, it is my contention that where there is 'no mission' there is 'no church' because the church's being originates in the trinitarian missions of God. The church, and the Christian, is vivified in missional obedience, and conversely can lose its ecclesial or Christian identity by decisively abandoning its missionary vocation. To substantiate this claim, I shall first further explain the church's missionary nature and then I shall discuss the inter-relation between missionary faithfulness and ecclesial or Christian existence by drawing on the Johannine and Pauline *corpora*. In the course of the argument I intend to clarify what 'decisive abandonment of missionary vocation' means and relate this whole discussion to the bedrock of Christian faith—salvation by grace alone.

Explaining the church's missionary nature, Barth says "It is with a task, and to fulfil this task, that the community is sent into the world and exists

---

107. See 1 John 3:17; 4:20–21.

108. Greene, "Trinitarian Tradition," 69.

109. For an in depth study of the implications of worship for ecclesial living, see Wannenwetsch, *Political Worship*.

for it."[110] Similarly, Newbigin says of the church, "It has no life except in this sending."[111] The church's missionary task and the church's being do not independently exist but co-exist. Therefore, the church is never more itself than when it gives itself in its mission of evangelism, love, and service to the world. In Andrew Lord's view, "Mission is the life-blood of the church and the natural expression of life in the Spirit."[112] Both the church and its members (Christians), are fully alive as they engage in the *missio ecclesiae* for which they have been created and redeemed. Speaking of the church, Barth explains

> It does not exist before its task and later acquire it. Nor does it exist apart from it, so that there can be no question whether or not it might have to execute it. It exists for the world. Its task constitutes and fashions it from the very outset. If it had not been given it, it would not have come into being. If it were to lose it, it would not continue. It is not, then, a kind of imparted dignity. It exists only as it has it, or rather only as the task has it.[113]

Barth is *not* saying that if a church denies its missionary nature, either theologically or in practice, then it is *in danger* of losing its own identity. The church is constituted by God's mission and exists only as it fulfils its role within the *missio Dei*, and so persistent, habitual, and systematic missionary unfaithfulness leads directly to ecclesial non-existence. A church that has decisively abandoned its missionary responsibility simply ceases to be a church. Similarly, John Flett argues that a church's "failure to act in this reconciling, missionary way ruptures the ontological relationship [with Jesus]."[114] Whilst concurring with his line of thought, this statement needs to be qualified, for in what does this failure consist?

It is vital to distinguish between churches that struggle with missionary faithfulness and lapse into unfaithfulness, and those which have abandoned their entire missionary vocation. Regarding the former, Wilbert Shenk says that "The church that refuses to accept its missionary purpose is a deformed church."[115] Whilst this is true, the situation is far more serious for such a church which has abandoned its missionary calling. The distinction between these two is based on a principle found in 1 John 3

---

110. Barth, *CD* IV/3.2, 795.
111. Newbigin, *Mission in Christ's Way*, 22.
112. Lord, "Mission Eschatology," 111.
113. Barth, *CD* IV/3.2, 795–96.
114. Flett, "*Missio Dei*," 13.
115. Shenk, "Lesslie Newbigin's Contribution," 6.

verses 6 and 9.[116] There, interpreters see John making a distinction between believers (and one could add churches) who commit acts of sin and unbelievers who sin as a settled habit or as a life orientation. In his commentary, Stephen Smalley says those who abide in Christ live for him but lapse into sin, whereas those outside of Christ have sin as a 'settled policy', for their "mind-set is therefore toward sin rather than toward God," and so are '(constantly) sinful' and 'sin habitually'.[117] The essence of this sin is a turning in on oneself (*incurvatus in se*), which can also be described as failing in self-giving love. Vincent Donovan suggests that "A church that turns in on itself is no longer a church. A church that turns in on itself will surely die. Many have died in history."[118] If a church irrevocably forsakes its mission to love then it breaks out of fellowship with the Triune God who is carrying out his mission of love to the world, and so abdicates its ecclesial identity. As the International Missionary Council said in 1952, "there is no participation in Christ without participation in his mission to the world."[119] Mission is so core to the being of the church that, says Kirk, "if it ceases to be missionary, it has not just failed in one of its tasks, it has ceased being Church. Thus, the Church's self-understanding and sense of identity (its ecclesiology) is inherently bound up with its [missionary] call."[120]

The church's mission can be characterized as its vocation to love the world, hence a church that has renounced its missionary responsibility has in some measure failed to love. Love is the being and nature of God, so failing in this means distancing, and possibly, in the end, severing oneself from the one who is love and the one who has life in himself (John 5:26). A clear

116. Verse 6: "No one who lives in him keeps on sinning. No one who continues to sin has either seen him or known him" (NIV). Verse 9: "No one who is born of God will continue to sin, because God's seed remains in them; they cannot go on sinning, because they have been born of God" (NIV).

117. Smalley, *1, 2, 3 John*, 156, 157. This distinction has been incorporated into the ESV, NASB and NIV Bible translations of 1 John 3:9. The distinction arises out of the attempt to resolve the hermeneutical tension between John's teaching that believers do not sin (1 John 3:6, 9) and his teaching elsewhere that believers can and do sin (1 John 1:8—2:1; 5:16). This distinction is based on the use of present tense for the verb 'sin', but does not by itself wholly resolve the matter.

118. Donovan, *Christianity Rediscovered*, 105.

119. Willingen Conference of the International Missionary Council, 1952, quoted in Newbigin, *The Open Secret*, 1. Teasing out the meaning of this statement, Flett asserts "There is no neutrality with respect to the cause of God: either one lives in active missionary fellowship with God, or one removes oneself from this fellowship" (*The Witness of God*, 270).

120. Kirk, *What Is Mission?*, 30. Similarly, Hauerwas and Willimon say the church has "significance *only* as God's means for saving the whole world" (*Resident Aliens*, 51, emphasis added).

example of this is the divine warning to the Ephesian church in Revelation 2:1–7. For abandoning love (2:4) God threatened to remove the lampstand from the Ephesian church (2:5), which according to David Aune "is nothing less than a threat to obliterate the Ephesian congregation as an empirical Christian community."[121] Consequently, vis-à-vis mission, Wilhelm Andersen states bluntly that "a Church without missionary activity can indeed for a period retain its form as a stiff and lifeless corpse, but the process of putrefaction will in time inevitably set in."[122] That this is possible and not definite is due to the grace of God that contends with obstinate humanity like a husband remaining faithful to his wife, despite the fact that humanity's covenantal fidelity can resemble that of a prostitute (see Hosea). The divine potter is always willing to change his plans for nations and kingdoms, and the reader might infer, churches and individuals, if they turn back to him (Jer 18:5–10). There is a dialectic between God refusing to give up on his covenant people, and certain individuals and churches disqualifying themselves from the covenant, and the one who is Judge is alone qualified to resolve this matter. However, one can affirm that a person cannot have fellowship with the God who is love and not love others.[123] The apostle John says, rather bluntly, "Whoever does not love does not know God, for God is love," therefore, "Whoever does not love abides in death" (1 John 4:8; 3:14b).

As it is sometimes appropriate for a person to make their calling and election sure (2 Pet 1:10), to examine themselves to see whether they are in the faith (2 Cor 13:5), so it is sometimes beneficial for a church to audit itself to know the state of its own health. In this regard, Eberhard Jüngel helpfully comments, "If the church had a *heart*, a living, beating heart, its pulse would be largely regulated by mission and evangelism."[124] There are many signs of a healthy church, including faith, hope, love, holiness, humility, generosity and so on, but there is something central about its missionary faithfulness. The church's apostolicity, which primarily refers to missionary nature, is one central mark of its ecclesiality. Barth is so confident about the centrality of the church's missionary nature that he says, "Certainly a Church which is not as such an evangelizing Church is either not yet or no longer the Church, or only a dead Church, itself standing in supreme need of renewal

---

121. Aune, *Revelation 1–5*, 147.

122. Wilhelm Andersen, *Towards a Theology of Mission*, quoted in Flett, *The Witness of God*, 270.

123. See the discussion on 1 John 4:12, 20 below.

124. Jüngel, "To Tell," 203, emphasis original.

and evangelization."[125] I contend that this is true of the church corporate, and so it also contains truth for individual Christians.

The church's missionary nature determines the nature of its members, so all Christians are missionaries because all have been called and sent by God to express his love for the world. Understanding missionary in a broad sense, I concur with Barth who says "every Christian is to be a missionary, a recruiting officer for new witnesses."[126] This is clear in Paul's letter to the Philippians where he describes the Philippians as functioning as a community of priests (2:16), and as lights (2:15) who, by virtue of being incorporated into Christ the light of the world (John 8:12), have themselves become lights to the world (see Matt 5:14). These are unmistakable descriptions of their missionary identity, and according to James Ware, in Philippians Paul understands "mission as an essential aspect of Christian identity," and "active verbal mission as an essential aspect of Christian faith and life."[127]

However, this can easily be misconstrued in quite damaging ways. Negatively, this does not mean that the Christian is saved by their missional faithfulness, as if salvation were dependent upon good works. Salvation is purely and wholly by God's grace, but God's grace is given for Christians to do good works (Eph 2:8–10), so that the latter gives expression to the former.[128] But these good works might not be forthcoming for numerous reasons. A Christian might not be missionally active because they are immature in the faith and are still learning to grasp the gospel and its implications. Christians may not be participating in God's mission to the world, because of fear of losing reputation, fear of the consequences of missionary obedience, selfishness, diminished capacity, difficulties in life that cause a person to be more inwardly focused, the entanglement of sin, and so on. In this regard, it would be erroneous to make the Pelagian suggestion that

---

125. Barth, *CD* IV/3.2, 874.

126. Barth, *CD* III/4, 505. Arguing the same point, Flett helpfully explains "Not every Christian will be called to a peculiar missionary vocation, but mission characterizes the whole of Christian existence" (Flett, *The Witness of God*, 239).

127. Ware, *The Mission*, 282, 287. Keown agrees and moves seamlessly from ecclesial to Christian missionary responsibility: "The church is to continue the evangelistic mission of Christ. All believers are called to be involved in supporting this mission . . ." (Keown, *Congregational Evangelism*, 279).

128. Making a helpful distinction, John Barclay prefers to speak of Christ as the *unconditioned* gift rather than the *unconditional* gift. Unconditional refers both to no prior conditions *and* no resulting obligations, whereas he argues that Paul understands Christ to be the *unconditioned* gift, without prior conditions but *with* 'strings attached.' For him, the gift of God in Christ is "a transformative gift that sets up new loyalties and commitments . . ." My argument is that in Christ God's grace is given which sets up new 'loyalties and commitments' that include participating in *missio trinitatis Dei*. Barclay, "Paul," 8.

lack of missional faithfulness puts a Christian's salvation into jeopardy. In Romans 10:13, the apostle Paul says that those who simply call on the name of the Lord will be saved; hence Peter Stuhlmacher comments, "Salvation is thus allotted to the one who confesses Christ as Lord."[129] It is imperative that the integrity and simplicity of salvation must be affirmed.[130] However, such a direction of thought *can* suggest that missionary faithfulness is an 'optional extra', which consequently *can* become an alibi for missionary responsibility by viewing missional faithfulness as *additional* to the Christian life, rather than at its very core.

The inseparability of loving God and people is most clearly taught in John's first epistle, where he says "if we love one another, God lives in us, and his love is perfected in us," and "Those who say, 'I love God,' and hate their brothers or sisters, are liars" (1 John 4:12, 20). The invisible reality of love for God is made visible and bears fruit in loving others, so that in the end these are two dimensions of one reality and are co-extensive.[131] John Thomas explains, "The thought here is not that one must love God in order to love one's brother or sister, or that one must love one's brother or sister in order to love God, but rather that love of God and love of brother or sister are impossible to separate."[132] Furthermore, as churches and individual Christians love the world through missionary faithfulness, God lives in them and his love is perfected in them (1 John 4:12). God's life-giving Spirit flows through the church to others (the doctrine of election) such that missionary faithfulness animates and vivifies those who carry it out. It appears that Newbigin grasped this truth experientially, for he says that

> faith can become cold and formal, can lose its power to illuminate my mind and warm my heart, and that there is only one way to prevent that happening, and that is to live in situations where it is constantly being matched against the powers of evil, and to have company with those who are being newly gripped by it. That means, in one sentence, that faith is kept strong by living on the frontier. *It is the church which lives on the frontier that will be ready to advance in strength.*[133]

---

129. Stuhlmacher, *Paul's Letter*, 157.

130. Indeed, Dunn says that "from very early on believers identified themselves simply as 'those who call upon the name of the Lord (Jesus Christ)'" (Dunn, *The Theology*, 257–58).

131. Lieu, *The Theology*, 66.

132. Thomas, *The Pentecostal Commentary*, 239.

133. Newbigin, *The Pattern of Partnership*, 44–45, emphasis original.

Participating in this trinitarian glorification means that the church partakes not only in the *missio Dei* but actually in God's loving nature (2 Pet 1:4), which cannot but animate the church. In summary, the church's ecclesial and missionary identity cohere because participating by the Spirit in the sonship of Christ is to participate in God's mission to the world.

This has a number of important consequences, two of which will be briefly mentioned. First, Newbigin, among others, has argued that Christendom was largely a non-missional entity.[134] This, then, bequeathed to the Western church, the heir of Christendom, patterns of ministry, theological training and structure which are all decidedly non-missional.[135] Hence, Newbigin's calls for "a profound transformation in the accepted patterns of congregational life, of ministry, of Christian action in the world."[136] Since the church's ecclesial and missionary identity coexist, to the extent that the Western church has abandoned her missionary vocation, she has undermined her ecclesiality. Might this go towards explaining why the Western church today is but a shadow of its former self?[137] Re-reading Donovan's words with the Western church in mind is sobering: "A church that turns in on itself is no longer a church. A church that turns in on itself will surely die. Many have died in history."[138]

Second, as the church is missionary by nature, so also is the church's theological task which serves the church's mission. According to J. Andrew Kirk, theology's "real identity and purpose are fulfilled by being a resource in the service of God's mission to bring all things into subjection to Christ."[139] Stating his position more fully, Kirk explains,

> My thesis is that it is impossible to conceive of theology apart from mission. All true theology is, by definition, missionary theology, for it has as its object the study of the ways of a God who is by nature missionary and a foundation text written by and for missionaries. Mission as a discipline is not, then, the roof of a building that completes the whole structure, already constructed by blocks that stand on their own, but both the

---

134. Newbigin, *Mission and Unity of the Church*, 7.

135. Newbigin, *Honest Religion For Secular Man*, 105.

136. Newbigin, *One Body*, 16.

137. Andrew Walls observes that the decline of the Western church in the second half of the twentieth century "has proved [to be] one of the largest and fastest movements away from the Christian faith ever to have taken place—much faster, for instance, than that in the Middle East which followed the rise of Islam" (*The Cross-Cultural Process*, 63).

138. Donovan, *Christianity Rediscovered*, 105.

139. Kirk, *The Mission of Theology*, 42.

foundation and the mortar in the joints, which cements together everything else."[140]

Unfortunately, one legacy of non-missional church structures is the marginalization of mission studies from the theological academy in both university departments and seminaries. Newbigin lamented over fifty years ago that our theological curricula perpetuate the illusion that the age of missions is over, and so focus on rival statements of Christian faith rather than non-Christian systems of thought.[141] The Western missionary movement has been a significant learning experience for the church, with knowledge advanced in countless fields including religion, anthropology, and linguistics. "Indeed," says Walls, "one is tempted to suggest that the missionary movement affected every department of scholarship—except theology."[142] Flett remarks that, "Approaching theological treatises with an interest in the missionary purpose of the church reveals an egregious blind spot. With few exceptions, mission is absent from the all-encompassing theological 'system.'"[143] Personally, I completed an undergraduate degree in theology without taking any courses on mission, because none were offered. Thankfully, publications such as Tennent's *Invitation to World Missions*, as an introductory textbook for mission studies, evidence a change has at least started. If this change does not continue then the consequences for the health of theology, and of the church communities it serves, are dire. Flett argues,

> If it is possible for a ministry candidate to progress through academic training—as much within a seminary as a secular university—without any dogmatic attention given to the purpose for which the Christian community exists, then this indicates the community's own radical disorder.[144]

The rediscovery of the church's inherently missionary nature, which has a broad ecumenical consensus, needs to translate into the church's ministry training programs and theological curricula. Theologians need to include mission alongside the other major dogmatic loci, and consequently, start to increasingly direct their intellect to engagement with non-Christian thought systems. This is vital for the health of the church worldwide, including the West, but it is only an outworking of the church's missionary nature.

---

140. Ibid., 50–51.
141. Newbigin, *The Mission and Unity of the Church*, 7–8.
142. Walls, *The Cross-Cultural Process*, 42.
143. Flett, *The Witness of God*, 296.
144. Ibid.

## THE CHURCH'S MISSION

### *The Breadth and Center of the Church's Mission*

Newbigin's distinction between the missionary dimension and intention (see 'The Church's Missionary Dimension and Intention' above) is closely related to the distinction he makes between *mission* (singular) and *missions* (plural). For Newbigin, mission is an all-encompassing term by which he means "the entire task for which the Church is sent into the world."[145] In this broad sense, mission "includes the task of preaching the gospel, of healing the sick, of teaching, of service to men in all their needs." He continues,

> It includes the task of prophetic witness in the face of wrong, of declaring the will of God in regard to the life of men both in their personal and domestic affairs and also no less clearly in their corporate life as nations, in business, in politics, in culture, in religion. All this is included in the mission of the Church understood in its broadest sense.[146]

Similarly, Verkuyl rightly says the church's mission must take the kingdom of God as its point of orientation, and so in its mission the church must seek to struggle against "the whole range of burdens and evils plaguing mankind."[147] Consequently, the church's mission is inescapably broad, as it seeks to bring the light and life of God's kingdom into this present evil age that lies within the domain of darkness under the power of the evil one (Gal 1:4; Col 1:13; 1 John 5:19). Mission (singular) closely equates to the missionary dimension of the church as God's love and life pervade all that the church does, with a view to the blessing of the nations (Gen 12:3 and Gal 3:16, 29). For Verkuyl, "participation in the fight against every vestige of evil plaguing mankind is an intrinsic part of our [the church's] calling."[148] Given the breadth of the God's mission in which the church participates, one could be tempted to conclude with Stephen Neill, "If everything is mission,

---

145. Newbigin, *The Gospel in a Pluralist Society*, 121. See also Newbigin, "Cross-Currents," 146.

146. Newbigin, "The Life and Mission," 60.

147. Verkuyl, "The Kingdom of God," 175. Offering a similarly broad description of the Church's mission, Kirk says mission is "announcing the good news in culturally authentic ways, struggling to right the wrongs caused by economic malfunctioning, environmental degradation and conflict, engaging with people of different beliefs, establishing new communities of disciples and seeking the unity of Christians and human communities..." (Kirk, *What Is Mission?*, 233–34).

148. Verkuyl, "The Kingdom of God," 173.

nothing is mission."[149] Whilst this is not without some truth, it would be an unfair assessment of the scope of the church's mission which is necessarily extensive, as it seeks to participate in God's mission of the redemption of all creation.

A Christian missiology that does not incorporate the full range of actions for liberation and reconciliation is highly impoverished. Nevertheless, it is simultaneously true that *only* speaking of mission in these terms is incomplete. According to the late Pope John Paul II, the *missio ecclesiae* does not *primarily* consist in "helping the poor, contributing to the liberation of the oppressed, promoting development or defending human rights." Whist these are necessarily part of the church's mission, "her primary task lies elsewhere: the poor are hungry for God, not just for bread and freedom. Missionary activity must first of all bear witness to and proclaim salvation in Christ, and establish local churches which then become means of liberation in every sense."[150] This 'primary task' is what Newbigin variously calls missions (plural), missionary intention, evangelistic mission, and mission in the narrower sense of the term.

"By 'missions,'" Newbigin explains, "I mean those specific activities which are undertaken by human decision to bring the gospel to places or situations where it is not heard, to create a Christian presence in a place or situation where there is no such presence or no effective presence."[151] In his autobiography, Newbigin explicitly invokes the language of missionary intentionality to describe what missions are, stating that "missions concentrate on the specifically missionary intention of bringing the Gospel to those who have not heard it and this must be directed to all six continents."[152] When Newbigin defines what he calls 'missionary intention' his definition is effectively the same as that of missions. Thus, missionary actions, which Newbigin also calls missionary in the narrower sense of the term, are those which intentionally cross the boundary, found in every country, between faith and unfaith, in order to see people come to faith in Christ. Intentional missionary actions chiefly refer to evangelistic activities such as proclamation, disciple-making and church planting.

A missionary dimension pervades all aspects of church's life because as the community of Jesus Christ, her very being bears witness to him. As important as this is, it is no substitute for intentional missionary activity.

---

149. Neill, *Creative Tension*, 81.

150. John Paul II, *Encyclical Letter Redemptoris missio*.

151. Newbigin, *The Gospel in a Pluralist Society*, 121. See also Newbigin, "Cross-Currents," 146.

152. Newbigin, *Unfinished Agenda*, 196.

Newbigin counsels that "unless there is in the life of the Church a point of concentration for the missionary intention, the missionary dimension which is proper to the whole life of the Church will be lost."[153] By way of illustration, he says the church reminds itself that all days are holy by treating one day as holy—the Lord's day. Hence Newbigin says, "The calling of men and women to be converted, to follow Jesus and to be part of his community is and must always be at the center of mission."[154] This is because the *missio trinitatis Dei* is a reconciled human fellowship, and intentional missionary actions work directly towards achieving that goal. This center of mission is often embodied in persons who have given their lives to full time missionary service, after the pattern of Paul and Barnabas (see Acts 13:1–3). The danger is that those who are like these apostles are seen to be 'real' missionaries thus downgrading and devaluing the missionary activity of the rest of the body of Christ. The CWME warns that "The church should not allow this specialized calling of the few to be an alibi for the whole Church, but rather it should be a symbolic concentration of the missionary vocation of the whole Church."[155] Since the whole church is missionary by nature, this missionary dimension is expressed in everything the church does, and finds concentrated expression in some actions of the church that are intentionally missional.

## THE MISSION OF THE CHURCH

In this chapter I have argued that the church is missionary by nature because its being originates in the *missio trinitatis Dei*, and its destiny is to be the human *koinonia* that reflects and participates in the Triune *koinonia*. This mission is primarily God's mission into which the church has been graciously incorporated. It is helpful to understand the church, first as participating in God's mission, and second (because of the first), as discharging its own distinctive mission within the *missio Dei*. The church best carries out her task by first attending to another task, that of abiding in Christ. The church is only effective in mission as she loves and prays and works and serves *out of* her relationship with the Triune God, whose mission it truly is. The unique relation between Christ and the church has been explored,

---

153. Newbigin, *One Body*, 43.

154. Newbigin, *The Open Secret* (1978), 136, quoted in Richmond, *Daring To Believe*, 151. Similarly, the WCC Commission on World Mission and Evangelism claims: "It is at the heart of Christian mission to foster the multiplication of local congregations in every human community" (CWME, "Mission and Evangelism," 68).

155. CWME, "Mission and Evangelism," 70.

showing that a healthy ecclesiology is dependent upon a healthy Christology, for the church is christologically determined. This determination has a double orientation toward God the Father and toward the world which he loves. Thus, the church is called to both worship and missionary activity (broadly understood). Like Christ, the church carries out her mission in the context of a hostile world such that persecution is inevitable. Nevertheless, like her Lord the church is only permitted to respond to evil with good. Rather than succumbing to violence, intimidation and fear the church is to live out her missional identity and calling faithfully and with all wisdom in the knowledge that in Christ's resurrection new creation has already dawned and the old is beginning to pass away.

The church's missionary nature is understood also to be grounded on its fulfilment of Israel's call to be a light to the nations, its commissioning by Christ himself, and as a natural consequence of faith in the uniqueness of Christ. The apostolicity of the church, whilst referring both to faithfulness to apostolic teaching and to historical church unity, is first to be understood in terms of the church's origin and participation in the sending of Christ. However, this does not mean that all church work ought to be intentionally missionary, even though a missionary dimension does pervade all aspects of ecclesial existence. Neither does this mean that the church can be reduced to her missionary vocation. Worship is central to the church's ecclesiality, and although it does rightly lead to mission, its worth does not belong to that. Rather, the significance of mission comes from the importance of worship, such that the church's mission is a participation not only in the *missio trinitatis Dei*, but also mutual glorification of the Triune Persons. Nevertheless, mission is understood to be so central to the church's being between the times, that a church which decisively abandons its missionary vocation is guilty of failing to love others, and is in danger of severing itself from the missionary God and thus from Life itself. This is in accord with the theologic of love being the source, reason and goal of ecclesial existence, and with the instrumentality of divine grace that moves the recipient to good works. As the church lives out this vocation by participating in the *missio Dei*, she is animated by the Spirit and confirms her own ecclesial identity. And finally, the church's mission itself is as broad as God's love for the world, but its center resides in intentionally evangelistic mission which seeks to make disciples of Jesus and establish new churches.

This exposition of the mission of the church stands alongside my accounts of the Triune being of the missionary God, the mission of the Son, and the mission of the Holy Spirit. Together these form a robust trinitarian theological foundation for mission.

CHAPTER 6

# Conclusion

## INTRODUCTION

IN THIS FINAL CHAPTER I bring together the insights and conclusions of this project as a whole. I will initially offer some broad reflections on Newbigin's theology, before providing a summary in which I draw together the threads of my constructive proposal in Part Two. I will then consider how this work relates to two recent publications in trinitarian missiology. Lastly, I will conclude this study of trinitarian missiology by turning once more to Newbigin's claim that 'the doctrine of the Trinity is the necessary starting point for preaching.'

## LESSLIE NEWBIGIN: AN APPRAISAL

As I investigated the Newbigin corpus of writings, published and unpublished, the scale and breadth of his theological vision was impressed upon me. His writings span a wide variety of genre including monograph, biblical commentary, poetry, diary, theological lectures, theological apologetic, historical analysis, missiology, instructional teaching, inter-faith dialogue, and socio-political analysis. In addition to Newbigin's expertise in missiology, he offered incisive and valuable contributions across a wide range of theological, ecclesial, social, and cultural concerns.

Newbigin's theological method is distinctly biblical in approach, rather than historical or systematic. Writing on eschatology, for example, Newbigin does not offer a historical account of this doctrinal area; nor does he offer a systematic study of its main theological coordinates (Christ's second coming, the resurrection, the final judgement, the new heavens and the new earth). Instead, he proceeds by expositing the main features of Mark chapter 13.[1] Furthermore, he theologizes in dialogue with contemporary world events, cultural developments, and current philosophical movements; his entire mission to modernity evidences this. Newbigin was the quintessential reflective practitioner, but for him the accent lies more on the activist than the academic. Accordingly, he wrote out of his lived experience of the local realities of places as different as rural South India and Geneva, Madras and Birmingham, all with a global perspective. His theology was both biblical and contextual, and it was also visionary. Despite his denials,[2] Newbigin's writings have a prophetic quality about them, demonstrating his ability to identify future issues ahead of time and to point the way forward for ecclesial and theological obedience.[3] His identification of the need for a trinitarian missiology, his pioneering mission to Western culture, his call for greater missional engagement with Islam,[4] and his declaration of the need for a restructuring of ecclesial patterns of ministry and training to reflect the church's missionary nature, all stand out. This study has attempted to address the first of these concerns.

There is, clearly, a consistency, openness and overall coherence to Newbigin's theology as it developed during his lifetime of ministerial service. The most notable change in his theology came during his formative years at Westminster College, Cambridge. Armed with numerous theological questions and confused about what to believe, he embarked on a detailed study of Paul's letter to the Romans, which he subsequently described as "a turning point in my theological journey. I began the study as a typical liberal," he continues, and, being influenced chiefly by James Denney, ended the study "much more of an evangelical than a liberal."[5] For the remaining sixty-five years of his life, Newbigin's theology remained remarkably con-

1. Newbigin, *Trinitarian Doctrine*, 41–50.
2. "I am no prophet" (Newbigin, "Mission in the 1980's," 154).
3. Sandy Millar. "Foreword" in Newbigin, *Discovering Truth*, vi; Tennent, *Invitation to World Missions*, 68.
4. See Newbigin et al., *Faith and Power*; Taylor, "Lesslie Newbigin's Understanding of Islam."
5. Newbigin, *Unfinished Agenda*, 30–31. Furthermore, Newbigin's theology remained *evangelical* in character throughout his lifetime. The central beliefs of Evangelicalism can be described as commitment to the core beliefs of historic, orthodox Christianity as expressed in the ecumenical creeds; the primacy, authority and sufficiency of Scripture; the uniqueness of Christ and his saving work through his death on the cross; the necessity and urgency of evangelism; and the need for personal conversion. These core evangelical beliefs feature prominently in Newbigin's theology. See Boyd and Eddy, *Across the Spectrum*, 7; McGrath, *Christian Theology*, 80.

sistent in areas of core Christian doctrine such as Christology, soteriology, ecclesiology, and missiology. He was not significantly swayed by fashionable currents of thought that swept so many others along.[6] Driven by his distinctly biblical theology, Newbigin did not desist from highlighting the importance of evangelism when this emphasis had fallen out of favor in WCC circles during the 1960s and 70s. Nor did he cease calling for organic church union when fashions in ecclesiology had moved on. No doubt his opponents would have interpreted this as stubbornness, but it might also be interpreted as Newbigin's commitment to his biblically inspired and prayerful theological vision. Newbigin combined theological constancy with an eagerness to learn; he remained a keen student open to new insights, even after his sight had failed.[7] Over the course of his lifetime Newbigin was strongly influenced by Charles Cochrane, Hendrik Kraemer, Roland Allen, Michael Polanyi, and Karl Barth among others.[8] These thinkers greatly enriched his theology, particularly regarding trinitarian theology, Pneumatology, missiology, and epistemology. This enrichment, however, did not constitute a fundamental change in Newbigin's theological orientation, but a deepening and supplementing of his existing theological commitments. This is true even of Newbigin's discovery of the importance of the doctrine of the Trinity. This discovery did bring about a change in his theological vision, in that what had been latent and implicit, became explicit and was brought into focal awareness. Accordingly, the lens through which Newbigin theologized was forever changed, and the essential content of Newbigin's theological vision was recast in alignment with that which is the *arché* of theology. His core theological convictions concerning, for example, salvation, the church, and mission, were deepened and broadened, but they were not fundamentally transformed.

The vitality of Newbigin's theology is also to be commended. His writings are the literary output of a life devoted to prayer and obedience. If Fiddes is right, that "True spiritual power is the power of increasing the faith of others" then this power is evident in Newbigin's writings.[9] To my mind this quality in his writings derives, in part, from Newbigin's formation by and

---

6. A partial exception to this is what Wainwright has called Newbigin's "secular flirtation." See Wainwright, *Lesslie Newbigin*, 341–54.

7. When Newbigin was well into his eighties and blindness had set in, a number of theological students from King's College, London, would regularly read him works of theology and biblical studies.

8. There are a few scholars whom Newbigin frequently names but whose contribution to his thought is largely limited to a single concept. For example, he often refers to Thomas Kuhn's notion of a 'paradigm shift', or Peter Berger's 'plausibility structures'.

9. Fiddes, *Participating in God*, 274.

commitment to the Reformed theological tradition. One of this tradition's greatest strengths is its emphasis on the centrality of God's sovereignty, an emphasis that formed the 'backbone' of all Newbigin's writings.

Newbigin stands as one of the greatest missiologists of the twentieth century with many achievements to his name, foremost of which was his pioneering missionary engagement with the tough new paganism characteristic of modern Western culture. Newbigin's legacy is likely to be enduring as the corpus of his writings continues to provide much stimulation, inspiration, and direction for those who wish to advance the church's mission. Whether or not Newbigin is indeed like a Father in the church, as a Russian Orthodox Bishop once suggested,[10] his writings and his example have proven to be a rare gift to the church as it seeks to carry out its mission.

## *Unfinished Agenda*

Newbigin's autobiography is aptly titled *Unfinished Agenda*, a reference, clearly, to the work that he perceived still needed to be done. It is also a helpful heading under which to view Newbigin's theology, which is rightly understood as indicative and not comprehensive. Accordingly, there are areas within Newbigin's missiology that need further development, two of which stand out.

First, Newbigin's missional engagement with modernity is based upon his analysis of its origin in the Enlightenment. It has been suggested, however, that this analysis, which is heavily indebted to Polanyi, is too simplistic and overlooks important complexity. Rejecting Newbigin's account, Hoedemaker suggests "It seems justified to regard Western Christianity and modernity as growing up together in kinship and rivalry, rather than as successive and fundamentally incompatible designs."[11] Offering a slightly different perspective, Walls observes "There was a Christian appropriation of the Enlightenment which was not all a betrayal of Christian faith. It was an indigenization of Christianity in Western terms."[12] Despite Newbigin's acknowledgement that there was good to be found in the Enlightenment, his presentation of it is overwhelmingly negative. He describes Enlightenment epistemology, beginning with Descartes, as "a small-scale repetition of the Fall."[13] To take the church's missionary engagement with modern culture beyond Newbigin's important pioneering work requires a more nuanced

---

10. Cited by Wainwright, *Lesslie Newbigin*, 390.
11. Hoedemaker, "Rival Conceptions," 21.
12. Walls, "Enlightenment," 150.
13. Newbigin, *Truth To Tell*, 27.

diagnosis of the Enlightenment and the current intellectual landscape. It will also require engagement with modernity's own evolution into late- or post-modernity. This remains one of the contemporary church's greatest missionary challenges.[14]

Second, one of Newbigin's great gifts to the church was his promotion of a self-critical awareness concerning Western plausibility structures and his call for the church to interpret culture in the light of revelation, rather than vice versa. Newbigin had the privilege of being a citizen of two diverse cultures. This enabled him to examine Western culture with both the deep understanding of one indigenous to this culture, and with the critical scrutiny of a cultural outsider. Nonetheless, in criticism of Newbigin's mission to modernity, "The reviewer of 'Foolishness to the Greeks' in *Theology* says that the attempt to criticize our culture in the light of 'The Bible' (his quotation marks) is like pretending to move a bus while you are sitting in it."[15] Newbigin acknowledges elsewhere that "It is a serious point."[16] Despite the fact that I too am a Westerner, sitting on the same bus, it is clear to me that Newbigin had an important cultural blindspot, and one he was not unaware of. He reflects:

> I was taking a group of village teachers through St. Mark's Gospel. My Tamil wasn't very good, but I was fairly confident about my theology, fresh as I was from theological college. All went well until we reached the first exorcism. Now Westminster College had not taught me much about how to cast out demons. My exposition was not very impressive. These village teachers looked at me with growing perplexity, and then one of them said: "Why are you making such heavy weather of a perfectly simple matter?," and proceeded to rattle off half a dozen cases of exorcism in his own congregation during the past few months. Of course, I could have said: 'My dear brother, if you will kindly let me arrange for you to come to Cambridge and take a proper training in modern science and then a postgraduate qualification in psychology, you will be able to understand that Freud and Jung and Co. have explained everything.' In other words, 'If you will permit me to induct you into my culture, you will see things as they really are.' But this was a Bible study, and Mark's Gospel was sitting there, saying what it does. Inwardly I had to

---

14. For indications of how such a challenge might be engaged with, see: Bauckham, *Bible and Mission*; Goheen, *A Light to the Nations*; Kirk, *The Future of Reason, Science and Faith*; Kirk and Vanhoozer, *To Stake a Claim*.

15. Newbigin, "Beyond the Familiar Myths," 2.

16. Newbigin, "Discussion Paper on Authority."

admit that he was much nearer to Mark than I was. Outwardly I
kept quiet and went on to the next passage.[17]

Newbigin's self-awareness did not mean that he could immediately escape his own cultural perspective. He remained reticent to engage in discussion of Satan or demons, and such charismata as healing, prophecy, or speaking in tongues receive little attention in his work. This is anomalous given Newbigin's biblical approach to ministry,[18] including theology, and the fact that healings, exorcisms, and the demonic are major motifs right through the New Testament. However, he is by no means unique in this regard.

The neglect of the miraculous, for example, is widespread in the Western, and particularly Protestant, church. The two primary causes for this, which are not unrelated, are the Protestant teaching on the cessation of miracles as taught by Luther and Calvin,[19] and the influence of Western cultural naturalism[20] on the church. These two influences often coalesce in the writings of biblical scholars such as Bultmann, who famously said, "It is impossible to use electric light and the wireless and to avail ourselves of modern medical and surgical discoveries, and at the same time to believe in the New Testament world of spirits and miracles."[21] In this view, says Boyd "miracles and modernity are mutually exclusive."[22] Or, as Burton Mack succinctly puts it, "Scholars and miracles don't mix well."[23] Of course, the word 'scholars' would have to be qualified to mean academics inducted into the naturalistic worldview of modern Western culture. Newbigin recognized the cultural blind-spot and rejoiced that the Western church's sight was starting to be restored. "I am happy," he writes, "that the long failure of Christendom to take seriously all that the New Testament so plainly teaches

---

17. Newbigin, *Christian Faith in a Secularized World*.

18. Gordon, "Newbigin," 88–101.

19. See "Excursus: On the Cessation of Miracles" in Williams, *Renewal Theology*, 1:158–68.

20. Boyd and Eddy explain that the naturalistic worldview "arose out of the scientific revolution and the intellectual Enlightenment that followed. The naturalistic worldview holds that everything that happens can in principle be explained by appealing to laws of nature. Miracles, therefore, are ruled out of court" (*Lord or Legend?*, 21).

21. Rudolph Bultmann, *Kerygma and Myth*, quoted in Boyd, *Cynic, Sage, or Son of God?*, 301.

22. Boyd, *Cynic, Sage, or Son of God?*, 42.

23. Burton Mack, *A Myth of Innocence*, quoted in Boyd, *Cynic, Sage, or Son of God?*, 224.

about miracles is now being ended."[24] Explaining the origin of this failure, Newbigin continues

> I am sure this was a surrender of the gospel to culture and that we are indebted to Third World Christians who (in my experience) expect and experience as a normal part of discipleship the kind of deeds of power that nineteenth century positivists have dismissed as mythical miracle stories.[25]

Newbigin succeeded in diagnosing the situation but he did not incorporate this diagnosis into his missiological writings; he continued to omit these matters even though he acknowledged that "One-fifth of all the material in the four Gospels is concerned with the healing of physical disease."[26] A holistic and biblically-grounded missiology needs to more clearly articulate the role of miracles, healing, prophecy, and deliverance from demonic oppression than Newbigin himself achieved.

## TRINITARIAN MISSIOLOGY IN REVIEW

Fifty years ago Newbigin called for the church-in-mission to bind itself afresh to the strong name of the Trinity, by pioneering an explicitly trinitarian missiology. This book, written in response to that call, has sought to develop a systematic theological account of mission in the tradition of Lesslie Newbigin.

For the past few decades, the church has enjoyed an ecumenical consensus that mission is primarily the mission of the Triune God into which the church has been graciously incorporated. Only this recognition provides permanent validity and a substantiated justification for the ongoing mission of the church. An account of the mission of the Triune God must begin with an examination of God's Triune self-revelation, encapsulated in the doctrine of the Trinity. This doctrine is the *arché* for Christian theology, bears witness to God's triune being and action, and is the starting point and abiding context for thought. God's communal being consists in the distinct Triune Persons in perichoretic loving relation to each other. These loving relations are constitutive of the divine life such that love is recognized as being *the* life-act of God. Consequently, this personal, relational and loving

---

24. Newbigin, "Lesslie Newbigin Replies," 154. Evidence of the growing appreciation of the reality of miracles by Western scholars includes Keener's *Miracles*. See also Stafford, *Miracles*.

25. Newbigin, "Lesslie Newbigin Replies," 154.

26. Newbigin, *The Light Has Come*, 63.

God can only be known through the mode of personal relationship; God remains unknown to the onlooker or spectator. This relationship is entered into through God the Son who, in the incarnation, became poor so that by his poverty we might become rich (2 Cor 8:9). The eternal processions within the divine life provide the foundation for the temporal missions of the Son and Spirit in revelation and in God's reconciliation of the world to himself. The *telos* of creation, and the *telos* of the *missio Dei*, is as Newbigin rightly says, creaturely participation in God's glorious, Triune, loving communion. God has granted extraordinary dignity to the church, since the completion of the *missio Dei*, which includes the church's mission, is linked to the eschatological consummation of the divine trinitarian life. Although there is no necessity in his doing so, God has bound himself to the church and enlists it as a partner in the working out of his own purposes.

The *missio Dei* centers on the Father's sending of the Son and the Spirit. Mission is ingredient to the identity of the Son and the Spirit in the economy since their very activity in the world cannot be understood without reference to mission. Both in the modes of sending and being sent, God is a missionary God. This is an outworking in the economy of God's eternal Triune being, which is holy love. The inter-relation of the missions of the Son and Spirit is mutual and reciprocal; each Person can and should be viewed from the perspective of the other Person's mission. The Son's revealing and reconciling historical mission centered in his call and training of the twelve, his vicarious obedience, his teaching and healing ministry, and finally, in his death and resurrection. The ongoing mission of the exalted Christ, carried out chiefly through the missions of Spirit and church, will be completed at his return when death is finally destroyed through the resurrection of the dead and he hands over the kingdom to God the Father. Jesus is God's missionary par excellence, so his unique life is the source, model, and standard for the church's message, messengers, and mode of communication. The church's mission is patterned after Christ's death and resurrection, which reveal that faithfulness in word and deed is both costly and eternally rewarding.

At the beginning of the proper mission of the Holy Spirit, the Day of Pentecost, the nature of his mission is evident. The Spirit glorifies the Son by creating communion between people and Christ, and consequently between persons, enabling creaturely participation in the divine *koinonia*. On the day of Pentecost the Spirit constituted the church in Christ and swept her up into *his* mission. The Spirit primarily advances his mission through the church, and so elucidation of the Spirit's mission necessitates speaking of the church. The asymmetrical inter-relation between the mission of the Spirit and the mission of the church is marked by commonality and distinctiveness and must be carefully delineated. The church's centrality to the Spirit's mission involves risk, the genuine and yet 'infallible' risk of God's decision to partner with his fallible, erring, and routinely disobedient, covenant people. The church's mission is shaped by the Person of the Spirit as he imprints his personal nature upon the church and leads and vivifies her in missionary obedience. Consequently, humility, self-effacement, and other-centeredness ought to be characteristic of the missionary church.

God seeks communion with his wayward creation and establishes in Christ, by the Spirit, a living creaturely echo of that divine communion—the church. The church exists in Christ, by the Spirit, for the Father. God's mission constitutes the church and determines her being. Moreover, the church has been graciously called and enabled to participate in the divine mission. Nevertheless, it is appropriate to speak of the church as having a mission because it is subject to a distinct sending, within the *missio Dei*. As Newbigin perceived, the Holy Spirit is the main actor in church's mission, and it is also true that God has left room for genuine creaturely contribution. The significance of that contribution is proportionate to the church's experience of being actively dependent upon and animated by the Holy Spirit. The church shares in the double orientation of her faithful High Priest, Jesus Christ, toward the Father and towards the world. Originating in the mission of God and itself a sent community, the church this side of the parousia is by nature missionary. This missionary identity is central to the church's ontological and existential makeup, such that a church that abdicates its missional responsibility forfeits its own ecclesial existence. Developing an insight from Newbigin, in practical terms the church's missionary nature is expressed in intentional missionary acts, and in a missionary dimension that pervades all ecclesial life. It is in this way that the church's missionary nature can be acknowledged while avoiding the danger of reducing all church activities to their missionary utility. The church's missionary nature must always be kept before the church because Barth's warning—that the church can become "an institution for private satisfaction in concert, or a work of sterile inbreeding"[27]—remains a live danger. The scope of the church's mission encompasses the entire task for which she was sent into the world, battling evil in its many manifestations, and yet clearly centers on crossing the boundary of faith with the intent of seeing people come to faith in Christ.

---

27. Barth, *CD* IV/3.2, 833.

## LOOKING FORWARD

The theological renaissance in trinitarian thought over the past few decades has been fruitful in most areas of Christian doctrine, with mission being a curious exception. The works of Tennent and Flett, together with this present work, begin to rectify this state of affairs. The discipline of theology needs to take mission seriously within its dogmatic framework, and mission studies needs systematic theology to provide a theologically robust account of mission that is located in, and determined by, the doctrine of the Trinity. The argument of our respective works is that *Christian* missiology should by definition be understood to be *trinitarian* missiology, as Newbigin said half a century ago. This work is offered in the modest hope that, in some measure, it might assist the missionary church to think through the theology of mission in a trinitarian manner. This is, I contend, essential in order for the church to successfully rise to the missionary challenges posed, in particular, by expansionist Islam and post-Christian secular humanism.

This monograph has been necessarily broad in scope in order to elucidate the central features of the mission of the Triune God. Nevertheless, this study constitutes a first step in constructing a thorough and comprehensive trinitarian missiology. What remains to be done, and the challenge continually to be taken up by the church, is to trace the implications of a trinitarian missiology for the ever-changing cultural context. Of particular importance in our own time is the challenge of Christianity's relation to other religions, the development of new mission strategies in the increasingly post-Christian West, and the ever-present challenge of articulating the gospel in ways accessible to our own age. Newbigin himself continually attempted to take up such challenges and so set an example for the church to follow.

## THE TRINITARIAN GOSPEL[28]

By way of a conclusion, let me take up once more Newbigin's claim that "the doctrine of the Trinity . . . is the necessary starting point of preaching."[29] I want to show, in particular, the importance of this claim for the church's mission of evangelism and thus to emphasize, in appreciative mode, the importance of Newbigin's insight. Preaching should not begin, Newbigin avers, by explaining the rich depths of trinitarian theologoumena, but rather with the truth represented by the doctrine of the Trinity concerning the being

---

28. My article, Dodds, "Newbigin's Trinitarian Missiology," contains an earlier version of what follows.

29. Newbigin, *Trinitarian Doctrine*, 35.

and action of God. Newbigin explains this claim, saying "one cannot preach Jesus even in the simplest terms without preaching him as the Son. His revelation of God is the revelation of 'an only begotten from the Father', and you cannot preach him without speaking of the Father and Son."[30] Newbigin goes on to stress the vital role of the Holy Spirit in the divine economy and particularly in evangelism. Evangelism begins by telling the story of God's self-presentation as Father, Son and Spirit. Newbigin's claim may be broken down into two related claims: the Triune nature of God is irreducibly bound up with the substance of the gospel, and evangelism begins with bearing witness to the Triune God.[31] Using the resources of trinitarian theology, how might these bold claims be evaluated?

## *The Gospel and the Doctrine of the Trinity*

*Prima facie*, Newbigin appears to be in broad agreement with modern trinitarian theological scholarship in affirming that the Triune nature of God is irreducibly related to the substance of the gospel. Early in the twentieth century, Adolf Schlatter said that "the Trinitarian name of God is the Christian Gospel."[32] Toward the end of that century Carl Braaten wrote, "The doctrine of the Trinity is the solid declaration of the gospel of Jesus Christ."[33] In similar vein, Robert Jenson says that the phrase 'Father, Son, and Holy Spirit' is a condensed telling of the gospel[34] while Colin Gunton describes the doctrine of the Trinity "as encapsulating the heart of the Christian Gospel."[35] Why is there this broad agreement that God's Triune nature is central to the nature of the gospel? The answer, as Newbigin suggests, is that the gospel concerns the actions of the Triune God. To be sure, the gospel centers on the life, death and resurrection of Jesus, but this same gospel does not describe Jesus apart from the Father and the Spirit.

---

30. Ibid., 36.

31. In a recent publication, Andreas J. Köstenberger also argues for a fundamental connection between the Trinity and mission in Johannine theology. "Rather than being one of several aspects or implications of John's trinitarian theology, mission is shown to be the nexus and focal point of his presentation of the Father, the Son, and the Spirit, individually and in relation to one another. Hence it can truly be said, not only that John's mission theology is trinitarian (which in and of itself is a significant statement), but that his trinitarian teaching is part of his mission theology—a truly revolutionary insight" (*A Theology*, 545).

32. Adolf Schlatter quoted in Barth, *CD* I/1, 302.

33. Braaten, "The Triune God," 424.

34. Jenson, *Systematic Theology*, 1:46.

35. Gunton, *The Promise*, 31.

The crucial issue at stake in evangelism is summed up in the question 'Who is Jesus?' The answer the evangelists give us is that Jesus is the only begotten Son of the Father. Pannenberg observes "The title 'Son' reflects Jesus' message of the Father. The reflection of the content of the message falls on his person."[36] The gospel declares that God, the Father of all humanity (Eph 3: 14–15; 4:6), loves his wayward children with a strong and persistent love that is undeterred by willful rebellion. From eternity, the Father and Son, with the Holy Spirit, have given and received love to and from each other. In the Father's sending of the Son by the Spirit, the Triune God continues to live his eternal life of perichoretic love in created space and time. In this sending, God the Father demonstrates that the love amongst the Triune Persons is so expansive that all humanity is invited to participate in the sonship of Jesus and to become adopted children of God. As children of God, humans can have security in the love of their heavenly Father, confidence when approaching God in prayer, and intimacy in relating to the Sovereign Creator and Ruler of all as Abba. Pannenberg is right to suggest that the content of the gospel is reflected in Jesus' person as the Son. Thus, the answer to the crucial question in evangelism is, Jesus is the beloved Son, the only begotten of the Father.

Jesus cannot rightly be identified without describing the Triune nature of God. This is because, says Moltmann, "The New Testament talks about God by proclaiming in narrative the relationships of the Father, the Son and the Spirit."[37] Although the gospel is the gospel of Jesus Christ, this gospel begins with the Father sending the Son who is conceived by the Holy Spirit. Stepping back from a close reading of the gospel narrative in order to discern the broader theological landscape, Gunton says, "The gospel is that the Father interrelates with his world by means of the frail humanity of his Son, and by his Spirit enables anticipations in the present of the promised perfection of the creation."[38] The Son was sent by the Father and lived to carry out his will. The beginning of the Son's mission—his conception and empowerment at baptism, and the climax of his mission—his atoning death and resurrection, were all accomplished in and by the Holy Spirit.[39] That is why Athanasius described the doctrine of the Trinity as "the summary (*skopos*) of our faith."[40] In what way does the doctrine of the Trinity summa-

36. Pannenberg, *Systematic Theology*, 1:309.
37. Moltmann, *The Trinity and the Kingdom*, 64, emphasis removed.
38. Gunton, *The Promise*, 72.
39. See Luke 1:35 (conception), Luke 3:21–23, 4:14 (empowerment), Heb 9:14 (atonement), and Rom 1:4; 8:11 (resurrection).
40. Athanasius, *De Decretis* 31, quoted in Anatolios, "The Immediately Triune God," 166.

rize the Christian faith? Daugherty explains that the doctrine of the Trinity "could be called the theological statement of the gospel; it is the gospel explained with reference to the being of God."[41] Consequently, Brunner is gravely mistaken when he states "the doctrine of the Trinity did not form part of the early Christian—New Testament—message, nor has it ever been a central article of faith in the religious life of the Christian Church as a whole."[42] The gospel of the Triune God is and always has been the central article of the church's faith.

The doctrine of the Trinity not only identifies this Triune God as the author of and chief actor in the drama of salvation, but goes further to say that this Triune God revealed in the gospel events *is* actually who God is in and of himself. The gospel reveals a God who loves (Rom 5:8), and "the doctrine of the Trinity is the teaching that God is love, not only towards us, but in his deepest and eternal being."[43] In other words, the immanent and economic trinities so truly correspond that God's loving actions in the gospel story are an economic echo of the eternal trinitarian love that God is. T. F. Torrance says,

> If the economic or evangelical Trinity and the ontological or theological Trinity were disparate this would bring into question whether *God himself* was the actual content of his revelation, and whether *God himself* was really in Jesus Christ reconciling the world to himself. That is the evangelical and epistemological significance of the *homoousion* . . . formulated by the Council of Nicaea in AD 325 . . . The trinitarian message of the Gospel tells us that . . . in Jesus Christ and in the Holy Spirit we really have to do with the *Lord God himself* as our Savior.[44]

The doctrine of the immanent or ontological Trinity safeguards the fact that the gospel *is* in fact the good news, that God really does love us because God *is* love. In other words, the doctrine of the Trinity ontologically underpins the truths of the gospel. Furthermore, this doctrine is also rooted in the events of the gospel in which God reveals himself as Father, Son and Spirit. Therefore, the doctrine of the Trinity is not speculation projected onto the divine being. "Trinitarian theology is not theory;" on the contrary, "it is an account of God's *being* which is tied to his *action*, and that action centers on a gospel rooted in the life, suffering and resurrection of Jesus."[45]

41. Daugherty, "*Missio Dei*," 162.
42. Brunner, *Dogmatics*, 1:205.
43. Gunton, *Father, Son and Holy Spirit*, 18.
44. Torrance, *The Christian Doctrine of God*, 7–8, emphasis original.
45. Gunton, *Father, Son and Holy Spirit*, xiv, emphasis added.

In this dialectic of divine being and action, is it appropriate to go as far as saying that the Christian gospel *is* the Triune God?

The gospel declares that the Triune God has judged all humanity in Christ out of his love for them. The 'No' of God has been spoken within an all-encompassing 'Yes', so that all humanity has been judged and forgiven and invited to participate in the loving relations that God is. Concerning the divine 'Yes' spoken to humanity, Barth says it is Jesus Christ who "pronounces a single and unambiguous Yes." Barth then goes further, saying of Jesus Christ, "He is this Yes, and therefore not merely its proponent, sign, symbol or cypher."[46] The gospel is not merely what Jesus pronounces, effects or enacts, but in his Person he is the gospel. Following Barth, T. F. Torrance argues that the atoning reconciliation and the death of death that Jesus achieves on behalf of all humanity does not occur externally from his Person. Rather, "atoning reconciliation," and one might add, the death of death, "takes place within the personal Being of the Mediator."[47] However, the atonement itself does not constitute the heart of the gospel. Torrance explains, "it is not the atonement that constitutes the goal and end of that integrated movement of reconciliation but union with God."[48] God became human in order to adopt all humanity into the divine life, an adoption that the ancient Eastern Fathers called *theōsis* or *theopoiēsis*. The good news is that the Triune God, Creator, and Redeemer, loves humanity even in its obstinate and defiant rebellion, and by way of the atoning reconciliation accomplished in and by the Mediator Jesus Christ; and by the Holy Spirit who unites us to this Mediator, humanity is beckoned into fellowship with God. The Triune God *is* the gospel, for in Jesus who is Emmanuel humanity discovers not only that God is with us, but that God is for us because this is God's nature. The gospel events are only good news inasmuch as they describe the actions of this God who is himself the gospel.

Nevertheless, it would be a false dichotomy to suggest that God is the gospel apart from the divine actions that the gospel describes. There is no division between divine being and act, for as the Psalmist addresses God, "You are good and do good."[49] It is of course by God's good deeds that God's being as the Triune God who is *good* is revealed. Describing the unity of divine being and act, Barth says, "God is who He is in His works . . . in Himself He is not another than He is in His works."[50] God's self-revelation is reliable

---

46. Barth, *CD* IV/3.2, 797.
47. Torrance, *The Mediation of Christ*, 73.
48. Ibid., 77.
49. Ps 119:68.
50. Barth, *CD* II/1, 260.

because God is truthful, so "we know that he is giving us himself and not an external manifestation whose internal structuring may be different."[51] The doctrine of the Trinity is indeed irreducibly bound to the substance of the gospel.

## Evangelism Begins With Bearing Witness to the Triune God

What of the second claim; that evangelism begins with bearing witness to the Triune God? Evangelism by definition is a communication of the gospel, and the gospel is both the being and the saving activity of the Triune God in the life, death, and resurrection of Jesus Christ. That is why Bavinck says "In the doctrine of the Trinity beats the heart of the whole revelation of God for the redemption of mankind."[52] Athanasius rightly called the doctrine of the Trinity 'the summary of our faith' but Bavinck adds to that, calling it the "kernel of the Christian faith, the root of all dogmas, the substance of the new covenant."[53] All Christian truths that one would seek to communicate in evangelism, such as creation, fall, salvation, eschatology and so on derive from the doctrine of the Trinity, for the works of God can only be rightly understood in the light of the nature and being of God. That is why Khaled Anatolios says, "Trinitarian doctrine is the hermeneutical key to Christian faith."[54] Therefore, evangelism must describe the Triune God of the gospel, communicating the truths contained within the doctrine of the Trinity without discussing the (important) obscurities of its theologoumena (see chapter 3). These truths, summarized in the patristic term *homoousion*, crucially include the fact that God actually *is* from and to all eternity the loving God revealed in the gospel, that the gospel is a gospel of salvation because *God* is its author, and that the Triune God who is love has so acted in the events of the gospel so that all may participate in the divine nature.

In *Trinitarian Doctrine* Newbigin observes,

> The vehemence of the doctrinal struggles which centered on the formulation of the trinitarian doctrine, and especially on the question of the relation of the Son to the Father, is evidence of the centrality of this issue for the whole Christian witness to the pagan world of that time.[55]

---

51. Gunton, *Father, Son and Holy Spirit*, 42.
52. Herman Bavinck quoted in Barth, *CD* I/1, 302.
53. Ibid., 302.
54. Anatolios, "The Immediately Triune God," 166.
55. Newbigin, *Trinitarian Doctrine*, 35.

The missiological significance of the doctrine of the Trinity, with its central Christological and pneumatological aspects, was clearly enormous during the patristic era. Missiologist Aasulv Lande acknowledges this fact, but proceeds to argue that the doctrine of the Trinity is inescapably culture-bound to its Greco-Roman context and that it should remain in its socio-cultural past. Lande believes that for our purposes in the twenty-first century the doctrine of the Trinity is irrelevant.[56] Lande is clearly not alone is this summation. The dismissal of the doctrine of the Trinity found earlier expression in Immanuel Kant's well-known claim that it was irrelevant whether a person worshipped three or ten persons, because "it is impossible to extract from this difference any different rules for practical living."[57] Against both Lande and Kant, it must be affirmed that God's being is not irrelevant to practical living, but is of the utmost importance. Fortunately, modern theology has generally rejected the sentiment expressed by Kant and Lande, and along with Newbigin, it is increasingly attentive the practical implications of the doctrine of the Trinity. A recent example is provided by Gary Simpson who argues that the doctrine of the Trinity possesses intrinsic relevance for missiology: "To my mind, it is not mere coincidence that we are developing a consensus regarding the dearth of missional imagination at the congregational level at the same time that some are deploring the non-trinitarian character of Christian theology, life, and practice." Simpson then sets out to investigate "the link between 'no Trinity' and 'no mission.'"[58] Given the relation between the doctrine of the Trinity and the gospel already sketched, a demise in the belief in and confession of the Triune God will inexorably lead to a partial and faulty understanding of the gospel. This is because, as Newbigin understood, the doctrine of the Trinity is built firstly on a Christological foundation, and so it theologically safeguards the church's central affirmation that Jesus is the beloved and only begotten Son who reveals God by showing us his love for and obedience to the Father.[59] Misunderstanding this good news, which contains within itself missional momentum, will result in a corresponding decline in missional consciousness and practice. By contrast, belief in *the* gospel will naturally lead to evangelistic action because the gospel testifies that Jesus is Lord and that in his resurrection from the dead God's new creation has begun. As such, the good news pertains to all people and so is to be preached to all the nations. Such evangelistic preaching will bear witness to the saving action

---

56. Lande, "Trinitarian Missiology."
57. Quoted in Moltmann, *The Trinity and the Kingdom*, 6.
58. Simpson, "No Trinity," 265.
59. Newbigin, *Trinitarian Doctrine*, 39.

of God the Father in sending his Son and Spirit to reveal who God is and to reconcile humanity back to God.

I have suggested that Newbigin's claim that 'the doctrine of the Trinity is the necessary starting point of preaching' involves two related claims. With the aid of modern trinitarian theology, I have assessed the claims that the Triune nature of God is irreducibly bound up with the substance of the gospel, and that evangelism begins with bearing witness to the Triune God. In the course of this discussion I have attempted to verify these claims and to deepen these insights in ways Newbigin himself, due to his vocational commitments, did not have time to achieve. In his being and action, the Triune God is the gospel, and so evangelism necessarily begins by bearing witness to this God whose being is in loving communion. More broadly, I hope to have demonstrated the necessity of missiology being thoroughly trinitarian, and the abiding significance of Newbigin's writings for continued missiological reflection, all in the service of the church carrying out her mission within the mission of the Triune God.

# Bibliography

Adams, Graham. *Christ and the Other: In Dialogue with Hick and Newbigin.* Farnham, UK: Ashgate, 2013.
Allen, Roland. *Missionary Methods: St. Paul's or Ours, A Study of the Church in the Four Provinces.* Grand Rapids: Eerdmans, 1962.
———. *The Spontaneous Expansion of the Church: And the Causes That Hinder It.* Grand Rapids: Eerdmans, 1962.
Althaus, Paul. *The Theology of Martin Luther.* Translated by Robert C. Schultz. Philadelphia: Fortress, 1966.
Anatolios, Khaled. "The Immediately Triune God: A Patristic Response to Schleiermacher." *Pro Ecclesia* 10/2 (2001) 159–78.
Anderson, Allan. *Spreading Fires: The Missionary Nature of Early Pentecostalism.* Maryknoll, NY: Orbis, 2007.
Anderson, Gerald H. "Modernity and the Everlasting Gospel: Assessing the Newbigin Thesis." *IBMR* 12/4 (1988) 1.
Arminius, James. *The Works of James Arminius: Volume 2.* Translated by James and William Nichols. London ed. Whitefish, MT: Kessinger, 2006.
Arnold, Clinton E. *Powers of Darkness: Principalities and Powers in Paul's Letters.* Downers Grove, IL: InterVarsity, 1992.
———. *Spiritual Warfare: What Does the Bible Really Teach?* London: Harper Collins, 1997.
Arthur, Eddie. "*Missio Dei* and the Mission of the Church." In *International Development from a Kingdom Perspective*, edited by James Butare-Kiyovu, 49–66. Pasadena, CA: William Carey International University Press, 2010. http://www.wycliffe.net/missiology?id=3960.
Aulén, Gustaf. *Christus Victor: An Historical Study of the Three Main Types of the Idea of the Atonement.* Translated by A. G. Hiebert. London: SPCK, 1961.
———. *The Faith of the Christian Church.* Translated by Eric. H. Wahlstrom. Philadelphia: Fortress, 1960.
Aune, David E. "Apocalypticism." In *Dictionary of Paul and His Letters*, edited by Gerald F. Hawthorne and Ralph P. Martin, 25–53. Downers Grove, IL: InterVarsity, 1993.
———. *Revelation 1–5.* Word Biblical Commentary 52A. Nashville: Thomas Nelson, 1997.
Badcock, Gary D. *Light of Truth and Fire of Love: A Theology of the Holy Spirit.* Grand Rapids: Eerdmans, 1997.

Barclay, John M. G. "Paul and the Subversive Power of the Unconditioned Gift." De Carle Open Lecture, University of Otago, Dunedin, March 30, 2010.

Barclay, William. *The Letters of John and Jude*. Daily Study Bible 15. Edinburgh: Saint Andrew, 1958.

Barrett, C. K. *The Second Epistle to the Corinthians*. New York: Harper & Row, 1973.

Barth, Karl. *Church Dogmatics*. Edited and translated by Geoffrey W. Bromiley and Thomas F. Torrance. 13 vols. Edinburgh: T. & T. Clark, 1957–75.

———. *The Göttingen Dogmatics: Instruction in the Christian Religion, Volume One*. Edited by Hannelotte Reiffen. Translated by Geoffrey W. Bromiley. Grand Rapids: Eerdmans, 1991.

———. *The Humanity of God*. Translated by John Newton Thomas and Thomas Wieser. London: Collins, 1967.

Barth, Markus. *Ephesians 1–3: A New Translation with Introduction and Commentary*. The Anchor Bible 34. New York: Doubleday, 1974.

Basil. *On the Holy Spirit*. Translated by David Anderson. Crestwood, NY: St. Vladimir's Seminary Press, 1980.

Bauckham, Richard. *Bible and Mission: Christian Witness in a Postmodern World*. Grand Rapids: Baker Academic, 2004.

BCC Study Commission. *The Forgotten Trinity Volume 1: The Report of the BCC Study Commission on Trinitarian Doctrine Today*. London: BCC, 1989.

———. *The Forgotten Trinity Volume 2: A Study Guide on Issues Contained in the Report of the BCC Study Commission on Trinitarian Doctrine Today*. London: BCC, 1989.

———. *The Forgotten Trinity Volume 3: A Selection of Papers presented to the BCC Study Commission on Trinitarian Doctrine Today*. Edited by Alasdair I. C. Heron. London: BCC, 1991.

Beasley-Murray, George R. *John*. Word Biblical Commentary 36. Waco, TX: Word, 1987.

Bellinger, Charles K. *The Trinitarian Self: The Key to the Puzzle of Violence*. Eugene, OR: Pickwick, 2008.

Berkouwer, G. C. *The Providence of God*. Translated by Lewis Smedes. Grand Rapids: Eerdmans, 1952.

Bevans, Stephen B. "God Inside Out: Toward a Missionary Theology of the Holy Spirit." *IBMR* 22/2 (1998) 102–5.

———. *John Oman and His Doctrine of God*. Cambridge: Cambridge University Press, 1992.

———. "Wisdom From the Margins: Systematic Theology and the Missiological Imagination." *CTSA Proceedings* 56 (2001) 21–42.

Blauw, Johannes. *The Missionary Nature of the Church: A Survey of the Biblical Theology of Mission*. Guildford, UK: Lutterworth, 1962.

Bloesch, Donald G. *Essentials of Evangelical Theology*. Vol. 1, *God, Authority and Salvation*. Peabody, MA: Prince, 2001.

Bonhoeffer, Dietrich. *Letters and Papers from Prison*. Edited by Eberhard Bethge. Enlarged ed. London: SCM, 1971.

Bosch, David J. *Transforming Mission: Paradigm Shifts in Theology of Mission*. Maryknoll, NY: Orbis, 1991.

Boyd, Gregory A. *Cynic, Sage, or Son of God? Recovering the Real Jesus in an Age of Revisionist Replies*. Wheaton, IL: Victor, 1995.

———. *God At War: The Bible and Spiritual Conflict.* Downers Grove, IL: InterVarsity, 1997.

———. *The God of the Possible: A Biblical Introduction to the Open View of God.* Grand Rapids: Baker, 2000.

———. *Satan and the Problem of Evil: Constructing a Trinitarian Warfare Theodicy.* Downers Grove, IL: InterVarsity, 2001

Boyd, Gregory A., and Paul Rhodes Eddy. *Across the Spectrum: Understanding Issues in Evangelical Theology.* Grand Rapids: Baker, 2002.

———. *Lord or Legend? Wrestling with the Jesus Dilemma.* Grand Rapids: Baker, 2007.

Braaten, Carl E. *The Flaming Center: A Theology of the Christian Mission.* Philadelphia: Fortress, 1977.

———. "The Triune God: The Source and Model of Christian Unity and Mission." *Missiology: An International Review* 18/4 (1990) 415–27.

Bria, Ion, ed. *Go Forth In Peace: Orthodox Perspectives on Mission.* Geneva: WCC, 1986.

Brown, Raymond E. *The Gospel According to John I-XII: A New Translation and Commentary.* The Anchor Bible 29. New York: Doubleday, 1966.

Bruner, F. Dale. *Matthew: A Commentary.* Vol. 1, *The Christbook.* Rev. ed. Grand Rapids: Eerdmans, 2004.

———. "The Son is God Inside Out: A Response to Stephen B. Bevans, SVD." *IBMR* 22/2 (1998) 106, 108.

Brunner, Emil. *Dogmatics.* 3 vols. Translated by Olive Wyon. Philadelphia: Westminster, 1950–62.

Buber, Martin. *I and Thou.* Translated by Ronald Gregor Smith. New York: Scribners, 1958.

Calvin, John. *Commentary on Corinthians.* Vol. 2. http://153.106.5.3/ccel/calvin/calcom 40.i.iii.html.

———. *Commentary on John.* Vol. 1. http://www.ccel.org/ccel/calvin/calcom34.i.html.

———. *Institutes of the Christian Religion.* Edited by John T. McNeill. Translated by Ford Lewis Battles. Philadelphia: Westminster, 1960.

Carr, Wesley. "Towards a Contemporary Theology of the Holy Spirit." *Scottish Journal of Theology* 28 (1975) 501–16.

Carson, D. A. *The Gospel According to John.* The Pillar New Testament Commentary. Leicester: Apollos, 1991.

Cartwright, Michael G. "Being Sent: Witness." In *The Blackwell Companion to Christian Ethics,* edited by Stanley Hauerwas and Samuel Wells, 481–94. Malden, MA: Blackwell, 2004.

Chan, Simon. "The Mission of the Trinity." *Christianity Today* (June 2007) 48–51.

Chaplin, Jonathan, et al. *Introduction to a Christian Worldview.* Unpublished manual for Open Christian College course on Christian Worldview. 1986.

Childs, Brevard S. *Biblical Theology: A Proposal.* Minneapolis: Fortress, 2002.

Clouser, Roy. *The Myth of Religious Neutrality.* Notre Dame: University of Notre Dame Press, 1991.

Cochrane, Charles N. *Christianity and Classical Culture: A Study of Thought and Action from Augustus to Augustine.* London: Oxford University Press, 1944.

Coffey, David M. "A Proper Mission of the Holy Spirit." *Theological Studies* 47 (1986) 227–50.

Cook, Michael L. *Trinitarian Christology: The Power that Sets us Free.* Mahwah, NJ: Paulist, 2010.

Cox, Harvey. *The Secular City: Secularisation and Urbanisation in Theological Perspective.* New York: Macmillan, 1966.
Cronshaw, Darren. "Saving Souls and Listening Hearts: Implications for Missional Leaders from Richard Rohr's *Immortal Diamond*." *Colloquium* 46/2 (2014) 242–54.
Curtis, Olin A. *The Christian Faith: Personally Given in a System of Doctrine.* Grand Rapids: Kregel, 1956.
CWME. "Mission and Evangelism: An Ecumenical Affirmation (MEEA)." In *"You are the light of the world": Statements on Mission by the World Council of Churches, 1980–2005*, edited by Jacques Matthey, 4–38. Geneva: WCC, 2005.
———. "Towards Common Witness to Christ Today: Mission and Visible Unity of the Church—Study Paper on Theme 8 of the Edinburgh 2010 Study Process." *IRM* 99/390 (2010) 86–106.
Dalferth, Ingolf U. "The Eschatological Roots of the Doctrine of the Trinity." In *Trinitarian Theology Today: Essays on Divine Being and Act*, edited by Christoph Schwöbel, 147–70. Edinburgh: T. & T. Clark, 1995.
Daugherty, Kevin. "*Missio Dei*: The Trinity and Christian Missions." *Evangelical Review of Theology* 31/2 (2007) 151–68.
Del Colle, Ralph. *Christ and the Spirit: Spirit-Christology in Trinitarian Perspective.* Oxford: Oxford University Press, 1994.
Dodds, Adam. "The Abrahamic Faiths? Continuity and Discontinuity in Christian and Islamic Doctrine." *Evangelical Quarterly* 81/3 (2009) 230–53. http://media.wix.com/ugd/546570_647340426c6547daaec0691beb9e08ba.pdf.
———. "The Centrality of the Church's Missionary Nature: Theological Reflections and Practical Implications." *Missiology: An International Review* 40/4 (2012) 393–407.
———. "The Mission of the Spirit and the Mission the Church: Towards a Trinitarian Missiology." *Evangelical Review of Theology* 35/3 (2011) 209–26.
———. "Newbigin's Trinitarian Missiology: The Doctrine of the Trinity as Good News for Western Culture." *IRM* 99/390 (2010) 69–85.
———. "Regeneration and Resistible Grace: A Synergistic Proposal." *Evangelical Quarterly* 83/1 (2011) 29–48.
Donovan, Vincent J. *Christianity Rediscovered: An Epistle from the Masai.* London: SCM, 1978.
Dunn, James D. G. *The Theology of Paul the Apostle.* Grand Rapids: Eerdmans, 1998.
Duraisingh, Christopher. "From Church-shaped Mission to Mission-shaped Church." *Anglican Theological Review* 92/1 (2010) 7–28.
Durie, Mark. *Which God? Jesus, Holy Spirit, God in Christianity and Islam.* 2nd ed. N.p.: Deror, 2014.
Edgar, Brian. *The Message of the Trinity: Life in God.* Leicester: InterVarsity, 2004.
Emery, Gilles. *The Trinitarian Theology of Saint Thomas Aquinas.* Translated by Francesca Aran Murphy. Oxford: Oxford University Press, 2007.
Escobar, Samuel. *The New Global Mission: The Gospel From Everywhere to Everyone.* Downers Grove, IL: InterVarsity, 2003.
Evans, C. Stephen. "Salvation, Sin, and Human Freedom in Kierkegaard." In *The Grace of God and the Will of Man*, edited by Clark H. Pinnock, 181–89. Minneapolis: Bethany, 1989.
Feddes, David. *Missional Apologetics: Cultural Diagnosis and Gospel Plausibility in C. S. Lewis and Lesslie Newbigin.* Monee, IL: Christian Leaders, 2012.

Fee, Gordon D. *The First Epistle to the Corinthians*. Grand Rapids: Eerdmans: 1987.

———. *Paul, the Spirit and the People of God*. Peabody, MA: Hendrickson, 1997.

Fiddes, Paul S. *Participating in God: A Pastoral Doctrine of the Trinity*. London: Darton, Longman & Todd, 2000.

Fitch, David E., and Geoffrey Holsclaw. "Mission amid Empire: Relating Trinity, Mission, and Political Formation." *Missiology: An International Review* 41/4 (2013) 389–401.

Flett, John. "*Missio Dei*: A Trinitarian Envisioning of a Non-Trinitarian Theme." *Missiology: An International Review* 37/1 (2009) 5–18.

———. *The Witness of God: The Trinity, Missio Dei, Karl Barth, and the Nature of Christian Community*. Grand Rapids: Eerdmans, 2010.

———. "'Who is Jesus Christ?' The Necessary Missionary Form of the Confession of the Trinity." In *Theology in Missionary Perspective: Lesslie Newbigin's Legacy*, edited by Mark T. B. Laing and Paul Weston, 260–76. Eugene, OR: Pickwick, 2012.

Forster, Roger T., and V. Paul Marston. *God's Strategy in Human History: God's Sovereignty and Man's Responsibility*. Minneapolis: Bethany, 1973.

Forsyth, P. T. *The Soul of Prayer*. Carlisle: Paternoster, 1998.

Foust, Thomas F., et al., eds. *A Scandalous Prophet: The Way of Mission after Newbigin*. Grand Rapids: Eerdmans, 2002.

Fretheim, Terence E. "Divine Dependence Upon the Human: An Old Testament Perspective." *Ex Auditu* 13 (1997) 1–13.

———. *The Suffering of God: An Old Testament Perspective*. Philadelphia: Fortress, 1984.

Gay, Peter. *The Enlightenment: An Interpretation*. Vol. 2, *The Science of Freedom*. New York: Alfred A. Knopf, 1969.

Gelwick, Richard. "Christian Faith in a Pluralist Society." *Tradition and Discovery (The Polanyi Society)* 27/2 (2000) 39–45.

George, Samuel. *The Gospel as Public Truth: An Indian Multi-Religious Perspective on Lesslie Newbigin*. New Delhi: Christian World, 2015.

George, Timothy. *Is the Father of Jesus the God of Muhammad?* Grand Rapids: Zondervan, 2002.

Goheen, Michael W. "'As the Father Has Sent Me, I Am Sending You': J. E. Lesslie Newbigin's Missionary Ecclesiology." PhD diss., University of Utrecht, 2000. http://igitur-archive.library.uu.nl/dissertations/1947080/full.pdf.

———. "The Finality of Christ and a Missionary Encounter with Religious Pluralism: Newbigin's Missiological Approach." In *Theology in Missionary Perspective: Lesslie Newbigin's Legacy*, edited by Mark T. B. Laing and Paul Weston, 244–59. Eugene, OR: Pickwick, 2012.

———. *A Light to the Nations: The Missional Church and the Biblical Story*. Grand Rapids: Baker Academic, 2011.

———. "The Missional Calling of Believers in the World: Lesslie Newbigin's Contribution." In *A Scandalous Prophet: The Way of Mission After Newbigin*, edited by Thomas F. Foust et al., 37–54. Grand Rapids: Eerdmans, 2002.

Goheen, Michael W., and Craig G. Bartholomew. *Living at the Crossroads: An Introduction to Christian Worldview*. Grand Rapids: Baker Academic, 2008.

Gordon, Kenneth D. "Newbigin as Preacher and Exegete." In *Theology in Missionary Perspective: Lesslie Newbigin's Legacy*, edited by Mark T. B. Laing and Paul Weston, 88–101. Eugene, OR: Pickwick, 2012.

Greene, Colin J. D. "Trinitarian Tradition and the Cultural Collapse of Late Modernity." In *A Scandalous Prophet: The Way of Mission After Newbigin*, edited by Thomas F. Foust et al., 65–72. Grand Rapids: Eerdmans, 2002.

Grenz, Stanley J. *The Social God and the Relational Self: A Trinitarian Theology of the Imago Dei*. Philadelphia: Westminster John Knox, 2001.

Guder, Darrell L. "Incarnation and the Church's Evangelistic Mission." *IRM* 83/330 (1994) 417–28.

Gunton, Colin E. *The Christian Faith: An Introduction to Christian Doctrine*. Oxford: Blackwell, 2002.

———. *Enlightenment and Alienation: An Essay Towards a Trinitarian Theology*. Grand Rapids: Eerdmans, 1985.

———. *Father, Son and Holy Spirit: Essays Towards A Fully Trinitarian Theology*. London: T. & T. Clark, 2003.

———. *The Promise of Trinitarian Theology*. 2nd ed. Edinburgh: T. & T. Clark, 1997.

———. *The Triune Creator: A Historical and Systematic Study*. Edinburgh: Edinburgh University Press, 1998.

Habets, Myk. *The Anointed Son: A Trinitarian Spirit Christology*. Eugene, OR: Pickwick, 2010.

Hart, Trevor. "Tradition, Authority, and a Christian Approach to the Bible as Scripture." In *Between Two Horizons: Spanning New Testament Studies and Systematic Theology*, edited by Joel B. Green and Max Turner, 183–204. Grand Rapids: Eerdmans, 2000.

Hasker, William. "Foreknowledge and Necessity." *Faith and Philosophy* 2/2 (April 1985) 121–57.

———. *God, Time and Knowledge*. Ithaca, NY: Cornell University Press, 1998.

———. *Providence, Evil, and the Openness of God*. New York: Routledge, 2004.

Hauerwas, Stanley, and William H. Willimon. *Resident Aliens: Life in the Christian Colony*. Nashville: Abingdon, 1989.

Heim, S. Mark. *The Depth of the Riches: A Trinitarian Theology of Religious Ends*. Grand Rapids: Eerdmans, 2001.

Hill, Andrew E. "A Response to Terrence Fretheim's 'Divine Dependence Upon the Human.'" *Ex Auditu* 13 (1997) 14–16.

Hill, William J. *The Three-Personed God: The Trinity as a Mystery of Salvation*. Washington, DC: Catholic University of America Press, 1982.

Hodgson, Leonard. *The Doctrine of the Trinity*. Digswell Place, UK: James Nisbet, 1943.

Hoedemaker, L. A. (Bert). "The People of God and the Ends of the Earth." In *Missiology: An Ecumenical Introduction—Texts and Contents of Global Christianity*, edited by F. J. Verstraelen et al., 157–71. Grand Rapids: Eerdmans, 1995.

———. Review of *The Open Secret: Sketches for a Missionary Theology*, by Lesslie Newbigin. *IRM* 68 (1979) 455–57.

———. "Rival Conceptions of Global Christianity: Mission and Modernity, Then and Now." In *A Scandalous Prophet: The Way of Mission After Newbigin*, edited by Thomas F. Foust et al., 13–22. Grand Rapids: Eerdmans, 2002.

Hong, Young-Gi. "Church and Mission: A Pentecostal Perspective." *IRM* 90/358 (2001) 289–308.

Hunsberger, George. "Apostle of Faith and Witness." *The Gospel and Our Culture (North America)* Special Edition (1998) 1–2.

———. *Bearing the Witness of the Spirit: Lesslie Newbigin's Theology of Cultural Plurality*. Grand Rapids: Eerdmans, 1998.

———. "The Church in the Postmodern Transition." In *A Scandalous Prophet: The Way of Mission After Newbigin*, edited by Thomas F. Foust et al., 95–106. Grand Rapids: Eerdmans, 2002.

———. "Faith and Pluralism: A Response to Richard Gelwick." *Tradition and Discovery (The Polanyi Society)* 27/3 (2000) 19–29.

———. "The Newbigin Gauntlet: Developing a Domestic Missiology for North America." *Missiology: An International Review* 19/4 (1991) 391–408.

———. "Renewing Faith During the Postmodern Transition." *The Bible in Transmission* Special Issue (1998) 10–13.

Hunsinger, George. "Election and the Trinity: Twenty-Five Theses on the Theology of Karl Barth." *Modern Theology* 24/2 (2008) 179–98.

Jacob, Sijo. *Religious Pluralism and the Finality of Christ: Christological Reflections from Lesslie Newbigin*. New Delhi: Christian World, 2016.

Jenkins, Philip. *The Next Christendom: The Coming of Global Christianity*. 3rd ed. New York: Oxford University Press, 2011.

———. *The New Faces of Christianity: Believing the Bible in the Global South*. New York: Oxford University Press, 2006.

Jenson, Robert W. *God After God: The God of the Past and the God of the Future, Seen in the Work of Karl Barth*. Indianapolis: Bobbs-Merrill, 1969.

———. *Systematic Theology*. Vol. 1, *The Triune God*. Oxford: Oxford University Press, 1997.

———. *Systematic Theology*. Vol. 2, *The Works of God*. Oxford: Oxford University Press, 1999.

———. *The Triune Identity: God According to the Gospel*. Philadelphia: Fortress, 1982.

John Paul II. *Encyclical Letter Redemptoris Missio: On the Permanent Validity of the Church's Missionary Mandate*. 1990. http://www.vatican.va/holy_father/john_paul_ii/encyclicals/documents/hf_jp-ii_enc_07121990_redemptoris-missio_en.html.

Jüngel, Eberhard. "To Tell The World About God: The Task for the Mission of the Church on the Threshold of the Third Millennium." *IRM* 89/353 (2000) 203–17.

Kalu, O. U. "Charismatic Movements." In *Dictionary of Mission Theology: Evangelical Foundations*, edited by John Corrie, 43–45. Nottingham: InterVarsity, 2007.

Keener, Craig S. *Miracles: The Credibility of the New Testament Accounts*. 2 vols. Grand Rapids: Baker Academic, 2011.

Kelly, J. N. D. *Early Christian Creeds*. New York: David McKay, 1964.

Kenneson, Philip D. "Trinitarian Missiology: Mission as Face-to-Face Encounter." In *A Scandalous Prophet: The Way of Mission After Newbigin*, edited by Thomas F. Foust et al., 76–83. Grand Rapids: Eerdmans, 2002.

Kenoly, Ron. *High Places: The Best of Ron Kenoly*. Hosanna! Music, 1997.

Keown, Mark J. *Congregational Evangelism in Philippians: The Centrality of an Appeal for Gospel Proclamation to the Fabric of Philippians*. Milton Keynes: Paternoster, 2008.

Keskitalo, Jukka. "Church and Mission: Lesslie Newbigin's Missionary Ecclesiology." PhD diss., University of Helsinki, 1992.

Kettle, David. "Unfinished Dialogue? The Reception of Lesslie Newbigin's Theology." In *Theology in Missionary Perspective: Lesslie Newbigin's Legacy*, edited by Mark T. B. Laing and Paul Weston, 19–32. Eugene, OR: Pickwick, 2012.

Kim, Kirsteen. "Mission Theology of the Church." *IRM* 99/390 (2010) 39–55.

King, Martin Luther, Jr. "Letter from a Birmingham Jail." 1963. www.africa.upenn.edu/Articles_Gen/Letter_Birmingham.html.

———. *A Testament of Hope: The Essential Writings and Speeches of Martin Luther King Jr.* Edited by James M. Washington. San Francisco: HarperSan Francisco, 1986.

Kirk, J. Andrew. *The Future of Reason, Science and Faith*. Aldershot: Ashgate, 2007.

———. *The Meaning of Freedom: A Study of Secular, Muslim and Christian Views.* Carlisle: Paternoster, 1998.

———. "Mission in the West: On the Calling of the Church in a Postmodern Age." In *A Scandalous Prophet: The Way of Mission After Newbigin*, edited by Thomas F. Foust et al., 115–27. Grand Rapids: Eerdmans, 2002.

———. *The Mission of Theology and Theology as Mission.* Christian Mission and Modern Culture. Valley Forge, PA: Trinity, 1997.

———. *What Is Mission? Theological Explorations.* London: Darton, Longman & Todd, 1999.

Kirk, J. Andrew, and Kevin J. Vanhoozer, eds. *To Stake a Claim: Mission and the Western Crisis of Knowledge.* Maryknoll, NY: Orbis, 1999.

Köstenberger, Andreas J. *A Theology of John's Gospel and Letters.* Grand Rapids: Zondervan, 2009.

Kovacs, J. L. "'Now Shall the Ruler of This World Be Driven Out': Jesus' Death as Cosmic Battle in John 12:20–36." *Journal of Biblical Literature* 114 (1995) 227–47.

Kraft, Marguerite G. *Understanding Spiritual Power: A Forgotten Dimension of Cross-Cultural Mission and Ministry.* Maryknoll, NY: Orbis, 1995.

Kreider, Alan. "*Ressourcement* and Mission." *Anglican Theological Review* 96/2 (2014) 239–61.

Küng, Hans. *The Church.* London: Search, 1968.

Ladd, George Eldon. *A Commentary on the Revelation of John.* Grand Rapids: Eerdmans, 1972.

Lai, Pan-Chiu. *Towards a Trinitarian Theology of Religions: A Study of Paul Tillich's Thought.* Kampen: Pharos, 1994.

Laing, Mark T. B. "Missio Dei: Some Implications for the Church." *Missiology: An International Review* 37/1 (2009) 89–99.

Laing, Mark T. B., and Paul Weston, eds. *Theology in Missionary Perspective: Lesslie Newbigin's Legacy.* Eugene, OR: Pickwick, 2012.

Lande, Aasulv. "Trinitarian Missiology." Audio Cassette AN812. Recording from "After Newbigin: A Missiological Enquiry in Honour of Lesslie Newbigin." November 2–3, 1998. Held at the Lesslie Newbigin Archives, University of Birmingham.

Letham, Robert. *The Holy Trinity: In Scripture, History, Theology, and Worship.* Phillipsburg, NJ: P & R, 2004.

Lewis, C. S. *Mere Christianity.* London: Fount, Harper Collins, 1997.

Lieu, Judith. *The Theology of the Johannine Epistles.* Cambridge: Cambridge University Press, 1991.

Longenecker, Bruce W. *The Triumph of Abraham's God: The Transformation of Identity in Galatians.* Edinburgh: T. & T. Clark, 1998.

Lord, Andrew M. "Mission Eschatology: A Framework for Mission in the Spirit." *Journal of Pentecostal Theology* 11 (1997) 111–23.

———. "The Pentecostal-Moltmann Dialogue: Implications for Mission." *Journal of Pentecostal Theology* 11 (2003) 271–87.

———. "The Voluntary Principle in Pentecostal Missiology." *Journal of Pentecostal Theology* 17 (2000) 81–95.

MacIntyre, Alasdair. *After Virtue: A Study In Moral Theory*. 2nd ed. Notre Dame: University of Notre Dame Press, 1984.

Mackay, John A. *Ecumenics: The Science of the Church Universal*. Englewood Cliffs, NJ: Prentice-Hall, 1964.

Marshall, I. Howard. *Acts*. Grand Rapids: Eerdmans, 1980.

Martin, Ralph P. *The Epistle of Paul to the Philippians: An Introduction and Commentary*. Leicester: InterVarsity, 1959.

McCormack, Bruce L. *Orthodox and Modern: Studies in the Theology of Karl Barth*. Grand Rapids: Baker Academic, 2008.

McGrath, Alister E. *Christian Theology: An Introduction*. 4th ed. Oxford: Blackwell, 2007.

McIntyre, John. *The Shape of Pneumatology: Studies in the Doctrine of the Holy Spirit*. Edinburgh: T. & T. Clark, 1997.

———. *The Shape of Soteriology: Studies in the Doctrine of the Death of Christ*. Edinburgh: T. & T. Clark, 1992.

McKnight, Scot. *The Heaven Promise*. Colorado Springs: WaterBrook, 2015.

Molnar, Paul D. "Can Jesus' Divinity Be Recognised as 'Definitive, Authentic and Essential' When It Is Grounded in Election? Some Dogmatic Implications of Bruce McCormack's Correction of Barth's Early Christology." Unpublished paper, University of Otago Theology Departmental Seminar, Dunedin, June 3, 2009.

Moltmann, Jürgen. *The Church in the Power of the Spirit: A Contribution to Messianic Ecclesiology*. Translated by Margaret Kohl. New York: Harper & Row, 1977.

———. *The Coming of God: Christian Eschatology*. Translated by Margaret Kohl. Minneapolis: Fortress, 1996.

———. *The Trinity and the Kingdom: The Doctrine of God*. Translated by Margaret Kohl. London: SCM, 1981.

———. "The World in God or God in the World? Response to Richard Bauckham." In *God Will Be All In All: The Eschatology of Jürgen Moltmann*, edited by Richard Bauckham, 35–41. Minneapolis: Fortress, 2001.

Morris, Leon. *The Atonement: Its Meaning and Significance*. Leicester: InterVarsity, 1983.

Murray, Andrew. *Key to the Missionary Problem*. Fort Washington, PA: Christian Literature Crusade, 1979.

Neill, Stephen. *Creative Tension*. London: Edinburgh, 1959.

———. *A History of Christian Missions*. 2nd ed. Penguin History of the Church 6. London: Penguin, 1990.

Newbigin, J. E. Lesslie. "The Basis and the Forms of Unity." *MidStream: The Ecumenical Movement Today* 23 (1984) 1–12.

———. "The Basis, Purpose and Manner of InterFaith Dialogue." *Scottish Journal of Theology* 30/3 (1977) 253–70.

———. "Beyond the Familiar Myths." *The Gospel and Our Culture (U.K.)* 1 (1989) 2–3.

———. *The Bible: Good News For Secularised People*. Unpublished, 1991. Available at www.newbigin.net and held at Lesslie Newbigin Archives, University of Birmingham.

———. "The Bible and Our Contemporary Mission." *The Clergy Review* 69/1 (1984) 9–17.

———. "Can a Modern Society be Christian?" In *Christian Witness in Society: A Tribute to M. M. Thomas*, edited by K. C. Abraham, 95–108. Bangalore: Board of Theological Education, Senate of Serampore College, 1998.

———. "Can the West Be Converted?" *Princeton Seminary Bulletin* 6/1 (1985) 25–37.

———. "Certain Faith: What Kind of Certainty?" *Tyndale Bulletin* 44/2 (1993) 339–50.

———. "Christ and the Cultures." *Scottish Journal of Theology* 31/1 (1978) 1–22.

———. "Christ and the World of Religions." *Churchman* 97/1 (1983) 16–30.

———. *Christ Our Eternal Contemporary*. Madras: Christian Literature Society of India, 1968.

———. "The Christian Faith and the World Religions." In *Keeping the Faith: Essays to Mark the Centenary of Lux Mundi*, edited by Geoffrey Wainwright, 310–40. London: SPCK, 1989.

———. *Christian Faith in a Secularised World*. Unpublished, 1985. Available at www.newbigin.net and held at the Lesslie Newbigin Archives, University of Birmingham.

———. *Christian Freedom in the Modern World*. London: SCM, 1937.

———. *The Christian Message*. Unpublished, December 1993. Available at www.newbigin.net and held at Lesslie Newbigin Archives, University of Birmingham.

———. "A Christian Vedanta? Review of 'A Vision to Pursue', by Keith Ward." *The Gospel and Our Culture (U.K.)* 12 (1992) 1–2.

———. *Christian Witness in a Pluralist Society*. London: British Council of Churches, 1977.

———. "Christianity and Culture." Unpublished paper, 1990. Available at www.newbigin.net and held at Lesslie Newbigin Archives, University of Birmingham.

———. "The Church As A Servant Community." *National Christian Council Review* 91 (1971) 256–64.

———. *Come Holy Spirit—Renew the Whole Creation*. Birmingham, UK: Selly Oak Colleges, 1990.

———. "Context and Conversion." *IRM* 68/271 (1979) 301–12.

———. "Conversion." *National Christian Council Review* 86 (1966) 309–23.

———. "Crosscurrents in Ecumenical and Evangelical Understandings of Mission." *IBMR* 6/4 (1982) 146–51.

———. "Culture and Theology." In *Blackwells Encyclopedia of Modern Christian Thought*, edited by Alister E. McGrath, 98–100. Oxford: Blackwell, 1993.

———. "Culture, Rationality and the Unity of the Human Race." *The Gospel and Our Culture (U.K.)* 3 (1989) 1–2.

———. *Discovering Truth in a Changing World*. London: Alpha, 2003.

———. "Discussion Paper on Authority." Unpublished, 1989. Available at www.newbigin.net and held at Lesslie Newbigin Archives, University of Birmingham.

———. "Ecumenical Amnesia." *IBMR* 18/1 (1994) 2–5.

———. "The Enduring Validity of CrossCultural Mission." *IBMR* 12/2 (1988) 50–53.

———. *England As A Foreign Mission Field*. Unpublished, 1986. Available at www.newbigin.net and held at Lesslie Newbigin Archives, University of Birmingham.

———. "Episcopacy and Authority." *Churchman* 104/4 (1991) 335–39.

———. *A Faith For This One World?* London: SCM, 1961.

———. *The Finality of Christ*. London: SCM, 1969.

———. *Foolishness To The Greeks: The Gospel and Western Culture*. Grand Rapids: Eerdmans, 1986.

———. "Foreword." In *Everyman Revived: The Common Sense of Michael Polanyi*, edited by Drusilla Scott, iv–v. Grand Rapids: Eerdmans, 1995.
———. "From the Editor." *IRM* 54 (1965) 145–50, 273–80, 417–27.
———. "The Gathering Up of History Into Christ." In *The Missionary Church in East and West*, edited by Charles C. West and David M. Paton, 81–90. London: SCM, 1959.
———. *The Good Shepherd: Meditations on Christian Ministry in Today's World*. Bedfordshire: The Faith, 1977.
———. "Gospel and Culture—But Which Culture?" *Missionalia* 17/3 (1989) 213–15.
———. *The Gospel and Our Culture*. London: Catholic Missionary Education Centre, 1990.
———. "The Gospel as Public Truth: Swanwick Opening Statement." *The Gospel and Our Culture: The Gospel As Public Truth* (1992). Available at www.newbigin.net and held at Lesslie Newbigin Archives, University of Birmingham.
———. *The Gospel in Today's Global City*. Birmingham, UK: Selly Oak Colleges, 1997.
———. *The Holy Spirit and the Church*. Madras: Christian Literature Society of India, 1972.
———. *Honest Religion For Secular Man*. London: SCM, 1966.
———. *The Household of God: Lectures on the Nature of the Church*. London: SCM, 1953.
———. "How I Arrived at the Other Side of 1984." *Selly Oak Journal* 2 (1985) 6–8.
———. "Human Flourishing in Faith, Fact and Fantasy." *Religion and Medicine* 7 (1988) 400–12.
———. "Integration—Some Personal Reflections." *IRM* 70/280 (1981) 247–55.
———. "Introduction." In *The Gospel as Public Truth: Applying the Gospel in the Modern World*. London: CEN, 1992.
———. "Is There Anyone In Charge Here?" *Reform* (March 1990) 6.
———. *Journey into Joy*. Madras: Christian Literature Society of India, 1972.
———. "Journeys End in Lovers Meeting." *Reform* (October 1990) 13.
———. "Lay Presidency at the Eucharist." *MidStream: The Ecumenical Movement Today* 35 (1996) 177–82.
———. "Lesslie Newbigin Replies." *IBMR* 6/4 (1982) 154–55.
———. "Letter to Charles C. West." Unpublished, June 17, 1988. DA29/2/21/66. Held at Lesslie Newbigin Archives, University of Birmingham.
———. "Letter to Rev. Bob Mayo." Unpublished, September 7, 1990. DA29/1/3/74. Held at Lesslie Newbigin Archives, University of Birmingham.
———. "Letter to Roy Clouser (i)." Unpublished, November 1, 1994. DA29/1/4/47. Held at Lesslie Newbigin Archives, University of Birmingham.
———. "Letter to Roy Clouser (ii)." Unpublished, November 19, 1994. DA29/1/4/34. Held at Lesslie Newbigin Archives, University of Birmingham.
———. "Letter to URC Ministers." Unpublished, Easter 1991. DA29/2/12/7. Held at Lesslie Newbigin Archives, University of Birmingham.
———. "Letter to Wm. B. Eerdmans, Jr." Unpublished, March 6, 1995. DA29/1/14/48. Held at Lesslie Newbigin Archives, University of Birmingham.
———. "The Life and Mission of the Church." In *We Were Brought Together*, edited by David M. Taylor, 59–69. Sydney: Australian Council for the WCC, 1960.
———. *The Light Has Come: An Exposition of the Fourth Gospel*. Grand Rapids: Eerdmans, 1982.

———. *Living Hope in a Changing World*. London: Alpha, 2003.

———. *The Mission and Unity of the Church*. Grahamstown: Rhodes University, 1960.

———. *Mission in Christ's Way: Bible Studies*. Geneva: WCC, 1987.

———. "Mission in the 1980's." *Occasional Bulletin of Missionary Research* 4/4 (1980) 154-55.

———. "Mission in the 1990s: Two Views." *IBMR* 13/3 (1989) 100-102.

———. *Mission of the Church to All the Nations*. Geneva: WCC Ecumenical Centre Library, 1960.

———. *The Mission of the Triune God*. Unpublished, 1962. Pages not numbered. Available at www.newbigin.net and held at the WCC, Ecumenical Centre Library, Geneva, Switzerland.

———. "A Mission to Modern Western Culture." In *The San Antonio Report: Your Will Be Done: Mission in Christ's Way*, edited by Frederick R. Wilson, 162-66. Geneva: WCC, 1990.

———. "The Missionary Dimension of the Ecumenical Movement." *Ecumenical Review* 14 (1962) 207-15.

———. "A Missionary's Dream." *Ecumenical Review* 43/1 (1991) 4-10.

———. "Missions in an Ecumenical Perspective." Unpublished, 1962. Pages not numbered. Available at www.newbigin.net and held at the WCC, Ecumenical Centre Library, Geneva, Switzerland.

———. "The Nature of the Unity We Seek: From the Church of South India." *Religion in Life* 26/2 (1957) 181-90.

———. *New Birth Into A Living Hope*. Unpublished, 1995. Available at www.newbigin.net and held at the Lesslie Newbigin Archives, Birmingham.

———. *One Body, One Gospel, One World: The Christian Mission Today*. London: International Missionary Council, 1958.

———. *The Open Secret: An Introduction to the Theology of Mission*. Rev. ed. Grand Rapids: Eerdmans, 1995.

———. *The Other Side of 1984: Questions for the Churches*. Geneva: WCC, 1983.

———. *The Other Side of 1990*. Unpublished, 1989. pages not numbered. Available at www.newbigin.net and held at the Lesslie Newbigin Archives, University of Birmingham.

———. "The Pastor's Opportunities: VI. Evangelism in the City." *Expository Times* 98 (1987) 355-58.

———. *The Pattern of Ministry in a Missionary Church*. Geneva: WCC Ecumenical Centre Library, 1961.

———. "The Pattern of Partnership." In *A Decisive Hour for the Christian World Mission*, edited by Norman Goodall et al., 35-45. London, SCM, 1960.

———. "The Present Crisis and the Coming Christ." *Ecumenical Review* 6/2 (1954) 118-23.

———. *Proper Confidence: Faith, Doubt and Certainty in Christian Discipleship*. Grand Rapids: Eerdmans, 1995.

———. "Reflections on the 'Affirmation of Faith' Embodied in the Eucharistic Liturgy Proposed for Use in the Church of South India." Unpublished electronic file, June 2, 1997. Floppy disk DA29/6/2. Held at Lesslie Newbigin Archives, University of Birmingham.

———. "Religion, Science and Truth in the School Curriculum." *Theology* 91/741 (1988) 186-93.

———. "Religious Pluralism: A Missiological Approach." *Studia Missionalia* 42 (1993) 227–44.
———. "Response from Bishop Newbigin." *The Gospel and Our Culture (U.K.)* 8 (1991) 4.
———. "Response to David M. Stowe." *IBMR* 12/4 (1988) 151–53.
———. "A Response to the Responses." *Selly Oak Journal* 2 (1985) 33–36.
———. *The Reunion of the Church: A Defence of the South India Scheme*. Rev ed. London: SCM, 1960.
———. "Salvation, The New Humanity and Cultural-Communal Solidarity." *Bangalore Theological Forum* 5/2 (1973) 1–11.
———. *Signs Amid the Rubble: The Purposes of God in Human History*. Edited by Geoffrey Wainwright. Grand Rapids: Eerdmans, 2003.
———. *Sin and Salvation*. London: SCM, 1956.
———. "Socialism, Free Markets and Christian Faith." *The Gospel and Our Culture (U.K.)* 4 (1990) 1–2.
———. *A South India Diary*. London: SCM, 1951.
———. "The Summons to Christian Mission Today." *IRM* 48 (1959) 177–89.
———. "Teaching Religion in a Secular Plural Society." *Learning For Living* (1977) 82–88.
———. "Theism and Atheism in Theology." *The Gospel and Our Culture (U.K.)* 8 (Winter 1991) 1–2.
———. "The Threat and the Promise." *The Gospel and Our Culture (U.K.)* 7 (1990) 2–3.
———. "Toronto Blessing: 'like a monsoon.'" *Church Times*, February 3, 1995.
———. *Trinitarian Doctrine for Today's Mission*. Carlisle: Paternoster, 1998.
———. "Trinitarianism." In *Concise Dictionary of the Christian World Mission*, edited by Stephen Neill et al., 607. Nashville: Abingdon, 1971.
———. "The Trinity as Public Truth." In *The Trinity in a Pluralistic Age: Theological Essays on Culture and Religion*, edited by Kevin Vanhoozer, 1–8. Grand Rapids: Eerdmans, 1997.
———. *A Trinity Sunday Sermon*. Unpublished and undated. DA29/4/1/43. Held at the Lesslie Newbigin Archives, University of Birmingham.
———. *Truth and Authority In Modernity*. Valley Forge, PA: Trinity, 1996.
———. *Truth to Tell: The Gospel As Public Truth*. London: SPCK, 1991.
———. *Unfaith and Other Faiths*. Geneva: WCC Ecumenical Centre Library, 1962.
———. *Unfinished Agenda: An Autobiography*. Grand Rapids: Eerdmans, 1985.
———. *Unfinished Agenda: An Updated Autobiography*. Edinburgh: Saint Andrew, 1993.
———. "Unity and Mission." *Covenant Quarterly* 19 (1961) 3–6.
———. *A Walk Through the Bible*. London: Triangle, SPCK, 1999.
———. "Way Out West: The Gospel in a Post-Enlightenment World." *Touchstone* 5/3 (1992) 22–24.
———. *The Welfare State: A Christian Perspective*. Oxford: Oxford Institute for Church and Society, 1985.
———. "What Do We Mean By 'God.'" *Reform* (February 1990) 7.
———. *What Is the Culture?* Unpublished, 1990. Available at www.newbigin.net and held at Lesslie Newbigin Archives, University of Birmingham.
———. "Why Study the Old Testament?" *National Christian Council Review* 74 (1954) 71–76.

———. "Witnesses to the World." *Christian (U.K.)* (1987) 5–8.

———. *A Word In Season: Perspectives on Christian World Missions*. Grand Rapids: Eerdmans, 1994.

———. "The Work of the Holy Spirit in the Life of the Asian Churches." In *A Decisive Hour for the Christian World Mission*, edited by Norman Goodall et al., 18–33. London: SCM, 1960.

Newbigin, Lesslie, et al. *Faith and Power: Christianity and Islam in "Secular" Britain*. Eugene, OR: Wipf & Stock, 2005.

Newlands, George. "Letter to Lesslie Newbigin." Unpublished, December 12, 1988. DA29/2/21/82. Held at Lesslie Newbigin Archives, University of Birmingham.

Nikolajsen, Jeppe Bach. *The Distinctive Identity of the Church: A Constructive Study of the Post-Christendom Theologies of Lesslie Newbigin and John Howard Yoder*. Eugene, OR: Pickwick, 2015.

Niles, D. T. *Upon The Earth—The Mission of God and the Missionary Enterprise of the Churches*. London: Lutterworth, 1962.

O'Collins, Gerald. *The Tripersonal God: Understanding and Interpreting the Trinity*. Mahwah, NJ: Paulist, 1999.

Oden, Thomas C. *Life in the Spirit*. Systematic Theology 3. Peabody, MA: Prince, Hendrickson, 2001.

O'Donovan, Oliver. *Resurrection and Moral Order: An Outline for Evangelical Ethics*. Grand Rapids: Eerdmans, 1986.

Pachuau, Lalsangkima. "Missio Dei." In *Dictionary of Mission Theology: Evangelical Foundations*, edited by John Corrie, 232–34. Nottingham: InterVarsity, 2007.

Padilla, C. R. *Mission Between the Times*. Grand Rapids: Eerdmans, 1985.

Pannenberg, Wolfhart. *Systematic Theology*. Vol. 1. Translated by Geoffrey W. Bromiley. Grand Rapids: Eerdmans, 1991.

Pasquarello, Michael, III. *Christian Preaching: A Trinitarian Theology of Proclamation*. Grand Rapids: Baker, 2008.

Peterson, Robert A., Sr. *Calvin and the Atonement*. Fearn, Ross-shire: Mentor, 1999.

Petersen, Rodney. Review of *The Open Secret: Sketches of a Missionary Theology*, by Lesslie Newbigin. *Princeton Seminary Bulletin* 2/2 (1979) 191–93.

Pinnock, Clark H. *Flame of Love: A Theology of the Holy Spirit*. Downers Grove, IL: InterVarsity, 1996.

———. *Most Moved Mover: A Theology of God's Openness*. Carlisle: Paternoster, 2001.

———, ed. *The Openness of God: A Biblical Challenge to the Traditional Understanding of God*. Downers Grove, IL: InterVarsity, 1994.

Piper, John. *Let the Nations Be Glad! The Supremacy of God in Missions*. Grand Rapids: Baker, 1993.

Plantinga, Cornelius, Jr. "The Threeness/Oneness Problem of the Trinity." *Calvin Theological Journal* 23/1 (1988) 37–53.

Polkinghorne, John. *Belief in God in an Age of Science*. New Haven, CT: Yale University Press, 1998.

———. *Science and the Trinity: The Christian Encounter with Reality*. New Haven, CT: Yale University Press, 2004.

———, ed. *The Work of Love: Creation As Kenosis*. London: SPCK, 2001.

Power, Bernie. "'A Volf in Sheikh's Clothing?': How *Allah: A Christian Response* May Deceive both Christians and Muslims." 2015. https://www.academia.edu/11295836/A_Volf_in_Sheikh_s_clothing_How_Allah_A_Christian_

Response_may_deceive_both_Christians_and_Muslims_ALLAH_A_ CHRISTIAN_RESPONSE.
Pratt, Douglas. "Islam: A Challenge to Christianity." *Stimulus: The New Zealand Journal of Christian Thought and Practice* 15/2 (2007) 2–9.
Prebble, Edward. "Missional Church: More a Theological (Re)Discovery, Less a Strategy for Parish Development." *Colloquium* 46/2 (2014) 224–41.
Pryor, John M. "The Trinitarian Missiology of Jonathan Edwards: The Historical Implications of Edwards' Missiological Appropriation of the 'Grammar of Divinity.'" Phd diss., Asbury Theological Seminary, 2006. *Tren Dissertations* Paper 6553. http://place.asburyseminary.edu/trendissertations/6553.
Rae, Murray A. "Prolegomena." In *Trinitarian Soundings in Systematic Theology*, edited by Paul L. Metzger, 9–20. London: T. & T. Clark, 2005.
Rahner, Karl. *The Trinity*. Translated by Joseph Donceel. New York: Crossroads, 1997.
Raiser, Konrad. "Is Ecumenical Apologetics Sufficient? A Response to Newbigin's 'Ecumenical Amnesia.'" *IBMR* 18/2 (1994) 50–51.
Redman, Matt. *Facedown*. Six Step, 2004.
Reichenbach, Bruce. "God Limits His Power." In *Predestination and Free Will: Four Views*, edited by David Basinger and Randall Basinger, 101–24. Downers Grove, IL: InterVarsity, 1986.
Richardson, Don. *Eternity In Their Hearts*. Rev. ed. Ventura, CA: Regal, 1984.
Richebächer, Wilhelm. "Editorial." *IRM* 92/367 (2003) 463–67.
Richmond, Helen. "Daring to Believe: Exploring the Missiology of Lesslie Newbigin." Masters diss., Sydney College of Divinity, 1995.
Robinson, John A. T. *Honest to God*. Philadelphia: Westminster, 1963.
Rogers, Glenn. *A Basic Introduction to Missions and Missiology*. Bedford, TX: Mission & Ministry Resources, 2003.
Sanders, Fred, and Klaus Issler, eds., *Jesus in Trinitarian Perspective: An Introductory Christology*. Nashville: B. & H. Academic, 2007.
Sanders, John. *The God Who Risks: A Theology of Providence*. Downers Grove, IL: InterVarsity, 1998.
———. *No Other Name: An Investigation into the Destiny of the Unevangelised*. Grand Rapids: Eerdmans, 1992.
———. "On Heffalumps and Heresies: Responses to Accusations Against Open Theism." *Journal of Biblical Studies* 2/1 (Spring 2002) 1–44.
Sanders, John, and Christopher A. Hall. *Does God have a Future? A Debate on Divine Providence*. Grand Rapids: Baker Academic, 2003.
Sanneh, Lamin. *Translating the Message: The Missionary Impact on Culture*. Maryknoll, NY: Orbis, 1989.
Scherer, James A. Review of *The Open Secret: Sketches for a Missionary Theology*, by Lesslie Newbigin. *Occasional Bulletin of Missionary Research* (1980) 89.
Schleiermacher, Friedrich. *The Christian Faith*. Edited by H. R. Mackintosh and J. S. Stewart. English translation of the 2nd German ed. Edinburgh: T. & T. Clark, 1928.
Schmidt-Leukel, Perry. "Mission and Trinitarian Theology." In *A Scandalous Prophet: The Way of Mission After Newbigin*, edited by Thomas F. Foust et al., 57–64. Grand Rapids: Eerdmans, 2002.
Schreiter, Robert J. "Jesus Christ and Mission: The Cruciality of Christology." *Missiology: An International Review* 18/4 (1990) 429–37.
Schuster, Jürgen. *Christian Mission in Eschatological Perspective: Lesslie Newbigin's Contribution*. Nuremberg: Theologie und Religionswissenschaft, 2009.

Schwöbel, Christoph. "Christology and Trinitarian Thought." In *Trinitarian Theology Today: Essays on Divine Being and Act*, edited by Christoph Schwöbel, 113–46. Edinburgh: T. & T. Clark, 1995.

———. "The Renaissance of Trinitarian Theology: Reasons, Problems and Tasks." In *Trinitarian Theology Today: Essays on Divine Being and Act*, edited by Christoph Schwöbel, 1–30. Edinburgh: T. & T. Clark, 1995.

Scott, Waldron. *Karl Barth's Theology of Mission*. World Evangelical Fellowship Theological Commission. Downers Grove, IL: InterVarsity, 1978.

Seamands, Stephen. *Ministry in the Image of God: The Trinitarian Shape of Christian Service*. Downers Grove, IL: InterVarsity, 2005.

Sheikh, Bilquis. *I Dared to Call Him Father: The True Story of a Women's Encounter with God*. Grand Rapids: Chosen, 1980.

Shenk, Wilbert R. "Lesslie Newbigin's Contribution to the Theology of Mission." *The Bible in Transmission* Special Issue (1998) 3–6.

———. "A Tribute to Bishop Newbigin." *The Gospel and Our Culture (North America)* Special Edition (1998) 4.

———. *Write the Vision: The Church Renewed*. Harrisburg, PA: Trinity, 1995.

Sherman, Robert J. *King, Priest, and Prophet: A Trinitarian Theology of Atonement*. New York: T. & T. Clark, 2004.

Simpson, Gary M. "No Trinity, No Mission: The Apostolic Difference of Revisioning the Trinity." *Word and World* 18/3 (1998) 264–71.

Smail, Tom. "Trinitarian Atonement." *Stimulus* 15/2 (2007) 43–48.

———. *Windows on the Cross*. London: Darton, Longman & Todd, 1995.

Smalley, Stephen. *1, 2, 3 John*. Rev. ed. Word Biblical Commentary 51. Nashville: Thomas Nelson, 2007.

Stafford, Tim. *Miracles: A Journalist Looks at Modern-Day Experiences of God's Power*. Grand Rapids: Bethany, 2012.

Stott, John R. W. *The Contemporary Christian*. Leicester: InterVarsity, 1992.

———. *Epistles of John: An Introduction and Commentary*. Leicester: InterVarsity, 1964.

Stuhlmacher, Peter. *Paul's Letter to the Romans: A Commentary*. Translated by Scott J. Hafemann. Louisville: Westminster/John Knox, 1994.

Stults, Donald LeRoy. *Grasping Truth and Reality: Lesslie Newbigin's Theology of Mission to the Western World*. Cambridge: James Clarke, 2009.

Sunquist, Scott W., and Amos Yong, eds. *The Gospel and Pluralism Today: Reassessing Lesslie Newbigin in the 21st Century*. Downers Grove, IL: InterVarsity, 2015.

Swinburne, Richard. *The Coherence of Theism*. Rev. ed. New York: Oxford University Press, 1993.

Tan, Seng-Kong. "A Trinitarian Ontology of Missions." *IRM* 93/369 (2004) 279–96.

Tanner, Kathryn. *Jesus, Humanity and the Trinity: A Brief Systematic Theology*. Minneapolis: Fortress, 2001.

Taylor, Charles. *The Ethics of Authenticity*. Cambridge, MA: Harvard University Press, 1992.

Taylor, Jenny. "Lesslie Newbigin's Understanding of Islam." In *A Scandalous Prophet: The Way of Mission After Newbigin*, edited by Thomas F. Foust et al., 215–24. Grand Rapids: Eerdmans, 2002.

Taylor, John V. *For All The World—The Christian Mission in the Modern Age*. London: Hodder & Stoughton, 1966.

———. *The Go-Between God: The Holy Spirit and Christian Mission*. London: SCM, 1972.
Taylor, Nathaniel W. *Lectures on the Moral Government of God*. New York: Clark, Austin and Smith, 1859.
Tennent, Timothy C. *Invitation to World Missions: A Trinitarian Missiology for the Twenty-first Century*. Grand Rapids: Kregel, 2010.
Thielicke, Helmut. *Modern Faith and Thought*. Translated by Geoffrey W. Bromiley. Grand Rapids: Eerdmans, 1990.
Thomas, Joe M. *Christ and the World of Religions: Lesslie Newbigin's Theology*. Omaha: Ekklesia, 2011.
Thomas, John Christopher. *The Pentecostal Commentary on 1 John, 2 John and 3 John*. London: T. & T. Clark, 2004.
Thompson, John. *Modern Trinitarian Perspectives*. New York: Oxford University Press, 1994.
Tilley, T. W. "Incommensurability, Intratextuality, and Fideism." *Modern Theology* 5/2 (1989) 87–111.
Torrance, Alan J. *Persons in Communion: Trinitarian Description and Human Participation*. Edinburgh: T. & T. Clark, 1996.
Torrance, James B. *Worship, Community and the Triune God of Grace*. Carlisle: Paternoster, 1996.
Torrance, Thomas F. *The Christian Doctrine of God, One Being Three Persons*. Edinburgh: T. & T. Clark, 1996.
———. *The Mediation of Christ*. Grand Rapids: Eerdmans, 1983.
———. *Theology in Reconstruction*. Grand Rapids: Eerdmans, 1965.
Treier, Daniel J., and David Lauber, eds. *Trinitarian Theology for the Church: Scripture, Community, Worship*. Downers Grove, IL: InterVarsity, 2009.
Vatican II. *Ad Gentes*. Decree on the Mission Activity of the Church. 1965. http://www.vatican.va/archive/hist_councils/ii_vatican_council/documents/vat-ii_decree_19651207_ad-gentes_en.html.
Verkuyl, Johannes. *Contemporary Missiology: An Introduction*. Edited and translated by Dale Cooper. Grand Rapids: Eerdmans, 1978.
———. "The Kingdom of God as the Goal of the Missio Dei." *IRM* 68/270 (1979) 168–75.
Visser 't Hooft, W. A. "Evangelism among Europe's Neo-Pagans." *IRM* 66/264 (1977) 349–60.
———. "Evangelism in the Neo-Pagan Situation." *IRM* 63/249 (1974) 81–86.
———. *None Other Gods*. London: SCM, 1937.
———. *No Other Name: The Choice Between Syncretism and Christian Universalism*. London, SCM, 1963.
Volf, Miroslav. *After Our Likeness: The Church As The Image Of The Trinity*. Grand Rapids: Eerdmans, 1998.
———. *Allah: A Christian Response*. New York: HarperOne, 2012.
Walls, Andrew F. *The Cross-Cultural Process in Christian History*. New York: T. & T. Clark, 2002.
———. "Enlightenment, Postmodernity, and Mission." In *A Scandalous Prophet: The Way of Mission After Newbigin*, edited by Thomas F. Foust et al., 145–52. Grand Rapids: Eerdmans, 2002.
———. *The Missionary Movement in Christian History*. Maryknoll, NY: Orbis, 1996.

Walsh, Brian, and J. Richard Middleton. *The Transforming Vision: Shaping a Christian World View*. Downers Grove, IL: InterVarsity, 1984.
Wannenwetsch, Bernd. *Political Worship: Ethics for Christian Citizens*. Oxford: Oxford University Press, 2004.
Ward, Heather. "The Use and Misuse of 'Metaphor' in Christian Theology." In *A Scandalous Prophet: The Way of Mission After Newbigin*, edited by Thomas F. Foust et al., 73–75. Grand Rapids: Eerdmans, 2002.
Ware, James P. *The Mission of the Church in Paul's Letter to the Philippians in the Context of Ancient Judaism*. Leiden: Brill, 2005.
Watson, Frances. "Trinity and Community: A Reading of John 17." *International Journal of Systematic Theology* 1/2 (1999) 168–84.
Watt, W. Montgomery. *Islam and Christianity Today: A Contribution to Dialogue*. London: Routledge & Kegan Paul, 1983.
Webster, John. *Word and Church: Essays in Church Dogmatics*. Edinburgh: T. & T. Clark, 2001.
Wenham, Gordon J. *Genesis 1–15*. Word Biblical Commentary 1. Waco, TX: Word, 1987.
Westcott, B. F. *The Gospel According to St. John*. London: John Murray, 1908.
Weston, Paul D. A. "Ecclesiology in Eschatological Perspective: Newbigin's Understanding of the Missionary Church." In *Theology in Missionary Perspective: Lesslie Newbigin's Legacy*, edited by Mark T. B. Laing and Paul Weston, 79–86. Eugene, OR: Pickwick, 2012.
———. "Gospel, Mission and Culture: The Contribution of Lesslie Newbigin." In *Witness to the World*, edited by David Peterson, 32–62. Carlisle: Paternoster, 1999.
———, ed. *Lesslie Newbigin: Missionary Theologian—A Reader*. Grand Rapids: Eerdmans, 2006.
———. "Mission and Cultural Change: A Critical Engagement with the Writings of Lesslie Newbigin." PhD diss., University of London, 2001.
White, James E. *Christ among the Dragons: Finding Our Way Through Cultural Challenges*. Downers Grove, IL: InterVarsity, 2010.
Wiles, Maurice. *The Christian Fathers*. London: Hodder & Stoughton, 1966.
Wilken, Robert L. *Remembering the Christian Past*. Grand Rapids: Eerdmans, 1995.
Williams, J. Rodman. *Renewal Theology*. Vol. 1, *God, the World and Redemption*. Grand Rapids: Zondervan, 1988.
———. *Renewal Theology*. Vol. 2, *Salvation, the Holy Spirit, and Christian Living*. Grand Rapids: Zondervan, 1990.
Wolterstorff, Nicholas. "Unqualified Divine Temporality." In *God and Time: Four Views*, edited by Gregory E. Ganssle, 187–238. Downers Grove, IL: InterVarsity, 2001.
Wood, Nicholas. *Faiths and Faithfulness—Pluralism, Dialogue, and Mission in the Work of Kenneth Cragg and Lesslie Newbigin*. Paternoster Theological Monographs. Carlisle: Paternoster, 2009.
Work, Telford. "Witness to the Signs: More Reminders from Lesslie Newbigin." *Pro Ecclesia* 13/3 (2004) 352–58.
Wright, Christopher J. H. *The Mission of God: Unlocking the Bible's Grand Narrative*. Downers Grove, IL: InterVarsity, 2006.
Wright, N. T. *Evil and the Justice of God*. Downers Grove, IL: InterVarsity, 2006.
———. *Jesus and the Victory of God*. London: SPCK, 1996.

———. Review of *Lesslie Newbigin: A Theological Life*, by Geoffrey Wainwright. *Gospel and Our Culture Network Newsletter* 32 (2001) 3. http://www.gospel-culture.org.uk/2001.htm#Newsletter%2032%20%28Autumn%20% 2701 %29.

———. *Surprised by Hope*. London: SPCK, 2007.

Yannoulatos, Anastasios "Rediscovering Our Apostolic Identity in the 21st Century." *St. Vladimir's Theological Quarterly* 48/1 (2004) 3–20.

Yates, Timothy. "Lesslie Newbigin's Missionary Encounter with the Enlightenment, 1975–98." *IBMR* 34/1 (2010) 42–45.

Yong, Amos. "Pluralism, Secularism and Pentecost: Newbigin—ings for *Missio Trinitatis* in a New Century." In *The Gospel and Pluralism Today: Reassessing Lesslie Newbigin in the 21st Century*, edited by Scott W. Sunquist and Amos Yong, 147–70. Downers Grove, IL: InterVarsity, 2015.

Young, Frances. "The Uncontainable God: Pre-Christendom Doctrine of the Trinity." In *A Scandalous Prophet: The Way of Mission After Newbigin*, edited by Thomas F. Foust et al., 84–91. Grand Rapids: Eerdmans, 2002.

Zahniser, A. H. Mathias. "The Trinity: Paradigm for Mission in the Spirit." *Papers* 47 (2015). http://place.asburyseminary.edu/firstfruitspapers/47.

Zebiri, Kate P. *Muslims and Christians Face to Face*. Oxford: Oneworld, 1997.

Zizioulas, John D. *Being As Communion: Studies in Personhood and the Church*. London: Darton, Longman & Todd, 1985.

———. "The Doctrine of God the Trinity Today: Suggestions for an Ecumenical Study." In *The Forgotten Trinity: A Selection of Papers presented to the BCC Study Commission on Trinitarian Doctrine Today*, edited by Alasdair I. C. Heron, 3:19–32. London: BCC, 1991.

———. "The Doctrine of the Holy Trinity: The Significance of the Cappadocian Contribution." In *Trinitarian Theology Today: Essays on Divine Being and Act*, edited by Christoph Schwöbel, 44–60. Edinburgh: T. & T. Clark, 1995.

# Index of Persons

Allen, Roland, 42–44, 46–47, 74n77, 95–96, 105, 115, 131, 190, 224n192, 251, 290
Anatolios, Khaled, 136, 191, 192n44–45, 226n204, 228, 299n40, 302
Anderson, Allen, 245–46, 261n40, 270n84
Arminius, James, 22n107
Athanasius of Alexandria, 65–66, 68, 77, 122, 134–35, 138, 147, 149, 155, 177, 299, 302
Augustine, Augustinian, 5, 17, 37, 62n15, 68, 134, 142, 147, 154, 185–86, 197, 216, 225, 247
Aulén, Gustaf, 197, 199

Barth, Karl, vii, xiv, xviii, xxn47, 6, 12n46, 20, 59, 64, 82, 100n212, 109, 117, 121, 126n20, 127n25, 133–36, 138n73, 139, 142, 152–54, 158–60, 168, 174, 177, 185n13, 187–89, 191, 202, 204n97, 205, 219, 225, 227–28, 231n226, 233, 238–41, 253n5, 258–59, 261n43, 262n44&48, 263–64, 266, 273n98, 276–77, 279–80, 290, 296n27, 298n32, 301–2
Badcock, Gary D., 83n127, 142n90, 262n46
Barrett, C. K., 201–2, 259
Basil the Great, 122n5, 145, 152n133, 156, 163
Bevans, Stephen B., xix–xx, 59n3, 131n44, 237n251

Blauw, Johannes, 232n232, 239, 242–43, 248,
Bloesch, Donald G., 201n88, 227
Bosch, David J., xix–xx, 72, 93n170, 165n209, 194–95, 198, 224n193, 232, 236, 241n275, 246, 247n295, 253, 256, 260, 262n45, 264n58, 267n70–71, 269, 275
Boyd, Gregory A., ix, 91, 194, 197, 199, 203n95, 218n166, 220n175, 242n279, 250, 258n26, 289n5, 293
Braaten, Carl E., 187n20, 253n2, 255n14, 269n79, 298
Bruner, F. Dale., 126n17, 246, 261n41
Brunner, Emil, 5, 67n37, 78, 122n6, 168, 201, 238n255, 300

Calvin, John, 5, 25, 144, 149, 189, 192, 207n107, 208, 210, 249, 293
Cochrane, Charles N., 41, 58, 60, 64–67, 69, 77n92, 100, 114, 116–17, 136n65, 290
Coffey, David M., 142n88, 185

Dalferth, Ingolf U., 129n33, 137n70
Descartes, Rene, Cartesian, 8, 13n54, 69, 291
Dodds, Adam, viii, 13n56, 22n110, 160n183, 223n189, 265n60, 297n28
Donovan, Vincent J., 278, 282n138

Escobar, Samuel, 212n130, 214n141, 215n148, 221n180, 232n230, 274

*Index of Persons*

Fee, Gordon D., 90n160, 184n5, 205n100, 208
Fiddes, Paul S.,143n95, 153, 157n163, 161, 162n194, 171, 186, 198n76, 241, 258, 290
Flett, John G., xix, 64n26, 95n185, 109n249, 115, 164n206, 165–66, 172–75, 254n9, 264n54, 277, 278n119, 279n122, 280n126, 283, 297
Fretheim, Terence E., 241

Gelwick, Richard, 230
Goheen, Michael W., xvi–xvii, 19n88, 62n15, 72, 90–91, 164n205, 230, 237, 292n14
Greene, Colin J. D., 71, 179n273, 276
Gregory of Nazianzus, 123, 126, 128, 146, 151, 184
Gregory of Nyssa, 186
Guder, Darrell L., 213–14
Gunton, Colin E., xv, xviiin31, 63, 127n23&26, 128n27, 130, 142–43, 145–46, 150–51, 155n148&150, 156–58, 160n186, 163n201, 169n229, 186n14&17, 188n26, 194n52, 201, 226, 228, 237n254, 247, 253–54, 262n47, 298–300, 302n51

Hodgson, Leonard, 98, 125, 138, 147n116, 162n198, 170
Hoedemaker, L. A. (Bert), 104n226, 164, 165n209, 230n219, 291
Hong, Young-Gi, 249, 266n65, 270n84
Hunsberger, George, xivn7, xvn9, xvii, 4n10, 11, 59n3, 109, 163, 212, 220, 230–31
Hunsinger, George, 141, 174, 175n257

Irenaeus of Lyon, 126, 183, 192

Jenson, Robert W., xx, 122n7, 124, 129n32, 136, 138, 140, 147, 155, 166n219, 167, 169, 186–87, 193–94, 196, 207n105, 210, 222, 224n195, 254n6, 266n62, 270, 298
Jüngel, Eberhard, 178, 198, 279

Kettle, David J., xiii, xviiin27
Kim, Kirsteen, 224, 271
King Jr., Martin Luther, 230, 234
Kirk, J. Andrew, xxn46, 17n74, 154n145, 166, 190, 213, 239, 255n12–13, 266n65, 272n95, 274n101, 278, 282, 284n147, 292n14
Köstenberger, Andreas J., 148, 298n31
Kraft, Marguerite G., 220, 221n177

Lande, Aasulv, 75, 78, 303
Letham, Robert, 112n264, 127n24, 151n129, 154n143
Lewis, C. S., xvii, 127n24, 198, 250
Lord, Andrew M., 221, 224n194, 226n203, 261, 275, 277

MacIntyre, Alasdair, 230
McGrath, Alistair E., 123n9, 161n189, 289n5
McIntyre, John, 97, 196, 200, 235, 237, 243–44
Moltmann, Jürgen, 63, 121, 127, 129, 143n93, 145–46, 150, 161, 166, 168–69, 171–72, 178, 181, 187, 188n24–25, 202–3, 205–7, 209n118, 210, 224, 249, 266n63, 268–69, 299, 303n57

Neill, Stephen, 242n276, 284–85
Niles, D. T., 219, 221, 236, 250

Oden, Thomas C., 254, 257, 269n77, 272
O'Donovan, Oliver, 199n77
Origen of Alexandria, 138

Pannenberg, Wolfhart, 127n26, 128n27, 136–38, 144–47, 149–50, 157n161, 176–81, 186n14, 192n46, 198, 206, 299

Pinnock, Clark H., 161n193, 184, 192n42, 223–24, 229n216, 258n26, 263
Piper, John, 167, 169, 232n229, 274n102
Polkinghorne, John, xixn39, 162n200, 258n26
Pope John Paul II, 131n44, 285

Rae, Murray A., viii–ix, 63n20, 134n58
Rahner, Karl, xiv, xviii, 78, 112n263, 128n27, 143n93
Raiser, Konrad, 18, 56n283, 97, 165n214
Richmond, Helen, 25n126, 286n154
Rogers, Glenn, 86n144, 210n121

Sanders, John, 52n273, 240, 242, 258n26
Schleiermacher, Friedrich, 64, 77, 134–36, 138n77, 139, 243
Schmidt-Leukel, Perry, xxn48, 128–29
Schwöbel, Christoph, 130, 134–36, 158–59, 171–72, 183–84
Shenk, Wilbert R., xvi, 72, 277
Simpson, Gary M., 79n99, 303
Smail, Tom, 196n64, 202, 227, 247
Smalley, Stephen, 198, 278
Stott, John R. W., 159n176, 214n144, 234
Stults, Donald LeRoy, xviin14, xvii, 18–19

Tan, Seng-Kong, 126n18, 151n129, 171n240, 182n282, 225, 244, 247, 260, 264
Tanner, Kathryn, 168–69
Taylor, John V., 21, 193, 224n192, 247

Tennent, Timothy C., xivn6, xviin12, xixn40, 71, 93, 115, 218n167, 261n37, 262n48, 283, 289n3, 297
Tertullian, 145,
Thomas Aquinas, 62, 78, 147
Torrance, Alan J., ix, 156
Torrance, James B., xixn35, 143n93
Torrance, Thomas F., 126n19, 127, 132–34, 137, 150–51, 157–59, 162, 185n12, 191, 245, 253n4, 263n52, 300–301

Verkuyl, Johannes, 250, 274n100, 284
Visser't Hooft, W. A., xviin26, 61

Wainwright, Geoffrey, xiii, xvii, 14n59, 39n198, 56n283, 60n6, 69, 89, 110–11, 113, 132n46, 165n214, 290n6, 291n10
Walls, Andrew F., xix, 219n171, 220, 223, 235n243, 260, 266n64, 267, 271n85, 282n137, 283, 291
Watson, Frances, 226n202&205
Webster, John, 15, 175
Weston, Paul, xiii, xvii, 37n185, 68n47
Wiles, Maurice, 138n75, 196
Wilken, Robert L., 160n184, 184n4, 222
Williams, J. Rodman, 90n160, 194n51, 293n19
Wright, N. T., xiii, xix, 190, 255n13, 270n83

Yannoulatos, Anastasios, 268n73
Young, Frances, 110, 128–29, 183

Zizioulas, John D., 7, 112, 127n21, 155–56

# Index of Subjects

Anthropology, 6–10, 17, 104, 233–34
Arché, 66–68, 77, 81, 114, 136, 145–46, 149–52
Atonement, 15, 35, 179, 191–93, 196, 198, 199–202, 204–5, 211, 227, 301
Authority, xiv, 38, 90n160, 148, 194, 205–7, 219, 221

Baptism, 18, 43, 46, 75, 83, 100n212, 124, 186, 201
Bible, Scripture, 4, 14–16, 37, 43, 46, 187, 210, 292

Cartesianism. *See* Descartes
Charismatic Christianity. *See* Pentecostal
Christendom, 40–42, 53, 78–79, 241n276, 282
Christology, 65, 77, 97, 115, 123, 126, 133–34, 138–42, 262
Church, the,
  apostolic, 267–70
  and Jesus 189–90, 211–23, 262–63
  double orientation of, 263–64, 273–76
  mission of the, 24–25, 27, 47–51, 85–95, 236–44, 284–87
  missionary nature of, 24–27, 40–42, 173, 175, 247–48, 269–73, 276–83
  self-effacing, 245–47
  unity, 29–40, 251, 268
Colonialism, 72, 94, 130, 164

Creation, 99, 108–9, 112, 127, 141, 166–71, 181, 187–88, 191, 194–96, 210, 224, 228–29, 241n272, 295
Culture, xvii, 68n47, 69, 75, 79, 84–85, 220, 292–94

Death, 21–22, 182, 192, 196–203, 205–6, 208–9, 245, 279, 295, 301
Demons, 91–92, 107, 194–95, 197, 220–21, 292–93
Doubt, 69, 72
Doxology. *See* Worship
Dualism, 13, 62, 197, 221n177

Eastern Orthodoxy, 34, 138, 145, 185
Ecclesiology, 24–37, 40–42, 97–98, 173, 233, 252–87
Ecumenical movement, 29, 32, 98
Election, 4–11, 20, 23–24, 89, 101, 103–4, 109n248, 141, 174, 232–36, 281
End Times. *See* Eschatology
Enlightenment, 42, 69–70, 194, 291–93
Epistemology, 17, 66–68, 131–34, 161, 291
Eschatology, 91–92, 205–11, 275
Evangelical, 260, 268, 289
Evangelism, 22, 31, 47–51, 78, 92–93, 95, 267, 275, 279–80, 289, 297–99, 302–4
Evil, 194–95, 197–99, 211, 217–18, 220–22, 284

329

## Index of Subjects

Faith, 18–20, 22, 48–49, 51, 66, 68, 101, 132, 192, 216, 221, 281, 302
Fall, 112, 187, 291
Fellowship. *See Koinonia*
Forgiveness, 195, 200–201, 219
Freedom, 16–17

God. *See* Trinity
Gospel, 24, 25, 32–33, 36, 43, 46, 53, 68, 70, 75–80, 151, 171, 212, 231, 236–37, 253–54, 298–304
Grace, 22–24, 88, 141, 154, 175, 182, 201, 203, 212, 228, 253, 279–81

Healing, 49, 89–92, 193–96, 219–22, 273, 293–94
Hermeneutic, 136, 187, 302
Hinduism, Hindus, 52, 54–55, 76
History, 15, 37–41, 75, 86, 101–2, 114, 171–72, 178, 187, 204, 210, 224, 241, 270
Holy Spirit,
  and the Church, 27–29, 45–46, 84–85, 88, 96–99, 225–26, 231–51
  and Jesus, 27–29, 82–84, 102, 104–5, 141–43, 171–72, 176, 179–82, 183–86, 225–28, 255–57, 260–61, 263
  mission of, 83–85, 142, 185–86, 206, 223–51, 253, 295
  self-effacing, 229, 244–48
*Homoousios*, 66, 122, 139–41, 146, 150, 152, 155, 300, 302
Hope, 103
Human Being. *See* Anthropology
Humble, Humility, 152–54, 177, 234, 244–45, 264

Individualism, 8n29, 16, 19, 152
Indwelling, 33, 81, 111, 126, 190, 207. *See also Perichoresis*
International Missionary Council, 18, 55, 61, 73
Islam, Muslims, xivn8, 41, 52n272, 54, 79, 127n24, 160, 219, 282n137
Israel, 4, 190, 211, 222n187, 223, 255, 266, 270

Jesus,
  ascension of, 102, 179, 204
  baptism of, 75, 83, 124, 186
  death and resurrection of, 196–205, 217–18
  incarnation of, 76, 110, 129, 133–34, 140–41, 152–55, 155, 187–88, 192, 194, 206, 210, 214, 240, 262–63, 266
  ministry of, 81–83, 147–49, 188–211
  risen life of, 185, 204–5
  second coming of, 39, 205–9

Kingdom of God, 80, 91–92, 194, 196, 206, 214–16, 249, 269, 284
Knowing God, 12–16, 68, 161–63
*Koinonia*, Communion, 127, 150–51, 155–58, 162, 166, 168–70, 172, 175, 188, 200, 225–28, 233–34, 247–48, 253–54, 295–96

Language, 129, 133, 163–64
Love, 7–8, 22, 49–51, 59n3, 80, 99, 111, 127, 156–60, 168, 170, 175, 242, 247, 264–65, 268, 274–76, 278–81, 287, 299–300

Mediator, 149, 200, 207–8, 237, 265, 301
Ministry, Pastoral, 41–42, 44, 219, 282–83
*Missio Dei* theology, 115, 164–66
Mission, Missionary,
  mission comity, 29–31
  ecclesial nature of, 24–25, 225–28, 231–43, 253–55, 258–62
  foreign, cross-cultural, 40, 44, 86–87
  of God, 164–70
  incarnational, 211–23
  justification of, xiv–xv, 98–99, 130, 164, 294
  missionary intention and dimension, 26, 271–73, 284–87, 296
  missionary methods, 42–47, 96, 115

## Index of Subjects  331

motivation for, 50–51, 93, 246, 274–76
purpose of, 37–40, 166–70, 209–10, 284–87
of the Son, 81–83, 183–211
and unity, 29–37, 56, 71, 251, 268
and worship, 263–65, 271–76, 287
Modalism, 124–25, 143, 147, 162n198, 186
Modernity, xiv, 4, 17, 39, 68–70, 90, 291–93
Monotheism, 59, 63, 78, 123–24
Mystery, mysterious, 6, 22, 100, 102, 127, 129, 152, 185, 188, 201, 216, 231, 240
Myth, 9, 129, 294

New Creation, 182, 187, 195, 199, 207, 229, 270
Nicene Creed, 108, 138–39, 142, 146, 155

Pantheism, 127, 178
Panentheism, 127, 141, 177–78
*Perichoresis*, 7, 32, 81, 111, 126–27, 146, 151, 160–62, 176–78, 180, 184, 203, 240, 260, 264, 294, 299
Pentecostal, 28, 221, 245–46, 261, 270
Philosophy, 62n15, 66, 79, 155–56
Pluralism, xiv, 52, 98, 115, 236
Pneumatology, 28, 97, 115, 142, 185, 229, 236, 245
Political, 38, 41, 98, 217
Post-modern, xv, 132, 213
Principalities and Powers, 206, 211
Prophetic, viii, xvi, 56, 263, 284, 289
Protestant, 24, 56, 93n170, 142, 242n276, 293
Providence, 37–40, 80, 87, 114, 197n67, 240–42
Predestination, 5

Reason, 20–21, 23, 69, 83, 132n46
Reconciliation. *See* Salvation
Redemption. *See* Salvation
Reformed tradition, vii, 5, 16, 53, 291

Relatedness, 6–10, 16, 103–4, 127, 150–52, 156, 158–61, 169, 225, 233, 253, 294
Religion, xiv, 52–56, 106–9, 123
Resurrection, 68, 82n114, 104, 179n273, 182, 198–99, 205–6, 208, 221, 229, 270, 295. *See also* Jesus
Revelation, xivn8, 11–16, 20–21, 23, 52, 62, 82, 110, 112, 123, 125, 129, 131–34, 140, 162–63, 188–89, 227–28, 238
Risk, 178, 233, 239–43, 296

Sacrifice, 199–202
Salvation, Soteriology, 11–24, 81–83, 187–211
Science, 292
Secular, 17, 39, 42, 53, 61, 69–70, 89
Sin, 12, 16, 91, 112, 191–92, 195, 198, 200–202, 219, 233, 278
Spiritual, 8, 33, 52n272, 220–21, 290
Suffering, 87, 101, 217–18, 221–22
Supernatural, 50, 90n160, 221n177

Theology,
  apophatic, 129, 221, 229
  cataphatic, 229
  of inter-faith dialogue, 54n280, 105n235, 106–9, 116
  natural, 20, 62, 116
  of religion, xvii, 52–56
  openness, 258
  systematic, xvi, xx, 116, 136, 297
Trinity, Triune God,
  *anarchos*, 145–47, 149–51
  Augustine's theology of, 142, 147, 154, 185–86, 225, 247
  Cappadocian theology of, 157, 186
  as communion, 154–61
  being, substance, 124, 133, 151, 155–56, 160, 162–63
  economic and immanent, 110–13, 128–29, 136n66, 152, 171, 173, 175, 177, 181n280, 259–60, 300
  epistemology of, 121–24, 131–37

Theology, *(continued)*
    Father, 37–38, 80–81, 104, 108–9, 114, 125–26, 145–52, 176–80, 205, 207–8, 210, 273, 299
    is love, 7, 59n3, 80, 99, 111, 127, 127, 156–60, 168, 170, 247, 264, 300
    oneness of, 81, 124–25, 155–57, 160–61, 170
    *opera ad extra*, 84, 114, 185, 242n280, 274
    order, 81, 125–26, 143–52
    reciprocity, 126, 142–44, 149, 176–80, 184, 295
    relations of origin, 170–72, 176–80
    the Son, 138–41, 172–76
    the Spirit, 141–44
    subordination, 124–25, 138–39, 144, 146–47, 150–53, 184
    temporal missions, 171–82, 183–211, 223–51

World Council of Churches, 18, 55, 290
Worship, 263–65, 271–76, 287

www.ingramcontent.com/pod-product-compliance
Lightning Source LLC
Chambersburg PA
CBHW061424300426
44114CB00014B/1536